Indonesian Politics and Society

This is a book that will become a classic, not only for those whose interests lie in Indonesian politics but for those with broader and comparative interests in the political dynamics of change. Bourchier and Hadiz are able to draw out those statements, quotes and documents that capture the pivotal struggles and issues of Soeharto's New Order. They present us with a rich insight into the the collision of reactionary and radical populism, secular state corporatism and liberalism in these turbulent years.

Richard Robison, Professor of Political Economy, Institute for Social Studies, The Hague, Netherlands

Indonesian Politics and Society is an exceptional tool for understanding social and political change in Indonesia over more than three decades. It contains more than eighty translated extracts of carefully selected speeches, pamphlets, manifestos and poems, providing a unique insight into the social thought and political concerns of a wide range of actors intimately involved in the struggle to shape modern Indonesia following the triumph of Soeharto's New Order in the 1960s.

This volume introduces and assesses the thinking of state ideologues, modernising pluralists, social radicals, and of political Islam, during a period of tumultuous change and sometimes violent conflict. It also relates the ideas of the major protagonists in political struggles to important events in Indonesia following the fall of Soeharto.

Much of the material presented is made accessible for the first time to English-language readers. As such, the book is an invaluable text for scholars of modern Indonesia, and for those who seek to understand the ideas that continue to be relevant to the actors currently reshaping the country's social and political terrain.

David Bourchier is Chair of Asian Studies at the University of Western Australia. **Vedi R. Hadiz** teaches at the Department of Sociology, National University of Singa   :search Centre, Murdoch Universit

Indonesian Politics and Society
A Reader

Edited by David Bourchier and Vedi R. Hadiz

This book is a project of the Asia Research Centre, Murdoch University, Western Australia

RoutledgeCurzon
Taylor & Francis Group

LONDON AND NEW YORK

First published 2003
by RoutledgeCurzon
11 New Fetter Lane, London EC4P 4EE

Simultaneously published in the USA and Canada
by RoutledgeCurzon
29 West 35th Street, New York, NY 10001

Transferred to Digital Printing 2003

RoutledgeCurzon is an imprint of the Taylor & Francis Group

© 2003 David Bourchier and Vedi R. Hadiz for selection and
editorial material; individual authors for their contributions

Typeset in Sabon by Taylor & Francis Books Ltd
Printed and bound in Great Britain by TJI Digital, Padstow, Cornwall

British Library Cataloguing in Publication Data
A catalogue record for this book is available from the British Library

Library of Congress Cataloging in Publication Data
Indonesian politics and society: a reader / edited by David Bourchier
and Vedi R. Hadiz
p. cm.
Includes bibliographic references and index.
1. Indonesia–politics and government 1966–1998.
2. Indonesia–politics and government 1998–.3. Indonesia–social
conditions–20th Century. I. Bourchier, David. II. Hadiz, Vedi R.,
1964–.
DS644.4 .I496 2003
959.803–dc21

ISBN 0–415–23750–5 (hbk)
ISBN 0–415–26261–5 (pbk)

For Herb Feith (1930–2001)

Contents

Notes on the authors   xi
Glossary   xxiii
Acknowledgements   xxvii

Introduction   1
  Ideological conflict in Indonesian history 2
  Conceptualising political thinking 7
  The search for a political format, 1965–73 11
  The New Order at its height, 1973–88 13
  Tensions and contradictions: 1988–97 16
  Crisis and reform: 1997–9 18
  Legacies 21

PART I
The search for a political format, 1965–73   25

1 The organicist camp   27
  1.1 Api: keep attacking them 30
  1.2 Supersemar 31
  1.3 Banning communism 33
  1.4 Ali Moertopo: the dual function of the armed forces 34
  1.5 Soeharto: Pancasila democracy 37
  1.6 Abdulkadir Besar: the family state 41
  1.7 Ali Moertopo: national political history 43
  1.8 Ali Moertopo: the floating mass 45
  1.9 Soeharto: democratic rights may not be used as masks 49

2 Modernising pluralism   56
  2.1 Soemarno: a two-party system 59
  *2.2 Soelaiman Soemardi: the need for a progressive,
      independent force 64*

2.3 *A. Rahman Tolleng: voting and the composition
    of parliament 67*
2.4 *Kompas: the concept of the floating mass 70*
2.5 *Mahasiswa Indonesia: the holy anger of a generation 71*
2.6 *The White Group: boycott the elections 73*
2.7 *Arief Budiman: the moral force 74*
2.8 *Abadi v. Berita Yudha: polemic on the military's
    dual function 76*

3 Marginalised Islam   82
3.1 *Idham Chalid: protecting the umat 84*
3.2 *Hamka: the shocking draft bill on marriage 85*
3.3 *Nurcholish Madjid: Islam yes, Islamic parties no! 88*
3.4 *H.M.S. Mintaredja: development-oriented Islam 92*

PART II
The New Order at its height, 1973–88   95

4 Organicism ascendant   97
4.1 *Soeharto: Muslims who fail to understand 99*
4.2 *Soeharto: Pancasila, the legacy of our ancestors 103*
4.3 *Ali Moertopo: Indonesianising Indonesians 110*
4.4 *The law on social organisations 112*
4.5 *Abdulkadir Besar: the armed forces must not take sides 115*

5 Pluralist critiques   118
5.1 *ITB Student Council: White Book of the Students'
    Struggle 120*
5.2 *The Petition of Fifty 126*
5.3 *Indonesian Legal Aid Institute: threats to NGOs in the
    bill on social organisations 128*
5.4 *H.R. Dharsono: the promise of the New Order betrayed 132*
5.5 *Abdurrahman Wahid: we can be Pancasilaists and liberals 136*

6 Islam out in the cold   139
6.1 *K.H. Hasbullah Bakry: critique of Pancasila democracy 141*
6.2 *Sjafruddin Prawiranegara: don't let Pancasila kill Islam 144*
6.3 *The Indonesian Muslim Students' Association: no more
    political engineering 148*
6.4 *Amir Biki: let me die for the Islamic world! 151*
6.5 *Abdurrahman Wahid: choices facing the Muslim
    middle class 155*

PART III
Themes in the later New Order   159

7 Radicalism and new social movements   161
  7.1 Setiakawan: the need for an independent trade union 163
  7.2 Fazlur Akhmad: the Indonesian student movement –
    a force for radical social change? 167
  7.3 Taufik Rahzen: anti-violence manifesto 170
  7.4 SKEPHI: people-oriented forest management 172
  7.5 Nursyahbani Katjasungkana: gender equality,
    a universal struggle 175
  7.6 Wiji Thukul: a caution 179
  7.7 People's Democratic Party: manifesto 179

8 'Political openness' and democratisation   185
  8.1 Soemitro: aspiring to normal politics 188
  8.2 Soeharto: openness 192
  8.3 Gadjah Mada alumni: the state of emergency is over 195
  8.4 Democratic Forum: rekindle society's critical capacity 197
  8.5 LIPI: reforming the New Order 199
  8.6 Megawati Soekarnoputri: an agenda for reform 203
  8.7 Muhammad Shiddiq Al-Jawi: must Islam accept
    democracy? 207

9 State and society relations   212
  9.1 Kopkamtib: intelligence test 215
  9.2 W.S. Rendra: poem of an angry person 216
  9.3 Iwan Fals: Bento 217
  9.4 Marsillam Simanjuntak: speak out! 218
  9.5 International NGO Forum on Indonesia: democracy
    and the right to organise 219
  9.6 The Sirnagalih Declaration 223
  9.7 Abdurrahman Wahid: Islam and the state in the New Order 224
  9.8 Dawam Rahardjo: ICMI's vision 226
  9.9 Y.B. Mangunwijaya: communists 230

10 Human rights and the rule of law   234
  10.1 Hamid S. Attamimi: the separation of powers is alien
    to our constitution 237
  10.2 Padmo Wahyono: Indonesian human rights 237
  10.3 Harry Tjan Silalahi v. Adnan Buyung Nasution:
    human rights and the constitution 239

10.4 Harjono Tjitrosoebono: the concept of the integralist state hinders
democracy 241

10.5 Budiono Kusumohamidjojo: the need for a reliable
legal system 244

10.6 Juwono Sudarsono: the diplomatic scam called
human rights 246

10.7 Indonesian NGOs for Democracy: joint declaration on
human rights 248

10.8 Government of Indonesia: rights and obligations 250

11 Federalism, regionalism and the unitary state   255

11.1 Frans Seda: regional autonomy, a constitutional right 258

11.2 Manuel Kaisiepo: the trouble in Irian Jaya 260

11.3 Mohammad Daud Yoesoef: Aceh might still secede 263

11.4 Anonymous: if only I were free 265

11.5 Y.B. Mangunwijaya: federalism as an antidote to
separatism 269

11.6 Major-General Sudrajat: federalism is not right for
Indonesia 271

PART IV
Crisis and reform   275

12 Looking beyond the New Order   277

12.1 Amien Rais: succession in 1998 – an imperative 280

12.2 LIPI researchers: restore our dignity as a nation 282

12.3 People's Democratic Party: end the dictatorship! 284

12.4 Jakarta students: proposal for an Indonesian
People's Committee 285

12.5 Emil Salim: total reform 288

12.6 Indonesian professionals: no justice and transparency,
no tax 290

12.7 I. Sandyawan Sumardi: crimes against humanity 291

12.8 President B.J. Habibie: a new beginning 295

12.9 Media Indonesia: an ideology of tolerance 302

12.10 The armed forces: a new paradigm 303

12.11 Agus Wirahadikusumah: overhaul the military 306

Bibliography   310
Index   319

Notes on the authors

ABDULKADIR BESAR (b. 1926) was a leading military thinker, lawyer and writer during the 1960s and 1970s. Born in the central Javanese town of Magelang, Abdulkadir graduated from the Military Law Academy in 1958 and the Military Law College in 1963. He worked closely with General Nasution in the 1960s, first as intelligence assistant at the Armed Forces Directorate of Social and Political Strategy, and from 1967 to 1972 as secretary-general of the Interim People's Consultative Assembly. Abdulkadir then joined the teaching staff at the Army Staff and Command College, where he became known as a leading theorist of integralism and *dwifungsi*. In the late 1970s he fell out of favour with Soeharto and 'pragmatic' elements within the military establishment for arguing that the armed forces should scale back its participation in politics. He retired a brigadier-general and spent most of the 1990s teaching at the National Resilience Institute (Lemhannas), the University of Indonesia and Gadjah Mada University.

K. H. ABDURRAHMAN WAHID (b. 1940) is a religious scholar, a liberal intellectual and Indonesia's fourth president. The grandson of a founding member of Nahdlatul Ulama (NU) and the son of the minister for religious affairs under Sukarno, he is the inheritor of a strong but open-minded Islamic tradition. Born in Jombang in East Java, Abdurrahman (known popularly as Gus Dur) was educated in Islamic boarding colleges (*pesantren*), and later at the Al Azhar University in Cairo and at the University of Baghdad. In 1984, soon after being elected chair of NU, he withdrew the NU from the United Development Party (PPP), giving the organisation more leeway to pursue its social and political objectives. He became well known as a pluralist critic of the New Order, allying himself with secular intellectuals in Democratic Forum. After Soeharto's resignation he helped form the National Awakening Party (PKB), which won approximately 11 per cent of seats in parliament in 1999. Supported by a temporary coalition of Islamic parties, he was elected president in October the same year. In July 2001 he was impeached and replaced by his vice-president, Megawati Soekarnoputri.

AGUS WIRAHADIKUSUMAH (1951–2001) was a highly trained infantry officer who emerged in the 1990s as a leading military reformer. He graduated from the Military Academy in 1973 and served in several combat zones, including East Timor. In the 1980s he undertook studies and training in the US and Australia, and in 1992 obtained a master's degree in public policy and management from Harvard University. After this he served mainly in senior education and planning positions, where he developed a view that the military's political role should be wound back and that its territorial apparatus should be abolished. He put some of his radical proposals in a 1999 book that received the backing of President Abdurrahman Wahid but was unpopular with many of his fellow officers. In August 2000 the military leadership blackballed him, forcing him prematurely from his position as chief of the Army Strategic Reserve Command.

Muhammad Shiddiq AL-JAWI (b. 1969) is a Muslim scholar and senior member of Hizbut Tahrir Indonesia, the local chapter of a Middle Eastern-based Islamist group that supports the establishment of Islamic caliphates. After studying at several *pesantren* in Bogor and gaining a degree in biology at the Bogor Agricultural Institute, he now lectures in Islamic economics at the Surakarta State Islamic College while taking a postgraduate degree in Islamic Studies at the Indonesian Islamic University in Yogyakarta. He has written several books on aspects of Islam and translated books from Arabic, including *Demokrasi Sistem Kufur* (Democracy, System of the Unbelievers) by Abdul Qadim Zallum, the current leader of Hizbut Tahrir.

ALI MOERTOPO (1924–84) was a long-time intelligence aide to Soeharto and one of the chief architects of the New Order political framework. In his capacity as head of OPSUS, a powerful clandestine intelligence unit, Moertopo oversaw the creation of Golkar and the reorganisation of the party system. In 1971 he co-founded the Centre for Strategic and International Studies (CSIS), a Jakarta think tank that played a major role in formulating domestic and foreign policy in the 1970s and 1980s. Although Moertopo exercised power largely through his personal networks, he also occupied important government positions, including deputy head of the Intelligence Coordinating Agency (Bakin) from 1974 to 1978, minister of information (1978–83) and deputy chair of the Supreme Advisory Council.

AMIEN RAIS (b. 1944) Born into a pious Muslim family in Solo, Amien Rais attended a Muhammadiyah school. He graduated from Gadjah Mada University in 1968 with a degree in political science and spent much of his career there lecturing in politics. In 1974 he obtained a master's degree in politics from Notre Dame University in the US, and in 1984 a doctorate from Chicago University. In 1995 he was elected head of Muhammadiyah and was later appointed to a senior post in the government-sponsored Indonesian Muslim Intellectuals' Association (ICMI). After adopting an increasingly critical stance, in 1997 Amien was expelled from ICMI and in 1998 he became a central figure in the anti-Soeharto reform movement. Following Soeharto's resignation, he formed the pluralist National Mandate Party (PAN), which won 7.7 per cent of the national vote. In October 1999 he became chair of the People's Consultative Assembly.

S.M. AMIN was a Muslim lawyer aligned with the modernist Masjumi party.

AMIR BIKI (1948–84) was born in Gorontalo, Sulawesi, and died in Jakarta in the Tanjung Priok massacre in September 1984. Biki, an entrepreneur and informal leader in the port area of Tanjung Priok, studied at the University of Indonesia in 1966, where he had been a strong supporter of the New Order. He took part in the 1978 protest movement and in the early 1980s organised religious lectures critical of government policies.

A. Hamid S. ATTAMIMI (1928–95) was a constitutional lawyer and ideologue who enjoyed a long career in Soeharto's powerful State Secretariat. Between 1983 and 1993 he was deputy cabinet secretary. A holder of a doctorate from the law faculty at the University of Indonesia, Attamimi advocated the thesis that Indonesia was a 'village republic' that should be guided constitutionally by customary law principles. He was also a defender of a strong presidency.

Arief BUDIMAN (b. 1941) was a leading light among the '1966 generation' of student protestors that helped bring the New Order to power. He received his undergraduate degree in psychology at the University of Indonesia and a PhD in sociology from Harvard. By 1968 he had become increasingly critical of the corruption and heavy-handed tactics of the Soeharto regime. He was an outspoken critic of Madame Tien Soeharto's 'Indonesia in Miniature' project and led a movement to boycott the 1971 – and subsequent – New Order elections. From his base at Satyawacana University in the central Javanese town of Salatiga, he wrote widely on Indonesian sociology and politics, becoming known as one of the New Order's most articulate and popular critics. Professor Arief Budiman is currently head of the Indonesian Studies Program at Melbourne University.

BUDIONO Kusumohamidjojo (b. 1949) is a senior practising lawyer and lectures in legal and cultural philosophy at Parahyangan University in Bandung. He obtained a PhD from the State University of Würzburg in West Germany in 1982 and has written numerous articles and books on legal topics, international relations, defence, education, leadership and social change in Indonesia. He is currently a partner with the Jakarta law firm Soebagjo, Jatim, Djarot.

Mohammad DAUD YOESOEF is a lecturer in the faculty of law at Syiah Kuala University, Banda Aceh.

Mohammad DAWAM RAHARDJO (b. 1942) is an economist, a Muslim scholar and a former non-governmental organisation (NGO) activist. Educated at the faculty of economics at Gadjah Mada University in Yogyakarta, Dawam worked as a researcher at the Institute for Economic and Social Research, Education and Information (LP3ES), later becoming its director. He also edited the prestigious social and political affairs journal *Prisma*. He subsequently established LSAF (the Institute for the Study of Religion and Philosophy), where he published the religious and social affairs journal *Ulumul Qur'an* until 1998. Dawam was instrumental in founding ICMI, the Indonesian Muslim Intellectuals' Association, where he served as an expert adviser. He is currently an adviser to Amien Rais' National Mandate Party and a senior member of Muhammadiyah.

Hartono Rekso DHARSONO (1925–96) was one of the most prominent generals to fall out with Soeharto. As commander of the prestigious Siliwangi division, Lieutenant-General Dharsono had played a major part in delivering West Java to the New Order. Disagreement over the reorganisation of the party system saw him removed from active duty, and in 1976 he was appointed secretary-general of the Association of Southeast Asian Nations (ASEAN). Dismissed two years later for criticising the regime, Dharsono joined a group of like-minded retired officers. Following the Tanjung Priok massacre in 1984, Dharsono and others signed a white paper questioning the official account. In 1985 he was charged with subversion and sentenced to 10 years in gaol for having signed this document and also for having allegedly incited Muslim activists to participate in a bomb attack. Dharsono was released in 1992 and posthumously rehabilitated by President Habibie in 1998.

EMIL SALIM (b. 1930) is a veteran economist who served for more than 20 years as a cabinet minister under Soeharto. Born in South Sumatra, he was educated at the economics faculty at the University of Indonesia, and at the University of California, Berkeley, where he received his doctorate in 1964. From 1971 to 1973 he served as minister for the reform of the state apparatus, then as transport minister, minister for the supervision of development and for the environment and, from 1983 to 1993, as population and environment minister. After this time he became increasingly critical of the Soeharto regime, and in February 1998 formed Gema Madani, a civil society advocacy group. A long-time professor of economics at the University of Indonesia, Emil Salim later served as an adviser to President Abdurrahman Wahid.

Bacharuddin Jusuf HABIBIE (b. 1936) Indonesia's third president. Patronised by Soeharto from his boyhood days in South Sulawesi,

Habibie was given the opportunity to study, first in Bandung and later in Germany, where he pursued a brilliant career in aeronautical engineering. In 1974, after 18 years as a German resident, Soeharto enticed Habibie to Jakarta to help realise his vision of a modern, industrialised Indonesia. He was appointed research and technology minister, a position he kept for 20 years. In 1990 Habibie was appointed to head ICMI, the Indonesian Muslim Intellectuals' Association, and in 1997 became vice-president. When Soeharto resigned the following year, Habibie inherited his position. With little political support, Habibie recast himself as a reformer, presiding over a bewildering array of legislative changes and successfully managing the democratic general election of June 1999. Allegations of serious corruption, his failure to restore the economy and his decision to grant East Timor a vote on its future were key factors in the MPR's vote of no confidence on 14 October 1999, which spelt the end of his 17-month tenure.

HAMKA (1908–81) was born in Maninjau, West Sumatra, and was one of Indonesia's best-known Muslim politicians and scholars. After spending his early years as a novelist, journalist and an activist for Muhammadiyah, he was elected to parliament in 1955 as a member of Masjumi. Hamka, whose full name was Haji Abdul Malik Karim Amrullah, later attracted the ire of Sukarno for vehemently opposing his establishment of Guided Democracy. For his efforts, Hamka was arrested and imprisoned without trial in 1964. Released from prison by Soeharto, Hamka soon grew disillusioned with the New Order and spoke out against what he saw as the weak moral fibre of its leadership and its suspicion of Muslim politicians. He wrote several books on Islamic doctrine and served as head of the Indonesian Council of Ulama (MUI), the peak body of Islamic scholarly organisations, from 1975 until shortly before his death in 1981.

HARJONO Tjitrosoebono (1922–99) was a widely respected advocate and human rights activist. He belonged to an older generation of Dutch-speaking lawyers that included Suardi Tasrif and Yap Thiam Hien, sharing their commitment to the rule of law. Born into a political family in Malang, East Java, Harjono became a student leader in the 1950s, and in 1965 he joined the anti-Sukarno protests as chair of the Indonesian Graduates' Action Front. In the 1970s Harjono joined the Legal Aid Foundation and defended many people accused of political crimes. He chaired the Indonesian Advocates' Association (Peradin) from 1980 to 1985 and maintained a critical stance towards the Soeharto government. When Soeharto's military lawyers attempted to establish a rival bar association (Ikadin), Harjono foiled their plans by managing to have himself selected as its chair, a position he held until his death.

HARRY TJAN Silalahi (b. 1934) was born into a Chinese Catholic family in Yogyakarta and rose to become a prominent politician, entrepreneur and adviser to Soeharto's government. Christened Tjan Tjoen Hok, Harry Tjan played a key role in the anti-communist movement of 1965–6 and accepted a seat in parliament at the age of 33. With the backing of Ali Moertopo and Sudjono Humardani, he helped establish the Centre for Strategic and International Studies (CSIS). As deputy director of the CSIS in the 1990s he maintained a high profile as a conservative commentator and intellectual.

K.H. HASBULLAH BAKRY (1925–98) was a South Sumatran Muslim scholar who worked as a spiritual adviser to the military from the 1950s until the mid-1970s. He also lectured in Islamic colleges in Jakarta and Yogyakarta, as well as writing books on theological issues, Islamic law and secular law. He obtained a law degree in 1970 and worked as an advocate in Jakarta in the 1970s and 1980s. In the 1970s he was associated with GUPPI, the Association for Renewal of Muslim Education.

IDHAM CHALID (1921–98) was a politician and religious leader born in Setui, South Kalimantan. He received his education in the well-known Gontor *pesantren* in East Java, but also received an honorary doctorate from Al Azhar University in Cairo in recognition of his role as a religious scholar. Initially an educator, Idham Chalid entered politics and served as a member of parliament in the 1940s and 1950s. It was also during this period that he was named a deputy prime minister (1956–7). A long-serving leader of Nahdlatul Ulama, he was a leading political figure in the early New Order. He chaired the People's Consultative Assembly from 1972 to 1977.

IWAN FALS (Virgiawan Listianto) (b. 1961) was born in Jakarta, and is a singer-songwriter idolised by poor urban youths for his songs, which frequently deal with themes of social injustice and sneer at the corruption and hypocrisy of the powerful. The son of a retired army general, Fals began to garner a substantial cult following when he was still in high school. He was a superstar by the 1990s, forming the group *Swami* and *Kantata Takwa*, which included the musician Sawung Jabo, the poet Rendra and the businessman-cum-artist Setiawan Djody.

JUWONO SUDARSONO (b. 1942) After graduating with a PhD in political science from the London School of Economics in 1978, Juwono taught politics for many years at his alma mater, the University of Indonesia, rising to become dean of the social and political science faculty. For many years he was known as an urbane and independent-minded commentator on politics and international relations. He accepted a position as environment minister in Soeharto's last cabinet and was appointed education and culture minister by President B.J. Habibie. Juwono's close ties with the military saw him appointed deputy governor of the National Defence Institute and, in

Abdurrahman Wahid's first cabinet, as Indonesia's first civilian defence minister since the 1950s. In 2000 he returned to teach at the University of Indonesia.

Manuel KAISIEPO (b. 1953) is a Papuan journalist, commentator and, more recently, a government minister. Born and raised in Biak, his father was the second governor of Irian Jaya, Franz Kaisiepo. Manuel Kaisiepo moved to Yogyakarta in the early 1970s to attend Gadjah Mada University. He later studied politics at the National University in Jakarta and at the Catholic Driyakara School of Philosophy. After editing the social and economic affairs journal *Prisma* (1979–83) he joined *Kompas*, Indonesia's leading daily, in 1986. In the interim he was a researcher at the Indonesian Institute of Sciences. In August 2000 Kaisiepo was appointed junior minister for the acceleration of development in Eastern Indonesia in Abdurrahman's second cabinet, a position he continued to hold in the Megawati administration.

Yusuf B. MANGUNWIJAYA (1929–99) was a Catholic priest, architect, novelist, human rights activist, social worker and a well-known social and cultural commentator. Born in Ambarawa, Central Java, 'Romo Mangun' studied architecture in Germany for six years before returning to Yogyakarta in 1966 to teach at Gadjah Mada University. He won many prizes, including the Southeast Asian Writing Award in 1983 for his historical novel *The Weaverbirds* and the Aga Khan Award for Architecture in 1992 for his Kali Code complex in a poor area of Yogyakarta. Romo Mangun embraced liberation theology, but did not affiliate himself with any political group. People from all layers of society and religious denomination attended his funeral in Yogyakarta.

MEGAWATI SOEKARNOPUTRI (b. 1947) was born in Yogyakarta, the eldest daughter of President Sukarno and Fatmawati. After studying agriculture for two years at Padjadjaran University in Bandung, she enrolled in psychology at the University of Indonesia. Megawati was recruited by the Indonesian Democratic Party (PDI) in 1987 and helped to boost the party's fortunes in the 1987 and 1992 elections. In December 1993 she was elected head of the PDI, but was ousted from her position in June 1996 when the government endorsed a rival faction of the party. This led to a dramatic standoff that saw the party's headquarters destroyed, triggering riots in Jakarta. After Soeharto's downfall Megawati formed the Indonesian Democratic Party of Struggle (PDI-P), which attracted the support of the PDI's constituency as well as many former supporters of Golkar and NU. Under her leadership the PDI-P won the largest share of the vote (34 per cent) in the 1999 general elections. She won only second place in the presidential election, however, and took her place as Abdurrahman Wahid's vice-president in October 1999. On 23 July 2001 Megawati was sworn in as Indonesia's fifth president.

Haji Mohammad Sjafa'at MINTAREDJA (1921–*c.*92) was a Dutch-educated lawyer who headed the Muslim Students' Association (HMI) during the revolution. After working as an official at the Foreign Exchange Institute he served on the boards of several business enterprises. In 1965 he became assistant to the social affairs minister, and soon afterwards was appointed minister for liaising between the government and legislative institutions. In late 1970, while still serving in this position, he was installed as head of Parmusi, the newly created party for modernist Muslims. In this role he was known as a supporter of the New Order government's depoliticisation and secularist policies which saw the role of political parties, including his own, tightly circumscribed. He argued for a merger of Muslim political parties, and when the government engineered this in January 1973 Mintaredja was appointed the first leader of the PPP. He held this position until 1979.

NURCHOLISH MADJID (b. 1939) is a widely respected Muslim intellectual. Born in Jombang, East Java, he rose to prominence as head of the influential Muslim Students' Association (HMI) between 1966 and 1971. He later became president of the Southeast Asian Union of Islamic Students. In the 1970s Nurcholish (known as Cak Nur) became a leading figure in a movement to decouple Islam from party politics and apply it more flexibly to the modern world. Since his brand of neo-modernist Islamic thought was compatible with the New Order's priorities, he was treated well by the regime. In the early 1980s he moved to the US, where he completed his PhD at the University of Chicago, and in 1991 was appointed deputy chair of ICMI. He has held several teaching positions and is now dean of the University of Paramadina Mulya in Jakarta.

Adnan Buyung NASUTION (b. 1934) was perhaps the most prominent human rights lawyer during the Soeharto era. Born in Jakarta, Buyung worked as a prosecutor before studying law at Melbourne University and at the University of Indonesia. He took an active role in the pro-New Order demonstrations in 1966. In the late 1960s he established himself as an advocate and in 1970 helped to found the Indonesian Legal Aid Foundation. It was in this role that he became well known as a defender of political dissidents and an outspoken advocate of human rights. After being ruled in contempt of court in 1988 during the trial of H.R. Dharsono, he moved to the Netherlands, where he wrote a doctoral dissertation on constitutional history that was published in 1992. After the fall of Soeharto he defended several military officers accused of serious human rights abuses.

NURSYAHBANI Katjasungkana (b. 1955) is a prominent lawyer, feminist and human rights advocate. After working as a legal aid lawyer in the early 1980s, she became well known as head of the Legal Aid Institute's Jakarta office between 1987 and 1992. She subsequently set up her own legal aid organisation (LBH-APIK) devoted to helping poor women, and has been active in several other NGOs working with women, and on human rights and environmental issues. In 1999 she became a member of the People's Consultative Assembly as an NGO representative, where she campaigned vocally for human rights and civilian supremacy. Nursyahbani comes from a prominent nationalist family in Madura that has produced several political activists.

PADMO WAHYONO (1932–91) was a constitutional lawyer and a leading ideologue of the New Order. Born in Tulungagung, East Java, Padmo spent most of his career lecturing in law at universities and military academies. In the mid-1970s he was appointed professor of law at the University of Indonesia and dean of the law faculty. When the government set up its Pancasila indoctrination body (BP7) in 1978, Padmo was appointed as one of its deputy directors, a position he retained until his death. Padmo published numerous works on constitutional law, Pancasila, legal education and legal philosophy.

W.S. RENDRA (b. 1935) is the son of two performing artists: his father was an actor in Solo and his mother a dancer at the sultan's palace in Solo. As a student at Gadjah Mada University in nearby Yogyakarta, Rendra founded the Bengkel Theatre. In the 1950s he began writing plays and poetry. His collection of poems *Ballada Orang-orang Tertjinta* was awarded a national literary prize for 1955/6. In 1964 Rendra took up a scholarship to study for four years at the American Academy of Dramatic Arts. On his return he staged several original plays, such as *Bipbop* and *Perjuangan Suku Naga*, as well as adaptations from Sophocles and Bertold Brecht. His plays and poems denounced injustice and were banned on several occasions. Rendra now lives in a village near Jakarta with his wife, the actress Ken Zuraida.

I. SANDYAWAN SUMARDI, SJ (b. 1958) is a Jesuit priest long involved in humanitarian causes. For several years 'Romo Sandy' was director of the Jakarta Social Institute, a group that assisted and advocated for street children. In 1996 he was awarded the prestigious Yap Thiam Hien Award in recognition of his courageous work in helping the victims of the attack on Megawati's PDI headquarters in Jakarta. In 1998 he and his Volunteer Team for Humanity played a crucial role in gathering evidence about the rapes and riots in Jakarta.

Frans SEDA (b. 1926) is an economist, politician and businessman from the eastern Indonesian island of Flores. After studying economics in Holland in the 1950s, Frans Seda went on to lead the small Catholic Party from 1961 to 1968. In the 1960s and 1970s he was plantations minister, agriculture minister, finance minister, and transport and tourism minister, serving under both Sukarno and Soeharto. A former member of the

Supreme Advisory Council, he founded Atmajaya Catholic University in Jakarta and was chair of the Association of Textiles Producers. Seda has more recently served as economic adviser to Presidents B.J. Habibie and Megawati Soekarnoputri. He also holds a senior advisory position within the Indonesian Democratic Party of Struggle (PDI-P).

SJAFRUDDIN PRAWIRANEGARA (1911–89) was a Masjumi politician who served as prime minister and acting prime minister of the Emergency Government of the Indonesian Republic, formed in Sumatra in 1948 after the Dutch captured Yogyakarta. Having been trained in finance during the colonial era, he rose to become finance minister in the Hatta and Natsir governments, and was governor of the Bank of Indonesia from 1951 to 1958. He was arrested in 1961, however, because he was a key figure in the Sumatra-based Revolutionary Government of the Republic of Indonesia (PRRI), and was kept in close confinement until 1966. Initially a supporter of the New Order, he grew disenchanted and signed the Petition of Fifty in 1980.

Marsillam SIMANJUNTAK (b. *c.*1937) was a prominent youth leader in the campaign against Sukarno and then against corruption in the New Order. He was imprisoned in 1974, along with several other activists, for his alleged role in fomenting the Malari riots in Jakarta. A medical doctor by training, he also studied political science and law in Indonesia and in the US. In 1990 he was a founding member of the liberal, anti-sectarian Democratic Forum, a group that produced sharp critiques of the New Order during its last years. When Abdurrahman Wahid became president in 1999, Marsillam was his cabinet secretary, and in the last days of the Abdurrahman administration he served as attorney-general.

SOEHARTO (b. 1921) was Indonesia's second president. Born in Central Java, Soeharto began his career as a soldier in the army of the Dutch East Indies. He rose through the ranks of the Indonesian military, fighting the returning Dutch forces in 1945–9 and later taking a leading part in the operation to take control of West Irian. As commander of the elite Army Strategic Reserve Command in 1965, Soeharto seized control of Jakarta from mutinous forces on 1 October. From this position he assumed control of the army and presided over the massacre and mass imprisonment of supporters of the Indonesian Communist Party. On 11 March 1966 President Sukarno gave Soeharto powers to 'restore order', and it was on the basis of this that the general was able to expand his authority and, in 1968, take over as president. A cautious but resourceful politician, Soeharto centralised control over the state apparatus and used his powers of coercion and cooption to neutralise his political opponents. After presiding over three decades of relative stability and unprecedented economic growth, Soeharto came under increasing attack in 1997 as a result of his family's conspicuous corruption and his failure to manage the financial crisis. Soon after his resignation on 21 May 1998 his health deteriorated and he was confined mainly to his house. A corruption trial was aborted when investigators concluded that Soeharto was too sick.

SOELAIMAN SOEMARDI was an intellectual mentor to many in the Indonesian Socialist Party (PSI). He received a master's degree from Cornell University in the 1960s and subsequently taught sociology at the University of Indonesia. He was also a staff member of the National Development Planning Board, Bappenas.

SOEMARNO (1925–94) served as secretary of the West Java branch of the Indonesian Socialist Party (PSI) between 1948 and 1959. He was a member of the national parliament between 1950 and 1955, representing the PSI-affiliated All-Indonesia Workers' Congress (KBSI), and then served in the provisional parliament of West Java until Sukarno banned the PSI in 1960. During the early New Order Soemarno was a Golkar activist, managing its campaign in West Java in the 1971 elections, and then he represented Golkar in parliament. He lost his seat in 1974, and was subsequently gaoled without trial for two years for alleged involvement in the Malari riots.

SOEMITRO (1925–98) headed Indonesia's powerful internal security agency Kopkamtib between 1969 and 1974. Sharing a similar career path to Soeharto, he became one of his closest aides, holding not only the position of Kopkamtib commander but also deputy commander of the armed forces. Following the Malari riots in January 1974 he was accused by his rival, Ali Moertopo, of encouraging student opponents of Soeharto, which forced the 49-year-old general into retirement. After many years in private business, Soemitro came to prominence again in the late 1980s as a moderate commentator on military and political affairs. One of his main vehicles was the magazine he edited, *Teknologi Strategi Militer.*

SUDRAJAT (b. *c.*1948) is a Harvard-educated intelligence officer. He served as defence attaché in London and Washington before being appointed head of the Armed Forces Information Service in August 1999. Major-General Sudrajat lost this position in January 2000 after siding publicly with armed forces commander General Wiranto in his conflicts with President Abdurrahman Wahid.

TAUFIK RAHZEN is a Bandung-based peace activist and political commentator. He studied engineering at Yogyakarta's Gadjah Mada University and was associated with the Forum on Human Rights (Front) in the 1990s. He now directs the Indonesian Festival Alliance (Aliansi Indonesia Festival).

A. Rahman TOLLENG (b. 1937) is a former anti-communist student leader who played an important role in Golkar in the early New Order.

From 1964 to 1965 Tolleng worked for Sukarno's Supreme Operations Command (G-V, KOTI), where he met many of the administrative and intelligence officers who would form the core of the New Order regime. In 1967 he became chair of KAMI, the most influential student organisation of the time, and the following year was appointed a deputy chair of Golkar in parliament. At the same time he edited the West Java edition of *Mahasiswa Indonesia*, an important newspaper affiliated with the former Indonesian Socialist Party (PSI), and, from 1972 to 1973, Golkar's newspaper *Suara Karya*. Following the Malari riots of 1974, Tolleng was accused of conspiring against the government and imprisoned for 16 months. Released in 1975, he joined the publishing firm PT Pustaka Utama Grafiti, which he now heads. In 1991 Rahman Tolleng was one of the pioneers of the Democratic Forum.

WIJI THUKUL Wijaya (1963–*c*.98) was a poet and radical political activist. The son of a Solo pedicab driver with limited formal education, he worked odd jobs and helped his wife with her sewing from home. His confrontational poems and his position as head of the People's Democratic Party (PRD)-affiliated People's Art Network (JAKKER) made him a target of New Order surveillance and violence. When the PRD was outlawed in 1996 Wiji Thukul went into hiding and he was not seen again after 1998. The Commission for Missing People and Victims of Violence (Kontras) suspects that he was killed by the military during a purge in which 14 people disappeared. A collection of his poems was published posthumously under the title *Aku Ingin Jadi Peluru: Kumpulan Sajak Wiji Thukul* (2000).

Glossary

abangan	Nominally Muslim or spiritually syncretic community in Java
ABRI	Angkatan Bersenjata Republik Indonesia, the Armed Forces of the Republic of Indonesia; became TNI in 1999
ASEAN	Association of Southeast Asian Nations
azas tunggal	Policy requiring all social and political organisations to adopt Pancasila as their 'sole philosophical foundation'
Bakin	Badan Koordinasi Intelijen Negara, State Intelligence Coordinating Agency
CSIS	Centre for Strategic and International Studies
Darul Islam	Armed movement that fought for an Islamic state, mainly in West Java, Sulawesi and Aceh; sometimes appears as DI or with TII: Tentara Islam Indonesia, Islamic Army of Indonesia
DPR	Dewan Perwakilan Rakyat, People's Representative Council; Indonesia's 500-seat parliament, also referred to as the House of Representatives
dwifungsi	'Dual function' doctrine according to which the armed forces claimed a permanent right to participate in social and political affairs
G30S/PKI	Gerakan September Tigapuluh/Partai Komunis Indonesia, 30 September Movement/Indonesian Communist Party; the New Order's shorthand for the movement that led the mutiny on the night of 30 September 1965
GAM	Gerakan Aceh Merdeka, Free Aceh Movement
GBHN	Garis Besar Haluan Negara, Broad Guidelines of State Policy; a set of policy directives ratified every five years by the MPR

Gestapu	Gerakan September Tigapuluh (30 September Movement); the name given by New Order supporters to the 'movement' that initiated the kidnapping and murder of senior army officers in 1965
Golkar	Golongan Karya, New Order regime's corporatist election vehicle; transformed into a political party in 1998
Golput	Golongan Putih, the 'White Group' that advocated an election boycott in 1971 and subsequent elections to 1997
GUPPI	Gabungan Usaha Pembaharuan Pendidikan Islam, Association for Renewal of Islamic Education
Hankamnas Rata	Pertahanan dan keamanan nasional rakyat semesta, total people's national defence and security; longstanding component of military doctrine that stresses the need for close cooperation with civilians in national defence
HMI	Himpunan Mahasiswa Islam, Muslim Students' Association
ICMI	Ikatan Cendekiawan Muslim Indonesia, Indonesian Muslim Intellectuals' Association
IMF	International Monetary Fund
integralism	Philosophy of state organisation described by Supomo, which posited a unity of interests between rulers and ruled; the theoretical basis for the 'family state'
Javanism	Set of beliefs associated with Javanese spiritual practice
KAMI	Kesatuan Aksi Mahasiswa Indonesia, Indonesian Students' Action Front; the army-sponsored anti-communist students' association formed on 15 October 1965 in Jakarta
karya/ kekaryaan	Notion that different groups in society should play complementary functional roles rather than be in conflict or competition with each other
Kopkamtib	Komando Operasi Pemulihan Keamanan dan Ketertiban, Operational Command for the Restoration of Order and Security (disbanded 1988)
Korpri	Korps [Karyawan] Pegawai Republik Indonesia, Indonesian Civil Servants' Corps
LBH	Lembaga Bantuan Hukum, Legal Aid Institute
Lemhannas	Lembaga Pertahanan Nasional, National Resilience Institute
litsus	*Penelitian khusus*, 'special investigation' procedure into an individual's family background and political allegiances

LP3ES	Lembaga Penelitian, Pendidikan dan Penerangan Ekonomi dan Sosial, Institute for Economic and Social Research, Education and Information
Malari	Malapetaka Limabelas Januari, Disaster of 15 January; anti-government riots in Jakarta in January 1974
Masjumi	Majelis Sjuro Muslimin Indonesia, Consultative Council of Indonesian Muslims (banned August 1960)
MPR	Majelis Permusyawaratan Rakyat, People's Consultative Assembly; the super-parliament, consisting of the DPR and additional members
MPRS	Majelis Permusyawaratan Rakyat Sementara, Interim People's Consultative Assembly; the fully appointed parliament that met between 1966 and 1968
Muhammadiyah	Modernist Islamic mass organisation with a large following among urban traders and professionals in Java and the outer islands; Indonesia's largest modernist Islamic organisation
MUI	Majelis Ulama Indonesia, the peak body for Indonesian religious scholars
Nahdlatul Ulama	*See* NU
Nasakom	Nasionalisme-Agama-Komunisme, Sukarno's concept that willed the unity of nationalism, religion (Islam) and communism
negara hukum	State governed by law, a translation of the German/Dutch *Rechtsstaat*
New Order	Orde Baru, the political configuration under Soeharto between 1966 and 1998
NU	Nahdlatul Ulama, Resurgence of the Islamic Scholars; rural-based Islamic organisation that was also a political party until 1984
Old Order	Orde Lama, the Soeharto government's term for the Sukarno era
OPM	Organisasi Papua Merdeka, Free Papua Movement
OPSUS	Operasi Khusus, Special Operations
P4	Pedoman Penghayatan dan Pengamalan Pancasila, Directives for the Realisation and Implementation of Pancasila (Pancasila indoctrination courses)

PAN	Partai Amanat Nasional, National Mandate Party (formed 1998)
Pancasila	Five-point Indonesian state doctrine articulated by Sukarno in 1945: belief in one supreme God; just and civilised humanity; national unity; democracy led by wisdom and prudence through consultation and representation; social justice
Parmusi	Partai Muslimin Indonesia, Muslim Party of Indonesia; also known as PMI
PDI	Partai Demokrasi Indonesia, Indonesian Democratic Party
PDI-P	Partai Demokrasi Indonesia – Perjuangan, Indonesian Democratic Party of Struggle (formed 1998)
Permesta	Piagam Perjuangan Semesta, Charter of the Common Struggle; North Sulawesi-based autonomist revolt that came into the open in February 1958
pesantren	Islamic boarding college
PKB	Partai Kebangkitan Bangsa, National Awakening Party (formed 1998)
PKI	Partai Komunis Indonesia, Indonesian Communist Party
PNI	Partai Nasional Indonesia, Indonesian Nationalist Party
PPP	Partai Persatuan Pembangunan, United Development Party
PRD	Partai Rakyat Demokratik, People's Democratic Party (formed 1996)
PRRI	Pemerintah Revolusioner Republik Indonesia, Revolutionary Government of the Republic of Indonesia; a counter-government proclaimed in February 1958 in Padang, West Sumatra
PSI	Partai Sosialis Indonesia, Indonesian Socialist Party
santri	devout, *pesantren*-educated, Muslim community
syariah	Islamic law
SKEPHI	Sekretariat Kerjasama Pelestarian Hutan Indonesia, Network for Forest Conservation in Indonesia
TNI	Tentara Nasional Indonesia, Indonesian National Army; incorporating the army, navy and air force
ulama	Muslim religious scholars
umat	The community of Muslim believers

Acknowledgements

For their invaluable help and advice we would like to thank Herb Feith, Ian Chalmers, Rahman Tolleng, Daniel Dhakidae, Richard Robison, Harold Crouch, Robert Hefner, Greg Fealy, Mochtar Mas'oed, Hardoyo F.S., Muslim Abdurrahman, Bill Liddle, Burhan Magenda, Lance Castles, Max Lane, Ignas Kleden, Arief Budiman, Angus McIntyre, Ed Aspinall, David Reeve, Ben Abel, Arya Wisesa, Peter McCall, Ian Wilson, Catherine Mills and Laura Lochore. Special gratitude is due to the Asia Research Centre on Social, Political and Economic Change at Murdoch University, which sponsored the writing of this book and persevered with us throughout its long gestation. We would also like to thank Routledge, and Craig Fowlie in particular, for their patience. Many others – who we cannot name one by one – are also owed a word of thanks.

David Bourchier would like to say a heartfelt thanks to Elke Kaiser for her friendship and support during the years this book has taken. Vedi Hadiz would like to thank Lina and Karla for tolerating the amount of time and attention he has diverted from them and given to work throughout these years.

Permission given by all copyright holders and authors is gratefully acknowledged. The publishers and editors have made every effort to obtain permission for the reproduction of all material contained in this volume. The publishers welcome any further inquiries regarding such matters.

List of published sources

Chapter 1

'Pukul terus' (Api editorial, 7 November 1965) in Dewan Redaksi Api (1965) *Harian 'Api' Mengganjang Nekolim-PKI-Gestapu*, Jakarta: Merdeka Press: 67–8.

Ali Moertopo (1973) *The Acceleration and Modernization of 25 Years' Development*, Jakarta: Yayasan Proklamasi/Centre for Strategic and International Studies.

Soeharto (1967) *Pidato Kenegaraan PD. Presiden Republik Indonesia Djendral Soeharto Didepan Sidang DPR-GR 16 Agustus 1967*, Jakarta: Departemen Penerangan RI.

Abdulkadir Besar (1972) 'Academic appraisal tentang tata tertib MPR', in *Laporan Pimpinan MPRS tahun 1966–1972*, Jakarta: Penerbitan MPRS: 493–548.

Ali Moertopo (1970) *Politik Nasional: Strategi, Taktik dan Teknik Implementasinja, (Tjeramah Brigadir Djenderal TNI Ali Moertopo pada kursus up-grading karyawan teras ABRI tingkat pusat di Djakarta, tanggal 20 Agustus s/d 17 Oktober 1970)*, Jakarta: Departemen Pertahanan Keamanan.

Soeharto (1972) 'Democratic rights may not be used as masks', in R.M. Smith (ed.) (1974) *Southeast Asia: Documents of Political Development and Change*, Ithaca, New York: Cornell University Press: 235–40.

Chapter 2

A. Rahman Tolleng (1970) Speech to a plenary session of the Gotong Royong People's Representative Council in the name of the 'Fraksi-fraksi Karya Pembangunan (A), (B) and (C)', 22 November 1969, in Sekretariat Dewan Perwakilan Rakyat Gotong Royong, *Undang-undang Pemilihan Umum dan Undang-undang Susunan dan Kedudukan MPR, DPR dan DPRD*, Jakarta: Sekretariat Dewan Perwakilan Rakyat Gotong Royong: 120–32.

'*Kompas*: the concept of the floating mass [25 September 1971]', in R.M. Smith (ed.) (1974) *Southeast Asia: Documents of Political Development and Change*, Ithaca, New York: Cornell University Press: 233–5.

'The holy anger of a generation' (translation of an article in *Mahasiswa Indonesia* [Edisi Djawa Barat] 19 June 1967), in R.M. Smith (ed.) (1974) *Southeast Asia: Documents of Political Development and Change*, Ithaca, New York: Cornell University Press: 211–13.

'Penjelasan Tentang Golongan Putih', in Arbi Sanit (ed.) (1992) *Analisa Pandangan Fenomena Politik Golput*, Jakarta: Sinar Harapan: 46–8.

Arief Budiman (1971) 'Jawaban kepada Ali Sadikin tentang Golput' (from *Kami*, 15 June 1971), in Arbi Sanit (ed.) (1992) *Analisa Pandangan Fenomena Politik Golput*, Jakarta: Sinar Harapan: 140–1.

S.M. Amin (1970) *Polemik dengan 'Berita Yudha' mengenai Dwi-Fungsi ABRI dan Civic Mission*: Hudaya: 15–16, 19–20, 23–5, 33–4, 48–50, 52–3, 70–1, 78, 90.

Chapter 3

Idham Chalid (1969) 'Tjeramah Ketua Umum P.B. N.U. pada pendidikan instruktur kader N.U. di Tjisarua', in Amak Fadhali (ed.) (1969) *NU dan Aqidahnya*, Semarang: CV Toha Putra: 7–16.

Hamka (1973) 'Dari hati ke hati: RUU perkawinan yang menggoncangkan', *Harian Kami*, 24 August 1973.

Nurcholish Madjid (1970) 'Keharusan pembaruan pemikiran Islam dan masalah integrasi umat', in N. Madjid (1987) *Islam: Kemodernan dan Keindonesiaan*, Bandung: Mizan: 204–14.

H.M.S. Mintaredja (1973) *Islam and Politics, Islam and State in Indonesia: A Reflection and Revision of Ideas*, Jakarta: Permata.

Chapter 4

Soeharto (1980) 'Amanat tambahan Presiden Soeharto pada pembukaan rapat pimpinan ABRI 1980', *Kompas*, 8 April 1980.

Ali Moertopo (1983) 'Membina ketahanan ideologi Pancasila: Ceramah pada penataran P4 tingkat instansi pusat Departemen Penerangan RI, tanggal 24 Mei 1980, Jakarta', in Departemen Penerangan (1983) *Himpunan Pidato Menteri Penerangan RI 1978–1982, Peningkatan Penerangan yang Berwibawa*, Jakarta: Departemen Penerangan: 197–215.

Chapter 5

'White Book of the Students' Struggle' (1978), *Indonesia*, April 1978.

Yayasan Lembaga Bantuan Hukum Indonesia (1984) *Hukum, Politik dan Pembangunan: Pokok-Pokok Pemikiran Yayasan LBH Indonesia tentang Perundang-Undangan Pembangunan Kehidupan Politik*, Jakarta: Yayasan Lembaga Bantuan Hukum Indonesia.

Hartono Rekso Dharsono (1986) 'Demanding the promise of the New Order (Menuntut Janji Orde Baru)', *Indonesia Reports*, no. 17, August: 2–17.

Abdurrahman Wahid (1987) 'Pancasila dan Liberalisme', *Kompas*, 21 July 1987.

Chapter 6

Drs K.H. Hasbullah Bakry SH (1973) 'Masalah akselerasi pembangunan 25 Tahun di Indonesia (Suatu sumbangan pikiran buat buku Ali Moertopo)', *Harian Kami*, 9 and 17 August 1973.

Sjafruddin Prawiranegara (1984) 'Pancasila as the sole foundation', *Indonesia*, no. 38, October 1984: 74–83.

Pengurus Besar Himpunan Mahasiswa Islam (1984) *Pandangan Kritis terhadap RUU Keormasan*, Jakarta: Himpunan Mahasiswa Indonesia.

Amir Biki (1990) Speech, Tanjung Priok, 12 September 1984, *Indonesia Reports' Human Rights Supplement*, nos. 28–29, January–February 1990: 3–8.

Abdurrahman Wahid (1990) 'Indonesia's Muslim middle class: an imperative or a choice?', in R. Tanter and K. Young (eds) *The Politics of Middle Class Indonesia*, Melbourne: Monash University Centre of Southeast Asian Studies: 22–4.

Chapter 7

Fazlur Akhmad (1989) 'The Indonesian student movement 1920–1989: a force for radical social change?', *Prisma* no. 47, (English language edition), September: 81–95.

Taufik Rahzen (1989) 'Anti-violence manifesto', *Inside Indonesia*, no. 19, July 1989: 15.

SKEPHI (1990) *Selling Our Common Heritage: Commercialisation of Indonesia's Forest*, Jakarta and Penang: Network for Forest Conservation in Indonesia and World Rainforest Movement.

Nursyahbani Katjasungkana (1994) 'Relevensi otonomi dan persamaan gender', *Kompas*, 26 September.

Wiji Thukul (1986) 'Peringatan', in Wiji Thukul (2000) *Aku Ingin Jadi Peluru: Kumpulan Sajak Wiji Thukul*, Magelang: IndonesiaTera: 61.

Chapter 8

General Soemitro (1989) 'Aspiring to Normal Politics', *Far Eastern Economic Review*, 6 April: 22.

Soeharto (1989) *Pidato Kenegaraan Presiden Republik Indonesia Soeharto di depan Sidang Dewan Perwakilan Rakyat 16 Agustus 1989*, Jakarta: Republik Indonesia.

Soeharto (1990) *Pidato Kenegaraan Presiden Republik Indonesia Soeharto di depan Sidang Dewan Perwakilan Rakyat 16 Agustus 1990*, Jakarta: Republik Indonesia.

Tim PPW-LIPI (1996) 'Menuju reformasi politik Order Baru: Beberapa usulan perbaikan', in S. Haris and R. Sibudi (eds) *Menelaah Format Politik Orde Baru*, Jakarta: Gramedia: 182–91.

Chapter 9

'Intelligence Test', *Inside Indonesia*, no. 8, October 1986: 8.

W.S. Rendra (1978) 'Poem of an angry person', trans M. Lane, *Inside Indonesia*, no. 2, 1984: 25.

Iwan Fals and Naniel (1989) 'Bento', *Swami I*, Jakarta: PT Airo Swadaya Stupa Records.

Marsillam Simanjuntak (1990) 'Bicaralah, dan nyatakan!', *Tempo*, 15 September: 33.

Dawam Rahardjo (1995) 'Visi dan misi kehadiran ICMI: Sebuah pengantar', in Nasrullah Ali-Fauzi (ed.) *ICMI Antara Status Quo dan Demokratisasi*, Bandung: Penerbit Mizan: 25–43.

Y.B. Mangunwijaya (1996) 'Komunis', in Y.B. Mangunwijaya (1997) *Politik Hati Nurani* (compiled by Ignatius Haryanto), Jakarta: Grafiasri Mukti: 23–5.

Chapter 10

Padmo Wahyono (1989) 'Pengembangan hak dan kewajiban asasi warga negara dalam mengamalkan Pancasila dan Undang-Undang Dasar 1945', in Padmo Wahyono (1989) *Pembangunan Hukum di Indonesia*, Jakarta: IHC: 109–11.

'Adakah hak asasi manusia di dalam UUD 1945?', *Forum Keadilan*, no. 20, 21 January 1993: 66–7.

Budiono Kusumohamidjojo (1988) 'Harga birokrasi hukum dalam deregulasi', *Kompas*, 29 April.

Juwono Sudarsono (1997) 'A diplomatic scam called human rights', *Jakarta Post*, 11 April.

Government of Indonesia (1998) 'Human rights in Indonesia', Indonesian Department of Foreign Affairs homepage; available at http://www.dfadeplu.go.id/English/ham.htm (9 February 1998).

Chapter 11

Frans Seda (1996) 'Otonomi daerah', *Kekuasaan dan Moral Politik Ekonomi, Masyarakat Indonesia Baru*, Jakarta: Grasindo: 157–62.

Mohammad Daud Yoesoef (1999) 'Aceh masih mungkin pisah dari RI', *Serambi*, 7 March.

Anonymous (1992) 'If only I were a free person (Or: Soewardi Soeryaningrat lives again)', *Inside Indonesia*, no. 33, December: 7–8.

Y.B. Mangunwijaya (1998) 'Federal system best way to end separatism issue', *Jakarta Post*, 4 August.

Major-General Sudrajat (2000) 'Federalisme masih diperdebatkan', in B. Simorangkir (ed.) *Otonomi atau Federalisme: Dampaknya Terhadap Pembangunan*, Jakarta: Pustaka Sinar Harapan: 183–6.

Chapter 12

H.M. Amien Rais (1998) 'Suksesi 1998: Suatu keharusan', in M. Najib, Supan and K. Sukardiyono (eds) (1998) *Suara Amien Rais, Suara Rakyat*, Jakarta: Gema Insani Press: 21–47.

'People's Democratic Party calls for an end to New Order regime', trans. James Balowski, *Green Left Weekly*, no. 318, 20 May 1998; available at http://www.greenleft.org.au/(16 March 2002).

B.J. Habibie (1998) 'The era of awakening for democracy', *Jakarta Post*, 16 August.

'Ideologi yang toleran', *Media Indonesia* (editorial), 16 January 1999.

TNI Abad XXI: Redefinisi, Reposisi dan Reaktualisasi Peran TNI dalam Kehidupan Bangsa, Jakarta: Jasa Buma (fourth printing), June 1999.

'Jenderal pembuat heboh', *Gatra*, 23 December 1999: 69.

'Mayjen TNI Agus Wirahadikusumah, MPA: Jenderal-jenderal muda maunya pakai kekerasan', *Tajuk*, 31 December 1999.

'Mayjen TNI Agus Wirahadikusumah: Dominasi ABRI itu terlalu jauh', *Tempo*, 26 December 1999: 26–7.

Introduction

David Bourchier and Vedi R. Hadiz

Analysing the politics of a country as enormous and complex as Indonesia has always been a challenge.[1] This was particularly the case under Soeharto's military-backed New Order regime, which from the 1960s controlled political life to such an extent that political contestation all but disappeared from public view. Foreign observers accustomed to the hurly-burly of liberal democratic politics frequently mistook the nuanced language of public discourse in Soeharto's Indonesia for consensus, over-looking the country's bloody political past and the often desperate struggles which continued to swirl below the surface. Others depicted politics in Indonesia, equally misleadingly, as an encounter between tyrants and hapless victims. The mass demonstrations that forced Soeharto's resig-nation in 1998 and the turbulent political competition since that time confirmed in spectacular fashion the inaccuracy of both views.

A central purpose of this book is to look beyond homogenising stereo-types and present a rich, textured picture of Indonesian politics from 1965 until the immediate post-Soeharto period, which captures the flavour of domestic political struggles within and outside the confines of permissible discourse. Providing a fuller portrait of the dynamics of political life during these decades is a vital step towards understanding not only the Soeharto years but also their legacy – a legacy that Indonesians have to grapple with as they face the road ahead.

At the core of this book are 84 readings taken from speeches, news-paper columns, pamphlets, courtroom defences and other primary sources spanning the 34 years between 1965 and the end of 1999. Most we have translated from Indonesian. Others were written in English or appeared subsequently in English translation. While some will be well known to students of Indonesia, others are more obscure. The items have been selected because they represent either historical turning points or impor-tant positions in the debates that have shaped politics. Many are to some degree polemical, even emotive, although we have also included some more reflective and analytical pieces. Still others are statements by political actors dealing with timely issues. By presenting a rich diversity of opinions among Indonesians, we hope to convey some of the complexity of their debates on the present and future of the country. Ian Chalmers and Vedi Hadiz published a companion volume in 1997 on the politics of economic thinking in the Soeharto period, but this is the first general book-length anthology of its kind since the publication in 1970 of Herbert Feith and Lance Castles' classic text, *Indonesian Political Thinking, 1945–1965*.

In this introduction we begin with a brief survey of the ideological forces that shaped political contestation in modern Indonesia before the mid-1960s. We then introduce the key concepts that will be used in this book, before presenting an overview of the main political developments and controversies in the New Order and its aftermath. We conclude with some reflections on the ideological legacies that present and future governments in Indonesia are faced with.

Ideological conflict in Indonesian history

Conflict over ideology has been a feature of political life in Indonesia since the early days of the nationalist movement. The fault lines, though, have shifted with the vagaries of national and international politics. At times the crucial debates have been between proponents and opponents of an Islamic state. At other times the predominant cleavage has been between Java and the outer islands, between communists and anti-communists, or between pluralists and authoritarians. Just as Indonesia itself is not a 'natural' entity, there are no 'natural' or permanent factors that divide it. Any discussion of cleavages and streams of thinking must therefore be situated clearly within their historical context.

From the time Indonesia emerged as an idea in the early 20th century there were contending visions of what kind of nation-state it should be. Secular nationalists such as Mohammad Hatta envisaged a modern social democratic state committed to capitalist economic development, education and social justice. Indonesia's communists shared some of the ideals of the secular nationalists but took a harder line against the Dutch. Their popularisation of Lenin's idea that colonialism was the logical extension of capitalism did a great deal to unite Indonesians and mobilise them against Dutch colonial rule. A third stream, more diverse than the first two, was Islam. The most influential Islamic organisations were the modernist Sarekat Islam and Muhammadiyah, which were concerned first of all with promoting the interests of Muslim traders and with cleansing 'rural' or traditionalist Islam of its accretions. These organisations were a powerful grassroots force linking together hundreds of thousands, if not millions, of people who looked forward to an independent state based on Islamic principles. A fourth group were the cultural nationalists, with their origins in a kaleidoscopic array of ethnic associations predating Indonesian nationalism. The most enduring were the Javanese cultural nationalists associated with the colonial administrative elite, who envisaged an Indonesia based on traditionalist, even feudal, principles in which a hereditary caste would preside over a mass of contented villagers. There was also a populist variant of Javanese nationalism that underpinned a series of more or less egalitarian millenarian peasant movements.

The ideas of these groups ebbed, flowed and spilled over into each other. Communists and Muslims, for example, collaborated closely for some years before splitting in the early 1920s. Many of the secular nationalists had leftist sympathies and many – Hatta included – were devout Muslims. Sukarno, who emerged as the most powerful voice of Indonesian nationalism after about 1927, made a conscious effort to unite what he regarded as the three major streams of Indonesian thought, Marxism, Islam and nationalism, but included a good measure of Javanese populism as well (Sukarno 1966).

The harsh post-1927 crackdown following a communist uprising and the stringent political controls of the 1930s saw most communist and secular nationalist leaders imprisoned or exiled. The colonial authorities also targeted Muslim leaders, who had by this time already isolated themselves from the secular nationalists. Only the Javanists and the most 'cooperative' of nationalist parties were allowed to carry on political activities, and then only through the Dutch-dominated Volksraad or People's Assembly.

The Japanese invasion in 1942 changed everything. In order to support their war effort, the Japanese put great energy into mobilising and energising the youth. Sukarno and Hatta, by that time revered symbols of the nationalist struggle, were returned from exile and put in charge of mass organisations with access to radio and newspapers. Modernist and traditionalist Muslim parties were united for the first time and given considerable freedom to expand their influence. Leaders of the conservative traditionalist Parindra, which had been the most pro-Japanese party in the 1930s, were given high posts in the Japanese administration, but their lack of mobilisational skills meant that they were sidelined in favour of the more radical secular nationalists. Of all the major political groups that had made up the nationalist movement before 1942, only the communists and some socialists, such as Sutan Sjahrir, were completely prohibited from organising during the Japanese occupation.

Sukarno and Hatta proclaimed Indonesia's independence on 17 August 1945, shortly after the surrender of the Japanese to the Allies. The one-party state that Sukarno tried to establish was quickly discredited as a Japanese creation and Sutan Sjahrir, the most prominent of the non-communists untainted by association with the Japanese, rose to the fore. With the help of Vice-President Hatta, Sjahrir brought Sukarno's brief period of direct presidential rule to an end and introduced a parliamentary system in which people were free to form political parties (Anderson 1972; G.McT. Kahin 1952).

But Indonesia was not yet independent. The Allies had won the war and soon the Dutch returned to try to re-establish their empire. Between 1945 and 1949 the fledgling republican government fought on the diplomatic front for international recognition, while at the same time conducting an armed struggle against the Dutch. This armed struggle involved tens of thousands of young men and women, fired up by nationalist zeal, who organised themselves into Muslim, nationalist and leftist organisations and devoted themselves with religious intensity to the cause of independence. The older generation of secular nationalist politicians who were trying to convince the world of the credibility of the republic found themselves increasingly at odds with the militias, planting the seeds of a lasting suspicion between those who placed their trust in negotiation and those who put 'spirit' before all (see Anderson 1972).

The revolution was largely uncoordinated; in some places it had a class characteristic, while in others it deteriorated into a virtual civil war between armed groups affiliated with political parties. Secular nationalist groups pitted themselves against Muslim militias and later suppressed a communist uprising in Madiun in 1948, leaving scores dead. Secular nationalists emerged as dominant within the military, leaving within it a lasting legacy of anti-Muslim and anti-communist sentiment. A further legacy of the revolution was a crop of political leaders skilled in the art of mass mobilisation but with little feel for administration or law.

After winning formal independence from the Dutch in 1949, Indonesia put in place a parliamentary democracy in which a plethora of large and small parties competed for support. Indonesia was ruled by a series of coalition cabinets dominated by three parties: the secular nationalist Indonesian Nationalist Party (PNI); Masjumi, the party of modernist Muslims, drawing support mainly from outside Java; and Nahdlatul Ulama (NU), the traditionalist Muslim party based largely in Java. The social democratic Indonesian Socialist Party (PSI) and two conservative aristocratic parties, the Greater Indonesia Party (Parindra) and the Greater Indonesia Unity Party (PIR), were also well represented (Feith 1962).

The period of parliamentary democracy was remarkably open. Democratic values were widely espoused, the courts operated independently, and there were very few restrictions on the press. Indonesia's first general election, in 1955, still stands as its freest and fairest. But it did not establish clear winners. The poll showed roughly equal support for four parties: Masjumi, NU, PNI and the Indonesian Communist Party (PKI). Much to the chagrin of the intellectual and aristocratic elites, the PSI and the conservative traditionalist parties were all but ignored by the electorate.

Between 1956 and 1959 the elected Constituent Assembly devoted itself to the task of drawing up a new democratic constitution. The major sticking point in its deliberations was the question of whether the state should take a direct role in obliging Muslims to abide by the dictates of their religion. As debate over this and other questions dragged on for months, more urgent issues came to dominate the political stage. Military commanders on Sumatra and Sulawesi, dissatisfied with the centralisation of economic and political power on Java, set up leadership councils that refused to accept directions from the capital. These local councils developed into an inter-regional anti-Jakarta movement (PRRI/Permesta), and in 1957 proclaimed a counter-government. Fearing national disintegration, Sukarno gave the central military command wide martial law powers, which they used both to suppress their brothers-in-arms and to extend their grasp on the apparatus of state administration. Confident and increasingly assertive, in 1957 the military took over managerial control of strategic, newly nationalised British and Dutch companies, which had originally been seized by militant labour unions, especially those associated with SOBSI, the PKI-linked labour federation (Hadiz 1997: 53–4).

Thereafter, the centre of political gravity shifted away from the parties and the parliament to the army. The other beneficiary of the national emergency was Sukarno, who was deeply dissatisfied with his figurehead role under the parliamentary system. Frustrated also by what he saw as the endless bickering among rival political parties, Sukarno had voiced his displeasure with the parliamentary system as early as 1956, telling a meeting of youth delegates: 'we are afflicted by the disease of parties which, alas, alas, makes us forever work against one another!...Let us bury them, bury them' (Feith and Castles 1970: 81, 83). This anti-party rhetoric resonated strongly with the armed forces and remained an important element of political discourse within military circles for decades.

With the active backing of the army, Sukarno dissolved the Constituent Assembly and proclaimed 'Guided Democracy', a system in which he held wide-ranging executive powers and in which parliament would comprise representatives of 'functional groups' such as workers, women, youth and farmers. Such a system, he envisaged, would uphold the interests of society as a unified whole (Reeve 1985: 108–9). As the army moved into an increasingly hostile relationship with Sukarno it appropriated this corporatist mode of organisation and made these 'functional groups' the basis of its own political vehicle, Golkar, which was established in 1964.

During the Guided Democracy period (1959–65) the old ideological divisions gave way to a left–right polarisation, mirroring the Cold War struggle within which Indonesian politics became increasingly enmeshed. The army and the PKI emerged as the two main contending forces, with Sukarno attempting to prevent either from threatening his position. Of the major political parties, the PKI was the only one to maintain, if not increase, its power and influence. It did this in part by ingratiating itself with Sukarno, supporting his concept of Nasakom (the unity of nationalism, Islam and communism), his 'Confrontation' with Malaysia, his campaign to 'return' West Irian to Indonesia and his increasingly friendly relations with Mao Zedong's China (Mortimer 1974).

Meanwhile the military, fearful of the growing might of the PKI – especially in Java, where it had done well in the regional elections of 1957 – developed an alliance with the anti-communist forces. These included the right wing of the PNI, the Christian parties, and even the Masjumi and the PSI, which had been banned by Sukarno in 1960 for their alleged complicity with the PRRI/Permesta rebels. Military leaders also developed close ties with the United States, where large numbers of military personnel were being trained. The US administration saw the military as their strongest guarantee against the growing power of the PKI, which by 1965 was the third-largest communist party in the world.

Political polarisation also developed apace in rural areas, especially in Java. With the backing of the PKI, landless farmers attempted to enforce new land reform laws, bringing them into direct and sometimes violent confrontation with the largely NU-aligned Muslim landowners. Conflicts over land exacerbated religious–cultural tensions between the Hindu–Buddhist-influenced *abangan* population of peasants and the more pious Muslim, and often landowning, *santri* community, giving the land conflicts an explosive religious dimension (Lyon 1970).

Making the situation worse, the economy was in freefall. Sukarno's frequent changes of economic policy and his campaign in 1964 to make Indonesia self-reliant had led to stagnation and gross inefficiencies. By 1965 inflation had spiralled to 600 per cent, and Indonesia faced the prospect of sinking further into poverty and hunger.

In this febrile atmosphere of political polarisation and dire economic uncertainty, rumours spread of a group of US-backed generals plotting to overthrow the ailing Sukarno. In an apparent attempt to pre-empt this move, a group of middle-ranking officers loyal to Sukarno kidnapped and killed six of the country's most senior generals on the night of 30 September 1965. The left-wing officers, led by Lieutenant-Colonel Untung, a battalion commander of Sukarno's palace guard, seized several key buildings in central Jakarta. From the state radio station they broadcast messages denouncing the military leadership and announcing the formation of a 50-member revolutionary council that would act to safeguard President Sukarno. Before the end of the following day, however, Major-General Soeharto, who had been spared by the young officers, had used his troops from the Army Strategic Reserve to assert control in Jakarta and crush the mutiny.

Many aspects of the abortive Untung 'coup' and the sequence of events that saw Soeharto take control of the army remain contentious. According to the New Order account (rehearsed in school dramas, films and public ceremonies throughout the Soeharto years) the abduction and killing of key army leaders was masterminded by the PKI. While some scholars support this account, there is now wide support for the view that the PKI's involvement in the affair was negligible and that Soeharto took advantage of a confused situation to blame PKI for what was essentially an internal military struggle, using their 'treachery' as an excuse to smash the party and assume control himself (Anderson and McVey 1971). Wertheim (1979) went further, arguing that Soeharto was working in league with Untung from the beginning (a view that gained considerable currency in Indonesia after 1998).

What is beyond dispute is that 30 September 1965 was a watershed in Indonesian history. It led, first of all, to the army taking dreadful revenge on its communist enemies. In one of the 20th century's worst episodes of mass murder, hundreds of thousands of members of the PKI and its mass organisations were killed (Cribb 1990: 1). The PKI and dozens of its affiliates were completely destroyed. The abortive coup – or, more precisely, Soeharto's counter-coup – greatly strengthened the hand of the army and led eventually to the downfall of President Sukarno, who the army alleged had conspired with the coup plotters and the communists. On 11 March 1966 – again in unclear circumstances – Sukarno put his signature to a document transferring wide-ranging powers to Soeharto. This was the cue Soeharto needed to sideline Sukarno and outlaw the PKI and take over as the effective ruler of the country. By 1968 Soeharto had been named president, after having been appointed acting president the year before. Sick and demoralised, Sukarno died in 1970 under virtual house arrest.

Conceptualising political thinking

The New Order was to change Indonesia in profound ways. It also changed the ways in which politics was interpreted. Before moving to a survey of the post-1965 period, it is important to consider what new maps might be necessary to chart the ideological landscape.

Grappling with the tumultuous years between 1945 and 1965, Feith and Castles (1970) identified five main streams of political thought: communism, radical nationalism, democratic socialism, Islam and Javanese traditionalism. They plotted these streams, and their associated parties, on an intriguing chart combining a horizontal left–right axis and a vertical Western–traditional axis (1970: 14). At the left extreme of a pendulum-shaped series of elongated circles were communism and the PKI, which was also regarded as the most Western party, despite its *abangan* support base. Occupying the middle ground was radical nationalism, an ideological predisposition shared by people across a spectrum of parties but which was represented politically by the PNI. Slightly further to the right, but substantially more Western, was demo-cratic socialism. Democratic socialists had no mass base, and no political vehicle after the PSI was banned, but were likewise influential in a range of parties and organisations at the elite level. At the far right end was Islam, a large category circumscribing both Masjumi and the Nahdlatul Ulama. Within the Islamic category, Masjumi was repre-sented as more Western, reflecting the fact that modernist Muslims, though anti-secular, were heavily influenced by the ideas of democratic socialism; they shared with the PSI, for instance, an interest in moder-nity, economic development, and a willingness to cooperate with the West. Traditionalists associated with Nahdlatul Ulama, on the other hand, were depicted as more custom bound and closer in many ways to the radical nationalists. Feith and Castles' final category, Javanese traditionalism, represented those who drew their inspiration from the Hindu Javanese tradition. Like the democratic socialists, they had only a tiny party, PIR, but exerted their mainly conservative influence in other groups, namely the PNI, NU, the armed forces and among territorial administrators (1970: 16).

The most obvious difference between the era Feith and Castles described and the years after 1965 was the virtual disappearance of the political left. Not only was the PKI eliminated; left-leaning and Sukarnoist members of the PNI, the military and some of the smaller parties were also purged, seriously eroding the currency of radical nationalism. One consequence of the left's defeat was that the political centre shifted sharply to the right. But with communism gone and the economy on the mend, new coalitions of interest soon surfaced; and with them came new, or at least redrawn, lines of cleavage.

In our analysis of the post-1965 period, we discern four main streams of political thinking that we have called organicism, pluralism, Islam and radicalism. 'Islam' is the only category carried over directly from Feith and Castles, although each of their five traditions continued – and indeed continues – to influence Indonesian political culture. Our adoption of this classification reflects not only the dramatic changes precipitated by the events of 1965, but also the far-reaching social transformation which industrialisation and the integration with the global economic order have brought about in Indonesia.

Organicism is the term we use to describe the official ideology of the New Order. Its recurring concepts are order, harmony and hierarchy. Organicists, among whom we count Soeharto and many of his closest political allies, promoted the idea that authority within the Indonesian state should reflect the patterns found within traditional families and orderly village societies. They rejected both communism and liberalism as divisive, and therefore out of tune with Indonesia's national personality. This stream of thinking has its roots partly in Javanese aristocratic traditionalism and partly in anti-Enlightenment European thought, spread through the influence of Dutch legal reformers (Bourchier 1996: 14–40). It was articulated most famously as 'integralism' by the lawyer Dr Raden Supomo during the constitutional debates of 1945, and found support among conservative sections of the civilian and military elite in the 1950s and 1960s. Its most tangible legacy in Indonesia was the corporatist principle of political organisation promoted by the military and some of their anti-party allies during Guided Democracy, and which would become the basis of the political restructuring in the 1970s. It also helped underpin the doctrine of *dwifungsi* (dual function), according to which the military claimed a socio-political role on the basis that it was an integral part of the 'national family' (Reeve 1985).

We use the term organicism in this book, perhaps controversially, to include the New Order's brand of apolitical developmentalism. According to many of the regime's Western-educated economic advisers, it was the state's first priority to facilitate economic development and modernisation, and in order to achieve this it was necessary to minimise the influence of political ideology. Indeed, the archaism of the traditionalists who looked to Supomo appears to conflict with the modernism of the regime's technocrats. But Soeharto's ideologues managed to combine them to potent effect. Soeharto's official title as Indonesia's 'Father of Development' (*Bapak Pembangunan*) symbolised the fusion of the two sets of ideas. While presiding over a program of rapid economic development, Soeharto simultaneously presented his government as the guardian of the culturally authentic 'village' values of *musyawarah* and *mufakat* (consultation and consensus). Coupling developmentalism with the idea that the state and society were part of the same 'big family' enabled his government to constitute opposition to itself or its development programs as not only disloyal, but also an affront to Indonesian cultural norms. Organicism provided the grounds for a rejection of a whole range of practices, from adversarial party politics to the separation of powers and voting in parliament, which were all held to reflect liberal and individualistic modes of social organisation imported from the West.

Pluralism describes the ideological perspective of many of the urban civilian groups that rallied around the New Order in the early days. In contrast to the organicists, they aspired to a more democratic political system in which Indonesia's social and cultural diversity could be expressed. Pluralists espoused concepts such as the rule of law, political openness, transparency and human rights. Their vision of democracy, however, was tempered by a fear of communism and a determination to avoid a re-emergence of the 'primordial' politics of class, religion and ethnicity that characterised Indonesia in the 1950s.

Pluralism in Indonesia has its roots in the social democratic tradition that influenced a range of pre-New Order political parties including Masjumi and the PSI. Pluralist principles underpinned the democratic constitution of 1950 and were in fact publicly espoused by most parties during the parliamentary period. Sukarno, however, was hostile to the multi-party system, and following his resurrection of the authoritarian 1945 Constitution in 1959 and the banning of the Masjumi and PSI a year afterwards very few dared openly espouse pluralist philosophies. Support for pluralism nevertheless continued among the small class of independent professionals, intellectuals and party leaders who became an influential part of the New Order's constituency. In this book we use the terms 'modernising' or 'critical' pluralists to reflect the fact that the pluralists who supported the New Order during its first years later became some of its most articulate critics.[2]

Islam is a somewhat problematic category given the great variety of streams within Islamic political thought and the significant overlap between Islamic perspectives and the others discussed here. For this reason, we considered not including it as a distinct stream of political thinking at all. There is, however, a set of shared values and symbols that clearly distinguish Islamic from non-Islamic political discourse, and we ultimately decided to include Islam as a stream of its own rather than to dissolve it into the other categories. This does not, of course, mean that all Muslim thinkers in the book are treated as representatives of the Islamic stream, for they are well represented among the pluralists and radicals in particular. Our Islamic category is reserved for those directly concerned with promoting Islamic values in politics and society – and includes those for and against the explicit establishment of a state based on Islamic law. It incorporates representatives from both the modernist and traditionalist schools of Islamic thought, as well as those who attempted to transcend this division.

Radicalism is probably the most contentious of our categories because it appeared later and has been less influential than the other perspectives. But to leave it out would be to ignore a distinctive stream of political thinking that has informed the agenda of a range of influential non-governmental organisations (NGOs), student groups and political activists, and which has recently led to major political change. The central proposition of radicalism is that the existing order is fundamentally exploitative and that liberation should come about through a radical redistribution of economic and political power. Many radicals see themselves as continuing the left-wing and radical nationalist traditions so important during the anti-colonial struggle and the early independence period. As a political force, however, radicalism only made its presence felt from the 1980s, in reaction to the large-scale social displacement and marginalisation caused by rapid economic development and industrialisation. Its agenda – and its language – is influenced by post-1965 developments in Marxist, environmentalist and feminist theory, as well as Islamic notions of social justice.

While the four categories discussed above provide a useful way of viewing some of the major debates of the post-1965 era, we do not pretend that they are the keys to understanding Indonesian politics. Indeed, a browse through the contents pages reveals that only in the first half of this book do the chapters focus explicitly on debates among and between representatives of these ideological communities. The second half is organised around particular themes and controversies, such as democratisation, human rights and regionalism, and events – including the economic crisis and political reform post-Soeharto. Overall, we opted for a chronological structure, with each of the book's four parts dealing with a particular phase of recent Indonesian history. It is to these phases that we will now turn, setting the broad context for the chapters that follow.

The search for a political format, 1965–73

On a large canvas, this was a period in which the military established its dominance in Indonesian politics and, with the backing of the Western powers, reintegrated the country with the global capitalist system. It began with the anti-communist pogrom and ended with the imposition of a political architecture that would serve the New Order for a quarter of a century. Compared with later periods in the history of Soeharto's New Order, these formative years were characterised by relatively open debate. Questions regarding the shape and character of the political system were settled only after protracted argument both within the military and between the military and civilian politicians. Often these arguments were public, as the restrictions on the print media were not as tight as they would later become.

The New Order in its early years is best thought of as an alliance between the military and a range of civilian groups that included students, secular intellectuals, professionals, anti-communist party leaders and large numbers of rural and urban Muslims. These groups had been united by their fear of the communists and by their perception that Sukarno was to blame for the economic crisis that had eroded their material interests. In class terms, they were essentially the urban and rural petty bourgeoisie and the urban salary-earners who had been hardest hit by the hyperinflation of the late Guided Democracy period (Robison 1986).

The military leadership, which was clearly the dominant partner in the alliance, had little wish to see parties play a major role in the new political system. In their view, explored in Chapter 1, parties had only succeeded in dividing Indonesians along religious and ideological lines, threatening national unity and leading ultimately to political and economic ruin. But they did not agree how, or how quickly, the old parties should be dispatched. One group, sometimes referred to as the New Order hawks, wanted to see the immediate dissolution of the multi-party system and the construction of a controlled arrangement in which two non-sectarian, modern-minded parties would participate. In this opinion they were strongly supported by many of the PSI-affiliated pluralist intellectuals cited in Chapter 2. The PSI had been steamrollered in the 1955 elections, and saw the kind of mass politics that existed then as inimical to the interests of both democracy and modernity.

Soeharto, though, was wary of demolishing the parties too quickly. The PNI and NU, two of the pillars of Sukarno's Guided Democracy, still had mass support. Others, including many former supporters of Masjumi, had a strong sense of entitlement, stemming from their record of anti-communist politics and from the part they had played in helping to establish the New Order. Soeharto's more cautious approach prevailed. His response was to preserve the existing parties while doing everything possible to weaken them and install compliant leaders.

At the same time as hobbling the parties, Soeharto entrusted his intelligence aide and primary political adviser, Ali Moertopo, with the ambitious task of creating a political vehicle capable of winning an election. Moertopo was one of the most important organicist thinkers and a key architect of the New Order. With the help of several civilian intellectuals coopted from the student movement – many of them Christians – Moertopo rebuilt Golkar. Like the 1964 version it was structured on corporatist principles, but the new Golkar was much better funded and was able to harness the full resources of the state apparatus, including the revitalised military.

Soeharto attempted to reassure the nation in a 1967 address that the New Order would not degenerate into a military dictatorship, and that the rule of law, democratic principles and human rights would be upheld. It was not long, though, before serious doubts about the intentions of the government emerged in the ranks of both the pluralists and the Muslims. Corruption, heavy-handed political engineering, and the military's increasing domination of social and political life were all common causes for complaint within the alliance by the end of the 1960s. Disillusionment about the prospects for democracy only grew as the government intensified its intimidation of parties and civil servants in anticipation of the 1971 elections. Symbolising the growing distance between the pluralists and the organicists was the election boycott campaign led by Arief Budiman, one of the leaders of the coalition that had toppled Sukarno. The boycott had little effect, however, and Golkar gained an absolute majority, with 62.8 per cent of the vote (van Marle 1974: 58–9).

Deflated by their poor performance, the bargaining position of the parties was considerably reduced. Ali Moertopo wasted no time in initiating a large-scale reorganisation of the political system, forcing the nine opposition parties to fuse into two government-sponsored bodies given the nondescript names PPP (United Development Party) and PDI (Indonesian Democratic Party). The former brought together four traditionally fractious Muslim parties, while the latter was an amalgamation of the remaining Christian, socialist and nationalist parties. Riven by internal contradictions and micro-managed by the military, the new parties were roundly defeated by Golkar in the next six elections.

In an attempt to further depoliticise society, new rules were brought in preventing the parties from maintaining a presence below the district level. Party-aligned mass organisations were also disbanded and their members absorbed into new state-backed corporatist bodies purporting to represent broad 'functional groups' in society, including labour, the peasantry and youth. These bodies, in turn, were incorporated into Golkar, which presented itself not as a political party but as an association of functional groups. In accordance with the regime's organicist ideology, all components of Golkar were expected to subordinate their particular interests to the national interest.

Muslim groups were a particular target of the New Order's drive to homogenise politics. While the regime was generous with grants to Muslim schools and mosques, it soon made clear its opposition to any attempt to reassert Islam through politics. This stemmed, in large part, from the New Order's aversion to mass-based politics. It also reflected the elite's cultural prejudices. The mostly *abangan* military and their secular or Christian partners dreaded the prospect of Islamic parties emerging as a major political force. Many Muslims, especially former supporters of Masjumi, felt betrayed by the New Order and their former allies among the PSI intellectuals. Others, such as the young Muslim intellectual Nurcholish Madjid, accommodated themselves to the new strictures, arguing that Muslims should focus on cultural issues rather than politics (see Chapter 3).

The New Order at its height, 1973–88

By 1973 the New Order political system had finally taken shape. Quite fortuitously, OPEC hiked up the price of oil the same year, reducing Indonesia's dependence on foreign aid and greatly strengthening the Soeharto regime.[3] Although oil prices were to fall a decade later, the government's economic managers were able to sustain an economic growth rate of around 6 per cent between 1973 and 1988, as well as a steady expansion of state spending on education, health, infrastructure projects, the armed forces and the bureaucracy. This facilitated an increase in employment opportunities and a rising standard of living for both urban and rural dwellers. But, while the economy grew, the period was marked by an increasing concentration of political power and an attenuation of civil and political rights. Restrictions on the press were also tightened, narrowing the scope for public debate.

Precipitating the initial clampdown was a serious riot in Jakarta in 1974 that came to be known as Malari, the Indonesian acronym for the 'Disaster of 15 January'. The riots began with student-led demonstrations targeted at the government's close relationship with domestic Chinese and foreign investors, especially the Japanese. Many prominent PSI-linked figures were arrested in the wake of Malari and 12 publications were closed down, including the newspapers *Abadi* and *Indonesia Raya*, which had regularly criticised the growing practices of political cronyism and corruption (Hill 1995). The episode also brought to a head a conflict within the military between the forces loyal to security chief General Soemitro, who favoured a shift towards a more institutionalised style of rule, and the 'freewheeling' generals and intelligence operatives associated with Ali Moertopo. Suspecting that Soemitro sympathised with the student protestors, Soeharto forced him into retirement, signalling an important defeat for what Jenkins (1984: 30) called the 'principled' group of army officers.

The post-Malari crackdown marked the final break between the pluralists and the organicists. It was not pluralism, however, but Islam that emerged as the most potent opposition force in the 1970s. Compounding their frustration at seeing their parties dissolved and excluded from the government, sections of the Muslim community were upset by the New Order's economic policies and its attempt to introduce a marriage law that they felt contravened Islamic principles (Emmerson 1976: 223–58). Worried that the PPP could challenge Golkar in the 1977 elections, the security authorities engaged in widespread intimidation of Muslim voters, and ultimately relied on vote-rigging to ensure a large win for the government party (Mackie and MacIntyre 1994: 15).

Muslim anger only intensified in the late 1970s and early 1980s when the government launched a major campaign to indoctrinate Indonesians with the state ideology of Pancasila.[4] Invented by Sukarno in 1945 as a formula to unite the new nation, Pancasila was invested with almost sacred status by the ideologues of the New Order.[5] Soeharto himself became increasingly obsessed with the Pancasila, and in the early 1980s pushed to have all political parties and mass organisations acknowledge it as their '*azas tunggal*', or sole foundation (see Chapter 4). Several Muslim groups resisted what they saw as an attempt to subordinate 'God-given' Islamic principles to the 'man-made' Pancasila. Tensions came to a head in September 1984 when government troops shot and killed scores of Muslim demonstrators in the working-class port area of Tanjung Priok (Chapter 6).

When his *azas tunggal* policy became law in 1985, Soeharto saw it as a great, even an epoch-making, achievement of his administration. Uniting all political forces under the Pancasila, he believed, enabled Indonesia to put behind it the ideological and religious conflict that had torn at its fabric in the past (Soeharto 1989: 382–3, 408–9). No longer would it be acceptable to advocate any ideology that conflicted with the Pancasila as defined by the government. The *azas tunggal* legislation was passed as part of a parcel of laws on political parties and mass organisations which together seriously restricted their freedoms and effectively codified the government's rejection of the very notion of oppositional politics.

Support for Soeharto among his former military colleagues had also eroded seriously by the early 1980s. Ali Sadikin, a retired marine lieutenant-general and former governor of Jakarta, became a leading light of a group of former military officers, intellectuals, student leaders and religious figures which in 1980 issued the 'Petition of Fifty', accusing the president of abusing his power and abandoning the ideals of the New Order and of the constitution. Soeharto's belligerent response to the Petition of Fifty group and to similar criticism by one of the early heroes of the New Order, retired Lieutenant-General Dharsono (see Chapter 5), indicated the degree to which he had managed to alienate former allies due to his increasingly intolerant attitude towards dissent.

Another source of opposition and criticism in the New Order era were NGOs. While some NGOs operating during the New Order had their precursors in the 1950s and early 1960s, former student activists set up many important groups in the early 1970s. They were disenchanted, in particular, with the New Order's authoritarian tendencies and its technocratic, top-down model of economic development, which NGO leaders felt neglected the needs and capacities of ordinary Indonesians. With political parties and mass organisations effectively domesticated, NGOs emerged as an alternative vehicle to voice the aspirations of the poor and powerless.[6] One of the most important of these was the Legal Aid Institute (LBH), established in 1971 with some assistance from the Jakarta municipal government. Under the guidance of a series of high-profile human rights lawyers, including Adnan Buyung Nasution and Mulya Lubis, LBH soon went beyond its initial brief of defending the indigent to publicly exposing the gap between the regime's rule of law rhetoric and the injustices pervasive in the political and economic system it presided over. Other NGOs worked in the area of social research, rural development, the environment, labour and urban poverty. While the mainstream activists and intellectuals of the NGO community might best be described as pluralists in the social democratic tradition, populist and Islamic ideas were also influential[7] (see Chapters 5 and 7).

But the most important schism to open up in the 1980s was between Soeharto and the military leadership and involved a contest for ascendancy over the institutions of state and differences regarding the status of the military as an autonomous power centre within the regime. The rift between the two became public in 1988, when armed forces commander General Benny Moerdani attempted to resist Soeharto's appointment of Golkar chair Sudharmono as vice-president (Vatikiotis 1993: 85–6). Although Sudharmono was himself a military lawyer, he was deeply unpopular among the officer corps because he had worked with Soeharto to reduce the political and economic autonomy of the armed forces. Sudharmono used his very considerable powers during his long tenure as chief of the State Secretariat to steer state contracts away from military companies towards non-military indigenous enterprises. This enabled him to build up a significant power base among indigenous business people, who were prevailed upon to support Golkar (see Pangaribuan 1995). He also transformed Golkar from a mere government electoral vehicle into a state-led mass party base, which in 1987 claimed 28 million members and 9 million cadres (Cribb and Brown 1995: 141). In the process Sudharmono wrested control of many branch offices from military officers, a move that alarmed the military leadership, who feared losing their grasp over the organisation.

The split in the regime that surfaced in 1988 eroded Soeharto's absolute dominance and thereby changed the character of the New Order. From this time onwards, Soeharto was forced to depend increasingly on his own skills as a political tactician and his own personal networks to maintain power.

Tensions and contradictions: 1988–97

The late New Order period saw the regime's grasp on society become increasingly unstuck. There were several reasons for this. One was that Soeharto could no longer rely on the full support of the military. Benny Moerdani was retained in the cabinet as defence minister in 1988, but forces loyal to him in parliament and the intelligence services used their influence to fan criticism of the aging president. But on a broader level, it was because society had changed. Indonesians were more educated, more healthy, more mobile and more prosperous than they had been in the late 1960s. A prolonged period of economic growth and stability had produced a substantial middle class and a rapidly expanding urban working class. These people read newspapers and watched television; they knew about human rights and gossiped about the corruption of the elite. Many had grown cynical about the government's warnings about the 'latent threat' of communism and official rhetoric about the benefits of Pancasila democracy, Pancasila industrial relations and a Pancasila press. And few had faith in the corporatist bodies that were supposed to represent their interests. In short, the New Order began to lose its coherence because its political architecture could no longer accommodate the tremendous social changes that had taken place over the past two decades.

Soeharto was not blind to these changes. In an attempt to regain the initiative, he reached out to the Muslim community his government had marginalised in the 1970s and 1980s. Reversing a longstanding prohibition against religiously exclusivist political organisations, in 1990 he sponsored the formation of the Indonesian Muslim Intellectuals' Association, known as ICMI. Under the leadership of his long-time Minister of Research and Technology Dr B.J. Habibie, ICMI was warmly embraced by many middle-class urban Muslims, including a number of NGO activists and intellectuals who had previously been opposed to the government (Ramage 1997; Hefner 1993). The support of this important constituency helped dilute Muslim criticism of Soeharto during his last years in office (see Chapter 9).

The president also sought to make peace with his pluralist critics. Prompted by calls from military parliamentarians for an easing of political controls, and also, no doubt, by the changed international atmosphere brought on by the ending of the Cold War, the president signalled his support for increased political 'openness' (*keterbukaan*). This led to a significant relaxation of controls on the media and to a period of more open public debate in the early 1990s. Newspapers and magazines tested the limits, publishing previously unprintable views on government policy and politics. The army's massacre of demonstrators at the Santa Cruz cemetery in East Timor in 1991, for instance, was given widespread and critical coverage. Private television stations also proliferated in the early 1990s. Despite the fact these were all owned by Soeharto's cronies or his famously avaricious children, competition for market share saw them, too, tempt audiences with talk show programs dealing with sensitive political issues (Sen and Hill 2000: ch. 4).

Democracy was a favourite topic of debate in this period. One increasingly mainstream line of argument, adopted in part from US neo-liberal discourse, was that globalisation demanded transparency. Since the mid-1980s Indonesia had been pursuing a policy of accelerated economic deregulation and liberalisation. The logical corollary, many argued, was that the country's rigid and authoritarian political structures should also be broken down to allow for greater participation and accountability. Other groups were inspired more by the rising status of human rights in the post-Cold War world, pressing Soeharto to recognise the legitimacy of international human rights standards (see Chapters 8 and 9). The regime made some concessions to these pressures, setting up a National Commission on Human Rights in 1993. At the same time, however – like Malaysia and Singapore – it maintained that 'Western' standards could not be applied in Indonesia. In an attempt to buttress this position, the regime's ideologues revived the notion, enunciated by Supomo in 1945, that Indonesia was an 'integralist state' (*negara integralistik*) inspired and guided by indigenous Indonesian values of harmony and cooperation. By this logic, any attempt to import liberal notions such as individual human rights and the separation of powers was illegitimate from both a cultural and a constitutional perspective. This argument, and some of the responses it provoked from pluralist critics, is detailed in Chapter 10.

While these arguments were taking place at the elite level, radical activists were beginning to make an impact at the grass roots, mobilising farmers and workers. Radicalism had its beginnings in the student movement. After a crackdown on campus activities in the late 1970s, students had begun to organise in small, non-campus-based groups, where they read the Marxist literature that had been denied to them in their formal studies. Many also took a keen interest in the left-wing tradition that had played an important role in Indonesia since early in the century. In the late 1980s sections of the student movement sided openly with peasants dispossessed in land disputes, often joining them in confrontations with the security apparatus. By the early 1990s radicalised students, some of whom were linked with Islamic-based formal student organisations, were successfully assisting urban industrial workers to organise and take mass industrial action (Aspinall 1996: 229). These protests often provoked harsh retribution; the murder of factory worker/activist Marsinah in 1993 was the best-known example. The ability of a small core of radical activists to organise large student/worker protests during the period 1989–94 helped revive mass protest, which had been suppressed by terror in 1965, as a form of political action. This did much to pave the way for the demonstrations that weakened the Soeharto regime between 1996 and its end in 1998. It also helped convince a wider circle of activists of the efficacy of mass action, leading to the formation of the People's

Democratic Party (PRD) in 1994. Established in defiance of the law, PRD became the main mouthpiece for political radicalism in the late New Order (see Chapter 7).

Another sign of the New Order's waning authority, and of the increasing relevance of mass politics, was Megawati Soekarnoputri's surprise election as chair of the PDI in 1993. Soeharto always feared Sukarno's ghost, aware of the reverence Indonesia's first president continued to inspire among the poor. Megawati quickly emerged as a symbol of opposition, attracting both popular adulation and the backing of a coalition of liberal intellectuals, student radicals and labour activists. There were high expectations that the PDI would win a large share of the vote in the 1997 elections and that Megawati would challenge Soeharto for the presidency in the March 1998 session of the People's Consultative Assembly.

This was too much for the Soeharto government, however, which sponsored a 'rebel' congress in 1996 at which Soerjadi, the man Megawati had taken over from in 1993, was reinstalled as leader. Refusing to accept Soerjadi's leadership, Megawati's followers occupied the PDI headquarters in leafy central Jakarta, setting up a 'free speech podium' outside, where speakers routinely denounced the government. Conscious of Megawati's popularity in crowded Jakarta, the authorities were reluctant to act, leaving the occupation to continue for several weeks. With the regime's remaining legitimacy ebbing rapidly, the authorities decided to take the building by force. On 27 July 1996 soldiers and paid thugs launched a frontal assault that killed several PDI supporters and triggered serious rioting in Jakarta. As had happened on several previous occasions, 'extremist' masterminds were identified – in this instance the PRD – and held responsible for instigating the riots. A nationwide crackdown on the PRD saw its leaders imprisoned for long terms and its network of sympathisers persecuted, tortured and in some cases 'disappeared'.[8] Such tactics were used routinely against opponents in East Timor, Aceh and West Papua, but the regime's resort to violence and intimidation in its heartland was widely perceived as a sign of its increasing alienation.

Crisis and reform: 1997–9

Part IV of this book addresses the fall of Soeharto and some of the issues that burst to the surface in its wake. We have described above the erosion of Soeharto's political base over the years. Few predicted in 1997, however, that the regime was about to collapse. Indeed, Golkar won the 1997 general election and, through a cleverly managed series of transfers and promotions, Soeharto regained the support of the dominant factions within the military. He may well have lived out the rest of his years in office if it had not been for the currency crisis that wrought havoc across Asia in late 1997 and 1998.

Indonesia turned out to be the most vulnerable of the Asian economies. Between June 1997 and January 1998 its currency lost almost 80 per cent of its value, plunging from around Rp2,400 to the US dollar, to Rp16,500. The crumbling value of the rupiah sent interest rates to 60 per cent, paralysing the financial and industrial sectors and sending the price of basic commodities skyrocketing. This in turn led to massive unemployment and to a dramatic rise in absolute poverty. Income per capita, which was hovering at about US$1,000 before the crisis, was estimated at less than US$350 by early 1998 (*Jakarta Post*, 17 April 1998). Where only a year earlier Indonesia had been lauded internationally for its economic success, its exploding levels of foreign currency debt put it at the mercy of the International Monetary Fund (IMF). The IMF took the opportunity to force on Indonesia a number of far-reaching reforms as a condition of a rescue package, including the slashing of subsidies on fuel, electricity and food. This, however, made the situation for ordinary people worse, triggering food riots in several towns across Java.

More fundamentally, the IMF's conditions of assistance included policies which would have directly undermined the rent-seeking business interests of the Soeharto family and their cronies. Several times, Soeharto baulked at taking steps agreed upon with the IMF, convincing the IMF and Western creditors and governments that Soeharto was the main obstacle to the reforms they considered crucial for Indonesia's economic recovery.

Entrenched as he was, Soeharto was initially able to survive even the onslaught of the economic crisis. In March 1998 the People's Consultative Assembly unanimously elected him to yet another five-year term in office. But his appointment of a cabinet that included his daughter 'Tutut' and long-time crony Bob Hasan saw confidence in Soeharto plummet further. 'Corruption, collusion and nepotism' quickly caught on as the catch cry of the *reformasi* movement.

A turning point came on 12 May with the fatal shooting of four students at a demonstration at Jakarta's prestigious Trisakti University. This public breach of an unwritten taboo made the government appear desperate and witless, as did its failure to prevent the looting, pillaging and burning of ethnic Chinese areas of Jakarta over the next two days, which left more than 2,000 dead. Indeed, the violence that shook the capital was understood in many quarters to have been engineered by a section of the military itself in an effort to tarnish the opponents of the regime and justify a crackdown – and possibly a military takeover – by Soeharto's son-in-law Lieutenant-General Prabowo Subianto (see Richburg 1998; Sim 1998).

On 21 May 1998, after more mass protests, culminating in a five-day occupation of the parliamentary complex by students and workers, Soeharto finally agreed to resign. He handed over power to his vice-president, B.J. Habibie, an aeronautical engineer, who had, as a minister, been in charge of developing Indonesia's hi-tech industries. Habibie was admired by many Muslim intellectuals but, as a protégé of Soeharto with no expertise in economic management, his appointment was greeted with little enthusiasm either domestically or internationally.

Habibie's only hope of survival was to distance himself from his mentor as quickly and thoroughly as he could. Almost immediately he revoked laws governing the licensing of the press, as well as most restrictions on forming political parties, unions and professional bodies, demolishing at a stroke some of the central features of the New Order system. These moves had an enormously liberating effect. In the space of weeks dozens of new political parties were formed, revealing the diverse reality of the Indonesian political landscape after decades of straitjacketing. The media also took full advantage of the new freedoms, subjecting politics to a degree of scrutiny unfamiliar to journalists and public figures alike. Military officials in particular were taken aback by the sustained attacks on them in the press for their past record of corruption and violence. This anti-military sentiment played an important part in forcing the military to accept a series of reforms that reduced their political role and separated the national police from their control (Bourchier 1999, 2000; D.F. Anwar 1999).

One of the immediate challenges facing Habibie was the upsurge of demands for autonomy and independence in the provinces unleashed by *reformasi*. Relations between Jakarta and the provinces had long been beset by tensions stemming from the New Order's highly centralised system of administration. There had been little opportunity to express such grievances in the past, since Soeharto had always been quick to accuse regionally based movements of harbouring separatist ambitions – or of links with armed rebels in the case of East Timor, Aceh and West Papua. Habibie emerged as an enthusiastic advocate of decentralisation, initiating legislation that devolved considerable powers to the provincial and sub-provincial levels. On East Timor he went further, surprising the world, and many in his own government, by agreeing to a UN-supervised referendum on the future of the territory. This offer of independence to the East Timorese accelerated demands for independence in Aceh and West Papua, raising the spectre – in some minds at least – of national disintegration. Ethnic and religious violence in other areas, most notably West Kalimantan and Ambon, only reinforced the impression that Indonesia was fragmenting from within. In Chapter 11 we present a sample of views from the regions dating from both before and after the fall of Soeharto, as well as two examples from the debate that took place in Jakarta on how to prevent a break-up of the country.

Another important legacy of the Habibie period was Indonesia's first free general election since 1955. As expected, Megawati's PDI-P (Indonesian Democratic Party of Struggle) gained the most votes in the election, held on 7 June 1999. But her party was unable to win an absolute majority, gaining only 153 seats in the 500-member People's Representative Council. In second place was Golkar, with 120 seats. Most of the remaining seats went to six Muslim-oriented parties, the largest of which were PPP, PKB (National Awakening Party) and PAN (National Mandate Party), with 58, 51 and 34, respectively. After much backroom deal-making, the Muslim parties teamed up with sections of Golkar to defeat Megawati, who some feared would promote a secular nationalist agenda at the expense of Islam. Instead they chose Abdurrahman Wahid, who took over as Indonesia's first democratically elected president on 20 October 1999.

Megawati Soekarnoputri was anguished by what she saw as Wahid's betrayal, but accepted a role as vice-president. She did not have to wait long, though, because Wahid quickly alienated the coalition that brought him to power with his imperious and erratic style of rule. He had little more success than Habibie in restoring the economy, and his often clumsy attempts to reform the military, the judiciary and the political infrastructure only swelled the ranks of those seeking to unseat him. Wahid did manage some reforms – in weakening the military for instance – but with his party, PKB, controlling only 11 per cent of the vote in parliament, he was forced to spend most of his energy simply defending his position. This was especially so from mid-2000, when he was dogged by the threat of impeachment on two relatively minor corruption charges. The painful impeachment saga came to a head on 23 July 2001 when Wahid was voted out and a beaming Megawati was sworn in as Indonesia's fifth president.

Legacies

Soeharto's fall was heralded around the world as a victory for democracy. In one sense this is correct; Indonesia now has multiple parties, a functioning parliament, free elections and a free press. Power is also more decentralised, both within Jakarta and between Jakarta and the provinces. At the same time, Indonesian politics and society remains profoundly conditioned by its past, and particularly by its experience of three decades of authoritarian rule under Soeharto. In this last section we look briefly at some legacies and their implications.

Perhaps the most imposing inheritance is the state apparatus. The machinery of state grew enormously during the New Order period and came closely to reflect the regime's patrimonial culture. Forced to abide by what Ali Moertopo called '*monoloyalitas*' (exclusive loyalty to the government), it became a tool of vested interests. There was no room for bureaucratic independence or for centres of authority that could act as checks on state power such as an independent judiciary or auditing office. The state apparatus also came increasingly to serve itself (Anderson 1983). The result was an inefficient and often predatory civil and military bureaucracy with a substantial stake in perpetuating the status quo. Would-be reformers have found the inertia of the bureaucracy to be a major obstacle to building a more transparent and democratic Indonesia.

Post-Soeharto Indonesia is also heir to a systematically disorganised civil society. Years of political engineering and state surveillance eroded the confidence of civil organisations and effectively prevented the emergence of coherent coalitions of reformist forces. One consequence is that Indonesia has few people outside the old established institutions such as Golkar and the army with experience in running political organisations or the apparatus of the state. Most of the current political parties are internally fragmented and prone to concentrate on building new systems of patronage. In the current scramble to gain control of state institutions and resources, all the major parties have embraced predatory elements of the old regime, including former generals, politico-bureaucrats, entrepreneurs and state-connected hoodlums. Few parties have shown a real interest in concrete policy, let alone serious reform agendas (see Mietzner 2001: 41).

Another important legacy of the past is the constitutional framework. Indonesian politics continues to be governed by the 1945 Constitution, which Sukarno resurrected in 1959. The ground rules of politics in contemporary Indonesia thus more closely resemble those of the Guided Democracy and New Order eras than of the period of liberal democracy in the 1950s. Previous leaders did not hesitate to turn the ambiguities of the hastily drafted wartime constitution to their advantage, bypassing the few democratic guarantees it provides. Between 1999 and 2002, however, parliament passed some important amendments to the constitution curbing the powers of the president, introducing a directly elected presidency and ending the practice of appointing a number of soldiers, police and others to the legislature. Though most of Indonesia's political elites remain uninterested in the complete overhaul sometimes suggested by non-state critics, the changes recently implemented would have been unthinkable in the Soeharto period.

Many of the assumptions that colour Indonesian political discourse today also have deep roots. There is, for instance, a lingering suspicion of liberalism and capitalism that derives ultimately from the influence of leftist ideas on Indonesian nationalism early in the 20th century. Sukarno often articulated the widely shared notion that individualism, materialism, liberalism, capitalism, colonialism and imperialism were inextricably linked. Despite Soeharto's embrace of capitalism and his increasingly market-oriented policies, he rarely if ever spoke of individualism, liberalism or even capitalism in a positive light. The corollary of this was an ideological commitment to social justice and to the view that the state had a duty to redistribute wealth from the rich to the poor. It is significant that both Abdurrahman Wahid and Megawati Soekarnoputri maintained a similar public commitment to egalitarian principles.

The high value attached to self-reliance, both in an economic sense and in the world of international relations, is another important legacy of post-1945 history. As an ideal, self-reliance was again advocated most eloquently by Sukarno, but Soeharto too aspired to national self-sufficiency and, like his predecessor, refused to enter into defence pacts with major powers or to allow foreign military bases on Indonesian territory. The nationalist reflex is probably not as strong as it once was – Soeharto's attempt to rally nationalist sentiment against the IMF in 1998, for instance, backfired. But it is also true that Indonesians of many political stripes took personal offence when Habibie invited the United Nations to intervene in East Timor in 1999. Subsequent governments have taken pains to avoid being seen to do the bidding of foreign forces, particularly large and powerful ones like the United States.

A preoccupation with unity has been another enduring feature of Indonesian political thinking. This includes not only the will to preserve Indonesia's borders, but also a desire for ideological unity. In Sukarno's terms, this meant bringing together nationalism, communism and Islam. Soeharto went well beyond this attempt at synthesis, denying the very legitimacy of 'imported' ideologies and seeking to expunge their influence from politics. Neither leader, of course, had much success. As soon as the lid was lifted in 1998 the country's kaleidoscopic reality reasserted itself. The establishment of a multi-party democracy should not be interpreted, however, as signalling the triumph of pluralism. Indeed, the organicist impulse is still clearly present among some of the most powerful groups in contemporary Indonesia, including the military and Megawati's PDI-P. Some of this is reflected in the government's unease about broadening the scope of local autonomy. Continuing ethnic, religious and separatist violence in the regions, in combination with prolonged economic stagnation, may well strengthen this impulse, leading to a growing official intolerance of opposition.

This said, it is unlikely that there will be a headlong slide back into New Order-style authoritarianism. While there is some evidence of a growing nostalgia for the stability and order of the past among sections of the urban middle class, Indonesian society has changed too profoundly to turn back the clock too far.

Notes

1 Our thanks to Ian Chalmers for his comments on an earlier version of this Introduction.
2 The term 'critical pluralism' was used by Herb Feith in a 1989 paper to describe one of the four streams of political thinking he discerned in Indonesia in the late 1980s. His other categories, which influenced our thinking in preparing this book, were integralism, developmentalism and radicalism (Feith 1989: 2–3).
3 The value of Indonesia's oil and gas exports trebled between 1969 and 1974, and trebled again in 1975 (Chalmers and Hadiz 1997: 23). By 1981 a full 60 per cent of state revenues were derived from oil and gas (Robison 1986: 171).

4   The basic tenets of Pancasila are: belief in one supreme God; just and civilised humanity; national unity; democracy led by wisdom and prudence through consultation and representation; and social justice.

5   For an analysis of the New Order's use of the Pancasila, see Morfit (1981) and Bourchier (1996: ch. 6).

6   A comprehensive overview of NGOs in the New Order era can be found in Eldridge (1995).

7   Prominent NGOs influenced by Islamic ideas included the Development Studies Institute (LSP), the Institute for Economic and Social Research, Education and Information (LP3ES), and the Indonesian Society for Pesantren and Community Development (P3M).

8   For a good overview of these events, see Eklöf (1999: ch. 2). A useful collection of English-language articles, interviews and documents from this time can be found in Luwarso (1997).

Part I

The search for a political format, 1965–73

1 The organicist camp

This chapter presents excerpts from writings, speeches and documents that establish some of the distinguishing features of the official orthodoxy in political thinking during Soeharto's New Order. Among these features were a strident anti-communism, an aversion to party politics and an insistence on political stability guaranteed on a permanent basis by the armed forces. While modernisation and economic development were the overriding public priorities of the regime, the New Order's ideologues promoted a vision of state–society relations that drew heavily on familial, nativist and organic metaphors. Harmony, cooperation and consensus were the catch cries of Pancasila democracy.

Soeharto did not come to power with any clear blueprint for the future. He and his allies were in one sense all children of the Sukarno era and it took them some years to work out what sort of a system they would – or could – establish in place of Guided Democracy. But it is possible to discern early patterns of interaction and confluences of ideas that set the parameters of the New Order. The corporatist organising principles of the New Order were essentially a continuation of the strategy the army leadership had used since the late 1950s in its efforts to undermine the influence of the parties in general and the PKI in particular. The regime's managerial and developmentalist character grew partly out of Soeharto's close relations with Lieutenant-General Suwarto, the man who brought together Indonesia's first generation of US-trained economists and senior officers at the Army Staff and Command School (Seskoad). Soeharto also depended on a group of military lawyers led by Brigadier-General Sutjipto, who contributed much to the New Order's bureaucratic character and to its organicist ideology. Indonesian – or perhaps Javanese – military culture was another important ingredient, with its regard for hierarchy, order and its institutional prejudice against political Islam and regionalism.

Soeharto's first priorities were to establish control over the country and to convince the West to initiate flows of financial aid and investment to rescue an economy in drastic decline. The PKI stood in the way of both objectives and was the army's first target. Reading 1.1, from an army-run newspaper called *Api*, provides a taste of the anti-communist propaganda produced by the Soeharto camp in the weeks after the coup of 1 October 1965. It was published at a time of widespread killing of members of the PKI and its mass organisations, and was clearly designed to maintain that bloody momentum.

The New Order, however, did not officially begin until 11 March 1966, when Sukarno signed the document that became known as Supersemar. This document, included as Reading 1.2, was used as the basis for Soeharto's claim to power and signalled the beginning of his slow but steady marginalisation of Sukarno before being appointed president in 1968. Another seminal document was the decree of the Interim People's Consultative Assembly (MPRS) banning the PKI and the teachings of communism/Marxism–Leninism (Reading 1.3). This provided the formal basis of all persecution of communists and leftism under the New Order. It is a measure of the success of the Soeharto government's efforts to keep the communist threat alive that when President Abdurrahman Wahid attempted to have this decree rescinded in early 2000 he was opposed by most major party leaders.

A defining characteristic of the New Order was its claim that the military, as the ultimate guardian of the state, had a permanent right to participate in political affairs. While military leaders had spoken in these terms since at least 1957, it was not until the Second Army Seminar, held at Seskoad in Bandung in August 1966, that the doctrine of '*dwifungsi*', or the 'dual function' of the armed forces, was formally enunciated. *Dwifungsi* was the subject of frequent debate and controversy in the 1970s and 1980s, and, despite the formal renunciation of the doctrine in 2000, the military's role in politics remains a contested issue both within the armed forces and outside it. The most succinct statement of *dwifungsi* we could find appeared in a booklet published in 1973 by the Centre for Strategic and International Studies, an influential Jakarta think tank that had a direct input into government policy at this time (Moertopo 1973; Reading 1.4).

While warning against the evils of ideology, the New Order placed enormous rhetorical emphasis on the Pancasila and the idea of the family state. Reading 1.5 is taken from a 1967 speech in which Soeharto outlines the fundamentals of the system of government he called Pancasila democracy. The speech is striking for its mix of constitutionalist and organicist rhetoric. It foreshadows not only the simplification of the party system, but also Soeharto's campaign in the 1980s to force social organisations and parties to adopt Pancasila as their sole philosophical foundation. This is followed by an extract from a report to parliament written by Colonel Abdulkadir Besar, one of the army's foremost lawyers and ideologues (Reading 1.6). It has been included because it is one of the earliest and clearest attempts to establish the organicist character of the 1945 Constitution. Although Abdulkadir at this time was not closely aligned with Soeharto, the ideas he propounded here – particularly his identification of the ultra-conservative Dutch-trained customary law expert Supomo as the authentic source of constitutional thinking – became part of the ideological orthodoxy of the New Order. According to this vision, Indonesia's political and constitutional life necessarily reflected the country's agrarian and communitarian culture. Pancasila, as the product of Indonesia's indigenous culture and value system, was in contradiction to both liberalism and communism, regarded as alien and unsuited to the Indonesian 'national character'.

But of course traditionalism was only part of the story. At the same time the New Order was resolutely modernist in its appeal to development, progress and rapid economic growth. The skill of its leaders – including Soeharto's remarkable intelligence aide Ali Moertopo – was to combine these apparently contradictory features in such a way as to enable the regime to reap the benefits of capitalism while denying its cultural baggage of individualism and liberal democracy. The rhetoric of Soeharto and Moertopo in this sense embodied many of the characteristics of what Jayasuriya called 'reactionary modernism', in which 'images of the future are coded in the name of a past cultural or natural heritage' (1998: 84). The discourse of organicism or the 'family state' clearly helped to legitimise state-dominated corporatist arrangements that prevailed during the New Order and the regime's penchant for state intervention into all aspects of social, economic and political life.

Next to Soeharto, Ali Moertopo was undoubtedly the most influential figure in crafting the political architecture of the New Order. Famously wily and indefatigable, Moertopo and his networks of agents created Golkar, dismantled the political party system and restructured state–society relations along corporatist lines. He was also an expert propagandist. In Reading 1.7 Moertopo gives a confidential briefing to a group of military officers in 1970. This extract is a good example of the way the regime attempted to establish the legitimacy of the New Order regime by redefining the past. Such narrations of the nation, in which the government is presented as leading the nation back to the true path, became a staple of official speeches and school texts. Reading 1.8, 'The floating mass', is taken from Moertopo's unofficial manifesto of the New Order, a 1973 tract entitled *The Acceleration and Modernization of 25 Years' Development*. In contrast to Sukarno's efforts to mobilise the masses, the emphasis here is on winding back popular participation in politics for the sake of political stability and development. The term was first used in the Indonesian context by the Muslim scholar Nurcholish Madjid shortly before the 1971 general elections but was soon picked up by Moertopo and his assistants. This reading presents the best known formulation of the 'floating mass' concept, according to which political parties were forbidden to maintain a presence in villages except during election campaigns. Translated into Law no. 3/1973, the concept remained a crucial element of New Order politics for the life of the regime.

The chapter ends with a rare impromptu speech by Soeharto in 1972 (Reading 1.9) attacking students for criticising an 'Indonesia in Miniature' theme park project headed by his wife. In his 1967 speech Soeharto had promised to uphold basic rights for the common good of the state, society and the people. By 1972 it had become increasingly apparent that this common good was increasingly being defined by Soeharto himself. In this impassioned speech Soeharto revealed his extraordinary sensitivity to criticism that would mark the rest of his presidency and lead to serious strains with some of his early supporters.

1.1 *Api*: keep attacking them

Api was a virulently anti-communist broadsheet, which began publication on 1 October 1965, the day of the attempted coup – referred to here as the G30S affair (Gerakan 30 September, 30 September Movement). This article was part of the army's campaign of hatred against the PKI that saw as many as half a million suspected communists killed. The following reading is *Api*'s editorial of 7 November 1965, 'Pukul terus'. It is translated from Dewan Redaksi Api (1965: 67–8).

The G30S (alias PKI) must be eliminated physically, mentally and spiritually, albeit within the bounds of humanitarianism in keeping with the Pancasila. This is the basic message of Pak Harto, who was mandated by Bung Karno to restore security. Thanks to our *collective effort* and the intimate bond between Bung Karno, the people and the armed forces, significant progress has been made.

The physical, mental and spiritual blows must be intensified in order to display an understanding of Major-General Soeharto's statement about the radical and total struggle of humanity, especially in facing enemies of the revolution as fierce and cruel as these. As well as crushing these enemies of the revolution with physical violence, the broad public must be instilled with a sense of moral revulsion at the attitudes and practices of the barbarous PKI, whose members laughed openly as they witnessed the murder of six generals and a junior officer.

Let there be no compromise, no bargaining, and no wavering among our officials in taking firm and just measures against figures implicated in the G30S affair. By the same token, do not get in the way of those who unyieldingly and courageously devote their energy, and even their lives, to crushing the G30S. Do not create difficulties, either physical, moral or spiritual, for the members of the armed forces who are now carrying out a comprehensive cleansing of all evil people in our republic and their teachings: PKI-ism.

Because, to be frank, there are some among our officials who hanker after the PKI, who lament its fate, who have been hit by the deadly sledgehammer of the people. The PKI is obviously counter-revolutionary and aims to destroy the unitary state of Indonesia. This is evident in a document discovered by the authorities which reveals a plan to turn Indonesia into a fractured federal state.

These officials are usually the overly clever types, enabling them to justify all sorts of misdeeds, or those who are too dim to keep pace with these vibrant and dynamic times. Or else those affected by moral disorders, making them vulnerable to blackmail by PKI people, who are very cunning in using these kinds of tactics.

The best way to harden our resolve against the PKI and PKI-ism is to arm ourselves with a superior ideology: the Pancasila. Major-General Ibrahim Adji was quite correct when he said that we must have Pancasila morals, morals whose humanitarian character contrasts starkly with that of the PKI.

We urge you, therefore, with clean hands, with a pure heart seeking divine guidance, and with the blessings of Bung Karno: keep attacking the PKI and PKI-ism, keep attacking Durnoism[1], keep attacking traitorous thoughts and deeds, keep attacking them so that the Republic of Indonesia will be free of all blemishes.

1.2 Supersemar

On 11 March 1966, with unidentified troops surrounding the state palace, President Sukarno fled by helicopter to Bogor. There he was visited by three of Soeharto's generals, who, in circumstances that remain unclear, obtained Sukarno's signature to a document conferring power on Soeharto to 'restore order'. Soeharto's forces pressed their advantage, using the Executive Order of 11 March as a weapon to wrest power from Sukarno and as the foundation for their efforts legitimise the New Order constitutionally. The 'sacred' status bestowed on the document was underlined by its cleverly conceived official acronym Supersemar (*Surat Perintah Sebelas Maret*). Semar is a shadow puppet character beloved of the Javanese who in times of chaos transforms himself from a rambunctious jester into a mighty god and a restorer of cosmic order. The version below is translated from Dinuth (1997: 164–5).[2]

Executive Order of 11 March

President of the Republic of Indonesia

Executive Order

Considering:

1.1 The present stage of the Revolution, as well as the domestic and international political situation
1.2 The Order of the Day of the Supreme Commander of the Armed Forces/President/Leader of the Revolution on 8 March 1966

Bearing in mind:

2.1 The need for calm and stability in the running of government and the course of the Revolution
2.2 The need to guarantee the integrity of the Great Leader of the Revolution, the Armed Forces and the People in order to preserve the leadership and the authority of the President/Supreme Commander/ Great Leader of the Revolution and all of his teachings

Instructs:

Lieutenant-General Soeharto, the Minister/Commander of the Army
In the name of the President/Supreme Commander/Great Leader of the Revolution

1   To take all necessary steps to guarantee security and calm and the stability of the running of the government and the course of the Revolution, and to guarantee the personal safety and authority of the President/Supreme Commander/Great Leader of the Revolution/ Mandatory of the Interim People's Consultative Assembly [MPRS] for the sake of the integrity of the nation and the Indonesian Republic, and to carry out faithfully all of the teachings of the Great Leader of the Revolution.
2   To coordinate the execution of this order with the Commanders of the other armed services to the best of his abilities.
3   To report back on all matters relating to the above mentioned tasks and responsibilities.

Concludes

Jakarta, 11 March 1966
President/Supreme Commander/Great Leader of the Revolution/ Mandatory of the MPRS
Signed
SOEKARNO

1.3 Banning communism

The following decision of the interim parliament, the MPRS, reinforced and extended the ban on the PKI and its allied organisations issued by the army in Sukarno's name on 12 March 1966, the day after Supersemar. It is taken from Majelis Permusyawaratan Rakyat (1989: 179–81).

Decision of the Interim People's Consultative Assembly of the Republic of Indonesia No. XXV/MPRS/1966 regarding:
The dissolution of the Indonesian Communist Party, the pronouncement of the Indonesian Communist Party as a prohibited organisation in all parts of the Republic of Indonesia and the prohibition of all activities aimed at disseminating or fostering Communist/Marxist–Leninist concepts or teachings.
By the grace of almighty God, the Interim People's Consultative Assembly of the Republic of Indonesia.

Considering:

a   That Communist/Marxist–Leninist concepts or teachings stand in fundamental contradiction to the Pancasila;
b   That there is clear evidence that people and groups in Indonesia who embrace Communist/Marxist–Leninist concepts or teachings, especially the Indonesian Communist Party, have attempted to seize power from the legitimate government of the Republic of Indonesia on several occasions;
c   That strong action therefore needs to be taken against the Indonesian Communist Party and against the dissemination or fostering [of] Communist/Marxist–Leninist concepts or teachings.

Bearing in mind:

Article 1 section 2 and Article 2 section 3 of the 1945 Constitution.
After hearing:
The deliberations of Interim People's Consultative Assembly between 20 June and 5 July 1966.
Has resolved to pass:

THIS DECISION REGARDING THE DISSOLUTION OF THE INDONESIAN COMMUNIST PARTY, THE PRONOUNCEMENT OF THE INDONESIAN COMMUNIST PARTY AS A PROHIBITED ORGANISATION IN ALL PARTS OF THE REPUBLIC OF INDONESIA AND THE PROHIBITION OF ALL ACTIVITIES AIMED AT DISSEMINATING OR FOSTERING COMMUNIST/MARXIST–LENINIST CONCEPTS OR TEACHINGS.

Article 1

Welcomes and reinforces the policy of the President/Commander in Chief of ABRI [Armed Forces]/Leader of the Revolution/Mandatory of the MPRS to dissolve the Indonesian Communist Party, including all levels of the organisation from the centre to the regions, and all organisations that share its philosophy or are affiliated with it in any way, as well as his pronouncement prohibiting the Indonesian Communist Party in every region within the Republic of Indonesia as established in his Decision of 12 March 1966 no. 1/3/1966, and reaffirms that the above policy has become an MPRS Decision.

Section 2

Any activity that aims to disseminate or foster Communist/Marxist–Leninist concepts or teachings in any form or manifestation, and any use of any type of apparatus or media for the dissemination of such concepts or teachings in Indonesia is prohibited.

Section 3

The scientific study of Communist/Marxist–Leninist concepts or teachings may be carried out in institutions such as universities for the sake of safeguarding the Pancasila provided that such work is supervised and has the approval of the government and the DPR-GR, which will introduce regulations on this issue as a security measure.

Section 4

The above decisions do not influence the independent and active basis of Indonesian foreign policy.
Decided in: Jakarta
Date: 5 July 1966.
Signed[3]

1.4 Ali Moertopo: the dual function of the armed forces

In 1972 the Jakarta-based Centre for Strategic and International Studies (CSIS) published the seminal text *The Acceleration and Modernization of 25 Years' Development*, from which the following reading is taken. While it appears under Ali Moertopo's name, his team of largely US-educated advisers at CSIS undoubtedly had a major role in writing it. The text appeared in English in 1973 and was widely circulated. This extract is from the English translation (1973: 44–5), with minor emendations based on the Indonesian version (1972: 48–50).

In Indonesia the armed forces were born from the people and lived among the people from the first moment of the eruption of the physical revolution against colonialism to achieve our independence. After the achievement of national independence the armed forces joined the struggle shoulder to shoulder with the people to bring independence to fruition. Therefore the Indonesian armed forces are not only a professional army for the purpose of maintaining national defence and security but are also a social force. This idea has been an important factor in the history of Indonesia since independence. From its very beginning the armed forces have performed these two functions, which are known today as the *dwifungsi* (dual function).

It is also a fact of history that the armed forces are the guardians and defenders of Pancasila from all kinds of deviation and attempts to undermine it either by the extreme right or extreme left.

Since the emergence of the New Order in Indonesia after the PKI coup of 30 September 1965 and the collapse of the Old Order, the armed forces have played a dominant role in national life in several fields. Even more than that, the armed forces have emerged as the stabilising and dynamising force behind the policies of the New Order.

Apart from historical considerations, the armed forces' dual function also has a constitutional and legal basis, which has made it possible for the implementation of the dual function to be expanded and developed in a natural way and in accordance with Pancasila and the 1945 Constitution.

First, the preamble to the 1945 Constitution says: 'The struggle of the independence movement has now reached the hour of rejoicing by leading the people of Indonesia safe and sound to the gateway of independence of an Indonesian state which is free, united, sovereign, just and prosperous.' The struggle to achieve national independence was carried over into the struggle to maintain national unity, sovereignty, and a just and prosperous society. Therefore the armed forces, which played an active role in the liberation of the Indonesian people and state from colonial bonds, also have a responsibility to join in the struggle in the social, political, economic and cultural fields in order to secure, defend and fulfil the promise of national independence.

Second, it must be noted that Article 30, paragraph 1 of the 1945 Constitution states: 'All citizens shall have the right and the duty to participate in the defence of the state.' If the principle is established that all citizens, as well as performing their basic functions, have a right and a responsibility to defend the state...the armed forces whose basic function it is to defend the state should be able to perform other functions in all areas in order to protect and strengthen the state.

Third, Article 10 of the 1945 Constitution says: 'The President shall hold the highest authority over the Army, the Navy and the Air Force.' Its elucidation goes on to say: 'The President holds the powers provided in these Articles by virtue of his position as President' and 'After the MPR, the President is the highest executive of the State. Authority and responsibility are vested in the hands of the President.' On this basis it can be concluded that the President has the right to use the armed forces to build and defend the Pancasila state in all fields.

Fourth, Article 3 of MPRS decision no. XXIV/1966 states that the basic considerations of defence and security policy include:

1   The explanation given by the Defence Minister/Armed Forces Commander before the Gotong Royong Parliament (DPR-GR) dated 4 May 1966 and 24 May 1966 that affirms, among other things, the position of the armed forces as an instrument of the Revolution and an instrument of the State

and

7   The socio-political function of members of the armed forces, as citizens and supporters of the Pancasila Revolution serving in all fields to strengthen Ampera[4] and the Revolution, should be recognised and its continuity guaranteed....

Finally, the national defence and security doctrine and the doctrine of the struggle of the armed forces, which were produced by the first national defence and security seminar (12–21 November 1966) in Jakarta and ratified by the first Minister of Defence and Security no. KEP/B/177/1966 dated 21 November 1966, and the implementation of which by all armed forces members was ordered by General Soeharto on 31 March 1967, say in Chapter V, among other things:

In addition to its function as upholder of the state power in the field of defence and security, the armed forces should also contribute their efforts in fields outside defence and security. In this context the armed forces constitute a functional group and are to take part in the determination of state policy (General Introduction).

The main role of the armed forces as a functional group is to take an active part in all the efforts of the state and the people in the field of politics, economy and social affairs in order to attain the goals of the Indonesian Revolution for the sake of Ampera.

The Karya *function/functional role*

In carrying out their basic task as a functional group, the armed forces should take part in development and the support and securing of all aspects of ideological, political, economic, financial, spiritual and socio-cultural life for the strengthening of the Indonesian revolution.

1.5 Soeharto: Pancasila democracy

This historic state address was given before a session of the Interim People's Representative Council on 16 August 1967, the eve of independence day. Soeharto was then acting president. The extract is translated from an official transcript (Soeharto 1967: 12–26).

The goal of the New Order is to secure and purify the implementation of Pancasila and the 1945 Constitution. Every Indonesian, every organisation, every form of business which calls itself New Order must accept the twin foundation of Pancasila and the 1945 Constitution; not just accept them but also apply and give substance to them in their true form, as precisely and purely as possible in accordance with their spirit and strength.

Therefore the New Order is nothing less than an ordering of the entire life of the people, nation and state that has returned to the pure implementation of Pancasila and the 1945 Constitution. We underline the word 'returned' because the New Order was born and has grown as a reaction to and is a total correction of all the forms of deviation and corruption carried out by what has come to be known as the Old Order.

The corruption of Pancasila and 1945 Constitution during the Old Order period had deep and far-reaching consequences; it in fact destroyed the lifeblood of the nation and state.

Pancasila was corrupted with the birth of Nasakom, a concept that attempted to combine communism with the implementation of Pancasila. Communism, which is based on dialectical materialism, is clearly anti-God, whereas Pancasila professes a devout belief in the great, Almighty God. Religion was corrupted for political interests.

The principle of a just and civilised humanity was discarded; human rights all but disappeared, because all of them were determined by the will of the ruler. Legal guarantees and protection were practically non-existent. This happened because, whether consciously or not, we fell for the strategy of the Indonesian Communist Party, which accepted Pancasila only as a tool to be used for seizing power in the framework of international communism.

The principles of nationhood and unity faded because there were groups loyal to other ideologies. The strength of unity was shattered because of the doctrines of contradiction and class struggle.

All of this gave a space to the PKI in which to popularise itself, as if it were the only truth and the real defender of the people's interests.

The Indonesian nation does not recognise class, because we are not and will not be divided by class.

The principle of the people's sovereignty was obscured; what existed was the 'sovereignty' of the leader.

The principle of social justice was increasingly marginalised because the nation's wealth was used for personal interests and for prestige projects, which destroyed the economy of the people and nation. The system of a 'guided economy' became in practice a 'system of licenses' which benefited only a handful of people close to the powerholder.

A serious aberration of the 1945 Constitution occurred with the placing of unconditional power into the hands of one person, the head of state. The principles and foundations of a constitutional state were gradually left behind, until in the end we became a nation based upon power. The principles and foundations of a constitutional system became absolutist in nature. The highest state power was no longer in the hands of the Interim People's Consultative Assembly (MPRS), but rather in the hands of the great leader of the revolution. The president did not submit to the MPRS; on the contrary it was the MPRS who submitted to the president.

Indeed, it was a tragedy for the Indonesian people and nation when in 1959, filled with hope, they supported 'the decree returning to the 1945 Constitution', which plunged the nation into both inner and external suffering that reached its climax with the uprising of the 30 September Movement of the Indonesian Communist Party....

The democracy that we live by is Pancasila democracy, whose basic norms and laws have been laid out in the 1945 Constitution. Pancasila democracy means 'democracy', the principle of the people's sovereignty inspired by and integrated with the other principles of Pancasila. This means that in making use of our democratic rights we must maintain a sense of responsibility to Almighty God according to our respective religions, highly esteem humanitarian values in accord with human dignity and worth, strengthen and guarantee national unity, and take the opportunity to realise social justice. Pancasila democracy originates from an understanding of family values and mutual cooperation.

Because the origins of Pancasila democracy are to be found in family values and mutual cooperation, it does not recognise the absoluteness of a particular group due to either physical strength, economic power, authority, or number of voices.

Pancasila democracy must not be directed towards pursuing individual and group interests. Nor should it be used to destroy other groups, as long as these groups are citizens of the New Order, Pancasila and the 1945 Constitution. The foundations of Pancasila democracy have in fact already been constitutionally regulated with the inclusion of every group who has an interest in the life of the state and society via the processes of consensual decision-making....

It is therefore clear that the president as the head of government, and the People's Consultative Assembly as his institutional overseer, must work together on a daily basis in accord with the 1945 Constitution. Indeed opposition groups found in liberal democracies are unknown in the life of Pancasila democracy. Pancasila democracy recognises only consensual decision-making via representatives either in the People's Representative Council or the People's Consultative Assembly. In relation to this it is necessary that we are aware that the system of government according to the 1945 Constitution determines that the president holds full government power and is responsible to the People's Consultative Assembly, whereas state ministers are the servants of the president and are responsible to him....

In Pancasila democracy the implementation of human rights is constantly guaranteed within the limits laid out by Pancasila and the 1945 Constitution. As a result, the life of the party system is also guaranteed in order to provide healthy and constructive vehicles for the people's right to organise, associate and express themselves. Political parties implement the principle of 'rule by the people led by wisdom in deliberation and representation', as laid down in the preamble to the 1945 Constitution. As tools of democracy, political parties must also abide by a series of responsibilities, as we have explained above.

The rules governing internal party organisation and relations between the political parties must be based upon family principles. At this point we wish to emphasise that there is no point in concentrating too much on ideological problems. Our nation has little to gain from exacerbating conflicts since we have already established Pancasila as our philosophy of life, our collective ideology, and the ideology for every political party and all other organisations. Old Order-style physical compartmentalisation of party groupings must be discarded because it leads to a sharpening of ideological differences that results in conflict and suspicion.

If there are still nationalist, religious, and socialist Pancasila groupings in representative institutions, this is only in the interests of streamlining and simplifying deliberation for achieving consensus. There is no intention to accentuate the differences between these groups or their political ideologies because amongst these groups (groups in the New Order family) there are no ideological differences, only differences in the priorities of their programs of struggle; programs that give substance to independence and put into practice the tenets of Pancasila and the 1945 Constitution....

MPRS Decision no. XXII [1966] stated that parties, mass organisations and functional groups must move to simplify themselves. What this meant, in essence, was that we had to avoid any increase in the number of parties except where this was necessary to streamline the functions and tasks of parties for the sake of democracy and the welfare of the people.

On the basis of these thoughts regarding the essence of Pancasila democracy and the function and task of political parties, the government embarked on a policy that still allows for the existence of one new party. This matter is currently the subject of great public discussion. The existence of such a party would not necessarily conflict with and can still be justified by the principle of simplifying matters pertaining to political parties and mass organisations. There are currently large numbers of Islamic organisations that are not united in one Islamic Party. They feel that they have not been effective in channelling their political rights.

To this end, the concept of forming one new Islamic party that could assemble, direct, and unite all non-party Islamic organisations should be respected and endorsed. Forming a new party that doesn't fulfil the criteria mentioned above should not be allowed because it would conflict with the principle of simplification....

In exercising our freedom of religion, that is to say performing our religious duties as prescribed by our respective faiths, we should be vigilant to ensure that differences of opinion do not arise that could be exploited by the enemies of the New Order and the enemies of religion – the atheistic remnants of the PKI – to play us off against one another....

In the development of political life in accordance with the principles of Pancasila democracy, the functional group with real potential to play an active role in protecting and upholding Pancasila and the 1945 Constitution is the ABRI [Armed Forces] group.

The extent of ABRI's involvement depends upon several things: the dangers that threaten the wellbeing of Pancasila and the 1945 Constitution, the threats to the wellbeing of the people and the unity of the nation, and direct threats to the state, be they internal or external. ABRI does not ignore the fact that certain schemers in the past have drawn ABRI units into uprisings and other deviations from their duty. But history also records that these uprisings and deviations have always been subjugated by ABRI itself....

ABRI will not and could not possibly impose a military dictatorship because members of ABRI have all taken the soldier's oath and sworn allegiance to the Seven Principles that strongly assert the role of ABRI as defender of Pancasila and the 1945 Constitution.

ABRI's current role is not the result of a thirst for power. If indeed ABRI did want power, then they could have seized it when the opportunity arose, for example on 1 October 1965 when ABRI used physical force to annihilate the revolt of the 30 September Movement of the Indonesian Communist Party and their supporters, a time when there was a state of panic and a vacuum of government administration....

There has been talk of the 'greening' of the administration because of the number of ABRI officers involved in social and government activities. But don't jump to the conclusion that this is militarism. Look first at the standing of legal institutions, ask whether human rights and democratic rights are guaranteed by laws based on the constitution. Don't measure militarism simply by counting the number of ABRI shirts.

If at the present time many members of ABRI have become district heads, then this is because they were chosen by the parliament via democratic procedures and in accordance with the prevailing law. It clearly doesn't mean that ABRI wishes to control every position and post. ABRI members have been placed in various government institutions essentially because they have a civil role to play and because they are needed to implement the government's endeavours efficiently....

It seems clear that the issue of militarisation is groundless, for it is simply untrue. What is more, it is a dangerous issue, especially if it is used to negate the role of ABRI as a functional group, such as was previously done by the PKI. Nevertheless ABRI will continue to accept constructive and honest criticisms and suggestions with an open heart, for the good of ABRI itself and for our collective good.

In conclusion and as a guide for the implementation of Pancasila democracy, we wish to emphasise that Pancasila democracy will continue to hold in high esteem the basic human and democratic rights of every citizen, who in exercising them must be loyal to a greater good, that of society, the people, and the state. It would be ideal if in the implementation of Pancasila democracy one could always achieve a balance between individual and general interests, between the interests of groups and of the nation, and between the people and the state. But if a problem arises where there is a conflict between individual and general interests or the interests of specific groups and the national interest, then we must sincerely, voluntarily and unselfishly sacrifice the relevant individual or group interest for that of society and the nation. This is the just principle and law of Pancasila democracy, and this is in our opinion the most appropriate recipe for achieving a just and prosperous society materially and spiritually based upon Pancasila.

1.6 Abdulkadir Besar: the family state

This extract is taken from a 55-page document written while Colonel Abdulkadir Besar was secretary-general of the Interim People's Consultative Assembly. The document itself is dated 18 April 1968 but cites sources from 1969. It is translated from Besar (1972: 493–501).

The 1945 Constitution is based on the family state-concept [*Staatsidee kekeluargaan*]. This concept must therefore underpin all aspects of a government based on the 1945 Constitution. Such a system of government entails a sharing of powers between state institutions (which form parts of the overall system) and linkages (that form functional connections between the parts) between these state institutions....

The Indonesian state is based on a theory of popular sovereignty that is usually called democracy. The essence of democracy is the idea that the people are sovereign and the structures of government are set up to reflect the popular will. Governments around the world interpret this in different ways, depending on the state-concept they adhere to.

The 1945 Constitution is based on the family state-concept (known in political science as the theory of integralism), 'namely an understanding of the state as being at one with its entire people, transcending all groups in all walks of life' (Supomo in Yamin 1959: 113). Inherent in the family state-concept are the principles of unity between leaders and the people, and of unity within the state, both of which are in accordance with Eastern thought (that includes Indonesia).

With their agrarian background, the Indonesian people have a strong tendency to be spiritually attuned to the oneness of life. This starts with their own families, and because of their need to face dangers and the challenges of nature together, this is reflected in their broader social environment as well. Because natural disasters are so unpredictable, the assistance that people give each other is not calculated, and this means that we do not think in terms of profit and loss.

In times of natural disaster, the help that one community gives another is always underpinned by an intention to free the affected community from its troubles without counting the cost, because next time it could just as well be the first community's turn to be struck by disaster. This institution of mutual assistance [*gotong-royong*] gave rise to a spirituality of family-ness in Indonesian society.

From these practices of mutual assistance was born a philosophy of life as described by Prof. Supomo. According to Supomo, 'individuals are separated neither from other individuals nor from the world around them, from other groups, or even from other life forms. Everything is connected and interdependent' (Supomo in Yamin 1959: 113)....

The family state-concept affects our understanding of the popular will, namely that we need to talk about the will of the entire people, considering all the socio-political aspirations in society, including regional and group interests, *not* simply the will of the majority as happens in countries based on *individualistic* state-concepts. And neither the will of a minority claiming to speak for the collectivity, as happens in totalitarian countries whose state-concept is based on *class*....

Because the Indonesian state subscribes to the belief that the popular will must encompass the *entire* society, membership of the People's Consultative Assembly (MPR) must reflect the *manifestation of the entire society*. In the language of the family state-concept, *every member of the Indonesian national family* must have a place within the MPR.

Article 2, paragraph 1 of the 1945 Constitution and its elucidation refer to 'members of the family' as *political groups*, namely all members of the People's Representative Council (DPR)...as well as *regional groups* and *functional groups*. The 1945 Constitution refers to the latter two as 'delegates', meaning they are not elected through general elections.... The functional groups comprise people who contribute qualitatively to national life, such as intellectuals, farmers, labourers, members of the armed forces, but who, because they are not large enough or do not fulfil the conditions for being elected, would not otherwise be represented in the MPR....

The requirement that regional and group delegates be represented in the MPR is a consequence of the family state-concept that underpins the 1945 Constitution.[5]...

Based on the family state-concept, there is only one formulation of the will of the people in Indonesia: the Broad Guidelines of State Policy (GBHN). These guidelines can only be drafted by the MPR as the manifestation of the entire people – all the 'members of the family' – and only by unanimous agreement. This is because if it were only a majority that passed it there would be a minority who were not represented, and this would mean that the GBHN did *not* reflect the will of the entire society and would therefore conflict with the understanding of the 'popular will' based on the family state-concept. Rather, it would reflect the 'popular will' according to individualistic state-concepts....

The drafters of the 1945 Constitution consciously avoided basing our system of government on Montesquieu's theory of the separation of powers because they regarded that theory to be part of liberal democratic theory.

Because they based the 1945 Constitution on the family state-concept, they chose a system of government based on a division of powers. Under this system the highest state institutions each had a certain sphere of authority but were able to work together with one another. According to Prof. Supomo, this meant that our 1945 Constitution was unique.

1.7 Ali Moertopo: national political history

This reading is from a speech delivered by Brigadier-General Ali Moertopo at an upgrading course for senior military officers in Jakarta held between 20 August and 17 October 1970. It is translated from a 'restricted' manuscript published under Ali Moertopo's name entitled *Politik Nasional: Strategi, Taktik dan Teknik Implementasinja (National Politics: Strategy, Tactics and Techniques of Implementation)* (1970: 17–20).

In order best to understand the New Order's ambitions we should consider the recent history of our country and people.

1945–50

On 18 August 1945, the day after the proclamation of independence, the ideological base of the Republic of Indonesia was put in place. This is when we came to a consensus to accept the constitution and its elucidation. Since then we have known what our basis is and what our goals are. For five years we fought, armed and resolute in our unity, sacrificing heroes on the battlefield, destroying and burning anything which could be used by our enemies. We carried out our individual tasks on the front lines as well as behind the scenes with complete dedication to uphold the unitary Republic of Indonesia based on Pancasila and the 1945 Constitution. The [1948] communist uprising in Madiun had the potential to halt or divert our efforts.

This struggle, which cost us greatly, succeeded and our sovereignty was acknowledged by the world.

1950–9

After digressing briefly towards the creation of a Federal Republic of Indonesia, we soon returned to the path of the unitary state. Yet we were still infected by the disease of liberal democracy, which permitted communism to rear its head once more, allowing all kinds of uprisings, gridlock in the Constituent Assembly, and change after change of cabinet. Political stability was completely lost, the economy was in a state of chaos and development ignored.

1959–65

The return to the 1945 Constitution, as decreed on 5 July 1959, was a turning point. However, the constitution and the Pancasila were never really implemented.

Pancasila was turned into an empty vessel to be filled by Nasakom; democracy led by wisdom based on deliberation/representation became 'Guided Democracy'; popular sovereignty was exchanged for the voice of the 'people's spokesman'; the elected Parliament was dissolved; freedom of the press was stifled; constitutional law was replaced by revolutionary law; the president was elected by revolutionary law; prestige projects were given priority over planned national development; power changed hands from the MPRS to the 'great leader of the revolution'; principles for implementing world order based on independence, lasting peace and social justice were betrayed by confrontational politics; our free and active foreign policy was exchanged for one based on an alliance with Peking.

It is not surprising that amid such chaos the PKI was able to flourish and carry out the 30 September Movement [coup], which was intended to turn Indonesia from a Pancasila state into a communist state, a satellite of the People's Republic of China.

The New Order period

...Against this background, we can understand why the New Order insisted on the pure and consistent implementation of the Pancasila and the 1945 Constitution, and why a total ideological, political and governmental, legal, social and educational correction was needed.

Against this background we can understand why it was most important and necessary for a radical change in mentality, for a step-by-step return to Pancasila democracy, for a return to the priorities of the people over individual or group priorities, a return to national unity and solidarity, to the spirit of development and to a reawakening of our enthusiasm for program-oriented work....

There was a nationwide conflict between the Old and New Orders in which two major forces in Indonesian society stood in opposition to one another. This gave rise to a dualism that extended to every field – ideological, political, economic, social, cultural and military.

The Old Order battle-array comprised people whose dominant ideology was communist; PKI organisations and their affiliates; people wrapped up in Sukarno's personality cult; adherents of Sukarnoist concepts such as Nasakom, Revolution, Manipol, Nefo, Dekon, etc.;[6] people who used the opportunities provided by the Old Order to advance politically and economically, including profiteers like Karkam, Aslam[7] and others.

The New Order battle-array comprised anti-communist groups/people and their affiliated organisations; people who opposed Sukarno for personal reasons; people who opposed Sukarnoist/Old Order political concepts; and extremist groups.

This dualism continued until the inauguration of General Soeharto as president of the Republic of Indonesia in March 1968.

1.8 Ali Moertopo: the floating mass

This extract is from Ali Moertopo's *The Acceleration and Modernization of 25 Years' Development*, first published in 1972, with an English version in 1973 (pp. 51–2, 82–7, 94–6). The policy of the 'floating mass' was maintained throughout the New Order period but was abandoned after the fall of Soeharto. For a cautiously critical reaction to the policy, see Reading 2.4.

For Indonesia's society, which is still largely traditional, modernisation demands the carrying out of changes in, and overhauling of, value systems. Thus modernisation means changing norms which are no longer functional in the development of society and changing norms which hinder development. Change should be integral and should not be limited only to change in aspects of socio-cultural life, but should also include technical, economic, political and other aspects. There is the fact that in bringing about integral changes, the dynamics of each aspect are not always in synchronisation. Changes in technical aspects occur more readily than changes in custom. From a socio-cultural perspective, the problem of modernisation demands an open mind towards foreign influences and cultures, strong support from progressive leaders who can evolve an ethos of progress, and the need for enthusiasm for work. These all need to be reoriented towards a new era and future, leaving behind the idealisations of the past. The process of modernisation in itself will not be free from the conflicts it gives rise to. New norms will be in conflict with traditional norms. Therefore the process of modernisation requires planning of socio-cultural change and planning of change in general. Modernisation as planned change must clearly set out the direction to be taken. This aspect requires clarification of the model of the Pancasila state and the application of the principles of Pancasila in every field of life, every organ and body of the state, and embracing all levels of society both in the towns and in villages....

Political field

The political and social lives of society are closely interrelated. It follows that any discussion of the one will touch upon the other. In political life the aim to be achieved is...a reorganisation of socio-political forces and the political structure, and, simultaneously or gradually, to guide the way of thinking and the political mentality of society in such a way that a stable and viable socio-political basis may be attained to support the development of society. This would avoid sacrificing development for political purposes as has happened in the past.

Politics and development

Stimulated by the national ideal of independence, Pancasila democracy should be developed. But it should always be kept in mind that Pancasila democracy is not just...a mechanism to arrive at decisions through the deliberation of representatives, but it must constitute a way of thinking, a way of deliberating and a way of acting with full awareness of the interests of the people at large. It must also strive for the best and optimal results. It is the determination of the Indonesian people to reject liberal democracy, with its concept of 'majority rule', and also the concept of 'guided democracy', which leads to absolute power or dictatorship by a minority. These two forms of democracy have been experienced during the life of the nation and their failure was basically a reflection of the immaturity of Indonesian society.

At present the socio-political condition of Indonesia has gradually been able to formulate and find a proper form which is hoped to be able to meet the needs of the people, who consist mostly of honest, good-willed and simple peasants. Therefore political development should not lead the people into disorder and fanaticism in respect of the ideology of a political party. Rather it should direct them to open-mindedness towards other groups in society as partners in the establishment of democracy and in development.

Political development is an endeavour to encourage the positive participation of the people as a whole in the program of national development.
The people's consciousness of having a state should take the form of
participation in their own areas, solving the problems they are directly
facing. Such participation is the proper implementation of the national
development program, beginning from the village level up to the district,
town and provincial levels. This participation can be maximised through
their own efforts, functions and professions....

A healthy climate of political development and a proper political structure form an undivided unity. In order to create a healthy political life it is
necessary to bring about changes in the political structure, both at the level
of society in general, or the 'political infrastructure', and at the government level, or the 'political superstructure'. These two simultaneously
influence political life as a whole.

After experiencing life as a nation since the winning of independence,
it has become obvious that the political life to be developed should not
be force- or power-oriented. Rather it should be oriented to man. Human
and social development should take the form of the realisation of development in all fields of human life in order to increase the people's
welfare. It goes without saying that the development-oriented thinking
should be embodied in the political structure. Political infrastructure that
is oriented to an exclusive ideology is no longer in tune with the political
structure needed for development. Such an infrastructure has proved in
the history of the nation to be incapable of meeting the demands of the
people.

Organisations that are directly involved in political activities should be
restructured in such a way that their political activities are only focused on
their direct participation in the life of the state. Political organisations
should function to provide good, considered, alternative concepts. Thus it
is only proper that in the renewal of the political structure political organisations should simplify themselves, in number as well as in organisation. In
this way, it is expected that in the coming general election of 1976 there
may be only three emblems, namely two of the political parties and one of
the Golkar.

The floating mass

In this connection it is worth remembering that in the past the people in
general, particularly those in the villages with their own, often national,
ways of thinking, were played upon and involved in the political and ideological conflicts of the parties. The political parties were always trying to
marshal mass support by forming various affiliated organisations based on
the ideologies of their respective parties. The mass of the people, especially
those in the villages, always fell prey to the political and ideological interests of those parties. Their involvement in the conflicts of political and

ideological interests had as its result the fact that they ignored the necessities of daily life, the need for development and improvement of their own lives, materially as well as spiritually.

Such a situation should not repeat itself. Nevertheless, even now the parties continue to be narrowly ideology-oriented as before. Therefore it is only right to attract the attention of the mainly village people away from political problems and ideological exclusiveness to efforts of national development through the development of their own rural societies. For these reasons, it is justifiable that political activities are limited to the district level only (Level II autonomy). Here lies the meaning and the goal of the depoliticisation (the process of freeing the people from political manipulation) and the '*deparpolisasi*' [the process of freeing the people from political party allegiances] in the villages.

Nevertheless, this does not imply that people in the villages are debarred from maintaining political aspirations. Besides their opportunity to pour their aspirations into development of their own societies, in the general elections they can also vote for whichever political party or the Functional Groups (Golkar) they regard as capable of channelling their aspirations and whichever has platforms in accordance with their own aspirations.

In this way people in the villages will not spend their valuable time and energy in the political struggles of parties and groups, but will be occupied wholly with development efforts. Through this process there emerges the so-called 'floating mass', i.e. people who are not permanently tied to membership of any political party. This concept of 'floating mass' should lead to increased development efforts. It may also stimulate the other socio-political forces to prepare development programs that will be brought forth and evaluated in general elections. The group that has the development program that best suits the public interest will win the general elections.

Golkar and political renewal

In formulating efforts toward political development in order to establish a healthy political life that carries on development demands and integral development efforts, the political structure resulting from the general election of 1971 may be used as an asset, or at least as a starting point, for all development efforts. There will not be any immediate political change; this will be a gradual process of renewal. In this framework, Golkar has emerged as a force that is expected to be a modernising element and to lead the present political climate into a new form necessary for the realisation of development.

The efforts of Golkar are supported by modernising elements consisting of groups of professionals and functionaries, civil servants, experts and technocrats, non-party masses and the armed forces. As a modernising element Golkar itself cannot be separate from the renewal process. It is obvious therefore that the political structure that is established in this way will change the dimension of the activities of existing political elements. Given that politics does not lead but is led, political life can be adapted to the requirements of social life. The closer the two forms are to each other, the sooner the political structure is perfected....

Institutions, communications and mass media

A society functions through organisations, associations, institutions and other groups in towns as well as in villages. The different functions between town and village bring about differences in the institutionalisation of town and village society, resulting from their different cultural conditions. While in the village the organisation of society is tied to the structure of agricultural life, in the towns there are new and increasing demands. Development demands clearer, more effective and efficient groupings, and it is a national consensus that the emphasis in the institutionalisation of a developing society should be on groupings based on function and profession. Everyone should participate in these groups, without forgetting our commitment to society as a whole. Confused backgrounds and the prevalence of outdated and backward thinking whereby formalism is regarded as more important than function have resulted in the improper functioning of democracy. The re-institutionalisation of society along modern lines cannot develop automatically, especially when it is the result of a synthesis with other cultures, as was the case with our political parties that are in fact borrowings from the West.

This form of structuring demands a certain background of thinking and attitudes that have sometimes proved to be difficult to adapt to Indonesian social conditions. Therefore the task of restructuring will be a continuing process. It should always be carried out and judged in the light of the intrinsic conditions of society, taking account of external influences.

The groupings needed for modernisation can be seen as specialisations. The process of specialisation is already apparent in Indonesian society in the shift from '*paguyuban*' [community] towards '*patembayan*' [association]. This change has resulted in the fact that the daily needs of man are not necessarily fulfilled by his own family members. There has been a division of labour in many areas of activity, from the agricultural sector to the service sector.

New organisations should be formed in all fields of social, economic and political life to accommodate these changes.

1.9 Soeharto: democratic rights may not be used as masks

The following speech was delivered at the opening of the Pertamina Hospital in Jakarta on 6 January 1972, following student protests against the 'Beautiful Indonesia in Miniature' theme park on the outskirts of the capital. It is taken from an official transcript translated in Smith (1974: 235–40). Several leaders of the student protests were arrested shortly after the speech.

It is quite unexceptionable for there to be differences of opinion in Indonesia, as long as these remain within the limits dictated by the need to maintain democratic harmony. Differences are the spice of democracy. But they must be kept within the limits of democratic harmony. People should not exercise their democratic rights if the end result is undemocratic. It seems that this sort of thing is happening in Indonesia, particularly in relation to the 'Beautiful Indonesia in Miniature' project.

It is actually quite natural that differences of opinion should arise in relation to this project. But these differences should not be blown up to the point where they endanger democracy itself. Conflicts between pro and con factions could come to threaten public security and order and disturb national stability. This would create obstacles for development....

The Beautiful Indonesia in Miniature project has two main functions. The first, outwardly directed, is to act as means of communication, to introduce Indonesia to other nations, to show them the real aspirations of the struggle of the Indonesian people, and the nature of the Pancasila, which reflects their philosophy of life. As I have said before, we cannot isolate ourselves; we must make friends with other countries. Particularly if we want to play a role in building world peace, we have to be trusted by other nations. To be trusted, respected and liked, we must make known the personality of the Indonesian nation, which goes back to the eighth century.

Second, there is the inwardly directed function. It is impossible for the people of Indonesia to visit all parts of Indonesia – Sumatra, Kalimantan, Sulawesi, the Moluccas, Irian and the Lesser Sunda Islands. That is impossible. But by visiting this miniature project they will be able to see the whole country and also have a sense of pride in being a nation, a nation that is really rich in culture, in natural wealth, in flora and fauna, in its various art forms and so on. That will create an awareness of nationhood. And this awareness of nationhood is an absolute necessity if we want to live as a nation, to improve our strength as a nation – ideological, economic, as well as military. Thus it has the purpose of teaching us awareness of nationhood by showing us the magnificence of Indonesia.

Moreover, it has one further function: economic development. There are many people from other countries who would like to see Indonesia, to see it at close quarters. So we have to exploit this situation. We have to look to other countries. For development, we need foreign exchange, we need foreign exchange earnings. If we bring in visitors we bring in foreign exchange. That is what other countries do, like Italy, Spain, Switzerland and Japan. From tourism alone we could earn more than Rp1 billion in foreign exchange. More than from all our exports, oil as well as other goods. Why should we not get this sort of benefit from the beauty of

Indonesia when I am confident that people of other nations want to see our country?...

Another aspect of the Miniature Indonesia project, if it can be implemented, is its by-product of providing employment, not only within the project itself, but also in other fields, like service to visitors and the selling of ice cream, peanuts, cigarettes and so on. All these secondary activities will be opened up for the people, hence the project will contribute to employment. So, seen from the point of view of objectives and ideals, it does not run counter to the strategy of the nation's struggle to achieve a just and prosperous society based on the Pancasila. Nor does it run counter to development strategy as an effort to give body to our independence and achieve a just and prosperous society. And it will certainly not affect government finances, as it will not be financed from the government budget.

I am quite convinced that this project is important. But I certainly accept that the government must give preference to more important ones. That is why it has not been made into a government project. But since development is not the concern of the government alone, and the private sector has a role to play, I am suggesting to them that they carry out this project. If the private sector is willing to establish Beautiful Indonesia in Miniature – without getting favours or special treatment of any kind – then I say go ahead.

Ladies and gentlemen, I sometimes wonder why this Miniature Indonesia project...has become so controversial – mixed up with the issue of courage to criticise, no different from the Old Order, the exercising of democratic rights, and so on. If democratic rights are taken too far, exercised without caution, then democracy is no more, and the strategy of stability, which is necessary for development, is jeopardised.

Now just what is the principle in doubt? What people are afraid of is the obstruction of development. As the person responsible for development, I can state firmly: I guarantee that this project will not hinder development. Quite the reverse is true, since in no way does it run counter to the development strategy. Second, it is said that it will affect government revenues. Again, as the head of government I assure you that the government funds committed for development, to the amount of Rp231 billion for 1972–3, as I stated before Parliament yesterday, would not be much affected even if the Rp10 million for the project were to be taken from the development budget. But the government is quite firm on this point: it will not use funds from the development budget. Nor will government revenues be affected.

Well, what is the problem then? Perhaps it is that the Project Officer is Bang Ali [Jakarta Governor Ali Sadikin] and the sponsor Bu Harto, my wife. The impression has been created that the Miniature Indonesia project is a lighthouse project,[8] a project to prolong a term of office. My God! This is just not so! Institutions of this kind just do not exist.

If that is understood it is clear that the project itself is not the real problem at all. Rather, the Miniature project is being used to create a political issue.

Look at the facts. Look at the pattern of controversy since 1968 and 1969. The way issues have been put up has been just the same throughout, always twisting things into their opposites, creating antagonistic opinions and contradictions and confusing the people. The basic aim is to discredit the government. And, as it happens, it is the same people. The actors are the same, and I know that the people behind the [scenes] are the same, too.

What is their real political goal? We know what it is, and it is not the Miniature project. The real goal, in the short term, is to discredit the government, and also, of course, the person responsible, myself, as the head of government and the president. And in the long run they want to kick the armed forces out of executive activities and eliminate the dual function of the armed forces. They want to chase the armed forces back into their 'stable', that is, limit them to their security function.

If that is the target, it is not up to the Miniature project to answer its critics. The answer must be given by the armed forces, and the armed forces' answer is quite clear. As I have said repeatedly, the armed forces will not relinquish their dual function. On the basis of this dual function, the armed forces – together with the other social forces – will be able to safeguard our constitution and our democracy. Together with the other social forces it will occupy executive and legislative positions.

So it is the armed forces which will answer. If the aim is to discredit the government with a view to kicking me out, that can be easily done. That is very easy. It is not necessary to make a lot of fuss about it. I am the head of government in accordance with our constitution. The head of state is elected by the people's representatives, hitherto by the Interim People's Consultative Congress, henceforth by the People's Consultative Congress. God willing, the elected People's Consultative Congress will assemble next year, in March 1973, to determine the broad outline of state policy and choose a president and a vice-president. This will give them their opportunity if this is what they want. They can nominate themselves or somebody else in the People's Congress to stand for election as a president or vice-president. It is very simple. Instead of making such a lot of fuss about these things now, let them rather compete with each other in providing their services to the state and let the people choose. Persons with a reputation for service will be the ones trusted by the people and elected in March 1973, just 15 months from now, less a few days.

However, if they cannot wait till March 1973, perhaps because they are disgusted with me, there are things they can do earlier in a constitutional way, that is, by holding a special session of the People's Congress. The present parliament, the outcome of the general elections, has been incorporated into the People's Congress by the president. In a short time they will be joined by the representatives of the regions and of the political parties. That means a special session of the People's Congress can be convened at any time if this is what the representatives of the people request. So if they cannot tolerate me until March 1973, a special session can be held to replace me. It is simple; there is no need for fuss.

But let me just remind them of one thing. Everything has to be done in a constitutional way! The purpose of the New Order is precisely to uphold the constitution and democracy. If unconstitutional tendencies arise I will go back to the attitude I took on 1 October 1965, when I served the people by confronting the PKI, who wanted to trample on the constitution and the Pancasila.

At that time nobody came to me to encourage me. Did the leaders of the political parties offer me support? No. No one [from] the youth [groups] came to me either. No. Nor any of the students. But I did not care who was behind me. In fact there was only one person, my wife. She said to me simply: 'Be strong in your faith.' That was my wife's message to me on 1 October. That was my encouragement and it gave me enough strength to urge the people to overcome the PKI.

Later, after this had succeeded, the Pancasila Front and the Generation of '66 were formed and then the movement to hasten the process of overcoming the deviation. And I was urged to act unconstitutionally to speed up the process of correction.

This I firmly rejected. I already knew my mind. Acting according to the constitution was a matter of principle for me. Because all corrections had to be made by constitutional means, the special and general sessions of the Interim People's Consultative Congress were convened, and so on. Everything was done constitutionally, so the people were the ones who took the decisions. My responsibility was to ensure that the changes were not effected by unconstitutional means. And, thank God, I was successful.

After that there was more pressure on me to take steps outside the constitution. But, as I say, thank God, I was successful. If I had acted unconstitutionally in the situation at that time when divisions were so sharp I can just imagine what the picture would have been. There would have been civil war and our situation would probably be very different today.

Thank God, we were able to overcome those difficulties. I have been criticised for doing things too cautiously. I have been abused as a 'slow but sure' Javanese, as a Javanese who is like a walking snail, like a snail whose shell is too big and heavy for its body. Never mind. The main thing was to safeguard the state and the nation.

For that reason, if there are now people trying to act in defiance of the constitution, I will go back to the attitude I took on 1 October 1965. Quite frankly, I will smash them, whoever they are! And I will certainly have the full support of the armed forces in that.

And that goes, too, for those who make use of their democratic rights and use those as their masks, who use their rights to excess in any way that suits them. Those rights are like spices: used excessively, they spoil everything. And if the spoiling of democracy is going to result in the disturbance of order and the general security situation, the disturbance of national stability and the disturbance of development, that is something I will not stand for. Lest you do not understand what I mean by 'I will not stand for it', let me say frankly that I will take action. If those people take no notice of warnings and continue to act as they have been I will take action. And if there are legal experts who hold that it is no longer possible for the president to do that, that it would be against the law for me to act against those responsible for these violations – if they want to be stubborn about it – all right, that is simple. In the interests of the state and the nation, I can invoke the Order of 11 March 1966, to declare a State of Emergency. If necessary I can do that even without the existence of an emergency. If those people are going to continue to create chaos I will take it upon myself to act, in my responsibility to the people and to God.

As I said before, it is unexceptionable for there to be differences of opinion in a democratic state, in a democratic environment. But there are limits to differences of opinion. The limits are set by the need for democracy to be in harmony with the calling of our struggle. The calling of our present struggle is to develop, to give content to independence. For development, political and economic stability are essential. And political stability requires order and security.

Notes

1   Durno is a Machiavellian character from the Mahabharata, well known through *wayang* stories. Thanks to the efforts of *Api*, the label came to be associated with Sukarno's intelligence boss and Foreign Minister Subandrio (Paget 1967: 215). Subandrio was sentenced to death in 1966 but released from prison in 1995.

2   Note that Soeharto's State Secretariat claimed in the 1980s to have lost the original document. At least two different facsimiles of it have appeared in print, one in *Tempo* (15 March 1986), another in the newspaper *Buana Minggu* (16 March 1986). While the text in these two documents was the same, the formatting and the signature of Sukarno were not.

3   MPRS Chair General Dr A.H. Nasution and four Deputy Chairs, Osa Maliki, H.M. Subchan Z.E., M. Siregar and Brigadier-General Mashudi, as well as Major-General Wilujo Puspo Judo, Administrator of the Fourth General Session of the MPRS.

4   Ampera stood for 'The Message of the People's Suffering', a Sukarno era slogan

5   Unspecified sections of the text before this point are apparently taken from a document identified only as 'Naskah Seskoad NSS. 61–780–03: 20–1'.

6   Manipol [Political Manifesto] was the name given to Sukarno's Independence Day speech of 17 August 1959, regarded as the ideological blueprint of the Guided Democracy period; Nefo stood for the 'New Emerging Forces' in the world, including Indonesia; while Dekon stood for Sukarno's *Deklarasi*

Ekonomi, according to which the capitalist phase of development would give way to a prosperous socialist phase.

7 Karkam and Aslam were businessmen who profited from their close relationship with Sukarno.

8 Soeharto used the term lighthouse (*mercu suar*) to refer to grand projects that would demonstrate Indonesia's status in the world. To his critics, however, it implied extravagant self-aggrandisement.

2 Modernising pluralism

The period covered in this chapter was characterised by intense debates regarding the establishment of a new political format after the fall of Sukarno. Among the more prominent protagonists were representatives of the 'modernising pluralist' stream of political thinking. This included urban intellectuals who were either anti-party or associated with one of the anti-communist parties banned by Sukarno – the Indonesian Socialist Party (PSI) and, to a lesser extent, the modernist Muslim party Masjumi. Some of the contributions to the debate included here are sharply critical of the military leadership under Soeharto, but it is important to note that they were part of a conversation being carried out *within* the New Order alliance.

Modernising pluralists had a vision of a modern, industrial Indonesia free from the sort of primordial political attachments which dominated 1950s politics in particular, as well as from the influence of radical nationalism or communism. All of these were regarded as impeding Indonesia's march towards modernisation and progress. The pluralists' concern was to establish a political system with the basic features of a democracy (elections, political parties, the rule of law, etc.) and which would effectively ensure that a technocratic, modernising elite would hold the reins of power and steer the country forward.

In order to do this they had to ensure the domestication of the surviving political parties of the 'Old Order'. They were especially concerned to reduce the influence of the large parties that they argued had exploited cultural and religious cleavages in Indonesian society to gain mass followings, the Indonesian Nationalist Party (PNI) and the Nahdlatul Ulama (NU). Following Soeharto's far-reaching purges of Sukarnoists in the PNI in the mid- to late 1960s, the NU and other Islamic parties became their main, although often unspoken, targets. Organised Islam became increasingly marginalised within the emerging political framework of the New Order (see Chapter 3).

Modernising pluralists were particularly keen to establish a political party system that would limit the number of parties that could contest general elections. Many were in favour of a two-party system, with one party representing what they saw as the forces of progress (the New Order) and the other essentially representing the 'backwardness' of the past (the Old Order). The virtues of a two-party system were sometimes advocated with reference to the United States, where several of their leading lights were educated. Such ideas are particularly prominent in the writings of the PSI intellectuals Soemarno and Soelaiman Soemardi (Readings 2.1 and 2.2).

If Western-style 'modernisation' was an important reference point for PSI intellectuals, so was their memory of the parliamentary era. The poor showing of the PSI in the 1955 elections helped produce in its sympathisers an enduring disdain for the uneducated masses. This saw many early pluralists support efforts to constrain mass participation in politics. Economist Sarbini Sumawinata's 1966 argument that maintaining political stability was a prerequisite of economic growth remained a hallmark of the political thinking of the New Order elite.

Most modernising intellectuals represented in this chapter supported Golkar as an alternative to the party system, at least initially. But there was disagreement about the rules under which it would operate. Rahman Tolleng, a PSI-related figure who was then a member of parliament for Golkar, argued in 1969 that a US-style electoral district system ought to replace the inherited system of proportional representation. While Rahman Tolleng's proposal was defeated, this debate was to resurface many times in the course of the New Order and was partly adopted in the election law of 1999. An extract from a key speech in parliament he made is presented in Reading 2.3.

Golkar's victory in the July 1971 elections gave the New Order government new confidence, allowing it to press ahead with further efforts to reduce party influence by overhauling the party system and implementing the 'floating mass' policy, as discussed in Chapter 1. The heavy-handed tactics of the military gave rise to growing unease among the intelligentsia. A range of what could be called pluralist or right-wing liberal newspapers, including the Protestant *Sinar Harapan*, the Catholic Chinese *Kompas* and the Masjumi-linked *Abadi*, took the government to task over its 'floating mass' strategy, warning that depriving villagers of the opportunity for political involvement posed dangers for the health of the political system as a whole (Ward 1974: 190). Reading 2.4 reproduces a typically circumspect *Kompas* editorial on the topic from 25 September 1971.

In Readings 2.5, 2.6 and 2.7 we present voices from the student movement, which regarded itself as part of the New Order struggle. Students were the first element of the New Order alliance to criticise the government openly. They often did so in language that reflected their view of themselves as moral agents free of political interest. The first, dating from

1967, seethes with indignation at a political elite it regards as cunning and corrupt. At the same time it calls for the 'new generation' to seize the initiative in the name of democracy, technology and progress. The second is a statement from Golput, a group founded by former student leader Arief Budiman, calling for a boycott of the 1971 elections. Golput was active during several election campaigns and became a byword for opposition to the stage-managed nature of elections under the New Order. Reading 2.7, 'The moral force' is from a debate with the then Jakarta governor Ali Sadikin in which Arief Budiman contends that politics need not be a dirty business.

We have also included in this chapter selections from a polemic between *Abadi* and the military newspaper *Berita Yudha* on the subject of the military's dual function. This reading (2.8) could have appeared in Chapter 3, on the marginalisation of Muslims in the early New Order, but we wanted to draw attention to that stream of thinking among modernist Muslim intellectuals that prioritised democracy and the rule of law above any overtly religious issues. It also illustrates the relatively robust nature of political debate that was possible in the early New Order period.

January 1974 marked the final break between a significant section of the modernising pluralist stream and Soeharto's New Order, as student-led protests against growing official corruption and ethnic Chinese as well as Japanese dominance over the economy was blamed on many of its leading figures. Many of the modernising pluralists, including Rahman Tolleng, Soemarno and Adnan Buyung Nasution, were gaoled, together with numerous student and youth leaders. *Abadi* and several other newspapers were banned at the same time.

The so-called Malari riots represented the culmination of tensions that had been brewing between the modernising pluralists and a group of officers, businessmen and politicians that had coalesced around the Special Operations (OPSUS) group under Ali Moertopo. Moertopo had engineered the fusion of Old Order political parties into the PPP and the PDI (see Introduction) in 1973, as well as the creation of state-sanctioned corporatist organisations to oversee such groups as labour, youth and the peasantry. With Malari, Moertopo effectively claimed the political scalps of not only the modernising pluralists, but also their main patron within the armed forces, General Soemitro, who was head of the security organisation Kopkamtib, and widely seen as a potential successor to Soeharto. Moertopo's ascendancy marked the beginning of the heyday of the organicist stream of political thinking (see Chapter 4).

Following Malari, modernising pluralists were frequently at the forefront of opposition groups, although they largely continued to lack a mass base. They were, for example, instrumental in the establishment of the Democratic Forum in 1990.

2.1 Soemarno: a two-party system

In this 1967 reading Soemarno, a veteran PSI politician who was a Golkar activist in the early New Order period, emphasises the need for checks and balances in the new regime. The use of the term 'Pancasila socialism' was commonplace at the time but disappeared as the influence of PSI intellectuals waned in the early 1970s. This extract is from a typescript entitled 'Zaman Sesudah Sukarno' (The Post Sukarno Era), dated 18 February 1967. It appeared in the West Java edition of *Mahasiswa Indonesia* shortly afterwards.

We want to organise a state and society in which there can be no repeat of the Sukarno era and no chance of another tyrant like Sukarno emerging. One such tyranny is more than enough.

While attention is focused on the fall and destruction of Bung Karno's politics, we invite everyone who feels a responsibility for the outcome of the state, the nation and the people to think together about our future....

Goals to be achieved

General Soeharto has given a detailed account of what the 'new order'[1] is, saying 'the new order is a mental attitude'. We regard the 'new order' as being more than simply a 'mental attitude'. The 'new order' we are building is a Pancasila socialist society....

But Pancasila, or Pancasila socialism, means nothing in itself. What distinguishes the 'Old Order' from the 'new order' is not to be found in Pancasila socialism itself, but in its realisation, in the manifestation of Pancasila socialist principles in the practice of daily life. In the era of Gestapu/PKI,[2] with its slogans of Manipol, Usdek, Djarek, Tavip, Nasakom,[3] and Guided Democracy and so on [now] collectively referred to as belonging to the 'Old Order', the implementation of Pancasila socialism became *totalitarian socialism*, which amounted to communism.

What is meant by the 'new order' is of course the ordering of a Pancasila socialist society in a way diametrically and fundamentally opposed to the organisation of a totalitarian socialist society.

What kind of society, though, do we mean? We are familiar with *democratic socialism* as being the opposite of totalitarian socialism, and democratic socialism must be distinguished from social democracy. Accordingly, what is meant by 'new order' as the opposite of 'Old Order' is democratic socialism.

If under Gestapu/PKI, Guided Democracy (synonymous with dictatorship) was the basic principle for implementing Pancasila socialism, then under the 'new order' *democracy* will become the basic principle for implementing Pancasila socialism. The New Order is not just socialism and not just democracy, it is both socialism and democracy....

This kind of order has not yet existed on earth, nor has there yet been a conception of how properly to implement 'socialism and democracy'. There is no textbook on the subject, nor any experience of implementing it.... The welfare states in Western Europe and Scandinavia are manifestations of *capitalism and democracy*, so these examples are of little use.

We are compelled to be self-reliant in this matter, so we must search deeply and apply ourselves without the assistance of the theories and experiences of others, applying all our energies to erecting a new order, a socialist and democratic order....

Political parties

We have been familiar with the system of political parties in Indonesia since the struggle for independence....They did not disappear with the achievement of independence, but have proliferated.

The parties have since deteriorated and are now often based upon personal likes and dislikes. They no longer struggle for noble ideals, and for the interests of the nation, the people and society, as did the parties in the colonial era. Rather, they are more interested in vying for official positions and riches. When the people have needed guidance, the parties have not provided leadership. When party principles have been in conflict with the authorities, it is the parties that have made the necessary adjustments. Parties that ought to have been expressions of all the best aspirations of the people, as was the case in the colonial era, have been turned into vehicles for the material interests of their leaders and factions. These attitudes in the parties have easily given rise to hostility, and to the view that parties are superfluous and unnecessary....

It is in the nature of power that it will always absorb other forces, so that eventually there is no power outside itself. Such centralisation of power opens the way for arbitrary behaviour. *For this reason, power must always be balanced by other powers. Checks and balances are required to avoid the arbitrary exercise of power.*

Hence the people need some defence against the tendency of power to feed on and eclipse other sources of power. For this reason parties need to be maintained and nurtured. Their many negative aspects apparent in the past, though, need to be avoided as much as possible. Among these was the fragmentation of our nation into many small parties, which destabilised Indonesian politics. This feature may have been the result of parties coalescing around individuals rather than great aspirations. The parties in operation when Sukarno was in power acted with little regard for their rightful obligations and responsibilities.

How ought political life, especially in party politics, to be ordered in our country so that the ideals of the new order, of socialism and democracy, are realised? We share an awareness that democracy is possible only when there are political parties. Democracy without healthy parties is anarchy and dictatorship.

It is obvious that the practical realisation of socialism still permits the existence of parties. We have rejected a ONE-party system in the context of realising Pancasila socialism, while we have also rejected an excessive number of parties, which would fragment the attention of the nation and destabilise the political situation.

The recent [1966] army seminar has established a political platform for the operation of parties in the New Order, in which four parties are envisaged, namely an Islamic party, a Christian party, a nationalist party and a Pancasila socialist party. There are also the independent functional groups, which are supposed to affiliate with one of the four parties.

It seems this army seminar was still too influenced by old order ways of thinking, as it was not yet able to avoid compartmentalising the nation into political power blocks, albeit large ones....

[In that seminar], mass organisations were called functional groups, and seen as annexes to political parties. Such a structuring of political affairs would provide no fundamental change in the political life of our country...and could lead to a second Lubang Buaya[4] and to a monolithic political order.

In spite of these limitations, the army seminar was convinced that a New Order can only be constructed with a healthy party system. Such a conviction is very progressive, given that it was held by soldiers....

Two parties

The Pancasila socialist state is secular, which means there is a separation of state and religious authority. Any party that aims to make religion the purpose of the state, or to demolish the boundaries between the state and religion, is contrary to the aspirations of a Pancasila socialist state....We are all, without exception, committed to creating a society of Pancasila socialism. We have all expressed our loyalty towards a Pancasila socialist state....

If there are to be parties, then all parties have to aim to 'realise a Pancasila socialist society and state'. *The difference between one party and another lies in the strategy and tactics they use to realise this aim....*

It would be dangerous in any given situation to have only a single set of political tactics and strategies at hand, since this would undermine one of the key elements of democracy, namely balance. A TWO-party system, however, would give us two alternative conceptions for the practical implementation of Pancasila socialism. It would appear that all the diverse wishes and aspirations of strategy and tactics for implementing Pancasila socialism would be accommodated by two parties....

A system of only TWO parties would produce a natural opposition, an opposition that ought to be as highly respected as the governing party. The right of the opposition to effectively perform its function should be guaranteed either by law or convention. The opposition must not automatically be assumed to have bad intentions. Rather, it should be regarded as no higher or lower than the ruling party in serving the society, state and nation. Their difference lies in the opposition offering different policy prescriptions than those of the government. What they share is an effort to realise Pancasila socialism in daily practice, each in their own way.

Socialism and democracy are one and the same. Socialism without democracy is dictatorship, and democracy can be fully realised only in the context of socialism. Democracy without parties, without checks and balances, is inconceivable. Both democracy and socialism are endangered if they are not in balance. This balance should not be seen as absolute, to the extent of becoming stagnant, but should embody the possibility of social development and continuous progress.

For this reason, democracy must have a built-in apparatus able to regulate this balance. Regulations making a group or society homogeneous in thought and action apply only in barracks and in communist societies. Socialism and democracy must reject the possibility of this occurring.

Organising political life around *only* TWO parties ought to unite all differences of strategy and tactics for realising Pancasila socialism, and the necessary built-in apparatus would be provided within each party. The existence of only TWO parties should in itself encourage a system of checks and balances....

It is quite true that in such a political system economic development will be slower than it would be under totalitarianism. But the dangers embodied in the former will be far less than in the latter....

Mass organisations

Let us turn to the position of mass organisations, of functional groups as organisations. What is their relationship to political parties in the context of the new order?...

The generation of 1966 [action fronts] revive the best traditions of the 1945 struggle. Between the handing over of national sovereignty [in 1949] and 1965, though, mass organisations tied themselves to the narrow interests of party politics. The mass organisations let go of their sovereignty and identity, becoming extensions of the interests of particular political parties, each with their own worker, peasant, youth and women's organisations. Narrow partisan interests fragment workers, peasants, youths and women.

The guardians and pillars of the revolution became fragmented; the revolution deviated and lost its way. *We consider that workers, peasants, youths and women must belong to the nation.* It is unjustifiable that the interests of these groups be identified with political parties, that these groups be made the playthings of political parties....

The politics of the action fronts must be clearly demarcated and separated from party politics, so that seeds of division are not planted in their midst....*The action fronts must be left to determine democratically their own political priorities.* Mass organisations must likewise be able to decide where they stand on vital political issues....

In short, we want to depoliticise the action fronts or mass organisations so that they no longer carry out the bidding of particular political parties. We want them to devote their energies instead to vital, national, fundamental issues.

Achieving our aims

We are yet to see the new order reflected in our society and politics. Political, economic and social initiatives are still required to create the objective conditions for realising a new order. Physical operations, particularly socio-political ones, may still be needed here and there.

The politics of parties and mass organisations today continues to reflect the old order era. Mass organisations are still controlled by political parties. Party politics are unbalanced, since they represent only the religious communities. Parties usually referred to as 'leftist', such as the PKI, have been destroyed; the Murba Party is in dire straits, and centrist parties, such as the PNI, are in a state of confusion and in the process of being destroyed.

Regardless of their size, NU, Partai Sarekat Islam Indonesia (PSII; a minor Muslim party) and Muhammadiyah can hardly be said to represent the Indonesian nation and people. To retain the current religious parties is to defend and protect the rights of some of us, while leaving the rest without any political rights....

Furthermore, there can be no fundamental political change by retaining the current party system. If we wish to realise the ideals of socialism and democracy, the current parties, religious ones included, ought to be disbanded, together with their affiliated mass organisations.

After all, it was these current parties that were directly involved in creating, developing and defending the political architecture of Nasakom and Guided Democracy. Retaining these parties would not provide a good education to the next generation and those who will establish new parties. Moreover, it is not conducive to establishing parties with a healthy sense of accountability and character if the PKI is banned while their partners in crime are left untouched....

A socio-political operation to destroy the old order is now under way, targeting first of all the political position of President Sukarno, the mastermind behind Gestapu. But obliterating the vestiges of the old order must go further, in a clean-up operation no less vigorous and drastic. Together with the banning of political parties, there must also be a cleansing of *state and community officials, vested interest groups, corrupters, crooks and manipulators.*

2.2 Soelaeman Soemardi: the need for a progressive, independent force

In this reading, Soelaeman Soemardi, a Cornell University graduate well respected in PSI circles, outlines what he sees as the key political priorities for progressive Indonesians. The extract is translated from a typescript entitled 'Penstrukturan Politik' (political structuring) issued to students of an Intermediate Leadership Training Course held by the Jakarta Students' Association (Ikatan Mahasiswa Djakarta, or IMADA), Ciloto, West Java on 25–8 January 1968. Soelaiman Soemardi's name does not appear on the manuscript.

1   The interplay between progressive and conservative forces is a natural part of the social process...

It is a fact that those forces that seek change, whether rapid or gradual, will eventually always prevail over conservative forces. At any given time the conservative and progressive forces will be in balance, but at the same time always moving towards a new equilibrium in which the progressive forces are more prominent. Ultimately the role of the progressive forces will become much more pronounced while the conservative forces will diminish.

2   Progressive forces are those that seek modernisation, a widening of opportunities for members of a society to more freely decide what is the best way to organise themselves without being merely bound by tradition, i.e. ties inherited from the previous era that offer no alternative than to follow old patterns.

Modernisation is the process of creating alternatives for people in the community, making progress more possible. In the economic sphere this involves raised living standards and improved provision of basic needs (clothing, food and housing). Providing alternatives in the political sphere entails a greater range of political representatives from which to choose and a broadening of political participation: in short, a situation in which decisions affecting society are to a greater extent made by, for and of the will of the people themselves. Alternatives in the social field would provide for greater participation in community life free of the bonds of traditional affiliations (aristocrat or commoner, indigenous or non-indigenous, ethnic and religious exclusivism). Cultural alternatives include greater provision of education and appreciation of ethical and aesthetic values.

3   A feature of modernising forces is the priority given to concrete programs in all fields of development.

Modernising forces emphasise realistic programs that are implemented pragmatically, especially in the economic field, without neglecting social and cultural spheres. Unclear, not to mention utopian, ideas and aims are undesirable. Rather, goals must be rationally attainable in the medium term and able to be implemented in phases. Justifications based on unclear and completely unrealistic ideological formulations are undesirable. Programs should be formulated with clear priorities.

4   The strengthening of progressive and modern social forces, together with the decline of conservative social forces, is naturally and automatically reflected in the political process.

The modern perspective is that political influence, power and authority are nothing more than *instruments* which are able to ensure the implementation of development programs. The conservative political mode is to accumulate power for power's sake, while the modern political mode requires that influence, power and authority be utilised directly to realise a development program that is beneficial to the people. Social, economic and cultural development are the ends.

In saying all this, it remains imperative that progressive and modern social forces be truly reflected in the political structure and process. The political system will only become stable if the political structure and process are able to reflect interaction between progressive and modern social forces on one hand and conservative social forces on the other. The political process will always move in a progressive direction. Indeed it is this progressive dynamic that makes ongoing development possible.

5   In other words, the restructuring of political life is an effort to provide opportunities for forces of renewal to present themselves in the natural course of an institutionalised political process.

Restructuring in the political field is a process that begins with the appearance of modernising forces in politics. Given the opportunity, it is certain that these modernising political forces will gradually increase in strength, because they bring the progressive forces of their own society with them. It may even be that such forces will suddenly and significantly expand in the near future. This is because at the present time there is a great deal of frustration within society itself due to disappointment with the pace of development.

Providing opportunities for the emergence of modern forces in politics is crucial for social, economic and cultural construction. This opportunity should not be provided half-heartedly: it will not be realised by recommending that current political parties 'rejuvenate themselves' because the modernising elements in the current parties remain very minimal. The psychology of power will clearly not enable the conservative elements that are still very dominant in each of these parties' organisations voluntarily to make way for progressive elements among them. The internal processes within the respective parties are little by little headed towards modernisation, but at most this must be regarded as a secondary process in Indonesia's politics.

6   What Indonesian political life needs most is an INDEPENDENT force to act as a vehicle of modernisation.

To pioneer the modernisation process there is a need for a new force unencumbered by the current political constellation. It needs to be independent in the sense that it is able to stand outside and above contemporary political affiliations with their narrow and artificial pigeon-holing of party ideologies, together with their semi-traditional ideological groupings (nationalist, religious, communist, socialist, etc). The pervasive distinction between religious and secular must also be transcended.

7   INDEPENDENT forces are able pragmatically to initiate, even pioneer, the renewal of political life in a positive, development-oriented way.

INDEPENDENT forces aim to carry the community with them as they pioneer an approach to politics that is always directed towards achieving development. Every existing political force has the potential to be engaged immediately and directly in development efforts, rather than being used simply as a means to accumulate yet more power. A concrete development program stands before all political forces. Politics is merely the instrument by which this program can be implemented.

INDEPENDENT forces need not make enemies of any political force whatsoever, nor should they be confrontational towards existing political parties. While attacks on the independent forces by those that misunderstand them can be anticipated, it is important that the independent forces continue striving for the implementation of the development programs before them.

The most important thing to remember is that the INDEPENDENT forces, as pioneers of modernisation, will certainly become stronger over time, and that the other forces will gradually be inspired to orient themselves to modern ways as well. The growing waves of modernisation in society and in political life, including the process of internal transformation of current political parties, can only be of benefit to all the people.

Nevertheless, a force that is not part of the existing semi-traditional political constellation must pioneer this modernisation process.

For this purpose, an INDEPENDENT MOVEMENT for development must be brought into being immediately.

Jakarta, end of December 1967

2.3 A. Rahman Tolleng: voting and the composition of parliament

Rahman Tolleng was a PSI-linked intellectual who represented Golkar in the appointed interim parliament. This is an extract from a speech he delivered to a plenary session of the Gotong Royong People's Representative Council on 22 November 1969. Development Factions A, B and C refer to the military, bureaucratic and civilian streams within Golkar. The extract below was translated from Sekretariat Dewan Perwakilan Rakyat Gotong Royong (1970: 120–32).

Honourable chair, government representatives, and other honourable members, in the name of the Development Factions A, B, and C we wish first to convey our position regarding the two draft bills concerning the election of members of the People's Consultative Assembly [MPR], the People's Representative Council [DPR], and the Regional Legislatures [DPRD].

The 1945 Constitution does not specify whether our legislative bodies are to be constituted through elections or through a system of appointments. It specifies that a statute governing the composition and status of the national, provincial and regional legislatures will determine this....

Why does the draft bill on the composition and status of the national, provincial and regional legislatures specify that our legislatures are constituted through both elections and a system of appointments? Because we have already agreed that these legislative bodies must fulfil two basic principles:

1   To guarantee the unity and integrity of the nation.

2   To channel and develop society's dynamics.

In order to achieve an objective guarantee that these two principles will be implemented, our faction sees the need for a reorganisation of the political structure in line with the preamble of Resolution no. XLIV, which reads: 'That political stability in accord with the aspirations of the New Order can only be achieved via political structures radically different from those of the Old Order.'

Our faction believes that without doing this we will waste time, energy, and money. However, it is apparent that the prevailing conditions do not yet enable the implementation of that goal. In the interim, constitutional life must go on.

Honourable chair and respected members, as I presume we are all aware, the practice of supplementing elected members of legislative bodies with appointees, as determined in the draft bill, is not a new idea. Neither is it intended as an interim measure. Even industrialised countries with mature democracies recognise the practice of appointing members of parliament as a means of improving the quality of assemblies constituted primarily through 'quantitative' means, i.e. general elections....

Concerning the general elections, I think we all agree that the human right of every citizen to vote and be elected – both as an individual and as part of a collective entity – must be guaranteed. This principle must be firmly upheld if we want our general election truly to function as an instrument of democracy, truly to reflect the dynamics of our society. By upholding this principle we certainly do not rule out the possibility that there may be exemptions for those whose right to vote has been revoked or those who are not considered competent to carry out their voting rights as regulated by law....

In the [1966–7] 'consensus' regarding the draft bills on the composition of legislative bodies and general elections there are matters that cannot be justified either constitutionally or from a legal perspective. We wish, first, to draw the assembly's attention to Article 2 of the draft bill on general elections, which reads:

> Indonesian citizens who are former members of the outlawed Indonesian Communist Party, including its mass organisations, or those who were involved either directly or indirectly in the Counter-Revolutionary 30 September Movement or other outlawed organisations, do not have the right to vote or be elected.

Are we fully aware of the consequences if this Article was to be implemented to the letter? It would be dishonest not to address the problems which arise from Article 2, clause 1, such as:

- How are we to control the members of an outlawed organisation such as the Indonesian Communist Party, including all its mass organisations, which have such large memberships?
- How are we to interpret the following criteria for determining indirect involvement in the G30S/PKI as provided by the official elucidation of article 2?:
  1 Those who have indicated, either in word or deed, their sympathy with the aforesaid Counter-Revolutionary Movement.
  2 Those who have consciously indicated, either in word or deed, opposition to the measures taken to crush the G30S/PKI.
- What or who exactly is being referred to when it says 'other outlawed organisations'? Is this supposed to refer to the former political party Masjumi and the Indonesian Socialist Party? Active debate about this issue outside this plenary session and in the press shows up the inadequacies in the wording of the two draft bills.

Proportional representation versus an electoral district system

The success of a general election as a democratic tool for managing the dynamics of a society in a healthy way depends largely on the electoral system. In a broad sense one can differentiate between what is called a proportional 'list' system and an electoral district 'member' system, both of which have many variants.

If our faction had to choose between these two electoral systems we would choose the district member system. Why, honourable chair, do we favour the district system? As with the idea of reorganising the political structure to better implement Pancasila programs, we are not proposing that Indonesia slavishly imitate a system practised in certain Western democracies. We want to emphasise this, because in our opinion *all* practices associated with modern democracy originate in the West, including the holding of general elections (based on either a proportional or a district system) and the formation of political parties.

Honourable chair, there are good logical reasons why we favour a district system:

- it forges a direct relationship between those who are elected and their constituents, because the candidates are not merely symbols or pictures as in the proportional system, but real people;
- establishing a direct relationship between those who are elected and their constituents will eventually improve the quality of candidates and make them more accountable to those who voted for them;
- as a consequence of the above two points, a district system would be inherently educative and will help the people to get used to democracy;
- it would help simplify the party system as required by Decision no. XXII/1966 of the Interim People's Consultative Assembly [MPRS];
- it is much simpler, more efficient and economical.

This is the position of our faction concerning the electoral system. Yet time and again we have been presented with a 'consensus' that cannot be criticised. Based upon this consensus we are now faced with a draft bill on general elections based on the proportional system....

Honourable chair, it is ironic indeed that, while we support the declaration in the draft bill on general elections and the composition of parliament to defend the 1945 Constitution and the Pancasila, the very same bill contravenes it. On the one hand, we persevere in defending the right to strike and the right of civil servants...to belong to a political party and, on the other hand, when dealing with the draft bill on general elections we do the exact opposite. Does this not mean that democracy will be allowed to prevail only as long as it does not threaten our interests? And that democracy will not be allowed if we do not like it?

2.4 *Kompas*: the concept of the floating mass

This editorial appeared in the 25 September 1971 edition of the Catholic daily *Kompas*. It was a response to a speech by Central Java military commander Major-General Widodo in favour of the 'floating mass' idea first proposed by the Muslim intellectual Nurcholish Madjid in June the same year (Ward 1974: 189). This translation is from Smith (1974: 233–5).

The idea has been proposed before: organised party activities should be limited to the centre, province, and *kabupaten* [district]. There is no need for them lower than the second level of local government.

This opinion has been repeated by the commander of the Diponegoro military command, Major-General Widodo. In Limpung District, Batang, he said it was enough for there to be party organisations in the centre, province and *kabupaten*. More was not necessary.

We comprehend the good intention behind this concept: communities outside the *kabupaten* do not need to be split up by political groupings. Let them live in calm, to work and construct. It is sufficient if there is political activity there when there is a general election.

There are further considerations too. It is not necessary for people to bind themselves organisationally to one of the parties. Just let them choose the one that suits them, the one they consider good, at every general election. In other words, let them form a 'floating mass'.

We do not reject this concept. But the following questions remain unanswered:

- Whatever their deficiencies, the parties (and this goes for Golkar as well) serve the function of protecting the interests of the mass of the people. If, for instance, the interests of the majority of the people in the villages are damaged by some individual in authority, to whom shall they turn for political protection?
- Moreover, the community of the villages cannot live just to work. They, too, need food for the mind and the heart. They, too, have a disposition to think about the common lot. Who is to provide that 'food' and how is it to be channelled? If the people are not satisfied with their conditions, who is to channel their dissatisfaction?

In practice, the civil service and its complementary instruments are not able to do all these things alone. Let it not happen that clandestine forces then find a way to the people's hearts and minds through various non-political organisations!

If the political parties (including Golkar) are not operating in areas below the *kabupaten*, this does not mean that there are no political activities there or that the need for political activities has disappeared. Political parties are inherent in the nature of humans as social beings. Parties are only one of the kinds of channel for them.

So thought must be given to the kinds of channels which are to be allowed to develop in areas below the *kabupaten*. What forms of political creativity should be promoted as something better to take the place of party politics? Farmers' associations, merchants' associations, teachers' associations, other kinds of associations?

2.5 *Mahasiswa Indonesia*: the holy anger of a generation

This extract is from an editorial in the West Java edition of *Mahasiswa Indonesia* [the Indonesian Student] of 19 June 1967. Founded a year earlier, the journal had been a vocal supporter of efforts to de-Sukarnoise the government. By 1967, however, disillusionment with the military was clearly evident. This translation is reproduced from that by Herbert Feith and Alan Smith in Smith (1974: 211–13).

On 19 June 1967, we completed our first year and embarked on a second. It is not for us to criticise or praise what we have done. Our task is to do what we promised ourselves we would do and complete what we have begun; that is what drives us to work. Those whose sleep was disturbed by the sound of our voice and who want us quiet – let them be on their guard...for our voice will continue loud and clear....

We have called for justice a hundred times and we shall call for it again and again. It is sad when men are locked up like wild animals as a result of the rule of law, sad to see men forced to live in isolation behind iron bars or forced to kiss the dust on which they have trampled. But it is a thousand times sadder when millions of people are cheated, insulted and exploited, sacrificed to the pleasure of rulers who play at being gods above the law.

It is not for revenge that we demand an immediate implementation of justice, but because to deny justice is injustice.

Some say: 'Yes, the law must be upheld. But more important still is order and tranquillity.' What kind of order and tranquillity is this that would try to postpone justice? Without justice, what sort of order can be kept, but one full of complaints and resentments, full of the wrath of men held in contempt? Where can tranquillity be found where each mouthful of rice costs men their self-respect? Shall this nation which once craved nobility and greatness be allowed to sink further, to become a gang of swindlers, black-marketeers, thieves and pickpockets, spending the rest of their history as a pack of wolves who deceive each other and gobble each other up?

You who have been entrusted by the people to uphold and implement the law, do not look the other way. Answer.

And what of that big word that is tossed about in our country like a toy, democracy? What is democracy, if it is not a symphony of life based on respect for human values and the principles of law? There is no democracy if millions of men are turned into horses for the pleasure of a handful of riders who never pay.

Ah, power, how many rupiahs it can furnish and how much indulgence! And how many there are who obtain it only through cunning, deceit and corruption, by licking the feet of the tyrant!

There are those who say, 'Our groups are upholding and implementing true democracy.' But we say: Can trees whose only fruit are empty slogans, conflict and tyranny be called trees of democracy? No, indeed, trees like this must be felled and destroyed to the roots and replaced by trees of a new kind. Let those who call themselves the defenders and implementers of democracy get busy with planning and work to produce wellbeing for the whole people, to put an end to wailing and sighing.

Here we stand, and we voice the holy anger of a generation.

We see before us an Indonesia which is old and broken and poor, bent down by sufferings and foreign debt. If this Indonesia wishes to live on, she must shake off her decrepitude and throw it back into the past. She must absorb new ideas and new values and undergo a complete rebirth.

'But what about our identity?' some people ask. 'Must we throw that into the dustbin?' Our reply is: Can a nation go on living with half its body buried in the past? How can any nation pride itself on its identity if it is unable to create anything new? A nation without creative power and capable only of boasting of its past – this is not a nation with identity. It is simply stupidity.

Identity is not a permanent cocoon. Identity is the principle which moves us to surmount one obstacle after another, to smash one form after another in the creation of something new. In the past Indonesia could boast a great identity because she was open to new ideas and new values. Let us too be open to receive all that is new and marvel at inventions and creations. Let us throw off whatever obstructs this renewal as a butterfly throws off its cocoon, to fly high and far and taste life in all its fullness.

Let things new come from any direction whatsoever, for we are not stepchildren in the world....

How sad that fate of a nation which has yet to learn the ABCs of democracy – after 22 years of independence! How sad the condition of a nation which still has prehistoric vehicles creeping along its countryside, in an age when modern technology is concerning itself with the launching of spaceships, a nation most of whose citizens still live in darkness, untouched by the progress of civilisation! How sad the state of a nation which after a quarter century of independence cannot free itself from the most basic problems of subsistence, with most of its citizens forever forced to worry about food for the next day, their thoughts never rising beyond their bowl of rice!

Let this generation arise then to put an end to this rottenness. Let it arise along with those others whose conscience has not yet been buried under riches and power. When will renewal ever start if not today?

There are those who say, 'The earth is a field in which the Devil sows sin. Light the way toward Heaven, ye children of this dark world.' But we say: Light up this earthly life, grace it with prosperity and abundance, with a million lights and colours, so that the way to Heaven is broad and bright. Earth is the one place where the spirit can rise through challenge after challenge to ever greater heights. No one can make light of the importance of this earthly life without scorning the power of God who is its foundation. How could earth remain solid under our feet but for God's power working in its every atom? How could earth provide us with riches but for God's love acting in and upon it? Men who toil for a new and better life, who wipe the sweat off their brow, know that the earth on which they stand is holy ground.

2.6 The White Group: boycott the elections

The White Group, or Golongan Putih, more commonly known as Golput, was set up prior to the 1971 elections by former student leader Arief Budiman and others in protest against the government's use of the military and the bureaucracy to ensure a Golkar victory. The following reading, written in May 1971, is a Golput manifesto published as 'Penjelasan Tentang Golongan Putih' in Sanit (1992: 46–8).

1   The White Group is not an organisation. It is an identity, an identity for those who are not satisfied with the present situation because the rules of democracy have been trampled upon, not just by political parties (for example when they initiated the general election regulations), but also the Golongan Karya [Golkar], who in their endeavour to win this election utilised government agencies as well as undemocratic methods.

2   To show that someone identifies with the White Group, they will wear a white five-sided badge with a black border. They can make these badges themselves using a piece of card and a safety pin.

3   The White Group does not act outside the law because one of the movement's objectives is to strengthen obedience to the law. It carries out its protest within the limits of existing laws.

4   The White Group carries out political education for the general public, especially the younger generation. It does not aim to make people follow any particular political stream but to encourage them to think critically and creatively in confronting their environment. One way in which this political education is carried out is by

providing translations and holding discussions concerning current political issues, by openly sharing thoughts and so on. The White Group movement in itself already constitutes political education, by implanting awareness within society that in a general election every citizen has the right not to vote.

5   Furthermore, to those who feel that they have been forced to vote for a particular political party or functional group, even though they did not want to vote, they need only complain to a legal organisation in order to bring the case to court. In Jakarta this legal organisation is the Legal Aid Institute headed by Adnan Buyung Nasution S.H. In the regions complaints can be lodged with a local legal organisation.

6   The objective of the White Group is to safeguard the democratic tradition, that is the protection, in any situation at all, of opinions that differ from those of the rulers. Indonesian society must protect this tradition. It must not become accustomed to a situation in which the government is free to do whatever it likes.

7   This movement is therefore a cultural movement, in the sense that what we are struggling for is not political power but a social tradition whereby basic rights are always protected from arbitrary power.

8   The White Group recommends that in protest against the undemocratic 1971 general election the Indonesian people simply become good spectators.

9   Not voting is the right of every citizen because it is protected by the constitution, as is evident in the dialogue between Arief Budiman and the president: 'If, for example, I did not agree with the present general election and I was to write articles that expressed my opposition to it, and did not vote in it, would I be arrested? Or would my stance be considered that of a loyal critic?' Pak Harto answered that it was 'my right to do all of these things. The important thing was that I did not use methods outside of the law, or sabotage or obstruct other people from voting. So long as my oppositionist attitude remained within the boundaries of the law, it was my basic right.'

Jakarta, 28 May 1971
The White Group

2.7 Arief Budiman: the moral force

Arief Budiman once likened the student movement to Shane, the former gunslinger in the eponymous 1953 Western, who, after saving a group of farmers from gangsters, spurns all blandishments and rides off alone into the dawn. The image of students as a moral force remained remarkably powerful throughout the New Order and allowed them far greater leeway to protest than other groups. The following extract was first published on the eve of the general elections in the student newspaper *Harian Kami* on 15 June 1971 under the title 'Response to Ali Sadikin concerning Golput'. The version translated here is from Sanit (1992: 140–1).

[Jakarta] Governor Ali Sadikin has said that because Golput [Golongan Putih or the White Group] have involved themselves in the election campaign, they have already overstepped the mark and become politicised....As pure moralists they should keep their ideas to themselves and not try to spread them or influence others....Politics is always a game of rough and tumble. It is full of intrigues and dirty play. This is what Ali Sadikin was reported as saying.

There are several matters of interest here:

1   Is Golput really a political movement? Let me relate an incident that occurred during the Sukarno era. At that time the Sukarno government was busy working to unite the 'New Emerging Forces'. The edifice for it, Conefo [Conference of the New Emerging Forces], was in the process of being built. People were forever being urged to talk about Nasakom, Panca Azimat Revolusi [the Five Talismans of the Revolution] and the like. The economy had been totally neglected, to the point that people could no longer buy rice to eat. One day an ordinary person said, 'Mister, I'm hungry. I don't want to spend all my time going to political rallies, I want to eat.' Without any questions, this man was arrested on charges of engaging in politics, more specifically anti-government politics.

What was really happening at that time was that politics in Indonesia was *over functioning*, permeating every aspect of life. Whenever anyone said anything it always had political consequences. Politics had taken over everything.

This is still the case. The people are forced to vote on the basis of religious decrees, threats of dismissal from their job, or through force of arms. The common people who see all this say, 'Brother, please don't bully us. Pity the poor people who get pushed around all the time.' To which the bullies reply angrily, 'So you want to get political, do you?' The common people are the White Group.

2   Can moralists not campaign on the basis of their morals? I think it is immoral if moralists do not try to promote their moral ideas. Indeed, the moment a moralist ceases to campaign he is no longer a moralist but an egoist.

The fact that moralists have taken part in a campaign does not mean at all that they have 'overstepped the mark' and become politicised. It may be true that the moralists' campaign has political consequences, especially in a country in which politics has become divorced from morality. If moralists who campaign for their views are all politicians, then Buddha, Jesus Christ, the Prophet Mohammad SAW, Krishnamurti and Bertrand Russell must all be big-time politicians as well.

3   Must politics always be full of intrigues and dirty play? That is the way it appears if you look at Indonesian politics today. But it does not have to be that way. The White Group actually wants to create a healthier political atmosphere by, for instance, creating better ground rules and providing a fair referee. Lieutenant-General Ali Sadikin used to be a straightforward military man. When he was first appointed to a political position he may well have been RATHER SHOCKED to see how filthily the political game was played, both by the parties and by Golkar. I really hope that when he says 'politics is a dirty game', Governor Ali Sadikin has not simply given up hope. I call on Ali Sadikin to join the youths who want to see cleaner politics by fighting alongside the White Group.

2.8   *Abadi* v. *Berita Yudha*: polemic on the military's dual function

The following extracts are from an exchange between the Masjumi-oriented Jakarta newspaper *Abadi* and the military daily *Berita Yudha* in February and March 1970. The *Abadi* articles are written by S.M. Amin, a Muslim lawyer. No author is given for the *Berita Yudha* articles but they are likely to reflect the views of intelligence officer Colonel Aloysius Sugianto, the publisher of the newspaper, and ultimately those of his patron, Ali Moertopo. All are taken from Amin (1970: 15–16, 19–20, 23–5, 33–4, 48–50, 52–3, 70–1, 78, 90).

S.M. Amin, 18 February

We need to begin putting the national administration in order, by, among other things, immediately ceasing 'military infiltration' of all non-military offices. Slogans proclaiming the armed forces' 'civic mission', 'dual function' and its status as a 'child of the people' and everything that flows from them need to be stopped at once.

It is completely unnatural to retain them any longer. Give the Indonesian people the national duties for which they are qualified. The practices of 'civic mission', 'dual function' and the concept of the military as a 'child of the people' can no longer be justified.

Imagine what would happen if civilians succeeded in promoting their own 'military mission', 'dual function' and themselves as 'children of the people'. Imagine them appointing a professor of ophthalmology as a regional military commander, an officer responsible for national security over a particular region tasked with conceptualising, evaluating and determining all matters of tactics and strategy in national security planning! God preserve us from such a disaster!

Berita Yudha, 21 February

Mr S.M. Amin may have got himself title of Mr [Master of Laws] but there are still many fields of knowledge that he has not yet mastered. Because of his inadequate knowledge, he feels entitled to call for an immediate end to sloganeering about dual function and civic mission. On the basis of our expertise (which Mr S.M. Amin lacks) we agree that there should be no more sloganeering about the civic mission and the dual function, but we also believe that the contribution that the civic mission and dual function make to society must continue. Mr S.M. Amin's misconceptions about the civic mission and the dual function stem from his ignorance or his inadequate understanding of HANKAMNAS RATA [total people's national defence and security][5] and its place in the philosophy and study of national defence in Indonesia. A more interdisciplinary approach between the sciences would help avoid misunderstandings and potentially damaging conflicts.

Ill informed as he is, S.M. Amin cannot be blamed for his emotional outburst about the civic mission and dual function or for going as far as using terms such as 'military infiltration in non-military affairs'. Mr S.M. Amin forgets that the military have never accused civilians who involve themselves in military affairs of 'infiltrating the military', because, based on our knowledge of HANKAMNAS RATA, the important issue is not whether someone is military or not, but to ensure that every national asset is maximised, that everyone plays their part in building national resilience.

S.M. Amin, 28 February

Do I really need to elaborate on the intentions behind slogans such as dual function and civic mission as they are used these days? These slogans have been used to justify 'military infiltration' (there is no better term to describe it) in every area of government.

Do the facts still need to be presented? Here are some indisputable facts: the daily *Harian Kami* (20 February 1970) carried an analysis of appointments of district heads and mayors in Central Java. Of a total of 35 positions, *Harian Kami* found that civilians fill 17, while 18 are from the military. Fourteen of the latter are from the army, one from the navy and three from the police.

The situation is more astonishing in regions like Aceh and North Sumatra. In Aceh, of a total of seven district heads and mayors, five are from ABRI, while in North Sumatra, of a total of 11, nine are from ABRI.

How many provincial governors and regional heads throughout Indonesia are from ABRI? How many government ministers, secretaries-general and section heads of government departments are military officers? How many ambassadors posted overseas, or heads of state corporations?

'Military infiltration' is an appropriate phrase in the circumstances, and we should not be in the least surprised to hear accusations from overseas that this nation of ours is under a military regime.

No one would object if the 'civic mission' and 'dual function' were geared to assisting village communities, for instance by upgrading roads, aiding victims of natural disasters and so on.

I accept that not everyone has expertise in every field of knowledge, and of course I also acknowledge my 'ignorance or inadequate understanding of HANKAMNAS RATA', as was pointed out in *Berita Yudha*'s editorial response.

Indeed, it is quite beyond me who or what HANKAMNAS RATA might be, or what position and rank he currently holds. I am aware of this short-coming, but it should also be understood that I have never claimed or regarded myself to be an expert in military matters. My statement in *Abadi* that ABRI's 'dual function' and 'civic mission' slogans, together with all their consequences, need to be stopped is based upon knowledge of law.

Legislation in a state based on democratic governance or popular sovereignty – our country in this case – must fulfil a number of essential criteria if that state is to be regarded as a democracy, not merely in theory but in fact.

One of these essential criteria, which we must struggle to affirm with all the means at our disposal, especially in light of the current drive to 'purify the 1945 Constitution' and to uphold the 'rule of law', is the clear and strict separation of powers between the legislature, executive and judiciary.

The separation of duties and responsibilities between officials within these three branches of government cannot possibly be realised while 'military infiltration' of every area of government not only continues to occur but also increases in comparison with the Sukarno era....

S.M. Amin, 14 March

The principles behind the dual function and civic mission – and all their consequences – derive from a number of 'instructions' and decrees by President Sukarno. These were issued not long after the Decree of 5 July 1959, which, as we have all experienced, changed the basis of government, which was initially based upon democracy in accordance with the 1945 Constitution, to become a 'Guided Democracy' which paved the way for an undermining of the law and led eventually towards a dictatorship.

These 'instructions' and decrees were accompanied by speeches intended to prepare the public to accept a new element in government, namely the military. 'The Indonesian armed forces,' he said, 'is a functional grouping that also has duties in the political, economic, social and cultural fields.'

President Sukarno was aware that this 'new element in government' could not be reconciled with the 1945 Constitution, which quite clearly indicates a separation of powers between the judicial, executive and legislative branches. Moreover, within each branch there is a division of duties; within the executive, for instance, there is the civil service, the military and the police. However, this was no obstacle for him.

Sukarno declared that the principle of *'trias politica'* [the separation of powers], an essential condition for a democratic state, did not apply in his 'guided democracy'. *'Trias politica,'* he claimed, 'belonged to the era of liberal democracy.'

'The posting of members of the armed forces to non-military positions is indeed inappropriate,' he said. 'Yet,' he continued, 'it is only inappropriate if we still think in liberal democratic terms. In the socialist sphere it is normal for a general to occupy a non-military position.' He took as his example the case of Shanghai (in a communist state), where the mayor was a high-ranking military officer.

Berita Yudha, *19 and 20 March*

It is wrong to talk about 'infiltration' with regard to people deeply committed to striving together to foster and ensure cooperation in national and community life through spiritual and material development in accordance with the norms of Pancasila. While there might still be differences of opinion, we must not allow these to obstruct our common aim to implement development. It is unbefitting a Pancasilaist to label this effort to foster a common basis and common direction 'infiltration'. Unless, of course, he is only playing at being a Pancasilaist for political reasons, like the PKI people used to.

So it is that, in accordance with the dual function, we do not make an issue about whether someone is military or non-military, or about military infiltration of non-military fields, since the dual function is in essence the fostering of cooperation among people participating and striving together in the development of a Pancasila society. It is wrong to claim that the dual function began to be implemented only in recent years, and it was certainly not ex-President Sukarno's creation....

Anyone familiar with the struggle for independence from the time of the proclamation will note that the dual function has been in operation from the outset – even though they may not have been aware of this. Whether we were seizing weapons and headquarters from the Japanese forces after independence was proclaimed, seizing government offices, setting up public kitchens and organising the Red Cross, or even forming armed units, we never made a distinction between military and non-military. Even in battle we did not refer to the units deployed as being military or non-military....

The politics [of the freedom fighters] were simple, the politics of nationalism, building and fostering national unity and resilience to confront the forces that threatened independence and the national interest. At that time politics possessed its original meaning, namely to wrench power from foreign hands and to uphold and defend the sovereignty of national power. Once the foreign power and its officers had left our homeland, it ought to have been apparent that it was unnatural, indeed illogical, for the guardians of Pancasila to go on to play politics and engage in political rivalry.

S.M. Amin, 27 March

Berita Yudha's editors have written at length about the sacrifices, dedication and close cooperation between our armed fighters and other groups in society, including students, graduates, Islamic leaders and their followers, workers, peasants, women and so forth in the physical confrontation with the Dutch military during our independence struggle. Nobody can deny this because it is an indelible historical fact....

[But] the kind of cooperation that took place during the struggle for independence between various groups in society, whether armed or unarmed, was inspired by a spirit of sacrifice and selfless dedication, without any expectation of reward. The dual function, on the other hand, has nothing to do with cooperation. It is a system that militarises the civilian government apparatus by sanctioning the takeover of civilian positions by military officers....

Sometimes it seems to us that the editors of *Berita Yudha* are living in a dreamland (sorry!). So much praise do they heap on dual function that it is as though they think of it as an Aladdin's lamp capable of curing all problems. Their view of dual function seems almost cult-like – something that has no place in the New Order. Under the Old Order we were all familiar with the personality cult surrounding the 'Spokesperson of the People', the 'Great Leader of the Revolution' and so on. Let us not allow the emergence of a cult of the dual function of the armed forces in the New Order period.

Notes

1 Inconsistent renderings of 'new order' and 'old order' here reflect the original text.
2 Gestapu/PKI [the 30 September Movement/Indonesian Communist Party] was the Soeharto regime's designation for the failed mutiny that took place in the early hours of 1 October 1965.

3   Usdek stands for the 1945 Constitution, Indonesian Socialism, Guided Democracy, Guided Economy, Indonesian Identity; Djarek was the title of Sukarno's 1960 state address and means 'the March of our Revolution'; Tavip (Tahun Vivere Pericoloso) was the Year of Living Dangerously; while Nasakom was a favourite Sukarno formulation willing the unity of nationalism, Islam and communism.

4   Lubang Buaya was the site of the well into which the bodies of the generals killed on 1 October 1965 were dumped.

5   The Hankamnas Rata doctrine stresses the need for close cooperation with civilians in national defence (see Lowry 1993: 88).

3 Marginalised Islam

When Soeharto came to power, Muslim parties looked forward to a new era. Masjumi leaders welcomed the overthrow of the man who had banned their party in 1960 and Nahdlatul Ulama (NU), through its youth wing, Ansor, actively collaborated with the army in the physical destruction of their common enemy, the Indonesian Communist Party. But both groups, the modernists and the traditionalists, misread the nature of their alliance with the new government. While Soeharto's army was glad of the support it received from Muslim groups in toppling Sukarno and eliminating the PKI, it was also deeply suspicious of political Islam. Soeharto and his fellow officers had spent much of their careers fighting Muslim insurgents in West Java, Sumatra and Sulawesi. They also shared many of Sukarno's doubts about Masjumi, especially since it had aligned itself with the CIA-backed PRRI–Permesta rebellions in the 1950s.

Muslim groups soon found themselves struggling for influence. Soeharto appointed very few pious Muslims to important positions, preferring to take advice from Christians or Javanists like himself (Karim 1999: 43–5, 117). In 1967 the new regime dealt a crushing blow to Masjumi when it prohibited the party from re-establishing itself. An attempt by former vice-president Mohammad Hatta and the Masjumi figure Deliar Noer to establish an alternative modernist party was also thwarted. As a compromise the New Order created a new modernist party in February 1968 called Parmusi (Muslim Party of Indonesia) but prevented former Masjumi leaders from occupying senior positions within it (Ward 1970).

The other major party in the early New Order period was NU. Although NU was historically more willing to accommodate itself to the prevailing political dispensation, it had deep roots in rural Java and was less amenable to manipulation. Despite bearing the brunt of physical intimidation and state violence in the 1971 elections, NU's support base was more or less intact; it won 18.67 per cent of the vote, almost exactly what it had won in the democratic general elections of 1955.

The first extract (Reading 3.1) is from a speech given by Idham Chalid, chair of the executive board of NU, to a group of NU cadres in 1969. He tells the story of two renowned *ulama* facing a hostile inquisition in the ninth century. The first defends his interpretation of the scriptures dogmatically and is tortured, while the second answers more diplomatically and is spared. Idham's speech, which would have been understood by his listeners as a parable about Masjumi and NU, provides a valuable insight into the political thinking of NU (Fealy 1998: ch. 2). NU's flexibility on political matters has typically been interpreted by outsiders as opportunism. But as Fealy (1994, 1998) has argued, there is a particular logic behind NU's accommodationism, one that draws on classical Islamic thinkers such as al-Mawardi and al-Ghazali. In essence, it involves putting the wellbeing of the *umat* (community of believers) above all else. This does not mean that NU was always willing to compromise with those in power. When its leaders perceived a threat to the *umat*, as was the case when the New Order drafted a new marriage law in 1973 which would have facilitated easier marriage across religious boundaries, NU reacted strongly, leading a walkout of parliament (Feillard 1999: 190–8; Emmerson 1976: 223–58).

The draft marriage law is the focus of the second reading (3.2), a 1973 polemic by the renowned West Sumatran modernist Hamka. Hamka was a frequent critic of the New Order's emphasis on rapid economic growth and modernisation at the expense of morals and ethical principles. He was particularly outspoken on the government's de facto legalisation of prostitution and gambling, as well as the profit it reaped from sales of alcohol. In this article Hamka expresses his frustration with the marginalisation of political Islam and argues that the marriage law threatened to 'completely destroy Islamic principles'. Vocal opposition from both modernists and traditionalists saw the marriage bill substantially altered, marking one of the few political victories won by Muslims in the first two decades of New Order rule.

Represented here also is a stream of Islamic thinking that was later to be called Islamic renewal or neo-modernism. Its most articulate proponent in this period was Dr Nurcholish Madjid, a University of Chicago-educated Indonesian and head of the large and influential HMI (Muslim Students' Association) from 1966 until 1971. Reading 3.3 is from an important speech he made to a group of Muslim intellectuals and activists in Jakarta in January 1970. This speech, entitled 'The need to renew Islamic thought and the issue of the integration of the Islamic community', is often referred to as the starting point for the reform movement in Indonesian Islam. In it, Nurcholish proposed abandoning the struggle for an Islamic state – as distinct from an Islamic society – and called for secularisation and liberalisation. If there was to be no Islamic state, he argued, there was no need for Islamic political parties. Hence the slogan 'Islam yes, Islamic parties no!', which originated with this speech. While the government clearly welcomed these ideas, Indonesian Muslims fiercely debated them. Many attacked them as un-Islamic, but Nurcholish was supported by a number of intellectuals, including Utomo Dananjaya, Usep Fathuddin and Dawam Rahardjo (M.S. Anwar 1995: 56). Nurcholish's anti-sectarian ideas became popular among Indonesia's new Muslim middle classes in the 1980s, and helped to underpin the convergence, at least at the elite level, of modernist and traditionalist Islam in the 1990s.

The last reading (3.4) is from an article written in about 1971 by H.M.S. Mintaredja, a modernist Muslim intellectual who was appointed by Soeharto to lead the modernist Parmusi in 1970. Mintaredja was at the time a government minister, and his installation was widely seen as an attempt to put an end to efforts by former Masjumi supporters to control the party. As Parmusi chair, Mintaredja was an outspoken supporter of the government's policy of depoliticisation and the separation of religion and politics. This extract from a pamphlet originally published under the title 'Islamic society and politics in Indonesia' articulates what was essentially the government position: that Muslims would be better off concentrating on social and economic development than struggling for an Islamic state. Mintaredja's unpopularity among former Masjumi voters was evident in its poor showing in the 1971 elections. While Masjumi had won almost 21 per cent of the vote in the 1955 elections, Parmusi won only 5.36 per cent in 1971 (van Marle 1974: 53, 58). Mintaredja was, however, the kind of Islamic leader the New Order favoured, and when the four Muslim parties were forcibly merged into the PPP in 1973 Mintaredja was made its leader.

3.1 Idham Chalid: protecting the *umat*

This extract is from a speech by the chair of Nahdlatul Ulama to cadres at an NU training session held at Tjisarua, West Java, on 20 February 1969. It was reproduced in a small paperback titled *NU dan Aqidahnya* (Fadhali 1969: 13–16).

Imam Hambali [Ahmad ibn Hanbal] held firmly to his convictions, but his imprudence prevented his teachings becoming widely known. His dogged consistency led to Imam Hambali being imprisoned for almost his entire life and tortured continuously. If I am not mistaken this was due to his opinion regarding the problem of whether the Qur'an is *qodim* [the 'uncreated' word of God] or *hadith* [the 'created' sayings of the Prophet Muhammad]. Mutazilites [in the ninth century] were of the opinion that the Qur'an was *hadith*, whereas Sunni theologians argued that the Qur'an was the divine word of God.

When Imam Hambali was asked by the Caliph al-Makmun whether he thought the Qur'an was *hadith* or *qodim*, he answered, with total consistency, '*qodim*' and as a result he was re-incarcerated and tortured. Imam Sjafi'i, in contrast, gave a diplomatic answer. Pointing to his clenched fist, he said that all five of these, the Qur'an, the Old Testament, the New Testament, the Psalms and Suhuf [scriptures revealed to the Prophet Noah], were *hadith*. The meaning of his answer was that it was not the Qur'an which was created, but his fist. The caliph, who held absolute power at that time, felt satisfied and freed Imam Sjafi'i, giving him the opportunity to spread his teachings to all corners of the globe, the outcome of which is that 45 per cent of the world's population adhere to them.

This means if you have to choose between two truths, one that involves an excessive degree of risk, and another that involves a small degree, then choose the latter, for this is a prudent decision which will ensure the well-being of the *umat*. If you become a leader, don't make a habit of creating difficulties for people. As the prophet Muhammad said, if you are an *Imam* preaching to a large congregation, especially if there are old and infirm people present, do not read a long *sura* [division of the Qur'an]. This is called prudence. If you pray alone it is up to you if you want to read 15 *Juz* [chapters of the Qur'an] for the first *rak'aat* [part of prayer] and 15 more *Juz* for the second, so that you recite the entire Qur'an during a single prayer. This is permissible, but if you try it while leading prayers there will not be much left of the congregation by the time you have finished. At the same time, do not choose too short a verse.

Prudent leadership that ensures the wellbeing of the *umat* is therefore essential. The prudent approach of Nahdlatul Ulama is not a concoction of its leaders but an application of the morality of Imam Sjafi'i along with the companions of the Prophet in their quest. This is the way of the Sunni.

What is the good of holding resolutely to one's convictions if it makes you a victim? There are indeed great rewards in the hereafter for those who die a martyr's death whilst fighting for Islamic principles. If they are fighting alone, let them die, it is not a problem. But if leaders insist on holding fast to their opinions their many followers will suffer. Leaders must not be driven only by their own interests....

If Imam Sjafi'i had acted in accord with his own personal interests, then his teachings would never have been disseminated. If a leader acts consistently simply for the sake of being known as consistent, without weighing up the consequences of his actions, the *umat* he leads will be destroyed.

3.2 Hamka: the shocking draft bill on marriage

This article appeared on the front page of the Masjumi-aligned newspaper *Harian Kami* on 24 August 1973. It illustrates well the intensity of feeling generated by the government's proposed changes to the marriage law but also the disillusionment of sections of the Muslim community with New Order policies more generally.

In writing this article I have not forgotten myself. I am well aware that my community, the Muslims, is in a very weak position. Politically weak, economically weak, weak in every respect. There remains only one area in which we are not weak, our faith! It is precisely at this time, when other groups see the Muslims as being outwardly weak and readily manipulated, that a piece of draft legislation on marriage has been thrust upon us. The essential point of this legislation is to compel Muslims, who make up a majority in this country, to abandon the *syari'ah* [God-given laws] of their own religion with respect to marriage. This legislation is intended to displace *syari'ah* and completely destroy Islamic principles.

This legislation was not drafted in ignorance. Its authors must surely have been aware what Islamic *syari'ah* means to us before they planned and drafted this marriage bill. According to Islamic doctrine the *syari'ah* has jurisdiction over five areas of life: religious belief; the soul; the intellect; future generations; and material possessions. In the fourth of these areas, 'the nurturing of future generations', the purpose of *syari'ah* is twofold: first, to ensure that humankind continues to develop and perpetuate future generations and prevent its annihilation through human folly; and, second, to ensure that future generations are legitimately naturalised as belonging to their parents. For this reason it follows that MARRIAGE is a precept of the Prophet, while adultery is contemptible. Those who drafted this legislation that will be tabled in parliament understand full well that this is a cardinal truth for Muslims. They must know that marriage in Islam is covered by *syari'ah*. Marriage in Islam is a part of religious observance and practice.

Previously they succeeded in gagging Muslims who persisted in mentioning 'the Jakarta Charter', because this Charter contained a phrase which was deliberately deleted [from the preamble to the 1945 Constitution], namely 'with an obligation upon adherents of Islam to abide by the *syari'ah*'. Any mention of the Charter these days is taboo! Bring up the subject and you can be accused of belonging to the 'extreme right', or even the '30 September Movement'! In their weak position, Muslims go along with this situation. They keep quiet, no longer mentioning the Camiharter. This is because there are still many Muslims who profess Islam but who do not want to abide by Islam's *syari'ah*. What can we do about it?

Now they are taking things a step further! Not only are Muslims no longer permitted to mention the 'obligation upon adherents of Islam to abide by the *syari'ah*', but they have even begun drafting a law that obliges Muslims to depart from the *syari'ah* of their religion with respect to marriage, requiring them to abide by a new regulation, a new law, a so-called 'National' law, under which it would be permitted to marry simply through registration, without further need of recourse to the five prerequisites of an Islamic marriage! Although the *syari'ah* prohibits marriage between first cousins, if you were to make use of the proposed marriage law, your marriage [to a first cousin] would be validated by the state. Under this bill, a child born out of wedlock, the result of pre-marital sex between an 'engaged' couple, may become their legitimate child, even though Islam regards this child as illegitimate! The bill validates the *free sex* recommended by pornographic magazines! You could go to a hospital and adopt an illegitimate child someone had brought to the hospital and this bill would sanction that child becoming yours. This means the adopted child would have a right to your inheritance, despite the Qur'an not recognising the child. Why not just forget the Qur'an and go along with the law? After all, the prohibition in question is only found in Islam, which does not apply in a National Pancasila State!

According to this marriage bill, a widow or divorced woman must wait 306 [days] before being able to marry again. However, the Qur'an stipulates a waiting period of four months and 10 days in the case of widows, and three months or three menstruations plus 10 days in the case of divorced women. You will be obliged to throw out these Islamic regulations. It is emphatic. You will be prohibited from carrying out the regulations of Allah and His Prophet, since those who embrace Islam will no longer be allowed to follow the *syari'ah*. You will have to submit to the national law of your own state! Pancasila law!

They say the bill has already been put forward for submission to the upcoming DPR session. The story goes that the Minister of Religious Affairs did not participate in the drafting of this bill, and that even the Justice Minister was not involved. This is supported by the fact that the bill does not bear the names of these two ministers. Instead the bill bears the name of President Soeharto, [a tactic designed] to smooth its passage and avoid further deliberation. But our president has already explained in his 16 August state address before the DPR, in a speech that was heard by the entire people of Indonesia, that he is still of the view that marriage is always intertwined with the religion we embrace. This means our president is still on our side. Naturally there has been an attempt to expedite acceptance of the bill, because the stamp of presidential approval has preceded the bill's submission for legislative deliberation.

They say that the Ministers of Religious Affairs and Justice will provide further explanation to the floor of the DPR on 30 August. We trust these two ministers have studied the reaction of the Muslims to this draft bill over the last few days. We also trust that the tone of their explanations will not be in breach of their own consciences as committed and aware Muslims. Because if there is an attempt to fast-track a bill like this through the DPR simply by relying upon power and the courageous valour of a majority vote, we wish to remind people in all humility that the Muslims will not stand in opposition, nor will they rebel, because it is strikingly obvious that they are weak.

But for the sake of religious awareness, this law will not be accepted, and neither will it be implemented. Moreover, *ulama* who regard themselves as having inherited the wisdom of the Prophets will issue a *fatwa* that it is FORBIDDEN [HARAM] for Muslims to marry under this law, and will require that marriage take place only in accordance with Islamic practice. And that Muslims who observe this marriage law are admitting that there is a regulation superior to the laws of Allah and His Prophet. Where such recognition is given, the judgement of the *kafir* [unbeliever] will be upon it. And for those *ulama* who have become entangled with Golkar, while they will not have the courage to issue a *fatwa* as adamant as that above, even they should not be so foolhardy as to make statements to the effect that the proposed legislation is in accordance with the will of Allah and His Prophet!

I recognise that my community, the Muslims, are in a thoroughly weakened position, and that I myself am also included in this category of the weak. But among this weak group there is still one utterance that can strengthen our resolve: '*Hasbunallahu wa ni'mal Wakil.*' Allah is our guarantor, and to Him the greatest surrender.

3.3 Nurcholish Madjid: Islam yes, Islamic parties no!

This much-quoted article was first published in 1970. The extract translated here appeared in Madjid (1987: 204–14).

A heartening reality about Islam in contemporary Indonesia is its rapid development, especially in terms of its number of adherents, at least in the formal sense. Regions previously unfamiliar with Islam are now familiar with it, to the extent that it has become the main religion of their inhabitants, together with those religions that had established an earlier presence. In addition, there is now a greater interest in Islam shown among people of higher social status, at least in terms of their official dispositions. However, it remains an open question to what extent this development is the result of a sincere attraction to the ideas of Islam as presented by its leading proponents. Might not this quantitative development of Islam be judged as nothing more than an indication of social adaptation in response to recent political developments in Indonesia, namely the defeat of the communists, which conveys an impression of victory for Islam? (We should remember that such social adaptation also occurred during the Old Order, when President Sukarno always displayed with great enthusiasm his interest in Islam, as well as in Marxism, however one might judge the motive behind his expression of interest.)

The answer to the question raised above may very well lie in another question: to what extent are these people interested in Islamic parties or organisations? Except for a few, it has become clear that they are not at all interested in such parties or organisations, to the extent that their attitude might be formulated thus: Islam yes, Islamic parties no! If Islamic parties are the vehicles for Islamic-based ideas, it is clear that there is no longer much interest in those ideas. In other words, Islamic ideas and thinking are in the process of becoming absolutely fossilised, having lost their dynamism. Islamic parties have failed to construct a positive and sympathetic image, and indeed the image we now have is quite the opposite. (Certain sections of the Muslim *umat* have a reputation for corruption that is bad and getting worse.)

Quantity versus quality

It is a truism that quality is more important than quantity. And yet the Muslim *umat* in Indonesia is pursuing the opposite, emphasising quantity over quality. It is indisputable that the aims of a struggle are better achieved through unity than fragmentation. But can this unity be forged dynamically and become a dynamic force unless the ideas it is based upon are also dynamic? (According to Lenin, there are no revolutionary actions without revolutionary theories.) Whatever the case, dynamism has more impact than inertia, even though the latter affects the majority of humankind. The recent paralysis of the Muslim *umat* is caused, *inter alia*, by the fact that it has closed its eyes to its own flaws, which can only be eliminated by a new movement of reformist ideas.

Contemporary liberalisation of views of 'Islamic teachings'

... Renewal must proceed from two interrelated initiatives, namely to extricate ourselves from traditional values, while searching for future-oriented values. Nostalgia must be replaced by a forward-looking vision, which requires the application of a process of liberalisation to current 'Islamic teachings and views'. This involves other processes:

Secularisation

Secularisation does not imply the application of secularism, since secularism is the name for an ideology, a new closed worldview which functions very much like a new religion. In this context, what is meant by secularisation is every form of liberating development. Such a process of liberation is needed because the Muslim *umat*, as a consequence of its own history, is no longer able to distinguish from among the values it assumes to be Islamic, those that are transcendental, and those that are temporal. Furthermore, this hierarchy of values is often inverted, [so that] all that which is transcendental is regarded as eschatological, without exception. While Muslims might not say so explicitly, and even deny the suggestion, such an approach is nevertheless reflected in their daily actions. The result is well known: Islam has come to be equated with tradition, and to be Islamic amounts to being a traditionalist.

Since defending Islam has become the same as defending tradition, the impression emerges that Islam is a traditional force of a reactionary nature. It is their hierarchical blinkers that have made the Muslims incapable of responding naturally to intellectual developments in the contemporary world.

So secularisation does not imply the application of secularism or turning Muslims into secularists. Rather it refers to accepting those values that really belong to the worldly domain as being profane, and to liberating the Muslim *umat* from the tendency to attach a sacred or eschatological value to them. In this way, Muslims would attain a mental preparedness to always examine and re-examine the truth of any value in the light of material evidence, whether of a moral or historical nature. Furthermore, secularisation involves strengthening the worldly duty of humankind as 'God's representative on earth'. This duty provides scope for the freedom of humanity to self-determination and choice of method and action in the course of improving human life on earth, and at the same time confirms the fact of humankind's accountability for its actions before God.

However, what is happening now is that the Muslim *umat* has lost its creativity in worldly life, giving the impression that it has chosen to remain passive and quiet. In other words, it has lost the spirit of *ijtihad* [contextual interpretation of the Scriptures]....

Intellectual freedom

Through a lack of intellectual vitality, we have lost our *psychological striking force*, since we lack a facility for free thinking which would focus our attention upon the immediate demands arising out of continuously developing social conditions, whether in the economic, political or social fields. Nevertheless, it must be acknowledged that our Islamic-based ideas would be best able to resolve problems in these fields were these ideas adjusted, renewed and organised (coordinated) to be made relevant to the realities of the current age. For example, Islamic teachings about the process of '*syura*' or deliberation in decision-making have become generally accepted in the Muslim *umat* as being equivalent or close to Western notions of democracy. On the other hand, the principal Islamic teachings concerning social justice and defence of the weak, the poor and the oppressed, which are found throughout the Holy Book, have yet to be worked into dynamic and progressive formulations for practical application. This is because the Muslim *umat* still seems to find socialist terminology taboo, even though, like democracy, it is of Western derivation and quite compatible with Islamic teachings. This psychological blockage in the Muslim *umat* can only be due to the absence of intellectual freedom. As a consequence, the Muslim *umat* is incapable of taking the initiative, which is always seized by others, who then take possession of strategic positions in the field of ideas to the exclusion of Islam. It is important to understand that this occurs precisely as in military operations, where a position is seized in the battlefield and defended to prevent it from falling into the hands of the enemy. It is in this regard that we can see the main weakness of the Muslim *umat*. Again, this is entirely the consequence of an absence of freedom of thought and confusion between sacred and profane domains. Our system of thought is still thick with taboos and a priori attitudes.

The idea of progress and an attitude of openness

...In accordance with intellectual freedom, we must be prepared to pay attention to human ideas across the broadest possible spectrum, and then select which ones, through objective criteria, contain the truth....

The need for a 'liberal' reformist group

Reform movements have appeared on the historical stage, both in Indonesia and throughout the world. In Indonesia we are familiar with organisations with reformist aspirations, such as Muhammadiyah, Al-Irsyad and Persis. But the historical record shows, and we must honestly confess, that these organisations have ceased to be reformist. Why? Because they have, in the end, become static through their apparent inability to grasp the spirit of the idea of renewal itself, namely its dynamism and progressiveness. Organisations histo rically considered to be counter-reformist, on the other hand, such as NU, Al-Wasliah and PUI, have come to accept values that had previously been the monopoly of the reformists – albeit perhaps half-heartedly and more as a result of historical pressures than out of a genuine commitment. Stagnation has now over-come the entire Muslim *umat*. Islamic organisations founded to oppose tradition and sectarianism have now become traditionalist and sectarian themselves. Other organisations that initially rejected innovations now accept them, but have never sought to make innovation their principal orientation. For this reason, a new liberal reformist Islamic movement is required, one that is necessarily non-traditionalist and non-sectarian....

Nowadays, the struggle to improve the lot of humanity is not the exclusive concern of the Muslim *umat*. All of humanity, using the rationality available to them, has become involved in efforts to find the most effective ways to improve the collective life of humankind. These efforts have found their expression in this modern age under the often-heard rubrics of democracy, socialism, populism, communism and so on. Regardless of how erroneous such ideas may subsequently prove to be, these efforts constitute the pinnacles of human reflection upon the social and historical contexts out of which they have emerged. We must learn to make use of the best of these ideas according to Islamic criteria, and attempt to develop them further with the same intellectual realism and diligence. This is the essential meaning of *ijtihad*, or renewal, that we seek. Thus, *ijtihad*, or renewal, must be an ongoing process of original thinking, informed by assessments of social and historical circumstance and subjected to periodic review....

It may be concluded that the task of renewal belongs to those in society most able to understand and comprehend. In other words, it is the task of the educated. So the educated really do have a great and weighty responsibility towards humanity in history, and before God in the life to come....

3.4 H.M.S. Mintaredja: development-oriented Islam

This extract is from a May 1973 booklet by Mintaredja entitled Islam and Politics, Islam and State in Indonesia: A Reflection and Revision of Ideas *(1973: 75–9, 100). His book was a translated version of the second edition of Mintaredja (1972). The English in this reading has been lightly edited.*

The main aim of life under the New Order is to bring about a frame of mind oriented towards national development, both physical and mental, with ideology relegated to second or third place. In the past (1945–65) the Islamic and other parties virtually only aimed at success in a spiritual struggle, with physical or economic development given second place. Any propaganda about economic development was in practice only lip service, with little or no evidence in reality.

The people, and especially the Islamic community, were, it seemed, fed up with this state of things, and were very keen indeed for physical development to get under way so that our common aspirations of the last 27 years might be realised as soon as possible. But what actually happened? Up to 1965 there was nothing but ideological struggle, causing suffering. As the author has already mentioned, Islam stresses a balance in life – a state of equilibrium between our present world and the world to come.

With all this in mind, Parmusi (of course now meaning its successor, Partai Persatuan Pembangunan) is determined to place the emphasis in its political struggle on balanced development....

In this context, the writer would like to bring the Islamic younger generation to an understanding of politics and its place in Islam, by presenting the origin (*asbabul wurud*) of the hadith which runs, '*antum a'lamu biumuri dunyakum*' – it is you who know best the affairs of your world.

Its meaning is that secular matters are the affair of us here in the world, and not the concern of those in the world hereafter. Of course it is difficult to separate politics based on faith from the Islamic religion.

Difficult, but not impossible.

For the writer, the proof is as follows:

Politics is not religion, but religion is politics. Politics is based on reason, judgement and wisdom, while religion is based on divine revelation. Clearly, politics is a secular matter, and it is we ourselves who are affected by it and knowledgeable about it....The writer obtained a clear and definitive explanation of the origin of the hadith above from the late Kiyai Fakih Usman: the Prophet was once visited by a date farmer, who related to him his plans to improve his crop by crossing two varieties of palms in order to produce fruit that was prolific, large and sweet. One of these varieties grew in soil with abundant water and yielded plenty of fruit, but they were small and sour. The other variety grew in soil with little water, and bore few fruits, but they were very large and sweet. The farmer asked the Prophet for advice and received the following reply: 'Matters of religion you may hand over to me. In secular matters it is you who know best the affairs of your world.'

This hadith clearly emphasises that secular matters are not the concern of religion in the narrow sense. Thus we are free to think about and deal with them in the best interests of the Islamic community, our religion, people and nation, providing of course that this does not conflict with the Qur'an and Hadith....

To achieve the results so urgently needed and eagerly awaited by the mass of the people, we must undertake development in all fields, particularly and immediately in the economic field. The New Order government, without much ado, has formulated a realistic and practical development plan, the first phase of which stresses development in agriculture and supportive industry. We are all beginning to feel the results of the first five-year development plan....

For these reasons, the Islamic parties no longer want to follow a formal politics approach [formal ideology with no content]. Parmusi, and now the PPP, have committed themselves (in particular after the 1971 general elections) to work together with the armed forces and align themselves with the development- or program-oriented group. In other words, they are going to follow a material politics approach, without forgetting their foundation in Islam, so that development of the whole man is achieved, with happiness both now and in the life to come.

Parmusi has stated unequivocally that it has no intention or aim of establishing an Islamic or any other sort of new state. (In all the writer's examinations of the Qur'an, in Indonesian, Dutch and English translations, he has so far never encountered the command that the Islamic community is obliged to establish an Islamic state.) Because of its conviction that this policy is in accord with religious doctrine, Parmusi will defend the state proclaimed in 1945 with its constitution and Pancasila philosophy.

Part II

The New Order at its height, 1973–88

4 Organicism ascendant

The years between 1973 and 1988 were, in retrospect, halcyon days for the New Order and its supporters. Sustained Western support and a flood of petrodollars gave the regime the freedom to pursue more nationalistic economic policies and to expand greatly the size and reach of the state bureaucracy. One consequence of this was to reinforce the patrimonial character of the regime (Crouch 1979). Vast patronage networks – of which Golkar was the primary example – became a key means by which the New Order bought loyalty and coopted dissent.

Revenues from oil and aid, as well as an elaborate apparatus of military repression, also insulated the government from domestic political pressures, allowing it to make sweeping changes to the political system. The two-party plus Golkar arrangement established by Ali Moertopo in the early 1970s passed into law in 1975, as did a series of laws governing the elections and the composition of parliament. These laws entrenched the 'floating mass' system, prohibited the formation of any new political parties and gave Golkar a range of privileges which effectively secured it a permanent majority in the legislature. The 1975 laws, then, cemented in place the building blocks of a new authoritarian order.

It has become common for Muslim scholars to identify the era covered by this chapter as the bad old days when the government was dominated by non-Muslims and pursued anti-Islamic policies. This is justified up to a point. For most of the period in question the government was preoccupied with containing the influence of Islamic organisations, which it feared would provide the focus for a popular struggle for an Islamic state. Ali Moertopo and subsequently his Catholic protégé Benny Moerdani oversaw a number of military intelligence operations targeting Muslim activists. The most dramatic confrontation came in September 1984, when troops from the Jakarta military command opened fire on working-class Muslims demonstrating near the port of Tanjung Priok, killing and wounding hundreds.

Soeharto's campaign to separate religion – read Islam – from politics also had a strong ideological dimension. Pancasila indoctrination, known generally as the P4 program, began in earnest in 1978 and was expanded in the 1980s to encompass tens of millions of Indonesian schoolchildren, university students, civil servants, businesspeople and bureaucrats. If the main aim of this huge and expensive program was to create an environment in which the expression of overtly sectarian views was unacceptable, Soeharto saw it as a means of inscribing his organicist vision on the nation. In Reading 4.1 Soeharto speaks frankly about his frustration with the Muslim PPP's resistance to his ambition to have it adopt Pancasila as their ideological basis. This 1980 speech also sparked controversy for its wholesale condemnation of political ideologies, including nationalism, and was roundly criticised by a range of nationalist figures in the Petition of Fifty group the same year.

Reading 4.2 is another rare but revealing extemporaneous speech by Soeharto, this time to Golkar youth leaders. It is included here because it illustrates the president's personal obsession with Pancasila and his idiosyncratic view of Pancasila as a product of ancient Javanese wisdom. The speech helps explain the preoccupation of New Order ideologues with 'discovering' indigenous traditions that could be used to buttress the regime's rhetorical emphasis on stability, consensus and order.

This is followed by a short extract from a talk by Ali Moertopo in which the veteran strategist puts forward a number of 'confidential' explanations for the government's Pancasila indoctrination program (Reading 4.3). His perspective is blunt and instrumentalist. The point of the Pancasila indoctrination program, he argued, was to rid Indonesians of the unconscious residues of communist ideology and to make them truly Indonesian again. Fortified with Pancasila, people would be inoculated against other ideologies and 'quarrels would be impossible'.

In both the Soeharto extracts in this chapter, the president depicts himself as having been long committed to bringing all parties and groups in society under the umbrella of the Pancasila. In the early 1980s he pushed this theme hard, sponsoring a controversial law requiring all social and political organisations to agree to ensconce Pancasila as their 'sole philosophical basis' (*azas tunggal*). When he finally achieved this and it was legislated as the law on social organisations in 1985, he wrote of it in his autobiography as one of his regime's proudest achievements (Soeharto 1989: 382, 408–9; Elson 2001: 239–40). Although regarded by some as mainly symbolic, the law on social organisations (sections of which are reproduced in Reading 4.4) profoundly affected the character and boundaries of legitimate political discourse in Indonesia. It was passed as one of five political laws regarded at the time as cementing the final political format of the New Order. The laws, which regulated political parties, elections, the composition of parliament and the holding of referenda, were a frequent target of reformers during the last decade of the New Order and were all revised after 1998.

Much of the politics of the New Order took place behind the ramparts of the New Order itself. One subject of serious dispute in the late 1970s and 1980s was the degree to which the military should involve itself in mobilising electoral support for Golkar. So-called 'pragmatic' generals around Soeharto argued that since Golkar was essentially the army's creation it had a right to participate directly in its activities. 'Principled' officers, meanwhile, such as Brigadier-General Abdulkadir Besar, (Reading 4.5), argued that the armed forces owed its allegiance to the state, and should therefore not dirty its hands by getting involved in day-to-day politics. This final extract has been included here because it is crucial to understanding the growth of discontent among some senior and retired generals which manifested itself in the Petition of Fifty controversy, discussed in Chapter 5.

4.1 Soeharto: Muslims who fail to understand

In these extemporaneous comments delivered after an address to an assembly of top military commanders in the South Sumatran city of Pekanbaru on 27 March 1980, President Soeharto offended several groups. Some saw them as a betrayal of the military's professed commitment to neutrality, while others interpreted them as an assault on nationalism and/or Islam. Following a public outcry, the government claimed that Soeharto had not said that the Pancasila had been submerged 'by' nationalism or religion, but rather 'in' them. The extracts translated below are from the earliest official version of the speech, printed in *Kompas* on 8 April 1980. It was supplied to the editors of *Kompas* by the department of defence and security and contains the phrase 'submerged by' (*tenggelam oleh*).

On this very valuable occasion I would like to add several points that I hope might assist the armed forces of the Republic of Indonesia to enhance its experience and vigilance in discharging its duties, particularly in its dual function duties, and more specifically to implement its function as a social force by contributing to the survival of political and economic democracy based on Pancasila.

You are of course aware that...Indonesia's national struggle was greatly influenced by various political ideologies. Inevitably these ideologies had a great bearing on the coalescing of interest groups and influenced the leaders of these groups. Consequently, prior to the emergence of the New Order we sensed that our national ideology was submerged by various ideologies of the time, whether Marxism or Communism, socialism, Marhaenism, nationalism or religion. Only our national ideology could unify our nation.

We also had to face the fact that once these groups had fallen under the sway of their respective ideologies, they felt able to consolidate their strength. This led them to want to impose their will on other groups by force. So unending rebellions broke out, like the DI/TII [Darul Islam/Indonesian Islamic Army] in West Java, Central Java, Sulawesi and Aceh, or the rebellions staged by the G30S/PKI starting with the Madiun affair. There was also the rebellion staged by the PRRI and Permesta.[1]

All of these events obstructed our struggle to realise a just and prosperous society based on Pancasila. In the process we have witnessed no small number of victims, whether among our beloved soldiers or the people themselves. This is why we do not wish to see such events repeated. And this is why the New Order has committed itself totally to rectifying deviations from Pancasila and the 1945 Constitution, and in so doing implementing Pancasila and the 1945 Constitution in their original form.

Our aim is to defend Pancasila and the 1945 Constitution. In fact we have reached a consensus that we do not wish to revise either the 1945 Constitution or Pancasila. So we have to focus on the question of how to implement this consensus to defend Pancasila and the purity of the 1945 Constitution.

Of course we must agree unanimously that the Pancasila we wish to defend and preserve is the same Pancasila that was accepted the day after independence was proclaimed....The system of democracy embedded within Pancasila is democracy led by wisdom in representative consultation.

So we must truly understand that sovereignty is in the hands of the people in accordance with our constitution. We were able to discover a mechanism of national leadership in which the People's Consultative Assembly would act as the supreme representative institution embodying the sovereignty of the state and the nation. The People's Consultative Assembly consists of the People's Representative Council supplemented by representatives of the regions and of groups. It is this Assembly that has the duty to formulate the broad guidelines of state policy and elect the president and the vice-president.

It has, in addition, a special authority, namely the authority to revise the constitution. Article 37 of the 1945 Constitution states that in order to revise the constitution at least two-thirds of the members of the People's Consultative Assembly shall be present and any revision must be supported by at least two-thirds of those present. These are the conditions under which revisions of the 1945 Constitution are warranted.

I think many questions can be raised whether this implies that only the 1945 Constitution is open to revision or whether the Pancasila can also be changed, since the 1945 Constitution consists of the preamble, the main body and the elucidation. If it is possible for the body of the constitution to be changed, who is to say that the preamble, and by extension the Pancasila as the basis of the state, cannot also be changed?

While ABRI is aware of the New Order's determination not to alter Pancasila or the 1945 Constitution, the constitution itself leaves open the possibility that it can legitimately be revised if two-thirds of the votes of two-thirds of the members present agree to the changes. How should it be defended in a way that can truly be accounted for constitutionally? ABRI long ago made its position clear. Together with the socio-political forces, ABRI pledged and committed itself not to change the constitution.

Everything is there in the Sapta Marga [Soldiers' Sevenfold Pledge]. The first pledge says that we are citizens of the unitary Republic of Indonesia based on Pancasila, which means that Pancasila is the one and only ideology that we accept as the foundation of the state.

The second pledge says that we are Indonesian patriots who faithfully support and defend the state's ideology without surrender. So it is clear that under no circumstances can we allow the Pancasila and the 1945 Constitution to be threatened. It was this resolve that summoned us all to confront the G30S/PKI.

The third pledge is that we are Indonesian warriors [*satria*] who believe in God Almighty and defend honesty, truth and justice. All these bind ABRI never, in any circumstances, to acquiesce in the replacement of the 1945 Constitution or Pancasila – even if this means taking up arms. But it is clear that if we do take up arms there will be casualties among the soldiers and the people. So we have to seek ways in which this commitment can be safeguarded by constitutional and democratic means.

We reached a consensus with all political parties at the time that ABRI be given an opportunity to do just this by being granted one-third of the seats in the People's Consultative Assembly in exchange for sacrificing its right to vote and to be elected. This did not contravene the constitution because it was still possible for two-thirds of the members to effect the change if they wished to do so. However, since ABRI did not wish to see any change and would be compelled to use its weapons if there was a change, I told all the political parties at the time that rather than using weapons to forestall a change of the 1945 Constitution and Pancasila it would be better for us to kidnap one member out of the two-thirds who wished to change it, because a decision by two-thirds minus one would be constitutionally invalid. This was accepted by the social-political forces, resulting in a consensus to appoint one-third of the members of the People's Consultative Assembly to safeguard Pancasila in the face of the article of the 1945 Constitution which allows the Assembly to alter the 1945 Constitution and Pancasila.

We know that the People's Consultative Assembly consists of the People's Representative Council as well as representatives of the regions and of groups. So there are appointees not just in the People's Consultative Assembly but also in the People's Representative Council. But the function of these latter appointees is different. Their function is to stabilise and dynamise democratic life. Only 100 of the 460 members of the People's Representative Council, or 22 per cent, are appointed. Out of this allotment of 100 seats we gave 25 to the non-ABRI, non-party and non-mass organisation functional groups.

The entire consensus was successfully cemented in law: the law on the composition of the People's Consultative Assembly and the People's Representative Council. This is Law no. 16, which is still in force.

As to whether the law can be changed, I think it can. But the consensus must be changed first. Neither the government nor the People's Representative Council can change that consensus. Only the People's Consultative Assembly is empowered to do this. So long as the original consensus stands, the composition of the People's Consultative Assembly, the People's Representative Council and the local legislative bodies remains as stipulated by Law no. 16.

Therefore we are still holding firm to the law. As I have said, however, the seats that ABRI has obtained for sacrificing its rights still makes it possible for the two-thirds to change the constitution. In order to face the challenges ahead, then, we must seek, together with the other social-political forces, to strengthen the one-third, because the one-third cannot possibly be increased but has to be supplemented by other social-political forces that legally accommodate the trust of the people. Naturally, this depends very much on the composition and structure of political life, the political parties and the functional groups.

Ever since the birth of the New Order the People's Consultative Assembly has assigned me the task of reforming political life and simplifying the party system. At that time we inherited nine political parties and the Sekber-Golkar [Joint Secretariat of Functional Groups], which did not function as it does now. The nine political parties and one functional group were very much influenced in their struggle by different ideologies, leading them to accentuate their differences. In order to foster unity the Interim People's Consultative Assembly [MPRS] instructed me to simplify the life of the political parties. What we had to do was of course based on the original consensus, namely that we wished to restore Pancasila as the state ideology, which meant that our social-political forces should also be based on one principle and one ideology, namely Pancasila....

After the general election in 1971 the general session of the MPR instructed me to repeat the earlier mission so that the simplification of the party system would truly be realised. We therefore continued our efforts through continuous consultations, and in 1975 finally succeeded in promulgating the law on parties and functional groups. The reality was, however, that one of the points we achieved agreement on, that all political parties and the functional groups base themselves on one ideology, Pancasila, turned out not to have been successful, because there was still a political party that added another principle to the principle of Pancasila. This naturally raised the question of why they did not yet fully trust Pancasila as an ideology. However, because of democratic developments we were compelled to accept the situation while continuing our attempts to bring them around.

Doubts about Pancasila were still evident in the process of drafting the law on parties and functional groups prior to the general session of the MPR. This was even more apparent in discussions in the MPR regarding MPR Decision no. 2 [1978] on Guidance to Understanding and Implementing Pancasila [P4], which led to the walkout [by the PPP]. So too the recent effort to formulate, or rather revise, the law on general elections, which still did not demonstrate a joint effort and commitment as some [Nahdlatul Ulama members of the PPP] staged another walkout. All this must at least indicate to us or alert us to the need to be vigilant in the framework of safeguarding the Pancasila and the 1945 Constitution.

In order to make a success of the dual function, [ABRI] and other socio-political forces have abided by democracy and avoided using weapons. Until we succeed in bringing them to their senses, we must always step up our vigilance and choose partners – friends who truly defend Pancasila and have no doubt whatsoever about Pancasila!

I hope that all our experiences during the New Order will alert us to the need to constantly step up vigilance for the sake of the safety and security of Pancasila and the 1945 Constitution, and therefore also for the success of our struggle to realise a just and prosperous society based on Pancasila, bearing in mind particularly our legacy to the younger generation. We of the 1945 generation – like myself – who have resigned from active service but who still feel connected with ABRI's struggle through our membership of Pepabri [the Veterans' Association], will keep supporting the struggle of ABRI in the discharge of its dual function.

I want you to truly reflect on this annex to my speech in the performance of your mission. We do not mean to be hostile to the party or group that does not yet trust Pancasila 100 per cent. Not at all. But we are obliged to persuade them so that all the social-political forces will base themselves on our national ideology, Pancasila, with no additions whatsoever. Hopefully, you will then be able to help take them, constitutionally and democratically, in the direction we wish to go. If that can be brought about, then the proclamation that took the Indonesian people to the threshold of independence, unity, sovereignty, justice and prosperity will be realised.

4.2 Soeharto: Pancasila, the legacy of our ancestors

This extract is taken from a transcript of a candid talk President Soeharto gave at his Jakarta home to leaders of the Golkar-affiliated youth organisation, the National Committee of Indonesian Youth (KNPI), on the evening of 19 July 1982 (Soeharto 1982b). Parts of it were reproduced in the small-circulation spiritual journal *Mawas Diri* (October and November 1982), but the mainstream media was forbidden to publish it, presumably because of Soeharto's overtly Javanist interpretation of Pancasila and his apparent contempt for Muslim politicians who did not share his vision of a Pancasila society.

We have to learn from history. Among other things, we have to learn about Pancasila, about our ideology, about the basis of our state. If we really want to be consistent in our desire to implement the Pancasila and 1945 Constitution we have to accept the fact that after the proclamation the purity of the constitution was unanimously ratified with the Pancasila as the basis of the state, as our national ideology and as our worldview. So we must abide by it.

If we are to be consistent, Pancasila is our sole ideology. This is especially apparent when we look at history, from the struggle for independence up until the G30S/PKI revolt. What caused this revolt? One factor was that we were not consistent in accepting Pancasila as the foundation of the state, as our sole ideology, our worldview. Despite its irrefutable incorporation as the foundation of the state, Pancasila was applied merely as a tool to unite all ideologies, whether communism, socialism, liberalism or religion. I think we really have to conclude that this is impossible, as history has proved.

This takes me back to an encounter with the founder of the republic, the man who unearthed Pancasila: Bung Karno. In 1956, just after the general elections, I was regional commander in Semarang and Bung Karno was making a presidential visit to Central Java. As regional commander I met him at the airport and after escorting him to his hotel I took the opportunity to ask him about the election, which had been won by PNI, Masjumi, PKI and NU. I asked him, '*Pak*, the PKI won a victory here. Doesn't this endanger Pancasila?' That was how I put it to him. He admitted this was the case, adding, 'The reality is that the PKI have gained the support of the people. So naturally we have to acknowledge that. What we have to do now is make the PKI an Indonesian or Pancasila PKI.' I asked whether this was feasible. He replied, 'That's my challenge, leave it to me. I will strive to turn the PKI into an Indonesian PKI, a Pancasila PKI.'

Naturally we respect and appreciate the determination of Bung Karno to transform the PKI into a Pancasila PKI, and after that I actually went along with it. Nasakom and other policies were indeed intended to turn the PKI into a Pancasila PKI by attempting to accommodate it. But as it turned out this did not succeed in inculcating the PKI with Pancasila. Rather the PKI made use of this opportunity to strengthen itself and eventually rebelled.

So you see I was on the right track, wasn't I? It just was not possible, it could not succeed. He then asked my opinion. 'So what are you doing about it in Central Java, Har?' I reported that since I did not believe the PKI could be Pancasila-ised in the way he described, I had been trying to separate the PKI from the people by working for the development of Central Java, of the fourth regional command. 'Good for you. Keep it up,' he said. 'Yes sir'.

So we kept an eye on Bung Karno's policies in the context of Nasakom while at the same time trying to separate the people from the PKI. The point here is that history has shown that it was impossible to use

Pancasila, the foundation of our state, our ideology and our worldview, as a means of uniting all ideologies. And in making corrections we should leave behind and not repeat what has been unsuccessful.

We must now return to the New Order's determination to position Pancasila as the foundation of our state, our national ideology and world-view. What remains now is to realise this in the life of the Indonesian people....

In times past, during the Sriwijaya and Majapahit eras, we were a glorious nation. But due to internal conflicts and squabbles we could be colonised. Were this to happen again we would eventually be colonised by another nation. Would that not be sinful – all our sacrifice in vain? So let us now strive to correct ourselves, so we do not bequeath to future genera-tions the preconditions for internal conflict, the opportunity to shatter the unity of the nation.

The main thing we have to do is to really seriously implement the New Order's resolve to return to the authentic purity of Pancasila and our constitution. It goes without saying, then, that we must find a way to convince our people now, our youth, of the truth of Pancasila. The realities of the past convince us that Pancasila is the right approach to take, rather than the approaches of modern ideological thought such as are found in Marxism, communism and liberalism.

But it would be wrong to see Pancasila as comprehensively overcoming all the shortcomings of such ideologies, as though it was a synthesis of the conflicts between Marxism, communism, liberalism, and religion. If we said that, well...eventually people would think Pancasila had been influ-enced by other ideologies. Consequently, in view of our experience, nothing good would come from such an interpretation. It would end in failure, because it would provide an opportunity for extremist elements to infiltrate every socio-political force. And these infiltrators would eventu-ally use this opportunity to consolidate their power to continue their struggle, leaving Pancasila behind. They would regard Pancasila as expe-dient, as something to be cast off, along with the '45 Constitution, to be replaced when it is no longer needed.

So how can we convince our people that Pancasila is truly the legacy of our ancestors? Actually the best way to do this is to look at the analysis of the founder of the republic, who formulated and gathered Pancasila from the precepts left by our ancestors. If I am not mistaken, Bung Karno himself said that he did not create Pancasila, but merely dug up the pearls of wisdom left by our ancestors and then gathered them together in the precepts of Pancasila. The order of these precepts as proposed by Bung Karno is different from that of the current Pancasila. But it is clear that Bung Karno himself admitted having excavated Pancasila's precepts from the pearls of wisdom left by our ancestors....

Subsequently I found the courage to suggest that we search for the theo-ries or methods used by our ancestors which eventually gave birth to

Pancasila. It turned out that the theories and science of our ancestors were very simple, indeed too simple for our scholars to understand. Such is the simplicity of these theories that it has not been easy to find comparable ideas in more modern theories – Marxist ideology, communism and so forth.

Our ancestors did have theories and science, in other words, but their very simplicity means it is difficult to understand, digest and absorb their meaning. Nevertheless I propose we study them, that we investigate the truth of these theories and science of our ancestors, who left us the pearls of wisdom that were eventually gathered together in Pancasila.

I am convinced that our ancestors did actually have theories and science, even though one intellectual has labelled them a form of black magic or mystical art. Our ancestors' way of life dates back to before the arrival of Hinduism, before Buddhism, before Islam, before Christianity and before the arrival of ideology. Our ancestors were [*thumbs-up gesture: stenographer*]. Really amazing. They had principles which they developed and which influenced the people. These were eventually socialised and came to be known as *gotong-royong*, mutual assistance. They are actually based on theory and science – very simple theory and science. This primary science of our ancestors concerns the science of truth [*ilmu kasunyatan*].[2] As I said, modern-minded people judge this to be magic or mysticism.

First of all, this science of truth concerns real facts. The Javanese here are of course familiar with this, but I am saying this in order for the non-Javanese to learn. The science of truth, of facts, then developed into the science of the origin and destiny of human life [*sangkan paraning dumadi*]. The science of the origin and destiny of human life later developed into the science of living perfection [*ilmu kasampurnaning hurip*].

Now let us look at the first basis of the study of truth, the study of actuality, because we only see realities that are visible to the eyes and hearts of living people. What is real? It goes without saying that the starting point is the universe and all it contains. So the universe and its contents really exist – the universe and all its contents, including humankind. Who made it all? We can only conclude that it must have been an extraordinary, colossal, omnipotent being we came to know as God or Allah. Javanese spiritualists call this being *Gusti Kang Murbeng Dumadi*, the Sublime Creator of the Universe....

This is where the role of religion comes in, for religion gives guidance to humankind to control their base desires and develop their spirituality. That is basically what religion is about. This is why our ancestors tolerated all the religions that came here. Hinduism was welcomed, Buddhism was welcomed, Islam came and was accepted, Christianity came and was accepted. It has been up to each individual to choose which of these they would follow in order to regulate the opposing dispositions of base desire and spirit. That is why there has been such tolerance. This is clearly the case with regard to Islam, and indeed all religions have been accepted. But Indonesian culture has never been disregarded.

Perhaps it was like, okay, Buddhism is here, so we will be Buddhists, but also Javanese, then Indonesian. And with Hinduism, okay, we are Hindus, Javanese Hindus, Indonesian Hindus. Even with Islam, it became Javanese Islam, then Indonesian Islam. That is right, isn't it? Christianity also followed the same process. This was due to the enormous influence of such an ingrained culture, a way of life which has permeated the soul of the Indonesian people and which cannot be separated from their lives.

Just look at Aceh, for example, where they really practise Islam thoroughly. Islamic teachings there still allow a space for ritual *tepung tawar*, purification offerings. *Tepung tawar* lives on in Aceh, it could not be discarded. Instead it was adapted through the addition of Islamic prayers.

So this is how things developed. But it is clear that our ancestors left us the elements of Pancasila. In *ilmu kasunyatan*, which we know is based on belief in God, with the completeness of life it provides and its influence on the spiritual development of Indonesian humanity, all religious requirements are fulfilled, in terms of both devotion to God and faith in God. By acknowledging only one God, and then by seeing the totality of human life, the human soul and spirit can be developed and influenced towards a socialistic togetherness, where people do not live apart because they are recognised as social beings in mutuality, unity, popular solidarity and social justice.

This is actually what has remained of this ancient theory we have been discussing. These are the things our ancestors left behind, which were subsequently lost – yet not completely, just buried. Yet they remained part of people's lives in Indonesia and were excavated after we proclaimed them to be the foundation of our state, our ideology and worldview. Thus if we want to be convinced of the truth, why should we search for other ideologies, be they socialism, communism, Marxism, or even liberalism and religion?

Talking about religion, time and again I have told Islamic scholars who are afraid because they worry that Pancasila will develop into a religion. That is impossible. Impossible. Pancasila as a worldview and as the foundation of the state and ideology guarantees tolerance and the way of life of all religions.

Thus religion will not be adversely affected. Rather, Pancasila constitutes its environment, its framework, and guarantees a cooperative unity between religions, rather than leading them to mutual enmity. Hence unity between religions and between communities of faith will be guaranteed within the framework of the Pancasila state. I think we really have to be convinced of this truth, for those who are not will surely never stop searching for the truth elsewhere.

We cannot just let this matter take its own course, or the next generation will end up in conflict. And then they will start searching, and experience something like what has happened in the past....

Once again, we must strive never to let this matter rest. Among other things, there is the issue of the simplification of political parties which we have already carried out, and which we indeed directed in view of these considerations.

Nine parties were turned into two parties, with one functional group. The basis of my thinking, which I put forward at the time, proceeded from the mandate of the people and was based upon our previous experience with various ideologies. When we had all those ideologies and only lip service was paid to Pancasila, we ended up with the rebellion of the 30 September Movement/PKI. This threatened national cohesion and unity and also the survival of Pancasila and the '45 Constitution.

The duty of simplifying political parties was mandated to me as president by the people's representatives, first by the provisional MPR and later by the MPR itself. Beginning as acting president with the provisional assemblies of '66 and '67, and then as a fully mandated president in the '68 assembly, I was entrusted with implementing the policy of simplifying political parties.

We deliberated, and, as it turned out, from a beginning in '66 the legislation was only realised in '75. This was because all aspects of party life had to be regulated by legislation, without which the system would have lacked effective force. So we deliberated with all the leaders of socio-political forces about how to implement the people's mandate to simplify political parties. This was done because the previous political parties did nothing to help our struggle. On the contrary, division continually afflicted our people and our nation.

So I emphasised to the leaders of the political parties at that time the need to return to the original purposes of the New Order. The New Order wanted to carry out a total overhaul and return to the purity of Pancasila and the '45 Constitution. This was one of the methods we employed. I reiterated time and again that we had to recognise and accept Pancasila as the sole ideology among all ideological and socio-political forces. What remained was to establish Pancasila as the sole ideology, and to develop a program for its implementation in the lives of the Indonesian people.

By now we ought to have chosen and determined – with total resolve – to agree that Pancasila is the sole ideology. All that remains now is to apply it in the life of Indonesians....

At the '73 general session of the MPR, in my capacity as the holder of the people's mandate, I was reminded of my task of simplifying the political party system. The MPR decree had to be in place prior to the subsequent general election. Because the election was due to be held in '77 I gave a deadline to the parties concerned that the process had to be completed by '75. It was because of this that discussions about the final form of Law no. 3, 1975 came to an end. All I strived for was full unanimity in accepting Pancasila. But while the parties were prepared to accept Pancasila as their basis, they still insisted on adding characteristics of their own.

This is really a sort of sickness, isn't it? I reminded Islamic teachers at the time, 'This sickness will spread and will lead us back to the situation before the New Order.' I could believe perhaps that the Islamic teachers would not exploit the situation, but you should understand that there were still extremist people around who were prepared to do so, and this would have reflected badly on Islam itself. And since there were some that seemed determined, and could not give any guarantees if the law was made any tougher, I had to go along with it. If that is the way they wanted it, okay, so be it. In the end Law no. 3 1975 allowed parties to include references to their own specific principles besides Pancasila.

Actually I complained, 'This is a sickness, a disease, a sickness, a disease, you know. If democracy is like this, well okay, we'll see how it goes.' It turned out later that the PPP still had not got the message. What saddened me was the way they responded to MPR Decree no. 2 by their walkout and so on. This was also unhealthy, since it boomeranged for a second time against the Islamic community. This response was subsequently regarded as signalling their lack of conviction in Pancasila as the foundation of the state. Why were they worried? 'Because we fear Pancasila will become a religion,' they said. 'Not so,' I replied. 'It will endanger religion.' 'It won't,' I repeated.

Rather, it should be seen as a challenge for all Islamic teachers to instil in their followers a trust, a trust in Pancasila. If this happened, there would be no danger, would there? It would just be over with. It is history, isn't it, that will bear witness.

During the PPP campaign in the '82 election, some non-NU characters just could not control themselves. Instead of sticking to the underlying principle [of Pancasila] or putting forward programs, they pushed their own principles [i.e. Islam]. This sort of thing can lead to disintegration, and if we are not aware of this and do not attend to it we will leave future generations to continue on in that way.

But if we are aware, then let us apply ourselves, because we have to be convinced of the truth that Pancasila is not against religion, and will not become an enemy of religion. On the contrary, Pancasila protects religion. In accordance with the constitution we guarantee the independence and freedom of religious communities to observe the precepts of their respective religions. This way, things will be peaceful. These are the sorts of things we need to think about when conducting political education, while at the same time sidelining criticisms that pose a danger.

Certainly it is up to the younger generation whether you continue to rally around other principles. Because with our socio-political forces in agreement, and with Pancasila firmly in place as the fundamental ideology of the state and other organisations, there will be room in future for mass organisations to be formed.

4.3 Ali Moertopo: Indonesianising Indonesians

Retired Lieutenant-General Ali Moertopo spoke on 24 May 1980 in his capacity as information minister to a group of his employees. His remarks provide a valuable insight into the purposes behind the Pancasila indoctrination program (P4). Like many speeches of this type, it says far more about what the P4 program was meant to counter than what it stood for. This extract is taken from a collection of Moertopo speeches published by the information ministry (Departemen Penerangan 1983: 200–1, 208–10).

Communism has long influenced Indonesia. Before any of you were born, before I was born, communism was already here. It was brought here not only by Indonesians. Even the Dutch who came here were influenced by communist teachings.

Communists were already active here at the end of the 19th century and communist ideology grew rapidly during the second decade of the 20th century. It was especially strong among the unions, particularly in the railway workers' unions. Indonesians have been influenced by communism as a system of thought for so long that it came to be identified as the Indonesian way of thinking.

You were not aware of the arrival of these concepts because they preceded you by two or three generations. Consequently you and your parents' generation considered them to be authentically Indonesian values, which is not the case. Information officers need to be aware of this, and need to be careful. If I were not speaking to information officers I would not be delving so deeply. So do not be mistaken.

After 1965 the unfolding political conflict demonstrated that Pancasila was victorious and communism was defeated. This is one proof that Pancasila is the real and living source of the aspirations of our society and nation. The proof is that, without being mobilised, Pancasila was still able to defeat the communists, who, I remind you, had already won power in 1965. This serves to demonstrate the potency and superior strength of Pancasila in society. In this process [of conflict between Pancasila and communism] we wasted far too much time, while neglecting to attend to the welfare of the people. After 1965 we wished to return to our original foundations, Pancasila and the 1945 Constitution, which were inspired by the spirit of the proclamation of the Indonesian nation. We felt that activities directed towards the creation of prosperity had yet to be realised, and we took the initiative to acknowledge this as the starting point for a joint decision to implement national development....

Pancasila as our national concept of culture

The reason I call Pancasila a concept of culture is that Pancasila has proven itself able to provide guidance in every sphere of national life. There are three things, or arenas, that are important in the life of our nation. The first is culture. If we accept Pancasila as a philosophy it means we accept it as our national culture. Second, we accept Pancasila as our state ideology.

Therefore it is all the same – our nation's philosophy is Pancasila and our state's ideology is Pancasila. It is all uniform, so conflict is impossible, quarrels are impossible, differences in values are impossible. Third, the way the philosophy and the ideology constantly interact and develop creates a certain atmosphere in the life of the Indonesian people. I mean it influences every individual, every good Indonesian citizen.

This is what we mean by way of life, or outlook. So Pancasila should be understood in three ways: as a basic philosophy; second, as the state ideology; and, third, as the outlook of every Indonesian citizen. We can conclude from all of this that, in essence, Pancasila is the Indonesian people's concept of culture.

Regarding basic human rights, every Indonesian, wherever they may be, is committed. And they are not committed only to the single precept of humanitarianism, but they have to be committed to all the values of Pancasila which are reflected in the life of the Indonesian nation. So Pancasila colours the life of the Indonesian nation to the extent that people view the Indonesian national culture as having a coherence which provides a firm grounding for mental resilience, cultural resilience and social resilience. Once individuals have been moulded in this way, with a state of mind, an attitude or perspective that Pancasila requires, it becomes impossible for them to be penetrated by communist ideology, or any other ideology.

With P4 we are reconsolidating the mental, political, social and cultural resilience needed to face all possibilities, whether external or internal. Such attacks may appear in the form of infiltration efforts from the outside, or insurgencies from within. This is why in this lecture you have occasionally heard the phrase 'from the outside'. I say to you that the purpose of the P4 program is none other than to Indonesianise Indonesians, by which I mean to make Indonesians truly Indonesian. So you have not become a complete citizen until you have mastered P4. This means that your ultimate duty in disseminating information is to Indonesianise all Indonesians. You have to take to society what you have undergone yourselves, albeit perhaps in a different manner. This was how I once responded to those who questioned the urgency and usefulness of P4 when we debated it at the national level.

What is the urgency and usefulness of the P4 program? My answer is simple: 'to Indonesianise Indonesians'. Is this really urgent? Why has it not been done before, why not do it later, why do it now?

I will tell you why it is urgent. First, the Indonesian nation is currently going through a period during which authority is being delegated from the older to the younger generation. The reminder not to forget Indonesia is a bequest from the old to the young, and the P4 program is our way of doing it.

Second, for the past 10 years we have all been pressured, pushed and when necessary compelled to achieve development outcomes. We have been drilled in order that development would succeed. And so automatically our way of thinking has also changed. Through being drilled, people have become economically oriented, and consequently materialistic. So when asked to do a bit of overtime people say, 'Oh, but the industrial relations law sets an eight-hour day, sir.' They will not do more than 10 minutes extra. This is what is called a materialistic orientation....If Indonesians are allowed to continue like this they will abandon their humanitarian values and take on a materialistic outlook. This must not be allowed to happen. In practice, many humanitarian values have been dispensed with. This process must be halted. So a second reason for the P4 program is to prevent the process of dehumanisation occurring within our nation since it is inimical to our struggle.

4.4 The law on social organisations

This law was the cornerstone of the New Order's efforts to enforce its ideological hegemony over civil society. It imposed on all social organisations, including political parties, the requirement to adopt Pancasila as their sole ideological principle, as well as a range of other strictures that increased the power of the state to regulate their existence. After considerable protest both from Muslim groups and secular NGOs (see Readings 5.3 and 6.3), it was promulgated on 17 June 1985 as Law no. 8/1985.

By the Grace of God Almighty, the President of the Republic of Indonesia..., with the approval of the People's Consultative Assembly, has decided to enact the law on social organisations.

Chapter I: general provision

Article 1

In this law, a 'social organisation' shall mean an organisation founded voluntarily by Indonesian citizens on the basis of common activities, profession, function, religion and belief in God Almighty, so as to actively participate in development in order to achieve national goals within the framework of the Republic of Indonesia, having Pancasila as its basic principle.

Chapter II: principle and purpose

Article 2

1 All social organisations must have Pancasila as their sole principle.
2 The principle referred to in paragraph (1) above is the foundation of the life of society, the nation and the state....

Article 4

The social organisation shall be required to state the principles referred to in Article 2 and the objectives referred to in Article 3 in its articles of association.

Chapter III: functions, rights and duties...

Article 7

The social organisation shall have the following duties:

a to have articles of association and by-laws;
b to comprehend, serve and promote Pancasila and the 1945 Constitution;
c to foster national unity and unification.

Article 8

In order to be more effective in the performance of its function, a social organisation shall gather together persons in a single body as a channel for the guidance and fostering of those with similar interests....

Chapter VI: guidance

Article 12

1 The government shall give guidance to social organisations.
2 The provision of such guidance shall be regulated by Government Regulation.

Chapter VII: suspension and dissolution

Article 13

The government may suspend the executive or central board of any social organisation if it:

a   carries out activities that disturb public security and order;
b   receives foreign assistance without the approval of the government;
c   assists any foreign party detrimental to the interests of the nation and state.

Article 14

If a social organisation whose management has been suspended continues to undertake activities specified in Article 13, the government may dissolve the organisation involved.

Article 15

The government may dissolve any social organisation that does not fulfil the provisions of Articles 2, 3, 4, 7 and/or 18.

Article 16

The government shall dissolve any social organisation which professes, develops, or spreads the doctrine or teachings of Communism/ Marxism–Leninism or other ideologies, doctrines or teachings contrary to Pancasila and the 1945 Constitution in all their forms and manifestations.

Article 17

The procedure for the suspension and dissolution of a social organisation referred to in Articles 13, 14, 15 and 16 above shall be regulated by a Government Regulation.

Chapter VIII: transitional provision

Article 18

On the coming into force of this law, existing social organisations shall be given an opportunity to bring themselves into conformity with its provisions and they shall do so within two years from the date of the promulgation of this law....

Signed, President Soeharto
Minister/State Secretary
Signed, Sudharmono, S.H.
Promulgated in Jakarta
17 June 1985

4.5 Abdulkadir Besar: the armed forces must not take sides

This extract is from a widely circulated typescript entitled 'Dwifungsi ABRI' written in 1978 by the military ideologue and teacher Abdulkadir Besar (1978: 36–40). By this time a brigadier-general, Abdulkadir was a staunch defender of the dual function, and his warning that the military must not side politically with any particular group (i.e. Golkar) should be seen as part of a debate within the New Order elite. He was, however, roundly attacked for his stance by some of the more pragmatic generals around Soeharto.

We can well imagine the dangers of the armed forces as a social group participating in politics along with other social groups which are unarmed. Armed forces of this type can deteriorate into armed political parties, which objectively have a tendency to use their weapons or threaten to do so to achieve their political aims. It is this danger which liberal democracy goes to great lengths to prevent, developing doctrines of 'civilian–military relations'. The situation becomes critical when the armed forces concerned have their own political goals. On the other hand, if they do not have such goals, this danger automatically disappears.

This begs the question whether ABRI has its own political aims, beyond those of the state. ABRI's character is revealed in the first three precepts of the Soldier's Sevenfold Pledge [Sapta Marga], which commit ABRI members to be:

- citizens faithful to Pancasila
- patriots upholding the state ideology
- warriors upholding honesty, truth and justice

Since the substance of each of these pledges is embodied in the 1945 Constitution, ABRI does not have political aims of its own. This absence of political aims is not a temporary policy. It has become a value in itself in the course of ABRI's experience of political challenges and temptations, which have always been overcome throughout its history of struggle.

The second feature of the Pledge is that it does not allow ABRI to become dictatorial. What prevents ABRI from having its own political aims is the intrinsic value that has been its lifeblood since 1945, namely 'the constitution is the armed forces' principle and politics'.

This is what truly constitutes ABRI's credentials. Without it the Indonesian people could not possibly have permitted ABRI's political participation or allowed it to carry out its primary function. It needs to be remembered that, in accordance with the essence of ABRI's dual function, its primary function is as a social force.

But we need to reflect on how things would be if the reverse were true. If ABRI were to deny its own credentials and to be guided not by the 1945

Constitution but rather by a certain group with which it sympathised, or if ABRI itself or a small circle within it were to adopt a partisan position, ABRI would at once lose the basis of its philosophy and sociology for carrying out its primary function. If ABRI were to continue to perform its primary function but to deny its credentials, it could no longer claim to be carrying out its dual function. 'Dual portion' would be a better description. So far the unitary Pancasila state has to a certain extent been guaranteed by ABRI's dual function. If 'dual function' was to deteriorate into 'dual portion', the state and nation would be plunged into misery without end. The purity of ABRI's credentials must therefore continually be guarded, and for this purpose an authoritative and effective control mechanism needs to be created within ABRI.

Nine principles of ABRI's dual function

Nine principles can be distilled from ABRI's dual function that must be firmly adhered to. These nine principles are intertwined to the extent that, if any one were not implemented or, worse, denied, the essential meaning of ABRI's dual function would be changed. Such a change could in turn change ABRI's character, since it would no longer reflect the Soldier's Sevenfold Pledge...:

a   ABRI is oriented to the 1945 Constitution, not to any sectional interest, and not to ABRI as a sectional interest....

b   In attaining political aims, it is prohibited to use or threaten the use of weapons, or to abuse power in the political superstructure....

c   In carrying out political activities, ABRI must use persuasive and constitutional methods, and is prohibited from using coercive methods....

d   ABRI's fundamental participation [as a social force] must remain within the assembly representing the sovereignty of the people and within the legislature....

e   ABRI's participation in the executive branch of government is only to be performed in the course of stabilising and/or dynamising government administration....

f   ABRI's determination of policy positions is to be carried out through consultative deliberation among ABRI's leadership and a number of its other members based upon an assessment of their capacity to offer objective opinions according to their experience and expertise, regardless of what opinions might be sought by the leadership....

g   When serving in 'non-military' positions, power must be exercised in accordance with the following values:

- use authority without relying upon force
- enter the field of battle alone
- gain victory without humiliating the opponent
- be rich without relying upon material possessions...

h Leadership based upon the pleasure of disinterested service must be expressed in word, attitude and deed....

i Whenever a person or institution outside ABRI can adequately perform a task, they should be given the opportunity to do so.

Notes

1 PRRI was the Revolutionary Government of the Republic of Indonesia, a counter-government proclaimed in February 1958 in Padang, West Sumatra. Permesta stands for Charter of the Common Struggle, the name of a North Sulawesi-based autonomist revolt that came into the open in February 1958.

2 The root *sunyata* derives from Indian Mahayana Buddhist metaphysics and refers to a monistic 'void' from which phenomenal existence emanates.

5   Pluralist critiques

The clampdown in the wake of the January 1974 riots was a significant turning point in Indonesian politics. Soeharto's manifest preference for the 'pragmatic' approach to maintaining power associated with generals such as Ali Moertopo dismayed many erstwhile allies and supporters, including some of the major proponents of pluralist political thinking. Consequently, important sections of the pluralist intelligentsia – comprising academics, students and NGO leaders – began to speak in openly oppositional terms and to develop a stance that was more clearly politically liberal than ever before, emphasising such issues as constitutionalism, democracy and freedom of speech. Significantly, this modernising intelligentsia, which had supported Soeharto in his early years in power, was joined by some of his military colleagues – figures like retired Lieutenant-Generals Ali Sadikin and H.R. Dharsono, who were instrumental in the establishment of the New Order.

In the early years of the New Order, most modernising pluralists were as keen as the organicists on achieving political stability in order to set the conditions for successful economic development. Away from the centre of political power, however, they became increasingly critical of the centralising, homogenising and authoritarian features of the New Order. More specifically, many were disenchanted with Soeharto's growing personal dominance over politics, which allowed him to brush aside critics and rivals with impunity, and to reward those he favoured with politically or financially rewarding positions.

These pluralists – who after 1974 are perhaps better categorised as critical pluralists – took Soeharto's New Order to task on several counts. First was the personalised nature of politics, which was seen as providing ample opportunity for various forms of abuse of power by Soeharto and those closest to him. Second was the lack of democratic controls on the executive, especially due to the impotence of parliament and the judiciary. Third was the New Order's failure to abide by its own constitutionalist and rule-of-law rhetoric. Fourth was the ideological uniformity imposed particularly since the mid-1980s through the forced acceptance by political parties and mass organisations of Pancasila as the 'sole principle' of political and social life. The fifth, also stemming from the Law no. 8/1985, included in Chapter 4, had to do with the numerous regulations constraining social and professional organisations.

Most of the readings in this chapter are from the 1980s. We begin, however, with an important document from the student movement of 1978, the *White Book of the Students' Struggle*, issued by students from the Bandung Institute of Technology (Reading 5.1). This movement signalled a new wave of student activism after the setbacks of 1974, and a new focus. While the 1974 students had targeted a group of generals, including Ali Moertopo, who they accused of selling Indonesia out to Japan, the 1978 student movement formulated a more comprehensive critique of the New Order and demanded Soeharto's resignation. The *White Book* crystallised the views of the 1978 student movement. The harsh crackdown triggered by the widespread student demonstrations in 1978 and 1979 saw strict controls imposed on universities, leading to a long period of decline in campus-based activism. It would take close to a decade before students found ways to cope effectively with this repression by forming less structured groups and networks.

One of the clearest indications of Soeharto's loss of support among his former allies was the emergence in 1980 of a petition signed by 50 prominent intellectuals, lawyers, Masjumi politicians and, most notably, retired military officers. The so-called Petition of Fifty group, led by former Jakarta Governor Ali Sadikin, attacked the personal, arbitrary nature of Soeharto's power, accusing him of deliberately abusing Pancasila and the 1945 Constitution for his own ends (Reading 5.2). The petition also chastised Soeharto for using the armed forces for party political purposes, which was against the military's own doctrines. Infuriated by the personal nature of the criticism, Soeharto subjected several of the Petition of Fifty signatories to a campaign of harassment and became increasingly suspicious, if not paranoid, about dissent among his retired former colleagues. In 1984 Soeharto ordered the arrest of H.R. Dharsono, a former commander of the Siliwangi (West Java) military region whose reformist views were well known. The general, who had also served as secretary-general of the Association of Southeast Asian Nations (ASEAN) until 1978, was accused of involvement in a plot by Muslim extremists to bomb a number of buildings. In Reading 5.4 H.R. Dharsono defends himself in court against charges of subversion by detailing how he believed the New Order had betrayed its ideals. Dharsono is only one among many critics who commented caustically on the disjuncture between the New Order's constitutionalist and egalitarian rhetoric and its repressive practices.

Probably the most controversial political issue of the mid-1980s was the promulgation of five laws on politics and society that codified state control over political parties and mass organisations. One of the ways that this was achieved was through the imposition of Pancasila as the sole basis (*azas tunggal*) of social and political life. The requirement that all social organisations adopt Pancasila as their sole basis particularly angered some Muslim political groups (see Chapter 6), who believed that they had the right to base their organisations on Islam. Pluralists, however, were also critical of these laws, seeing them as an attempt by the government to exercise a monopoly on the interpretation of the Pancasila in a way that would stifle opposition. Indeed, the charge of being 'anti-Pancasila' was increasingly used as a weapon against a range of activists, from Muslim fundamentalists in the 1980s to the left-wing PRD in the 1990s. Concerns over this issue, and its implications for NGOs, are well summarised in the 1984 excerpt by the Indonesian Legal Aid Institute (Reading 5.3).

The last reading is by Abdurrahman Wahid, who was then the leader of the nominally 'traditionalist' Nahdlatul Ulama (NU), Indonesia's largest Islamic organisation. One of the country's most original political thinkers, Wahid decided in 1984 to disassociate the NU from the PPP. Rather than seek direct political power for Islamic forces, Wahid proclaimed that NU members should strive for fundamental social transformation, involving upholding democracy, the rule of law and social and political freedoms. In the 1987 article included here as Reading 5.5 Abdurrahman defended liberalism, arguing that the Pancasila and liberal democracy were not necessarily incompatible – contrary to the official dogma regarding Pancasila, and contrary to the misgivings of some Muslims about 'Western' political traditions. With Wahid's contribution, we see a bridge being built between traditional Islamic political thinking and that of secular pluralists. It was on this basis that Abdurrahman Wahid emerged as a political leader in the 1990s whose appeal went well beyond his natural constituency of NU followers.

5.1 ITB Student Council: *White Book of the Students' Struggle*

We present here a portion of a hard-hitting critique of social, political and economic policy under the New Order compiled by students of the prestigious Bandung Institute of Technology (ITB) in 1978. The movement prompted a government crackdown that saw hundreds of students arrested and several publications, including this one, banned. This reading is an excerpt from a translation published in the Cornell University journal *Indonesia* (*White Book of the Students' Struggle* 1978: 153–60). The text is reproduced as printed in the journal, although we have omitted the explanatory footnotes and section markers.

Merdeka!!!!!!!

The time has come for all of us to outline the struggle of the students amidst the unsatisfactory course the development our beloved country is taking.

We are not being overly dramatic when we state that all our efforts are a manifestation of our sense of responsibility as the younger generation which will have to give meaning to our country's independence.

This Book of the Students' Struggle, published by the [ITB] Student Council, endeavours to give a picture to the wider society of: why we have to struggle and what the struggle is all about???

As the tempo and the rhythm of the struggle are growing more and more rapid, we must communicate the principles for which we must struggle, now and in the future.

The problems faced by our country are too grave to be gambled with any longer. The errors in our development strategy over the past 10 years must be corrected as soon as possible.

This White Book does not merely discuss negative incidents caused by administrative errors. We want to emphasise rather that the development policies themselves are wrong. The incidents in question are simply the consequences of these erroneous policies.

We hope that through this book we can give a clear portrayal of the problems that we all face together.

We invite all readers of this book to unite in the struggle.

The present condition of our country

The defects that we see today are caused by the *National Leadership* and by the 'System of Government' that it has created. Improper mechanisms for the management of the state, which in turn have given birth to erroneous and uncontrolled policies and programs, have bred restlessness in society. Errors of leadership and in the system have taken place in all fields: Political, Economic, Sociocultural, Legal and other fields of development. All of this has generated a sense of oppression and injustice in society.

The political field

As a consequence of the political system that has been in operation up till now, government policies have been executed without any 'meaningful correctives' from the Political Parties and from Golkar, which are recognised administratively as the official political forces.

The *innermost voice of the little people*, who live under the *oppression* and *repression* of the 'elite' forces, never reaches the ears of the government. In turn, the government has never opened its heart to the pure and honest *'voice of the common people's heart'* [rakyat jelata]. Thus a system in which the *city people* exploit the *villagers*, the *rich* oppress the *poor*, *private cars* elbow *city buses* out into the slow lanes, wealthy *idiots* kick aside poor *bright people*, *non-native* businessmen kill off *native* businessmen, etc. goes on and on, and the oppressed have no way of stopping it. There aren't even any *complaints* about it in Parliament any more.

The prevailing situation is such that 'the top people' solely direct their eyes and ears further up. They all scramble to enjoy the *luxuries* that are indeed *freely* '*provided*' by the *liberal* economic system *practised* by the government!! These errors could develop to such a disastrous point because *control* functions have not operated as they should. State Institutions have in fact been 'fixed' so as not to interfere with the build-up of 'executive power'. For the sake of stability in economic development, the whole system and all the activities of the Highest State Institutions have been 'harmonised' with the tastes of the executive. Let us observe, one by one, the anomalies that are to be found in the Highest Institutions of our country.

PARLIAMENT

Up till now, Parliament is still not an institution capable of channelling the aspirations of the people, nor is it an effective institution for control. Parliament is simply a spectator to all the irregularities that are taking place within the executive! There have been many incidents, shameful to our nation and state, which have demanded active intervention by the people's representatives, but they have done absolutely nothing. Major cases, such as the reports in the foreign press about bribery in the acquisition of the 'Palapa Satellite', have degraded our country in the eyes of the world. Actually, Parliament should have been able to conduct an investigation to prove or disprove such allegations. But what did it do in fact? It simply conducted a few hearings for the sake of 'appearances', and after that the issue was considered as settled. In the meantime, the Government took the following steps to resolve the matter: first, the Minister of Communications, Emil Salim, announced that he had formed an 'investigative team'. After some time had elapsed, Minister Salim announced that there was evidently no proof that bribery had occurred in connection with the purchase of the Palapa Satellite. What a joke! In the Palapa case, the *Department of Communications* was the criminal suspect or the party charged with involvement in bribery. But then it was the very same Department of Communications that formed the 'investigative team', and declared that the Department of Communications was clean and that there was no 'Palapa Scandal', for in legal terms there was *no acceptable proof....*

Hundreds of other major cases, such as the Pertamina tanker affair, the Rp200,000,000,000 Bank Bumi Daya credits episode, and the like, all of which demanded action by the *people's representatives*, suffered the 'same fate'.

And so we have to consider why our Parliament is so inactive and why it can *no longer be trusted* to represent the people????

The reason, of course, is that Parliament has been, *'fixed'* by the national executive leadership to become *so paralysed*! Even at the time when the official *list of parliamentary candidates* from the Political Parties and from Golkar was being drawn up for the General Election, the individuals listed were picked by the Government. People thought to have *too much courage, integrity, and principle were considered dangerous* and were scratched off the list. Those who remained on the list of candidates 'blessed' by the government consisted of people who were either *weak* or, at best, *moderates*, ready to swing to the right or to the left; but the *majority*, of course, were *weak*. After they were elected and became members of Parliament, they were welcomed with various special facilities to 'soften them up'. The first 'softener' was a Rp90,000 suit, followed by accommodations, transportation (minimally *first-class* train tickets, not 'people's class'), honoraria, a Volkswagen on the instalment plan, and other things, such that the total value amounted to approximately Rp250,000 a month. Moreover, their time is by no means wholly taken up [with parliamentary duties], so that they can still pursue other lucrative occupations on the side! Remember, too, that no one can *check* the quality of the work of the individual members of Parliament. Whether they are often absent or work diligently, whether they speak frequently or never speak at all – there is not one person who makes an issue of it! The public can evaluate the quality of the work of Parliament as an institution, *but it cannot do so for the individual members of Parliament*, because the General Election [electoral] system follows the proportional representation, not the electoral district, system.

After the members had been selected and 'softened up' as individuals, Parliament itself, as a system or institution, was also 'softened up'. Parliament has been taken care of in such a way that it can no longer make use of its *right of enquête* [investigation], its *right of interpellation*, and its *right to determine the budget*. On utilising the right of enquête (investigating a problem), a rule was established that a separate law would regulate the realisation of this right. To prevent Parliament from using this right, to prevent Parliament from becoming a *nuisance*, to prevent Parliament from *making a fuss*, to prevent Parliament from being *nasty* enough to investigate such things as Pertamina, Bulog, the Bank Bumi Daya credits, Tapos, Mangadeg, the wealth of certain officials, etc., establishment of *any law regulating the right of enquête* was aborted!

So Parliament has never been able to use its right of enquête! To ensure that no such law was enacted was no big problem for Golkar, which holds a majority in Parliament and which is also reinforced by the Armed Forces faction appointed personally by the President.

Can the people expect anything from such a Parliament?...Consider the General Elections, for instance: the *Election Commission* was formed and appointed, not by Parliament, but by the *Government*, though in fact the

Government, through Golkar, was also a participant in the General Elections. Excesses, naturally, were unavoidable. Excesses such as referee Amir Machmud[1] 'joining the game', followed by *lurah* [village headmen] and *camat* [sub-district officers], all for the sake of securing victory for Golkar. The little people in the villages were pressured, and not just pressured, but even persecuted, with threats of being kidnapped – especially in crucial areas such as West Java, Central Java, and East Java. Nevertheless, *Mr President Soeharto* declared West Java the best election region! Whereas Jakarta, which had conducted the Election quietly and without incidents, was not declared such a region! Was this because the governor happened to be Marine Lt.-Gen. Ali Sadikin?...Or because the PPP won [in Jakarta], not Golkar?...*They really have no generosity of spirit at all....*

And this farce, too, took place before the noses of the *people's representatives* in Parliament, without any hindrance whatsoever.

Could the little people in the villages, who were pressured and persecuted during the elections, ask for help from the people's representatives in Parliament???...The simple answer is: *No!* Parliament's Committee II, in charge of dealing with the problem of excesses during the General Elections, could never meet to discuss all these incidents because there was never a quorum, since the Golkar members *never attended....*

Can the people expect anything from such a Parliament? Knowing what they do, the people were not at all surprised that during the work-period of the 1971 Parliament, during all those five years, it was only able to pass 43 laws, all of which were proposed by the Government. Parliament was not able to come up with even one law on its own! This is a record worse than that of the Gotong-Royong Parliament of the Old Order, which at least was able to complete two laws [of its own]. Some people may still put their hopes in the Parliament produced by the 1977 General Elections; but we should remember that the 1977 Parliament was born via the same process as the 1971 Parliament. The majority of the leadership consists of the same people, and the same internal protocol is still in operation.

THE MPR

The 1977 MPR is *unconstitutional*! According to Article 2 of Section I of the 1945 Constitution, *Sovereignty is in the hands of the People*, and is fully exercised by the People's Consultative Assembly. This means that it is an Institution consisting of the Representatives of the people that holds sovereignty. But 61 per cent of the members of the 1977 MPR are *not representatives of the people*!! They are appointed. The General Elections, conducted with so much effort at a cost of Rp60,000,000,000, in which people flailed at one another till blood flowed, elected only 39 per cent of the members of the MPR. So supposing that, in a general session of the 1977 MPR, the 39 per cent of the members elected through the General Elections *could not be present*, and those present were only the *61 per cent that were appointed*, that session would still be legitimate.

How does this *differ* from the general session of the Provisional MPR?! There is no difference. The Provisional MPR, the 1971 MPR, and the 1977 MPR are all *unconstitutional*. That is why their function as bearers of the people's aspirations is highly dubious. Many strange anomalies have occurred. *The Chairman of the MPR doubles as Speaker of Parliament. The President does not account to the MPR that elected him. The compositions of the GBHN* [Broad Outlines of State Policy] *consists merely of editing the government's draft, and so forth.*

Since the Speaker of Parliament doubles as Chairman of the MPR, the latter office assumes a status equal to the presidency. The fact that the President does *not* give an accounting to the MPR that elected him is more laughable than Srimulat.[2] Presidential accountability means that the President must answer for all his policies and [use of] his executive powers in carrying out the Broad Outlines of State Policy. The body that produced the GBHN is the same MPR that elected him. The body that followed the GBHN's implementation from day to day is also the MPR that elected the President, for his tenure of office coincides with its own term of life. It is for these reasons that the MPR which elected the President will have a better feel for the issues, in order to determine how far the President has carried out the GBHN, and also how far he has deviated from it. But then, all of a sudden, the above farce took place. And the climax of the farce came when the person who ended the debate on whether the President should account to the 1971 MPR or the 1977 MPR was Mr President Soeharto himself, during a visit to Kuala Lumpur, in a speech to the local Indonesian community there. The *constitutional* way would have been for the 1971 MPR to decide whether Mr President Soeharto should be accountable to the 1971 MPR or the 1977 MPR....

THE ACCOUNTING OFFICE [BPK]

The Chairman of the BPK should be appointed by the MPR. The BPK is the institution that scrutinises the finances of the Government. So it is anomalous if its chairman is actually appointed by the Government [itself]. On appointment, he is supposed to start scrutinising. Experience shows there are two subsequent possibilities. Either the appointee is a close friend [of the Executive], or, if he scrutinises too vigorously, he will be fired. Possibly things will not turn out quite this badly. But to avoid even the possibility, the Chairman of the BPK should be appointed by the MPR. Moreover, the BPK should report on its programs and their implementation to Parliament.

THE SUPREME COURT

The Supreme Court is the Judicial Body in the governmental system of a country. Accordingly, it must not be influenced by the executive to the slightest extent! But, in our country, the fate of the Chairman of the Supreme Court lies in the hands of the President. So he is forced to play along in safeguarding the authority of the Government!!

But political errors are not only present among the Highest Institutions of State. They also exist in the system of the Political Parties and Golkar.

THE POLITICAL PARTIES AND GOLKAR

In reality, the present official political forces, namely the Political Parties and Golkar, are not genuine political forces. It is true that they are classified administratively as official political groupings, but the real political power lies in the hands of the *Government*. The Political Parties and Golkar have to follow the will of this Government, whether they like it or not. If they are obstinate, the Government will immediately interfere and manipulate them to ensure they will no longer pose a threat to the Government. The most obvious example at present is the 'disaster' that has befallen the PDI. Possibly because the PDI was a bit recalcitrant towards the Government, it was 'coup'-ed [by the Government] via Isnaeni and Sunawar. From now on, it will be manipulated in such a way that it will no longer be so 'recalcitrant'. The Government has [here] conducted an 'amoral' policy of expediency!!! And Mr President Soeharto has *not refused to allow* all this to happen.

In addition, the parties are not allowed to operate in the villages, yet the villages are where 80 per cent of Indonesia's inhabitants live!!! If the parties are not allowed to operate in the villages, this means that *only 20 per cent* of the inhabitants of Indonesia will have their aspirations represented. Yet the Political Parties and Golkar always claim to speak for the entire People of Indonesia. This is not true! This is what we call manipulation! This is why so many 'incidents' which have happened in the villages have never gained the attention of Parliament. The reason why widespread famine can take place without the 'higher-ups' knowing about it is that the Political Parties and Golkar are not allowed to operate in the villages.

5.2 The Petition of Fifty

This document (see Bourchier 1987) was written in reaction to two speeches the president made to military audiences early in 1980, an excerpt from one of which was reproduced in the previous chapter (Reading 4.1). Its submission to parliament on 13 May 1980 sparked an extraordinary reaction from the authorities, including a media blackout and claims by security chiefs that the petition was part of a 'constitutional coup d'état' which also involved plans to assassinate 67 people, including Soeharto. Nobody was imprisoned directly on account of the petition, but its signatories, several of whom continued to collaborate as the Petition of Fifty Working Group, were harassed for years.

Statement of concern

With the mercy of the Almighty, we the undersigned, as voters in the last general elections, express the deepest disappointment of the people over remarks President Soeharto made in his speeches to the Armed Forces Commander's Call at Pekanbaru on 27 March 1980 and on the anniversary of the Kopassandha [Red Beret Commandos] in Cijantung on 16 April 1980.

We are concerned about these speeches of the president because they:

a   Assume that in our society, which is striving under an increasingly heavy burden to develop the country, there is a polarisation between those committed to 'preserving Pancasila' on the one hand and 'replacing Pancasila' on the other, which we fear could generate fresh conflict between groups in society;

b   Misinterpret Pancasila in such a way that it could be used as a means to threaten political opponents, when in fact Pancasila was intended by the founders of the Indonesian Republic as a means to unite the nation;

c   Legitimise the less than praiseworthy activities of those in power to systematically paralyse the 1945 Constitution, using as a pretext the Sapta Marga [Soldiers' Sevenfold Pledge] and the Sumpah Prajurit [Soldier's Oath], even though these two oaths cannot possibly outrank the 1945 Constitution;

d   Invite the Armed Forces to take sides; not to stand above all groups in society but, on the contrary, to choose between friend and foe as determined by the authorities;

e   Create the impression that there is someone who regards himself as the personification of Pancasila, so that every rumour about him is construed as anti-Pancasila;

f   Allege that preparations are under way for armed uprisings, subversion, infiltration and other unsanctioned activities as we approach the general elections.

Recognising that the thoughts expressed in these speeches of President Soeharto cannot be divorced from the management of the affairs of state or from the coming general elections, we urge the representatives of the people in both the People's Representative Council and the People's Consultative Assembly to respond to the presidential speeches delivered on 27 March and 16 April 1980.

Jakarta, 5 May 1980

Signed[3]

5.3 Indonesian Legal Aid Institute: threats to NGOs in the bill on social organisations

This extract is from a booklet published in 1984 by the Yayasan Lembaga Bantuan Hukum Indonesia (Indonesian Legal Aid Institute), one of Indonesia's most outspoken NGOs (1984: 37–50). It was originally presented to parliament in August 1984 as written testimony during hearings on the government's introduction of five important bills dealing with the composition of parliament, elections, parties and societies. The portion presented here takes the government to task over the proposed restrictions on NGOs and other organisations in the bill on social organisations (an excerpt from the final form of which is reproduced in Reading 4.4).[4]

The legislative regulation of social organisations cannot be understood outside the context of the workings of the political system in Indonesia during the New Order period.

In the process of providing legitimacy – increasingly demanded in the current phase of political power – the government has been directing its efforts at institutionalisation, on the one hand towards consolidating its hegemony, while at the same time maintaining its image of 'constitutionalism as far as possible', which follows from its stance that the law is the basis of a broad consensus. The process of consolidating its legitimacy has involved designing a 'normative' political architecture, beginning with the regulated fusion of political parties, the concept of 'the floating masses', 'Pancasila as the only principle' and other features which not only increasingly institutionalise the ideology but also operate very directly upon the political process.

The breadth and intensity of community participation – particularly in the articulation of political interests – has come under increasing control, while the components of the political system revolve around a status quo which distances itself from the process of democratisation....

When one reads the terms of reference of this bill on social organisations, it is evident that it will affect an enormous range of organisations. And the meaning of social organisations here seems unrelated to numbers of members. According to Article 1 it covers every organisation founded voluntarily by Indonesian citizens on the basis of common activities, profession, function, religion and belief in God Almighty, so as to actively participate in development. If this is so, this law will cover the following categories of social organisation:

1   Social organisations that play a direct part in the political system, such as Golkar and the political parties.
2   Social organisations affiliated to such groups, such as Kosgoro Mulitipurpose Mutual Assistance Co-operative, Soksi [Autonomous

Organisation of Indonesian Socialist Functionaries], and MKGR [Familial Mutual Assistance Conference].

3   Social organisations that mobilise their members to assure the stability of the current political system by incorporating certain social collectivities, such as KNPI [The National Committee of Indonesian Youth], FBSI [All-Indonesia Workers' Federation], Korpri [Indonesian Civil Service Corps], PGRI [Indonesian Teachers' Association] and Dharma Wanita ['The Duty of Women' Organisation of Civil Servants' Wives].

4   Professional associations such as Peradin [Indonesian Lawyers' Association] and IDI [Indonesian Doctors' Association].

5   NGOs such as those involved in the environment, population, legal aid, and so on.

6   Organisations involved in regional cultures and in leisure activities such as martial arts, hiking and local arts.

7   Religious organisations.

8   Organisations representing specific interest groups, but which cannot be categorised with those in Points 2 and 3, despite having the same organisational characteristics, such as HMI [Muslim Students' Association], PMKRI [Catholic University Students' Association of the Republic of Indonesia], GMNI [Indonesian Nationalist University Students' Movement], PII [Indonesian Islamic High School Students], and GPM [Marhenist Youth Movement]....

As well as signalling a tendency towards technocratic policy planning...it appears that the government is intent on imposing bureaucratic models on the reality of social diversity. The political system, through the intervention of bureaucratic mechanisms, will give precedence to preventing rather than developing opportunities for the effective participation of citizens. This will particularly apply to social organisations which have been undergoing quantitative and qualitative growth, such as NGOs. The diversity that characterises social organisations is disregarded in the bill on social organisations.

Several other regulatory features in this bill also warrant attention, including:

1   The tendency toward regimentation in the bill (Article 8). All organisational activities within an occupational group must take place within a single association. If everything has to be centralised in a single body agreed to by the government, it will be increasingly difficult to act and be creative within any particular field. While the existence of a single body will certainly promote stability, it will greatly hinder the growth of democracy. Such regimentation will also formally negate Article 28 of the 1945 Constitution on freedom of association, assembly, and expression, and it also contradicts President Soeharto's recent speech recognising the diversity of our

people. Article 8 of this shows us how strong this regimenting spirit is in our government. Without being aware of it, those in government are taking us further and further away from a democratic social climate.

2   The most worrying parts of the bill on social organisations are the articles on guidance, suspension, and dissolution of social organisations (Articles 12 to 16). These articles provide the government with the authority to exercise guidance through as yet unclear forms and means which are still to be determined in the form of an executive regulation. It is by no means impossible that this executive regulation on guidance will be so tight that social organisations and NGOs will not feel guided, but rather feel they are under surveillance, controlled and constrained. This executive regulation on guidance might mean repression of the freedom and creativity of social organisations and NGOs. A climate devoid of freedom will emerge, with social organisations and NGOs forced to exercise self-censorship or face the real risk of being suspended and dissolved by the government (Articles 13, 14, and 15).

The bill gives three grounds for suspension of social organisations and NGOs:

1   carrying out activities which disturb public security and order;
2   receiving foreign assistance without government permission;
3   giving assistance to foreign parties detrimental to the interests of the nation and state (Article 13).

Furthermore, Article 14 states, 'If a social organisation whose management has been suspended continues to carry out activities specified in Article 13, the government may *dissolve* the social organisation involved.' And government authority reaches its culmination in Article 15: '*The government may dissolve social organisations that do not fulfil the provisions of this law.*'

Articles 12, 13, 14, and 15 of this bill on social organisations will be minefields for social organisations and NGOs. No details at all are given on the criteria for suspension and dissolution, leaving their interpretation completely to government discretion. What does carrying out activities that disturb public security and order mean? What is meant by giving assistance to foreign parties detrimental to the interests of the nation and state? It is difficult to imagine social organisations and NGOs setting out to disturb public security and order, or assisting foreign parties to harm the interests of the nation and state.

These articles make bitter reading, arising as they do from a sense of suspicion. In social and political life we ought to adhere to the principles of mutual trust and the presumption of innocence.

Legal action can only be taken where there is clear evidence that the behaviour of a specific social organisation as an institution has harmed the interests of the nation and state. It is our impression that existing social organisations and NGOs love this country, and were established to help consolidate the independence of our country. So such tight control and oversight is unnecessary, including the matter of receiving assistance from foreign parties. Insofar as such assistance is used in the interests of the people in general, no problem arises since the social organisations concerned also thereby aid the government.

It is excessive to make permits conditional because very frequently permits are not issued. Public disclosure of a financial report audited by an accountant should more than suffice. If the instituting of permits is forced upon us, the impression that social organisations and NGOs are suspected, controlled, and under surveillance will be all the more confirmed. And this could be the beginning of the repression of our creative freedoms.

The formulations in the bill on social organisations that are left open to broad interpretation – concerning the functions, rights and obligations, guidance, dissolution and suspension – almost certainly constitute criteria which could be used as political instruments to constrain freedoms of association and expression guaranteed by the constitution.

In addition, bureaucratisation of the regulation and supervision of social organisations will reinforce the pattern of patron–client power relations that characterise a highly centralised political process. This in turn will weaken the potential of social organisations to struggle for the interests of their members. Moreover, in its implementation a law that is effectively applied but which is weak in terms of legitimacy – both because of its content and because the parties to be regulated have been excluded from the process of its formulation – will tend to appear repressive.

In view of these considerations it is altogether appropriate that legislation concerning social organisations must address the following matters:

1   Given that the political system has already been progressively consolidated, emphasis should now be placed on expanding community participation in the political processes. Accordingly, the provision of legal guarantees for exercising the rights to organise political interests and responses to political issues, in line with the values and norms of Pancasila democracy, should be an integral part of the regulation of social organisations.

2   The growth of social organisations in Indonesia, which essentially serve community needs across diverse fields of activity, constitutes a social reality that cannot be ignored. Organisations working in the areas of the environment, population, and legal aid, for example, have

proliferated rapidly over the last decade or so. With their unique characteristics in organising their activities and serving their target groups, the role that these organisations play is increasingly appreciated. On the one hand they fill voids in the development bureaucracy's fields of operation, and on the other hand they constitute vehicles for popular participation in opening up new development alternatives. It is inappropriate that this diversity be obstructed by regulations that impede community action and participation in the national development context.

3   In the implementation of national law it is appropriate that priority be given to the making of laws which are able to serve as the means of social emancipation, rather than prioritising laws which further expand the capacity for formal control over citizens. Moreover, in the present stage of development, there is an increasing demand for more legislation guaranteeing the implementation of citizens' rights contained *de jure* in the 1945 Constitution, particularly in Article 28. Legislation that deviates from the letter and spirit of Pancasila and the 1945 Constitution will clearly only reinforce authoritarian trends.

5.4 H.R. Dharsono: the promise of the New Order betrayed

The reading below is a translation of sections of a defence speech (*pleidooi*) by retired Lieutenant-General Hartono Rekso Dharsono in January 1986. The former secretary-general of ASEAN served six years of a 10-year sentence for subversion and was officially rehabilitated by President Habibie in August 1998. This passage is reproduced from a translation published in *Indonesia Reports* in August 1986.

Honourable judges of the court, public prosecutor, and legal counsel,
I will set forth several symptoms of the political life of the state, which clearly veer from the ideals of the proclamation and the promise of the New Order. These have been carried out through highly repressive and anti-democratic actions.

Such political acts frequently proceeded outside constitutional channels. Nonetheless, the government has done its best to legitimate its actions by manipulating the laws, which are, of course, contrary to Pancasila and the 1945 Constitution.

What is most disheartening is that the government has often acted in inhumane and unjust ways. Its actions can be direct and overt or indirect and concealed. At the highest levels of authority, the leadership can also undertake individualistic and institutionalised actions. And after 20 years of the New Order, it is evident how systematic and sophisticated their non-adherence to the promises they uttered 20 years ago has been....

The authorities' interference in finalising candidates submitted by political organisations in the general elections

Honourable judges of the court, public prosecutor, and legal counsel,
It would be normal and in accordance with their rights for every political organisation to select and appoint their own prominent figures and leaders to put forward in the general elections as candidates to be chosen by the people.

It appears that, due to uneasiness, when the political parties put forward worthy figures who can attract votes in the general election the authorities shamelessly and without legal justification are ready with their own ideas. This involves making a list of names of community figures and leaders, who can, the authorities aver, net the votes of electors for a political victory. A classic tactic always used is to label certain candidates as dangerous to the perpetuation of the Pancasila state. In the 1971 general election alone, no less than 2,500 popular figures were placed on a 'blacklist' of persons who could not be nominated in the general election by the political parties.

Aside from the deletion of names from the parties' lists as I have described above, the authorities have also tampered with the order of candidates on the parties' nominee lists for the general election. Even if a candidate's name is not on the 'blacklist', if the authorities doubt the candidate's loyalty, his rank on the nominee list is immediately reshuffled from near the top to near the bottom, making it impossible for him to be elected.

Can acts like these be considered anything but tyrannical?

Unequal treatment of Golkar and the political parties

Honourable judges of the court, public prosecutor, and legal counsel,
The regulations governing the general election state that Golkar and the political parties should receive the same treatment and services from the government in the general election. That's the way the provisions read. But how are they realised in practice?
Examine the facts:

- every government operative, from the village heads, the sub-district heads, the district heads, the mayors, the governors, the first echelon officials up through the ministers and even the president campaigns for a Golkar victory;
- even the military is mobilised;
- everywhere it is an open secret that the people are forced to vote for Golkar through various means, from gentle persuasion to intimidation, frequently incurring sanctions such as beatings, dismissals from civil service positions or other jobs, and, in some areas, killings;

- all civil servants have to join the Indonesian Civil Servants' Corps Korpri, which has declared itself part of Golkar, so that all civil servants have to vote and work for a Golkar win;
- the wives of all officials from village heads to ministers must help in 'fighting' for a Golkar victory, otherwise sanctions will be levied against their husbands;
- fraud abounds because the government, which should be the umpire in this, the New Order period, instead precisely is the main player in ensuring a Golkar victory....

The existence of the extra-constitutional institution Kopkamtib

Honourable judges of the court, public prosecutor, and legal counsel,
It appears that after Law no. 5/1963 and Law no. 11/1963 were established as a basis for their actions, the holders of state power still needed a 'physical device' to achieve their objectives.

The elections governed by Law no. 15/1969 and Law no. 16/1969 yielded an MPR in which 61 per cent of the members were appointed and only 39 per cent were elected by the people.

The MPR, so constituted, produced MPR Decision no. X/1973, which the president used to issue Presidential Decision no. 9/1973, establishing Kopkamtib. In Article 3 this decision states, 'The task of Kopkamtib is to restore security and public order resulting from the G30S/PKI, extremist activities, and other subversive activities'.

By this means, the president came to occupy two positions: first, as head of state based on the 1945 Constitution, and, second, as holder of authority to resolve problems of security and public order resulting from the G30S/PKI and other extremist and subversive activities.
Honourable judges of the court, public prosecutor, and legal counsel,
In [the] performance of his duties as head of state, the president's actions are clearly limited by the provisions of the 1945 Constitution. But in his other position as holder of authority to overcome the results of G30S/PKI and other extremist and subversive activities, all of the president's policies lie outside the limits set down in the constitution.

Through this crack in the door, the president has used the authority of Kopkamtib to enact whatever policies and take whatever actions he chooses without following the procedures specified in the constitution and without the supervision of the DPR.

Furthermore, MPR Decision no. X/1973 does not prescribe limits on the manner and content of the president's actions based on this law.

This is quite different from what is stipulated in Article 12 of the constitution, [which] states, 'The President may declare a state of emergency. The conditions and consequences of the state of emergency are determined by law.'

In accordance with the order of supersedure of the various levels of law, set out in MPRS Decision no. 19/1966 and MPRS Decision no. XXXI/1968, an MPR Decision may not be contrary to the contents of the 1945 Constitution, especially in matters of principle.

MPR Decision X/1973, through which Kopkamtib was later established by Presidential Decision no. 9/1973, is clearly inconsistent with the letter and spirit of the 1945 Constitution.

Because there are no limits placed on the definition of the phrases 'extremist activities' or 'other subversive activities' as used in Article 3 of Presidential Decision no. 9/1973, whoever is commander of Kopkamtib will be able to interpret this passage however he likes.

For this reason, during the New Order we have often witnessed or read in the newspapers or at least heard from various circles of society about Kopkamtib actions such as banning or ordering coverage of a story in the mass media through only a telephone call; carrying out arrests, detention, and interrogation against citizens without regard to the proper procedures delineated in law; inhumane treatment during questioning; carrying out executions performed without regard to legal procedures, more commonly known as 'mysterious shootings' or 'Petrus';[5] undertaking 'political screening' of citizens to determine their loyalty to the government, as in the case of prospective nominees in the general elections; depriving citizens of their civil rights without trial, such as forbidding signatories of the Petition of Fifty to leave the country and depriving them of the ability to earn a living by instructing all agencies and state banks not to honour their requests; the arrest and detention of religious teachers and so forth.

All of this has been done with the excuse that the individuals involved are suspected of engaging in extremist or other subversive acts....

Kopkamtib's actions would be appropriate if the country was in fact in a state of emergency. According to those responsible for the country's security, however, conditions here are now secure and stable.

Thus it is truly ironic that during a period of security and stability the holders of state power have continued to make use of their authority based on MPR Decision no. X/1973 through Kopkamtib. This gives rise to the impression that the country is under a state of emergency that continues without end.

With things as they are, perhaps it would be far better if the country was just declared to be in a state of emergency, for then there would be laws governing the conditions and consequences of such a declaration under Article 12 of the 1945 Constitution. Since the basis for this would be laws founded on the constitution, the DPR would be continually able to supervise actions taken by the government in connection with the implementation of these laws.

5.5 Abdurrahman Wahid: we can be Pancasilaists *and* liberals

By the standards of public discourse at the time, this article was a bold challenge to the prevailing orthodoxy. It was published under the title 'Pancasila dan Liberalisme' in *Kompas* on 21 July 1987.

In the past few years, senior officials of our nation have suggested more and more often that Pancasila rejects liberal democracy. This view is promoted not only by individual high government officials, including the head of state, but also – more formally – in Pancasila indoctrination (P4) materials. It is therefore clear that rejection of liberal democracy has become the standard view and basic attitude of the government.

But there has never been any systematic and objective survey of how the majority of the nation feels about liberal democracy. So things are not so simple.

On the one hand, we all accept the legality of the government. So we have to accept all decisions it makes through the constitutional process. In this way, the government's view becomes the view of the entire nation. The government can say that the rejection of liberal democracy was done by representatives of the people and has the force of law. On that basis the law can punish any behaviour with a whiff of liberal democracy about it.

On the other hand, the people have clearly not taken this decision on board in their daily lives. Liberal democratic practices are still widespread in society, even though only on a small scale. But while the scale may be small, such practices occur with great frequency and massive volume. The most concrete example is the behaviour of social organisations.

According to the Pancasila vision, competition is allowed and even encouraged for the sake of achieving progress. But it has to take place very politely, in an atmosphere of mutual respect and accommodation among the competitors. The winner should represent the interests of all parties through consensus-based decisions. In other words, competition is accepted as part of the process of achieving consensus; it is integralist.

To what degree is this [style of competition] already happening? It must be admitted that it has barely caught on yet. Every time it happens it is supported by the intervention of the government apparatus, as we have seen in the cases of the PDI and PPP in the last 10 years. Competing sides clearly do not take Pancasila political culture into account. Each side still wants to win outright. Furthermore, the winning side does not feel it necessary to be bound by consensus and in the end only imposes its own opinions. Is that not clear proof that the spirit of liberal democracy is still strong?

Why is it necessary, then, to measure the nation's acceptance of Pancasila's integralist view of democracy? There is clearly a need for it to consolidate the Pancasila outlook and for the sake of the political culture we wish to build for the future.

We still have to work out exactly what it is about liberal democracy that Pancasila rejects. In reality, government officials, especially at the local level, regard anyone who does not agree with official policy as challenging the government itself. Does that not kill the democratic impulses in Pancasila itself? How can a mature consensus of opinion emerge without a thorough dialogue on every government initiative? Are differences of opinion not an important part of achieving a meaningful consensus?

We are also yet to formulate in unambiguous legal terms a distinction between differences of opinion and subversive acts. Are differences of opinion allowed to be publicised beyond a small circle to society at large? If they are, what kind of act can really be said to incite the public against the government? If publicising personal opinions which differ from government policy was not regarded as inflammatory, would it not become clear that only truly subversive acts – acts calculated to provoke riots or overthrow the government – would be punished?

Until these issues are clarified, the public will of course be reluctant to express any opinions whatsoever. As a result, debate will be restricted to the tiny group of people brave enough to express opinions, on the one hand, and the government, on the other. The difficulty is determining what the majority of the people really want. In a procedural sense the government will always be right because it has a formal mandate from the people. But is anybody infallible, including the government's decision-makers?

What is the use of the representative institutions that we have gone to so much trouble to set up? With the wider society wholly silent, how is it possible for the people's representatives to measure public opinion and provide the feedback that is needed by the executive? Is it any surprise that most of the people's representatives at the central and regional levels only pay lip service to 'public opinion'? Are we not also to blame for having these kinds of representatives?

We need seriously to discuss our attitude towards liberalism. In our political culture we associate liberal democracy with competition for competition's sake and have rejected it because of the excesses it brought us. Many see the difficulties inherent in balancing individual and collective rights as a danger to Pancasila's integralist worldview. Liberal democracy considers contradiction to be the foundation of its political culture, whereas Pancasila specifically rejects it. At least that is our government's official interpretation.

But there is more to liberalism than the kind of adversarial politics associated with liberal democracy. It is also a philosophy that regards human rights as important. It believes in the absolute necessity of upholding the sovereignty of law and demands equal treatment of all citizens before the law without regard to ethnicity, culture, or religion. It even protects those who have different opinions than the majority. In other words, liberalism has the values that support a high civilisation. Indeed, if we are honest we have to admit that it embraces the same lofty goals and noble values as Pancasila!

We can be Pancasilaists and liberals at the same time. The two viewpoints do not necessarily conflict, even though they produce different political cultures. The logical conclusion is to figure out how to establish a mature relationship between Pancasila and beliefs like liberalism. Incongruence in one respect does not mean total conflict between Pancasila and such beliefs.

If we do not make an effort to establish this kind of relationship, Pancasila will end up in confrontation with beliefs like liberalism. Pancasila's efforts to correct the excesses [of other ideologies] will then lead to Pancasila chauvinism. Such exclusivism endangers the survival of Pancasila itself by turning it into an authoritarian and anti-democratic ideology.

But do we have the desire and the courage to do this? That is the basic problem. And it is the key to the question of how we are to live in the future.

Notes

1　General Amir Machmud was the Interior Minister who earned the nickname 'bulldozer' for his efforts to secure a Golkar victory in both the 1971 and 1977 general elections.
2　Srimulat is the name of a famous comedy troupe.
3　H.M. Kamal, A.Y. Mokoginta, Suyitno Sukirno, M. Jasin, H. Ali Sadikin, Prof. Dr Mr Kasman Singodimedjo, M. Radjab Ranggasoli, Bachrun Martosukarto, Abdul Mu'thi S.H., M. Amin Ely, Ir HM Sanusi, Mohammad Natsir, Ibrahim Madylao, M.Ch. Ibrahim, Bustaman S.H., Burnahuddin Harahap S.H., Dra S.K. Trimurti, Chris Siner Keytimu, Maqdir Ismail, Alex Jusuf Malik S.H., Julius Hussein S.H., Darsjaf Rahman, Slamet Bratanata, Endy Syafruddin, Wachdiat Sukardi, Ibu D. Walandouw, Hoegeng, M. Sriamin, Edi Haryono, Dr A.H. Nasution, Drs A.M. Fatwa, Indra K. Budenani, Drs Sulaiman Hamzah, Haryono S. Yusuf, Ibrahim G. Zakir, Erza Mth Shah, Djalil Latuconsina, Djoddy Hippy, Bakri A.G. Tianlean, Dr Yudilherry Justam, Drs Med. Dody Ch. Suriadiredja, A. Shofandy Zakariyya, A. Bachar Mu'id, Mahyuddin Nawawi, Sjafruddin Prawiranegara S.H., Manai Sophiaan, Moh Natsir, Anwar Harjono, Azis Saleh, Dr Haji Ali Akbar.
4　The editors wish to acknowledge that this translation is based in parts on one published by *Indonesia Reports* (Yayasan Lembaga Bantuan Hukum Indonesia 1987: 1–5).
5　Petrus refers to an army-run anti-gang campaign that saw thousands of suspected criminals executed without trial in 1983–5 (Bourchier 1990).

6 Islam out in the cold

It was obvious to most Muslim politicians by the mid-1970s that participation in Soeharto's New Order demanded compromise and more compromise. The government had prevented the resurrection of the modernist Masjumi and forced the remaining Muslim parties to dissolve themselves into a new entity with a decidedly non-Islamic name – the United Development Party (PPP) – and a pliant leadership. Malari, and the subsequent banning of Muslim newspapers, dealt a further blow.

Within the core institutions of the state, devout Muslims had been marginalised, sometimes to the point of exclusion. Javanist Muslims and Christians dominated the armed forces and the intelligence apparatus was under the sway of Ali Moertopo, Soeharto's political henchman who had stage-managed the wholesale transformation of Indonesia's political landscape. The key political think tank, Moertopo's Centre for Strategic and International Studies (CSIS), was effectively run by Chinese and Catholics. Golkar, too, preferred Christians and nominal Muslims, leaving many devout Muslim figures who had thrown in their lot with the government out in the cold. The frustrations this generated are illustrated in Reading 6.1, a 1973 newspaper article in which Golkar-aligned Muslim scholar Hasbullah Bakry warns the government of the explosive consequences of neglecting Indonesia's Muslim majority.

By the end of the 1970s little was left of the marriage between the army and Islam but memories of their post-1965 honeymoon and a shared loathing of the PKI, their vanquished but always latent foe. Disgruntlement and anger at the government were increasingly expressed during Friday prayer meetings in mosques and small prayer houses across the country, but particularly in urban slum areas. Frequently, recordings of sermons by popular figures like Tony Ardhie (later to be imprisoned) made their rounds in the political underground and even the general public. Many of these sermons protested at what was seen to be growing Chinese wealth through the development of business conglomerates enjoying state patronage. This was contrasted with the fate of the millions of rural and urban poor, the vast majority of whom were indigenous Muslims.

The issue that caused most consternation, if not outrage, among politically active Muslims in this period, though, was the government's push to make all political parties and social organisations adopt Pancasila as their sole ideological basis. Many organisations saw Islam as their reason for being, and interpreted the government's campaign as a direct assault on their religion. Why, they said, should they be forced to subordinate the holy precepts of Islam to the 'man-made' Pancasila? Why should they and their children be indoctrinated with 'Pancasila morality' when Islam already provided the guidance they needed? These sentiments are expressed forcefully in an open letter addressed to President Soeharto by Sjafruddin Prawiranegara, a former Masjumi politician and elder statesman of modernist political Islam (Reading 6.2).

While Sjafruddin's letter is reported to have greatly upset Soeharto (Awanohara 1983), the greater challenge for the New Order was to persuade religious youth organisations into the Pancasila fold. The most prestigious of these was the Muslim Students' Association (HMI), founded in Yogyakarta in 1947. In Reading 6.3 we present a 1984 statement by the HMI's leadership council rejecting the government's efforts to 'engineer' acceptance of its 'Pancasila as the sole principle' legislation. The 150,000-member national organisation was eventually cajoled into committing itself to Pancasila, but not before opponents set up a rival HMI, called the HMI–MPO, which outlived the New Order. Given the Islamist leanings of the HMI–MPO, it is interesting to note that the statement below consists almost entirely of constitutionalist and democratic arguments.

The massacre of dozens, possibly hundreds, of Muslim demonstrators in a crowded working-class neighbourhood near the Jakarta port of Tanjung Priok on the night of 12 September 1984 marked a historic low in relations between Muslims and the armed forces. Reading 6.4 is from a recording of a speech given only hours before the killings by Amir Biki, an informal Muslim leader who had enjoyed good relations with New Order figures dating from his participation in the movement to topple Sukarno. Tempers in the area were running high following reports that soldiers had desecrated a local prayer house by entering wearing muddy boots. Following a series of rousing speeches by Amir Biki and local preachers, angry crowds marched on a military post to demand the release of several people who had been arrested for setting fire to the offending soldier's motorbike. Some businesses were attacked and set alight along the way. The details of what happened were covered up, but most accounts suggest that the marchers, including Amir Biki, were simply gunned down en masse. Many Muslims blamed – and continue to blame – the massacre on Armed Forces Commander General Benny Moerdani, a Catholic whose failure to promote the careers of devout Muslims in the military led many to see him as hostile to Islam.

In the weeks after the Tanjung Priok killings, three bombs exploded in the Chinese-dominated business district of Jakarta, damaging two banks owned by Liem Sioe Liong, one of Soeharto's richest and most trusted business associates. The government arrested several prominent Muslims in connection with these bombings, including H.R. Dharsono (see Reading 5.4). The government's response to Tanjung Priok and to the bombings, however, only served to underline the degree to which it had itself become alienated from Muslim sentiment in the *kampungs* (urban neighbourhoods).

While those who marched at Tanjung Priok may have represented the urban underclass, there were also many Muslims who prospered under the New Order. Better funding for schools and universities opened up opportunities for those who could afford them, leading by the mid-1980s to the growth of a Muslim middle class not simply of traders, as in the past, but of doctors, lawyers, journalists and other urban professionals. This brought into being a new constituency, which Soeharto later decided to court by sponsoring the formation of the Indonesian Muslim Intellectuals' Association (ICMI) in 1990. In the last reading (6.5) the Nahdlatul Ulama leader Abdurrahman Wahid, writing in 1986, briefly charts the transformation of the Muslim middle class and warns of an emerging schism over the proper relationship between Islam and state power. He argues that Muslims should regard Islam as a source of inspiration and motivation, but not as the charter for an all-embracing social system backed by the state. As Hefner (1993) has pointed out, Wahid's article anticipated by four years the controversies that arose in the Muslim community with the formation of ICMI. Wahid himself was to play a leading role in opposing the cooption of Islam by the state in the 1990s.

6.1 K.H. Hasbullah Bakry: critique of Pancasila democracy

This reading comes from a critique of Ali Moertopo's tract *The Acceleration and Modernization of 25 Years' Development* (1973) published over two weeks in *Harian Kami*, one of several newspapers banned in 1974. Hasbullah Bakry, a well-known lawyer and Islamic scholar, wrote it at a time when Muslim groups were fighting a losing battle for representation in the new political dispensation. He was aligned with GUPPI (the Association for Renewal of Islamic Education), a minor organisation of *kyais* which was inflated into a nationwide body to mobilise Muslim support for Golkar. The following extracts are from *Harian Kami*, 9 and 17 August 1973. (Emphasis as in the original.)

It is now *eight years* since the 30 September Movement/PKI, the deaths of the PKI leaders and the ousting of their backers (Sukarno and Subandrio). The internal security situation in Indonesia is far more settled than it was then. There is now much less chance of PKI guerrillas threatening us. *Have we not now come to the point where we need to set aside intelligence*

*methods and do more to advertise the benefits of the Pancasila democracy
of which we are so proud?* In my opinion, the way to showcase *Pancasila
democracy* in this early phase is as follows:

Let *it not* be forgotten that Pancasila democracy is *democracy*, not
guided democracy and also not *prefabricated democracy*. It is essential
that in its day-to-day practice democracy provides leadership and allows
people the freedom either to support the government or to correct it (i.e. as
part of an opposition). It should always be remembered that a government
without an opposition is totalitarian. People speak through the political
parties, namely the Development Democracy Party (PDP)[1] and the United
Development Party (PPP), or through Golkar, which together make up the
representative bodies that either *support* or *oppose* the government. The
decision whether to support or oppose the government rests with the
central executives of these parties and Golkar. *Therefore the fate of
Pancasila democracy depends on whoever is chosen to lead these political
parties and Golkar. If they are people of strong character and democratic
conviction,* they will, God willing, reject all temptations to *betray democracy* or lead us towards a *sham democracy, even if this means their
removal from positions of luxurious opportunity such as were enjoyed
during Sukarno's Old Order.*

The track record of the executive bodies of the political parties and
Golkar is in my view neither democratic nor in accordance with the aspirations of their supporters. The formation of Golkar's central executive, for
example, has *greatly disappointed* its constituency, 95 per cent of which is
surely Muslim. (Statistics from the 1971 elections show that most
Christians voted for Partindo and the Catholic Party.) GUPPI, which
encouraged Muslims to vote for Golkar, did not get a single seat on
Golkar's executive. Christians, on the other hand, somehow happen to
account for around a third of the Golkar executive. Stranger still, most of
these Christians belong to one particular ethnic group. This undemocratic
stacking of the executive has led to undemocratic policies, such as the
*rejection of all GUPPI-nominated candidates for positions in the religious
affairs department.* Moreover, some of Golkar's activities both inside and
outside the legislature could be seen as *disadvantaging Islam.*

The story goes that Golkar is to convene a national congress this
coming September. According to *Sinar Harapan* (19 June 1973) the
congress organisers have been making arrangements not only for the 3,000
delegates but also for a team of 1,000 (note: *one thousand*) entertainers. If
this story is correct, I have my doubts that there will be much that is
democratic about the election of the new central executive at this very
important congress, because the delegates are to be serenaded until late
every night by the performances. I write this not to tarnish Golkar's reputation. On the contrary, I wish Golkar to successfully lead the way in the
building of democracy in Indonesia. It is in the *public interest*, in the state's
interest, to *strive for democracy*, and this *towers high above the interests*

of any particular organisation such as Golkar, GUPPI or individual departments. As for myself, as a GUPPI *ulama* I *appeal* to all Muslims to support Golkar, just as I have in the past. On nearly *50 occasions* I have stood before Muslim crowds applying all forms of Islamic argumentation and justification to urge them to *vote for Golkar* for the sake of national development in accordance with the teachings of Islam.

In the name of the Muslim community – which sponsored GUPPI – I request the attention of President Soeharto to personally *take the matter in hand* and reform the Golkar central executive following the congress. Should this appeal of mine not be heeded and GUPPI again be excluded from the Golkar executive, I am fully convinced that in the coming general election Golkar will have *great difficulty in winning over the Muslims* who voted for it in 1971. Why? Because only the hypocrites, the unenlightened syncretists among the Muslim community would want to vote for a group who they regard as being hostile to the interests of Islam in Indonesia. Muslims who vote for Golkar in such circumstances would certainly feel they had sinned.

There is no question that the armed forces [have] played a key role in preserving national unity in the face of political upheavals (such as the PRRI/Permesta rebellion) and in saving the state from ideological conflict (when confronting the Darul Islam rebellion and the PKI). The dual function doctrine helps the armed forces to continue in this role and we support them as long as they are regulated by law and are not arbitrarily and *cynically* exploited by one small group wishing *to further its own interests.*

State policy is armed forces policy. Therefore we expect to see armed forces policy reflect that of the state. Because the state is a national institution, the armed forces must also have a *national outlook*. If we accept that Islam should not be given favourable treatment, this should also apply to Christianity, for instance. And if we accept that preference should not be given to the Javanese, this should also apply to Bataks, for example. If we think nationally, it is only reasonable to start by looking at the numerical representation of various groups and religions in Indonesia. It is *rubbish* to claim that the followers of a certain religion or members of a certain ethnic group have a higher percentage of clever people than do those of another religion.[2] Such claims only mask the devious intentions of a small group seeking to ride roughshod over the opportunities that should belong to the numerically larger group.

I need to *stress* this point to stave off the *increasingly negative sentiment within the armed forces towards a certain ethnic group and a certain religion*. The danger posed by such sentiment is *much greater than that brought about by ideological differences*, because it will *tear the country apart* and lead to the kind of bloodshed that we are now seeing in India, Palestine and the Philippines. The dual function of the armed forces ought to help *neutralise* (rather than *stimulate*) this kind of sentiment.

On this last point I request the attention of the president, the *supreme commander*. As a military man I hope he will appreciate what is implied in this article – people whisper about it all the time – and *intervene to ensure that the armed forces' dual function is really and truly implemented in the national interest for the sake of the development of the nation and the state*.

6.2 Sjafruddin Prawiranegara: don't let Pancasila kill Islam

On 7 July 1983, 72-year-old Sjafruddin Prawiranegara wrote an open letter to President Soeharto to protest against the provision in the draft law on social organisations that required parties and societies to adopt Pancasila as their sole ideological foundation. As a committed Muslim, a former president of the Republic's Emergency Government in 1948 and an outspoken Masjumi politician in the Sukarno era, Sjafruddin was particularly angry about the impact he believed the legislation would have on Islam. His letter conveys in blunt terms the sentiments of several Muslim groups at the time. The extracts below are from a translation published by the editors of the Cornell University journal *Indonesia* (no. 38, October 1984: 74–83), with minor emendations based on a copy of the original text (Prawiranegara 1983: 7–18).

His Excellency
The President of the Republic of Indonesia
26 Ramadhan 1403H
Jakarta, 7 July 1983

With all respect,
Assalamu'alaikum w.w.

In connection with the efforts of the government of the Republic of Indonesia – after the MPR/DPR proclaimed that Pancasila was to become the *azas tunggal*, the sole foundation for the political parties and Golkar – to extend the enforcement of this principle to all types of social organisations in Indonesia, and also in view of the anxiety and unrest thereby aroused among the majority of the Muslim community, I feel compelled, in order to maintain a feeling of unity and justice in the Indonesian nation, to convey my opinion on the question of this 'sole foundation' to you, in the sincere hope that you will be willing to order the cessation of efforts to enforce the Pancasila as the sole foundation of all social organisations....

Pancasila was not intended to become the foundation of citizens' organisations, whether of a political character, or of a social or other character.

From the excerpts I have taken from Bung Karno's [1945] address, it is clear that Pancasila was intended to be the foundation of the state, and the basis for the *constitution*. This means that Pancasila principles have been incorporated in, have been realised through, the articles of the 1945 Constitution. Anybody who disagrees with the 1945 Constitution – and everybody who regards himself as a citizen of the Republic of Indonesia must agree with the 1945 Constitution – implicitly and automatically recognises and is committed to Pancasila. This means that whichever religion, belief, or ideology an individual or group of citizens espouses, they are committed to live and work in a harmonious and peaceful manner within and outside the Republic of Indonesia. Or, to borrow Bung Karno's words: 'The Indonesian state that we are founding must be a "*gotong-royong*" [mutual assistance] state.'

This idea of *gotong-royong* implies that each person joining in this *gotong-royong* preserves his own identity and personality. The Muslims remain Muslim, the Christians remain Christian, the Buddhists remain Buddhist, the Hindus remain Hindu, and so on. But if Christians are no longer permitted to form organisations based on Christian principles, whether Protestant or Catholic, and if Muslims cannot establish organisations based upon Islamic principles, and the same is the case for other citizens espousing other religions or ideologies, but all citizens are allowed only to have organisations based upon Pancasila, then Indonesia, this fertile and prosperous country, with its many hills and valleys, must, as it were, be transformed into a barren Sahara desert, consisting only of stones and undifferentiated particles of sand.

From a Pancasila State as conceived by the 'founding fathers' of our beloved Republic of Indonesia, a democratic republic, Indonesia will become a national-socialist, i.e. Fascist, state just as bad and brutal as a communist state.

If Pancasila has to be regarded not merely as the foundation of the state but as the basis of human life, then the religions revealed by Almighty God (or so perceived) will have to be exchanged for an ideology, an ideology that claims not to be a religion but which acts as though it wants to replace existing religions.

Just consider: there used to be no such thing as 'Pancasila morality' because problems of morality were left up to the individual religions. Then a committee was established consisting of people regarded as 'smart' – not a single *ulama* of good standing in the Muslim community was included – and this committee of smart people drafted a kind of holy writ filled with moral prescriptions that had to be studied and practised by all our citizens. Yet these prescriptions could not all be swallowed by Muslims, for many of them contained tenets in conflict with Islamic teachings.

Now that a 'Pancasila morality' has been drawn up, we are bound to start hearing about 'Pancasila law', 'Pancasila economics', etc.

Indeed, as you yourself, Mr President, have pointed out two weeks ago in your address during the 'Nuzulul Qur'an' commemoration on 27 June, Pancasila is not a religion and cannot ever replace religion. This is certainly true. However, even if Pancasila is not a religion, with the power that lies in your hands and with the support of the parliament – which reflects the sovereignty of the president more than that of the people – Pancasila is, in effect, being enforced as a comprehensive religion that touches on all aspects of the lives of Indonesian citizens....

In your address commemorating the Nuzulul Qur'an to which I referred earlier, Mr President, you yourself pointed out: 'Pancasila and religion are not in opposition to each other and must not be set against each other.'

If this was the situation, why must Islam, the foundation of the one remaining Islamic political party, the United Development Party, be replaced by Pancasila? And why does the Minister of Youth and Sports Abdul Gafur try with all his might to replace the Islamic basis of the Muslim Students' Association (HMI) by the Pancasila? After all, the Islamic basis of the political parties and social organisations has long existed and been recognised as not in conflict, but rather in accord, with the 1945 Constitution. Why only now must Pancasila replace Islam as their foundation? What crime has the PPP, or the HMI, or any other Muslim organisation committed?...

If Muslims are no longer allowed to establish Islamic associations – whether political organisations or social organisations – then Islam will come to be regarded as a private matter, which is completely contrary to Islamic teachings. The Islamic religion is not merely a private matter, but is also, indeed primarily, a matter of the *umat* [community]. The *sholat* [act of worship], for example, may be performed individually, but communal prayers are mandatory, i.e. where a number of Muslims wish to perform the required prayers, namely the five daily prayers. Community is also at the heart of the *zakat* [religious tax] which aims to bridge the gap between the rich and the poor, even though although those receiving the *zakat* do not have to be Muslims, but can be any poor person in need of help.

To put it briefly, if the Indonesian Muslim community is to be prohibited from establishing and maintaining Islamic associations, whether in the political field or in other social fields, this not only contravenes the 1945 Constitution – and thus the Pancasila itself, but in practice is an attempt to kill Islam – with Pancasila! As a human creation, Pancasila can be interpreted and applied according to the thoughts and wishes of people, namely the people in power, the power-holders controlling the armed forces! In the long run religious teachings – and it is Islamic teachings that I, along with tens of millions of Indonesian Muslims, am particularly concerned with here – will be suffocated by Pancasila morality, Pancasila economics, Pancasila law, and all other such Pancasila offspring. We are already seeing the results of this in alcoholism and narcotics, promiscuous sex and the proliferation of venereal disease in society, particularly among teenagers, rampant criminality and corruption, alongside measures to combat them, which on the one hand are completely ineffective, and on the other hand show symptoms of no longer being under the control of the law....

If this matter of the sole foundation is also to apply to all social organisations, the situation for Christians, whether Protestant or Catholic, will not be as bad as for Muslims. They have their priests and clergymen, who lead the organisation of the Christians known as the 'church'. The mosque is not the same as the church. A mosque is a place of worship, managed by a committee, whose members are not sacral officials such as priests or clergymen. But a church consists of people of a particular denomination led by a hierarchy of priests or clergymen. Every church has at least one, but usually several, even possibly thousands of individual churches spread throughout the world, as for instance the Roman Catholic church. Thus their 'church' is a fortress for the followers of a specific Christian denomination.

If Muslim social organisations are banned, mosques will be very fragile fortresses, because their committees can be captured by Golkar minions who profess to be Muslims but are more obedient to the president and to other superiors than they are to Allah, His Prophet, and His Holy Scriptures.

I cannot assess the position of the Buddhist and Hindu communities, but they also have their religious leaders, similar to the Christian priests and clergymen, and they too cannot easily be interfered with by Pancasila. The weakness, but also the strength of Islam, lies in the fact that its *ulama* and *kyai* are not like Christian priests and clergymen. Because of this it appears that Islam can easily be subdued and dominated by temporal rulers. But make no mistake! The True God ultimately protects Islam....

I hope that, after you have read this letter of mine, you will agree at the very least to halt the enforcement of Pancasila as the 'sole foundation' [for social organisations], in accordance with the recommendation offered by Mr Hardi in *Kompas* of last 4 July.

But it would be better still if the application of the sole foundation idea was also to be revoked for the political parties, particularly the PPP, and that all citizens be allowed to establish any organisation whatsoever, so long as they aim to work for the benefit of Indonesian society, and in pursuit of their objectives they refrain from all illegal actions, specifically the use of force. This would be in accordance with Article 28 of the constitution, which guarantees the principles of freedom of association and assembly and of the expression of opinion in speech and writing, as was laid out by Bung Karno in his address at the end of the BPUPKI's session on 1 June 1945,[3] and also in accordance with the promises of the New Order at the beginning of its career – namely your promises to implement the 1945 Constitution in a pure and principled manner....

Wabillahi taufiq wal hidayah
Wassalam
Sjafruddin Prawiranegara

6.3 The Indonesian Muslim Students' Association: no more political engineering

The refusal of the influential Muslim Students' Association (HMI) to accept Pancasila as its sole basis in 1983 caused the government a major headache. Following pressure from Youth Affairs Minister Abdul Gafur and serious conflict within the organisation, HMI general chair Harry Azhar Aziz dropped his opposition and agreed to the government's wishes in 1986. In this speech to a parliamentary hearing read on 20 September 1984, the HMI's leadership council details its objections to the social organisations bill. It is translated from a booklet entitled *Pandangan Kritis terhadap RUU Keormasan* (1984: 6–15).

Contemporary Indonesian politics is marked by a tendency towards the centralisation of power. This is being done through the engineering of political power structures, revealing a crisis in commitment to democratic values.

There are several [other] features that characterise contemporary Indonesian politics: pervasive political intervention in economic institutions; restrictions on the right to a basic level of social welfare; political forces that are simply accessories to the power structures; diminishing academic freedom caused by turning the heads of tertiary education institutions into undisputed rulers; the failure of people's representative institutions to carry out their true function of channelling the demands of the people; and the appropriation of judicial powers by the executive.

Political engineering of this kind is the product of a political culture so bereft of self-confidence that those who have been entrusted by the people could lose all sense of responsibility. Political engineering of this sort is driven by a desire for more power that could continue on, unconstrained by the popular will.

The five bills on politics that the government has presented, and which have become the 'issue of the day', are part and parcel of its political engineering effort. They seek to govern not only how organisations are run but also how to think. For example, the attempt to make Pancasila the sole principle of social organisations, and, even worse, of religious organisations or religiously oriented social organisations, can be read as a unilateral attempt to engineer political thinking, even social thinking.

In formulating the law on social organisations, the following matters should be considered:

1   A law on social organisations is essentially required to provide legal guarantees and protection of the basic rights of the citizen in social, national, and state life, on the basis of Pancasila and the 1945 Constitution. [It should] guarantee and protect the liberty and

freedom of the citizen to congregate, associate and express thoughts and opinions verbally or in writing....

2   As a law, the social organisations legislation is legally subordinate to the constitution. Therefore it cannot arbitrarily eliminate or diminish the freedoms and liberties of the citizen contained in Articles 28 and 29 of the 1945 Constitution....

3   The liberties and freedoms guaranteed and protected by the 1945 Constitution include:

  a   The freedom and liberty of citizens to congregate, which entails the liberty and freedom to hold and attend meetings, to hold conventions, congresses, conferences, and the freedom to hold consultations.

  b   The liberty and freedom of citizens to associate entails the freedom of citizens to form, shape, and sustain an organisation. Also, the freedom and liberty of citizens to join whatever organisations they are interested in.

  c   The liberty and freedom of citizens to carry out activities decided by an organisation.

  d   The liberty and freedom of a group of citizens to determine the foundation, principles, objectives, character, nature, and program of the organisation it forms.

  e   The liberty and freedom of citizens to embrace a religion and to worship according to their religion and belief entails the liberty and freedom to live according to the principles of their religion.

4   A law on social organisations should provide legal guarantees and protection of the right of every social organisation to manage and govern itself, not furnish the executive with the authority and legal right to disrupt and intervene in the freedom and liberty of citizens in their civic life....

6   Social organisations have the liberty to decide on their own organisational structure. Thus, every social organisation has the right to have a youth, women's, and professional section, as well as others, if they are deemed necessary.

7   A law on social organisations should guarantee to citizens who associate in religious organisations the freedom to live according to religious principles. Religious organisations must be given the liberty to make religion the source of their values and their behaviour, as well as their foundation.

8   The legal right of social organisations to exist implies that they cannot be frozen and disbanded. If a social organisation undertakes activities that are categorised as being against the law, it is the leadership of the organisation that should be penalised, not the organisation. And any such punitive action should be undertaken through the courts....

10 The Muslim Students' Association aims to realise the five noble values
   of Pancasila in national and state life (in fact they are already
   mentioned in HMI's charter) in the context of serving Almighty God.
   Thus, for the HMI, the realisation of Pancasila is a transcendental
   responsibility.
11 Placing Islam as the basis of the HMI is predicated upon the conviction that Islam is a true and perfect teaching. For the HMI, Islam is
   not just an organisational symbol or identity, but the source of the
   values and of the very process of thinking and acting. At the same time
   it is the source of the HMI's motivation to realise Pancasila. It is only
   with Islam as its basis that the HMI can be accountable to God and
   the people and nation of Indonesia in realising an Indonesian society
   based on Pancasila.

The central board of the HMI has found the following problems with
the social organisations bill presented by the government to the DPR:

1 The bill appears to be an attempt by the government to secure a legal
  right to intervene and interfere with the rights of social organisations.
  This will lead to the executive increasing its power, enabling it to
  erode both the individual and collective rights of citizens (see Articles
  8 and 12).
2 In its provisions on freezing and disbanding organisations it shifts
  authority from the judiciary to the executive, threatening to destroy
  the justice system in the Indonesian Republic, based as it is on the rule
  of law (see Articles 13–16).
3 The bill only governs organisations that already exist. There is nothing
  in it that gives an idea of how a new social organisation might be
  formed. Article 8 even enables the unification, merger and disbanding
  of social organisations so that they can be transformed into other
  organisations that the government approves of.
4 Article 8 also gives the executive the authority to limit the activities
  and operations of an organisation on the basis of how it is classified.
5 The Article (no. 13) that governs the freezing of an organisation's
  board or central board, contains no clear criteria, opening the way
  for interpretations that will disadvantage social organisations and
  eventually undermine the freedoms and liberties of citizens as a
  whole.

As one of the five political bills, the social organisations bill is part of a
concerted effort on the part of the government to manipulate non-government or non-bureaucratic social organisations. Making Pancasila the sole
principle of social organisations will drive all religious members of society
to think in a monolithic, apathetic, and apolitical way, without dialogue. If
this process continues, Indonesian national political life will be increas-

ingly undemocratic. Our national culture, in any case, contains authoritarian – even totalitarian – values, which we naturally do not want to encourage.

In principle, the involvement of the broad public in the national decision-making process is important for the government. With the public involved, the government can understand the intentions, interests, and wishes of those it governs, and, in turn, ensure that its decisions are really made for their benefit. But if the public is allowed to participate only on a monolithic basis and their opinions are never any different from those of the government, then the only source of political legitimation for the government's decisions will be the government itself, and of course this is no way to make effective decisions....

Nothing can eliminate the diverse and multi-religious character of social life in Indonesia. Both as individuals and collectively, citizens have a right to decide and to practise the teachings of their own religion, and this right needs to be protected by law.

6.4 Amir Biki: let me die for the Islamic world!

This speech, transcribed from a widely circulated tape recording, was made at a protest meeting in the poor Tanjung Priok area in north Jakarta on 12 September 1984 shortly before the speaker and up to 300 locals were gunned down by the military. The protest meeting was held to demand the release of four residents detained after burning a motorbike belonging to the neighbourhood non-commissioned officer (*Babinsa*) after the officer had allegedly ordered his men to enter a small prayer house (*musholla*) in their muddy boots. The following excerpts are reproduced here, with minor emendations, from a translation that appeared in *Indonesia Reports' Human Rights Supplement* (January–February 1990: 3–8). (Text in round brackets indicates crowd responses and atmospherics.)

Calm down please, calm down....I am not making jokes. This time there will be no jokes...I am asking you, my friends, is it appropriate for an officer to enter a *musholla* with his boots on??? (No!! No!! uproar)

Patience, my friends, patience...it is important that I tell you this so that all of you will understand why our preachers always say that the Islamic community is being discredited, the Islamic community is treated as nothing!!! My friends, they dare to do this while we are in a state of readiness, when we are in a heated mood, my friends!! My friends, perhaps I'll pass it on to the authorities from this pulpit. Do you understand the restlessness among the Muslim community? I'd like to pass it on from the pulpit tonight. Do you realise the restlessness of the Muslim community?...

You must understand that the social organisations law, or rather the social organisations bill that will be made law, deals with, among other things, the issue of Pancasila as sole principle. For a long time, (partially unintelligible) I was one of the generation of '66 leaders supporting the New Order. I told my friends that we should return to the Pancasila and constitution in a consistent way. We had practised this since we abandoned the Old Order. But what has happened, my friends? Lately our national leadership – let me frankly say it – Soeharto himself has deviated from the Pancasila. Perhaps you have often heard this from our preachers at youth Qur'an readings how he has deviated from Pancasila and the constitution, which were the very basis of the New Order. Consequently, my friends, I decided to leave my group, Fosko '66 [1966 Communications and Study Forum], and returned to join in the struggle of my preacher friends and all of you, leaving ourselves to the mercy of God by standing up for Islam, my friends!!...

My friends, from this pulpit I would like to stress that the Muslim community does not hate Christians. No, my friends. But in their judgements, or perhaps their treatment, or in issuing permits, our officials ought to be fair. I myself had a rather unpleasant experience during the construction of the Al A'raf mosque in Sukapura [built by Biki in Tanjung Priok]. It is necessary you know that at that time the committee was forced to pay one and a half million rupiah for the permit. We had to go through a long procedure during which our mosque was closed down on the grounds that it didn't have a permit to operate. So, my friends, what I have just told you was not because we did not agree or did not like it. If you want to build a church, you may certainly do so, but do it in your own community, not in the middle of a Muslim neighbourhood!! This contradicts the government's own regulations! (uproar) I know this strongly contradicts the decision of two ministers. I understand such things, believe me.

And so, my friends, I informed the authorities and went unheeded and damage occurred. What our friends did, our Muslim youth, was branded as coercive, as undermining the authority of the government. I ask you all, have we been undermining the government? (No!!!) We have never undermined the government. So why does it always make things so difficult for us??

My friends, here is some more information. Perhaps today if you read *Kompas* – read *Kompas* – you open its pages, and on the inner pages, if I'm not mistaken on page four, there are the readers' letters. In this section someone named Silitonga – they printed his address – mentioned an incident (rising voices)...I ask those sitting on my right to keep calm. I need to explain this so that we all know and perhaps won't be branded trouble-makers. The newspaper discusses who has the most right to defend the people. My friends, that reader's letter speaks about the taking over of land belonging to the people. I state this so that the authorities note that I read this in the newspaper. If this news is false, investigate the paper. This letter mentions the takeover of land belonging to the people. They were forced by local officials, local civil servants, to give up their land, to be sold to...who else if not Chinese.... Isn't this just too much, my friends!! (Biki's voice rises, huge uproar)

Be patient, my friends, patience. I don't need to hear your answers right now. I ask you to keep calm....The authorities can read that, the letter to the editor, about takeovers. Now, think of all the families uncertain about their future because they have lost their land, have no homes, and are in despair because the North Jakarta mayor's office pushed them out. We know these cases very well. In the area near Papanggo, my friends, Lati, in the area of Lati, in the area of Warakan, Papanggo [North Jakarta]...we see takeovers and evictions, again for the interests of the Chinese, my friends!!! (uproar)

Yes, in a little while you will hear instructions on what we have to do tonight. (uproar) Patience. Hear me out. I am asking you to be quiet for a moment. The rowdy ones are not our friends. (quieting down) Do try to be quiet.

Friends, I relate this all to you to make clear our views that have been misinterpreted by the authorities all this time. Then there is something else, friends, about what they call family planning. You see it on television; Pak Harto talking with mothers....But you know how many mothers have had to go to hospital because our civil servants forced them to join family planning. There are many stories about this in the villages, my friends, and in the city neighbourhoods.

If one does join family planning, what's the term...those who take the spiral [IUD], what's it called, I don't understand it...anyway, the acceptors. Those who don't become acceptors will have difficulties renewing their identity cards. They lose their access to certain privileges, all sorts of things. These are the things that have perhaps caused great restlessness in the Muslim community. It is necessary for me to inform the authorities about it from this forum.

Now, my friends, we go back to the incident that has troubled us all, the incident at the *musholla* in Alley IV. My dear friends, God willing there will be no downpour, my friends. Not even bloodshed will make us retreat from this place!!! (uproar) Do you agree??? (huge uproar)

I'll continue. Hang on, hang on, there will be some instructions in a moment. I know you are impatient. That incident in Alley IV, friends, is now being twisted around and soon may be spread through the media and presented as if it had damaged ABRI's image, as if the youths at the mosque had dared to oppose ABRI. This perhaps is what will be published in the papers. I was sure that the authorities were not that stupid, particularly our leaders, our elders who are serving in Hankam [the Defence and Security Ministry] or the Kodam [(Jakarta) Regional Military Command]. My friends, they have brains and surely they will determine the truth, I am sure of it. But as for those officials, those corrupt ABRI men, those ABRI men who terrorise the people, we plead with our authorities to punish them!! (Right!! uproar) Otherwise, the Muslim community will punish them!! (Right!! uproar) Do you agree? (Yes!! uproar)

You know the incident has already claimed victims, my friends. There have been victims. The motorbike belonging to the Babinsa was burned. The Babinsa's motorbike was burned, my friends. The Babinsa who ordered his men to enter the prayer house – his motorbike was burned. Then, the saddest thing, my friends, is that four of our colleagues are being held in detention at the Kodim [Sub-district Military Command]. (huge uproar)

I want all of you to be quiet!! Those on the left, be quiet!! Those on the right, be quiet!! Quiet, please!! I am going to tell you something that may be important for me and for all of us.

My friends, despite all the efforts of the caretakers of the *musholla*, of our youth, to explain, to clear up this matter, these ABRI people have only further infuriated the Muslim community. So, if I have said that they have twisted the facts around, these are the facts that speak, my friends. Many of our colleagues are willing, and have vowed before me, that they are willing to die or be killed so long as they stand on the side of truth, my friends. (uproar)....

So, my friends, I ask you, I ask you through this forum, I ask the officers...release our friends detained in the Kodim and Korem [Military District Command]. Do you agree?? (Yes!!)

Patience. Patience, my friends, patience. Once more, I ask you all. Through this forum, I ask the authorities, release our friends, whether from the Kodim or Korem. Do you agree?? (Yes!!) Are you with us? (Yes!!! uproar)...Wait! Wait, my friends. I ask you to wait calmly. Wait for your instructions. Quiet! (uproar) We ask you all to keep quiet....

Calm down, friends, calm down!!Those on the left will follow the orders which have been drawn up.... Then, those on the right will be led by the Pekoja group....You know the Pekoja group? (Yes!)...(unintelligible) If at 11 tonight our friends are not turned over to us, we will make blood flow in Priok!! (huge uproar)....

My dear friends, it is already too late for me personally. The authorities perhaps already consider me crazy. Let them see me that way, that is their business. And perhaps, friends, this first time I have been on stage will be the last time, my friends. Tonight, the rifles are already pointed at my head. (uproar) But I will state this. Let me die for the Islamic world!!! (uproar)

You need to know my view, friends. You need to know that I do not want to be arrested. I don't want to be summoned! I will go alone to the authorities. I said I don't want to be arrested. This means I don't want to have a warrant for my arrest sent to me, or the telephone ring with a voice saying, Amir Biki, please come to our office and me replying, I am coming. That's the way it is. If you intend to take me away by force, you will see what I am holding (unintelligible) to defend Islam!!! (uproar)

Allahu Akbar! (Allahu Akbar)
Allahu Akbar! (Allahu Akbar)
Allahu Akbar! (Allahu Akbar)
Friends, I ask you all to sit down. All sit down!! The time will be at 11
tonight. Wait for orders from the preacher. Now Syarifin Maloko will
come onto the stage and speak. We will give the preacher until 11 o'clock.
If at 11 they are still not here, then we will carry out the orders, my
friends. (uproar) We are ready to defy the flow of blood!!! (big uproar)

6.5 Abdurrahman Wahid: choices facing the Muslim middle class

In this article, written in 1986, Abdurrahman Wahid foreshadows an
important debate that was to emerge with the founding of ICMI, the
Indonesian Muslim Intellectuals' Association. Wahid, who was broadly
sympathetic to the government's attempts to detach religion from politics in the 1980s, argues here for an inclusive non-sectarian vision of
Islam in society. This lightly edited extract is taken from Wahid (1990:
22–4).

In the past, a Muslim middle class was clearly identified, in the rural areas,
with rich farmers and traders, and in the urban areas with manufacturers
of batik, kretek cigarettes, leather goods, silver and goldwares. This
entrepreneurial nature of the Muslim middle class stood in naked contrast
to the traditional indigenous ruling class in nearly everything. It looked as
though that middle class was as far away from that ruling class as was the
Chinese middle class. Even though it did not lose altogether the common
cultural perspectives of the indigenous peoples in that vast archipelago,
there was so little in common between the Muslim middle class and the
indigenous ruling class that common responses to the political rule,
economic domination and cultural penetration of the West were not able
to grow. In fact, the so-called *divide-et-impera* strategy of the Dutch colonial rulers was as much the result as the cause of so many rifts among the
indigenous rulers and the ruled.

When the political approach of the Muslim *ulama* counter-elite failed to
achieve the basic objective of an Islamic state, the Muslim middle class developed a dual response to colonial rule: it integrated itself into the political
struggle for independence led by the so-called nationalist leaders, but at the
same time maintained a certain distance from other indigenous groupings
culturally. It even used the second part of that dual response, i.e. nurturing an
independent cultural identity for Muslims, to augment the first part, resulting
in the use of Islam as a political as well as cultural resistance to colonial rule.
Even when it modified the dual response a little, as a matter of survival, by
sending its children to Westernised schools (in contrast to the *ulama* elite's
refusal to do so), the Muslim middle class insisted on maintaining its own

'cultural identity' by having its own literature (as represented by the works of Hamka and his like), arts (represented by Arabic calligraphy instead of paintings) and education (represented by 'Modern Islamic schools').

Just prior to, and right after, independence, the Muslim middle class set aside that dual response and demanded formalisation of Islamic teachings as the political ideology of the whole nation or, failing that objective, as the law of the nation. It did this by supporting political leaders with the same commitment, giving rise to such political leaders as M. Natsir, A. Wahid Hasjim and Abikusno Tjokrosujoso. This attitude culminated in the deadlock within the Constituent Assembly in 1959, when the body failed to ratify the 1945 Constitution as the basic legal framework of the state.

That failure resulted in political developments that have ended for now the aspiration to formalise Islam in the state's life. This situation is accompanied by the demise of Muslim entrepreneurs and the emergence of professionals, civil servants, intellectuals and military officers as the backbone of the Muslim middle class. This middle class has begun to reassert Islam's role in the life of its members. This rising consciousness of Islam takes place at a critical time for the nation, i.e. deciding what types of action need to be taken to ensure a democratic government, the rule of law and economic justice for Indonesia in the future.

Different Muslim groups have responded by formulating two main strategies to achieve those objectives. The first idealises Islam as the only feasible social system able to maintain true democracy, strict adherence to law and economic justice. The so-called 'Islamisation process' taking place in the life of the whole nation should be used to promote the idea of an 'Islamic society' in Indonesia. This strategy of struggling for an Islamic society in Indonesia naturally collides with the other strategy. According to the so-called 'soft' groups [on the other hand], Islam plays an important role in the life of the nation, if only for the reason that Muslims constitute the overwhelming majority of the population. But the role Islam should play is not derived from the idealisation of itself as the only alternative to the existing situation, but rather as the inspirational base for a national framework of a democratic society. As such, Islam is not an alternative to other social systems, but a complementary factor among a wide spectrum of other factors in the nation's life. Islam, according to this view, is not an imperative to be accepted automatically, but one among many choices available to construct the future.

A bitter debate is therefore unavoidable between those opposing views. Of course, the second view is subject to further division also, as to whether the democratisation process should take place through political strategy or a socio-political approach. Each choice has its own implications for the future, but for the most part those differences are as great as the difference between the idealisation of Islam as a social system and Islam as a complementary factor. As of now, it is not yet clear where the support of the Muslim middle class will go. But it has to decide soon, since such a choice is unavoidable.

Notes

1 When this article was written it was still undecided what the PDI would be called.
2 There was a relatively high proportion of Christian Bataks (from northern Sumatra) in the upper echelons of both Golkar and the army during the early New Order period.
3 BPUPKI stands for Badan Penyelidikan Untuk Persiapan Kemerdekaan Indonesia, or the Committee for the Investigation of Indonesian Independence. Established by the Japanese towards the end of the occupation, it was the venue of the debates which led to the drafting of the 1945 Constitution.

Part III
Themes in the later New Order

7 Radicalism and new social movements

Prior to the economic crisis of 1997, Soeharto's New Order was frequently cited as a shining example of a government successfully presiding over economic development. But while the growth charts jagged upwards, large numbers of people were pushed to the political and economical periphery. Industrial estates, housing complexes and golf courses ate into the country-side, forcing peasants off their land. Huge new populations of young rural migrant workers sprang up on the margins of the large cities to service the booming low-wage manufacturing sector. By the 1980s industrial strikes and demonstrations over land were common, with urban-based activists increasingly linking up with peasants and workers. At the same time, a host of new labour, environmental and women's organisations were formed, linking up with international movements and helping to transform the political agenda in Indonesia.

The readings in this chapter have been categorised under the broad rubric of 'radicalism and new social movements'. 'Radicalism' refers to the intention among some, but certainly not all, of the contributors to reclaim the radical nationalist, populist and socialist traditions of pre-New Order Indonesia. It also refers to a propensity to argue for alternatives that would require a considerable unravelling and overhaul of Indonesian (if not global) social, political and economic structures. Radical political actors often criticised 'capitalist development' vociferously, and demanded democratisation of life in all spheres. The 'new social movements' label refers to new groupings clustered around issues to do with the marginal-ising effects of rapid economic development, and should perhaps be understood particularly as a designation for the growing environmental and feminist movements of the 1980s and 1990s. However, not all new social movement activists have been radical, and many radicals have been involved in 'older' movements like those of students and labour, although these to an extent are also 'new' in the sense that they were revitalised during roughly the same period. What many actors referred to here have in common is the espousal of a much more egalitarian vision of Indonesia, based on a more fundamental criticism of the New Order than is professed by most of its mainstream critics.

Workers became particularly active in the 1990s, with strike action rising and the proliferation of illegal, or at least unsanctioned, unions. Its new activism had much to do with the gradual development of a new urban working class based on the low-wage, export-oriented industries which Indonesia began to rely upon to spur growth following the fall of international oil prices in the 1980s. The first serious attempt to establish an independent trade union came in September 1990, when a number of labour and human rights activists formed Setiakawan, a union that borrowed its name from Solidarnosc (Solidarity), formed a decade earlier in Gdansk, Poland. Setiakawan was less radical than some of the labour groupings that later played a part in the Indonesian labour movement, but its demand that the New Order recognise independent unions confronted head on the strategy of societal control through state-directed, corporatist representation. In Reading 7.1 Setiakawan outlines its position. The piece remains relevant given the attempts by workers to establish new independent unions following the fall of Soeharto and the partial unravelling of the corporatist system.

The essay by Fazlur Akhmad (pseud.), the anti-violence manifesto and the manifesto of the People's Democratic Party (PRD) (Readings 7.2, 7.3 and 7.7) provide good illustrations of how the student movement evolved in the 1980s and 1990s. Student activism was stifled in the late 1970s following a clampdown on campus organisations, but a new generation was finding new strategies of organising by the following decade. At first combining in informal off-campus 'discussion groups', some sections of the new student movement became increasingly radicalised, as much as they were being politically marginalised. The radicalisation could be attributed in part to first-hand, on-the-ground experience of joining with workers and peasants in their struggles and confrontations, often with state security forces. This kind of experience, in many ways, separated significant portions of the 1980s and 1990s generation of student activists from their 1960s and 1970s predecessors, who were more inclined to try to influence elite-level political developments directly.

The anti-violence manifesto (Reading 7.3) shows the growing criticism voiced by sections of the student movement in particular, but the political opposition in general, of state-initiated practices of violence and terror. It was common for striking workers, rebellious peasants or active students to have to face beatings by local security/military commands for their troubles. Influenced by the global peace movement, criticism such as this should be read, first, as being directed against the culture of militarism stemming from ABRI's omnipresence in various spheres both nationally and locally. Reading 7.2 provides a good summary of the history of the student movement, its ups and downs, from the perspective of its more radical elements, and professes the latter's faith in the virtues of joining in the concrete struggles of the oppressed. By the mid-1990s some of the more radical students had coalesced into the PRD, producing a manifesto that was clearly partly inspired by radical political traditions long suppressed by the New Order.

Reading 7.6 is a well-known protest poem by Wiji Thukul, the son of a pedicab driver who became head of the PRD-affiliated People's Art Network (JAKKER). It is included here to illustrate how a new generation of cultural activists with few links to the elite art community in major cities like Jakarta became increasingly politicised and contributed to the radicalisation of social movements. More than once the target of arrest or assaults by security officials, Wiji Thukul disappeared in 1996 and is presumed to have been killed.[1]

Environmentalism and feminism also emerged as vital forces within Indonesia's opposition movement in the 1980s. Both grew quickly into diverse movements engaged in their own debates over theory and practice, which cannot be adequately represented in the space available here. Reading 7.4 is from SKEPHI, a network of environmental organisations ostensibly specialising in forestry-related advocacy work, but which became intimately involved in grassroots organising against various development projects. Significantly, SKEPHI had ties with the student movement and at least one of its leaders helped establish the Setiakawan trade union. Nursyahbani Katjasungkana's contribution (Reading 7.5) links women's issues with wider debates on rights, law and class. As a leading figure in both the legal aid and women's rights movement, Nursyahbani's strong views on emancipation influenced many of the feminist groups that played an important role in the reform movement.

Compared with the other streams of thought discussed in this book, radicalism is neither very large nor very influential in its own right. But radical ideas continue to inform the political thinking of many nationalist politicians, including significant sections of the PDI-P and those in the NGO movement. Given the political and economic volatility of the post-Soeharto period, as well as Indonesia's legacy of radical political thinking pre-1965, the history of radicalism may be far from over.

7.1 Setiakawan: the need for an independent trade union

This extract is from a 1991 statement by the Supreme Executive Council of the Setiakawan Free Trade Union, the first independent trade union to be formed under the New Order. The unpublished typescript, entitled 'Thoughts and ideas presented to the Sixth Parliamentary Committee', is in English and has been presented here with slight emendations.

The process of development in Indonesia for over 20 years has given rise to some new factors of considerable concern. On one hand, gigantic companies have arisen, accumulating annual profits in the trillions of rupiah as a result of their capital strength and facilities made available to them by the government. On the other hand is the desperate plight of the workers. The wages they receive are very low, not even enough to supply their most basic needs, while working hours are extremely long, social welfare is minimal and so on. Furthermore, their rights that are guaranteed by law have in reality deteriorated, including their right to form unions.

The [official] trade union that has existed since 1973 has done little to deal with the problems of workers. In fact it has tended more to be an instrument to vindicate policies that are not in the interests of workers. The trade union took part in the ratification of Minister of Manpower Regulation no. 1109 in 1986 [legitimising military intervention in labour affairs]...has not done much to help determine minimum wage policies, and is not even making much effort to enforce the existing minimum wage regulations.

Workers have been waiting for more than 25 years to see the realisation of the good intentions of company owners, but developments have shown clearly that businessmen are more interested in expanding their businesses than they are in improving the lot of workers. Therefore we are of the opinion that it is impossible to improve the lot of workers without enforcing a basic right of workers enshrined in law, the right to form unions.

It is impossible for workers to organise themselves at the present time. All sorts of circumstances have them bound hand and foot. First, there are regulations that compel them to consult with company owners if they want to form a union at the company where they work. Second, it is impossible for them to develop inter-factory and inter-regional linkages, because all of these interrelating mechanisms are controlled by a formal organisation of which they have no ownership. Third, government policy only allows one union for workers in private companies. Fourth, the workers themselves are very weak in both economic and political terms, so it is impossible for them to take the initiative to develop unions by themselves.

Under conditions such as these, it is not wise and is even against the national ideals of the Republic of Indonesia, as set forth in the constitution and Broad Outlines of State Policy (GBHN), for us to sit idle.... On the basis of this responsibility we have formed the Independent Workers' Union 'Setiakawan' as a meeting forum for workers who realise that their lot will improve only if they themselves endeavour to make it happen....

Our main goal is not to be accepted, registered at the Ministry of Manpower, but to make a mark in the hearts of the workforce. This organisation is theirs and we will become a part of them.

Article 28 of the 1945 Constitution reads as follows: 'Freedom to associate and assemble, and to express thoughts both orally and in writing as established by law'...[This shows] clearly the democratic desire of Indonesia to enforce social justice....

However, in the decade of 1970–80 the understanding of freedom of association was narrowed. The number of political parties was cut back and civil servants experienced difficulty joining political parties. Labour and farmer organisations could only stand and move in unity with the government. At the same time the government also reduced the right of student bodies to form their own organisations.

We will not discuss the lot of civil servants. It is enough that the government demands they show their loyalty to the government by making them join Korpri.

In 1975 the Indonesian government declared that the right to form unions was governed by Law no. 18/1956, which states the right to form unions and carry out negotiations.... In 1966 the People's Consultative Assembly (MPR) expected the introduction of a comprehensive law that would govern employment, wages, salaries, social security and health, and the result was Law no. 14/1969, which in turn guaranteed the right to form and become a member of an independent union.

In the 1970s the government established tripartite councils and rationalised worker and farmer organisations and their affiliation to political parties. This is not something that we reject. However, it must be [said] that the formation of functional groups certainly assisted in the centralisation of supervision and control and the limiting of democratic decision-making.

Golkar's monopolisation of relations with the ILO [International Labour Organisation] and the ICFTU [International Confederation of Free Trade Unions], used to encourage membership of Golkar and compulsory membership of Korpri for civil servants, were severe blows for trade unions. In June 1971 [NU union affiliate] Sarbumusi submitted a complaint to the ILO about freedom of association...[explaining that] trade unions were forced to disband through the use of intimidation and misuse of authority.

On 5 November 1971 the government of Indonesia explained that it was continuing to pay attention to the rights of trade unions as a basic right enshrined in the 1945 Constitution. Strangely enough, the right of association and assembly guaranteed by the 1945 Constitution, quoted in defence of the government..., was temporarily frozen.

On 20 February 1973 all labour organisations joined together in the FBSI [All-Indonesia Labour Federation], whose leadership was appointed by the government....Under pressure from the government, farmer organisations were physically organised to become HKTI [the Cooperative Farmers' Association] on 26 April 1973. This, together with the prohibition of political parties to operate in rural areas, represents extremely rigid control over the lives of farmers. We consider this process of depoliticisation to have a negative effect on labour organisations, rendering them powerless in practice.

If the Broad Outlines of State Policy of 1973 still talked about the need for a struggle to defend the right of workers and unions, the 1983 version spoke delicately of peaceful cooperation between employers and employees....

Workers must not be considered only as a means of production, but as human beings. So there must be a humanising of Pancasila. For example [it must be established that]:

1   Workers are partners in profits and production.
2   They are partners in responsibility.
3   They are aware of their rights and obligations.

Indonesian Law no.14/1969 stipulates:

1   That every worker has the right to form and become a member of a trade union.
2   That the formation of a workers' union must be carried out on a democratic basis....

Ministerial regulations in 1967 guaranteed that a person *could not be dismissed from employment because of activity in a trade union.*

[But] membership in SPSI often does not guarantee that a person cannot lose his/her job.

Ministerial Regulation no. Per 01/1975 was also detrimental to the formation of trade unions by geographically limiting the membership and total area. Such provisions mean that a trade union can only be formed with assistance from the government. SPSI, YTKI and Korpri were all formed based on this principle.

The FBSI, which is often regarded as the forerunner of the SPSI,[2] was already tightly under the control of the government and received financial assistance. *SPSI's leadership is not responsible to the workers, but to the government....*

It is no longer a secret that many industrial disputes are settled with the assistance of security agencies. The right to strike exists, but it is extremely limited and also not very constructive, with the existence of arbitration [bodies] that can be forcibly influenced, or fines for employers that have no practical meaning, or extremely light prison sentences.

This is probably a good opportunity to touch on the issue of workers in the informal sector such as domestic maids and servants, street vendors, *bajaj* [motorised tricycle taxi] drivers, taxi drivers and *becak* [pedicab] drivers. They are often without any organisation and are totally dependent on their employers or the owners of the vehicles they drive.

For domestic maids and servants it could be said that the term forced labour or slavery is still very applicable.

For the informal workforce, possibly the norm is the same. Attention from the Indonesian trade unions in these sectors is minimal and little is done to fight for their lot.

We understand that hearing our opinions in the parliament will possibly not help a great deal to reach an understanding that freedom of association as guaranteed by Article 28 of the constitution and Laws nos 14/1969 and 18/1956 is a *conditio sine qua non* for a nation calling itself a Pancasila state under the rule of law. We shall continue to strive for the ideals of the proclamation because we are positive that this is the only truthful interpretation of the 1945 Constitution. Do not lose sight of this truth.

7.2 Fazlur Akhmad: the Indonesian student movement – a force for radical social change?

This article critiques the Indonesian student movements of the 1960s and 1970s and identifies the growth of a historical consciousness among the new, more radical generation of students in the 1990s. The section below follows on from an account of the cooperation between students and the military from the mid-1950s until the overthrow of Sukarno. The pseudonymous article was published in the English-language edition of the Indonesian social sciences journal *Prisma* (no. 47, September 1989) and an excerpt is reproduced here with minor grammatical changes.

Before 1970 the first activists to become aware of the shortcomings of this alternative [linking up with the military] were Soe Hok Gie of GEMSOS (Socialist Student Movement) and Ahmad Wahib of HMI (Muslim Students' Association).[3] However, like others in the generation of new activists in the 1970s who decided that this strategy was wrong, they made another strategic mistake; separated from popular power, they had no strong or broad mass base. The demonstrations against Taman Mini and corruption, the boycott of the 1971 elections, the 'Malari' affair of 15 January 1974, and the 1978 movement with its 'White Book' were just examples of frustration.

Some activists of the 1966 movement later entered state administrative structures; others went into business; only a few entered institutional structures able to revive their idealism. The critical faculties of this last group developed because most were in institutions able to accommodate their intellectual and idealistic sentiments: academia, mass media, NGOs. We can understand the sociological condition of the student and youth movements prior to the 1980s if we look at their historical background. Most activists of the 1966 movement were unfamiliar with leftist literature (except Hok Gie and Wahib, whose reading, even in primary school, reflected intellectual democracy). And they had no experience in political organising or dealing with the masses; their political actions were elitist and pragmatic. So it is not surprising that during the early years of the

New Order they were pacified with the idea that the Indonesian nation was in the process of building economic and political democracy.

Former 1966 activists are from a generation that, even now, has not been able to find a concrete alternative. They offer no firm alternative to the political, economic and cultural problems of the Indonesian people. And if they do, the majority have a middle-of-the-road, reformist alternative that does not provide a way out. Their strategy is *moral action* – to change the system from within (mostly by using the ideology and institutions of NGOs). No political action can strengthen their bargaining position [because] they see mass organisation for political pressure as taboo. They often shelter behind the word (it is only a word) *tactical*, but in reality they never take political action on the ground to mobilise the masses.

There is another category of 1966 activists, also in the centre, who linked up with a faction of the former Socialist Party of Indonesia (PSI), dissatisfied bureaucratic elements and military administrators. Their political ideal was to take political power, but they lacked the political boldness to become involved in mobilising people from all sectors of society. In the 1970s they usually remained behind the scenes, provoking university students to prepare the right conditions. In the case of Malari, the masses were told to retreat. In the 1978 movement, which had the same characteristics, mass mobilisation was even less well prepared.

An objective condition offered by capitalism in the 1970s was the NGOs and populist literature. But capitalism had reached an economic, political and cultural crisis – low productivity, poverty, the gap between rich and poor, populist education. These objective conditions, most of which were absorbed by former 1966 activists, then became their subjective condition, so they had no political alternatives. Their middle-of-the-road economic, political and cultural alternatives, and their moral strategy, were truly sterile, for they did not carry even a tiny fleck of history.

More recently, a culture of discussions, of social research, and of social action for charity and 'income generation' has been fostered by the popularity of NGOs; a condition of academic titles, of social science theories (especially concerning Indonesian society) brought in from overseas (especially the West). Bravo! For this cultivated the growth of NGOs and study groups (from around 1983), drawing responses from many moderate students of the 1980s generation and moderate ex-students of the 1970s. Several frustrated students of the 1970s became involved, tried to find satisfaction, or seek alternatives, but became lost in the ideological decadence. The first of the above categories, the 1966 generation of activists – the most extreme in its moderation – also bears responsibility for popularising this condition, so that succeeding generations have considered study groups and NGOs to be the alternative.

Until now, those students who have looked to this alternative in study groups have not been aware of their decay. A comparison with the

Studieclub of the 1920s shows that they were in fact superior to the study groups of the 1980s. The previous historical analysis clearly shows how the *Studieclub* responded to and stimulated objective political-economic conditions – the increasingly repressive colonial policies that became more liberal due to the changing economic status between Holland and the East Indies. In the political economic conditions of the New Order, however, the study clubs are not transforming themselves: they more closely resemble apolitical debating clubs in their activities. They wallow in theoretical issues and cannot act dialectically, responding to and stimulating objective change. As institutions, they never took action in response to the Tanjung Priok case, the Ujung Pandang student movement or recent student movements. If study groups continue as they have, the process of decay will not halt, will not be transformed into political organisation. It is crazy to conclude that they could become pioneers, dominating or even playing a tiny role in the student movement of the 1980s.

Even worse is the condition of the NGOs. Although they too never trigger political action, they have decayed more slowly than the study groups. Large and continual financial support, which continually demoralises social activists (even students) who are drawn into them, means that NGOs have remained in their original state. NGOs have in fact created their own stratification: the symptom of BINGOs and LINGOs [Big NGOs and Little NGOs]. The 'Group of 13' NGOs and the International Non-Government Group on Indonesia, 'INGI', is a symptom of concentration of BINGOs, which will make it difficult for them to reorganise themselves and transform their political agenda. One cannot conclude that a broad spectrum of NGOs exists, for they are controlled, first, by social democratic groups (linked to the PSI generation) and, second, by Protestant, Catholic or modernist Islamic groups (linked to the Masjumi or NU generations). Their political concepts and actions are the same: middle of the road.

The law of history leads us to the conclusion that in the 1970s and early 1980s the political-economic conditions were not yet ripe for promoting understanding, for taking a firm political stance or for developing skill in political action.

Recently, society's lack of action regarding the extremely negative objective political and economic conditions for political democracy and social justice has been successfully shaken up by the student movement, most of whose members come from the lower middle class. They are still more sectarian than in the Philippines or South Korea. Nevertheless, in view of their consolidated actions and issues the student movement is now more successful in forming public opinion and political bargaining than movements of workers, farmers or other social sectors. Other movements, especially those for workers or farmers, are only consolidated over issues, not in terms of actions, and even less of organisation. For Indonesia, this condition is natural in the early stages....

In terms of tactics and strategy, the Yogyakarta student movement is the best: they have been able to develop both their understanding of the people and their organisational skill. The majority never fall straight into 'activism' – they are aware that there can be no division between action and understanding, that both work dialectically to make the movement mature. From most, there is no regional chauvinism and they don't separate themselves from other progressive social sectors. They are intellectually honest and differences of opinion are always discussed openly in forums. They are aware of the broader political spectrum, so they understand which spectrum is progressive and which is reactionary. They therefore refuse to collaborate, even tactically, with the PSI generation, the military, NGOs, the Petition of Fifty group, or with politicians who want to coopt the movement once it has become effective. These are the means, mechanisms and subjective conditioning that has brought the Yogyakarta student movement to maturity.

Many factors have...provided the student movement of the 1980s with valuable experience in understanding and organising: discussions, the distribution of campus media, informal relations with youths in cities and demonstrations, leading to continual reconsideration of tactics and strategies. Also, objective political-economic conditions which have made the movement mature cannot be ignored, particularly the financial crisis caused by the fall in oil prices and national revenue. For example, the student movement in Jakarta in the 1980s initially had no effective political and populist political agenda. They always came out with sectarian student issues, such as increases in course fees or attempts to remove the rector – such as at the National University (UNAS). They have, however, recently become more political and populist after consolidating with students from Yogyakarta, Bandung, Salatiga, Semarang, Malang and Bogor.

Prospects for the student movement are now more encouraging – to the point where they have been able to win national and international public sympathy, where the issues they raise are more populist, where their bargaining position is stronger, and, unlike previous generations, where there is a very low level of collaboration with military administrators, bureaucrats, the three legal political parties, NGOs, social organisations and study groups.

7.3 Taufik Rahzen: anti-violence manifesto

This statement was read by its author during a large demonstration at Gadjah Mada University in Yogyakarta on 25 February 1989. It was formulated in response to the military's massacre of scores of civilians in Way Jepara in rural Lampung, southern Sumatra, the same month. Entitled 'Students' Statement of Belief: Violence and Conscience', it was translated and published in *Inside Indonesia* (no. 19, July 1989: 15).

We stand here, gathered together by a deep feeling of concern. Concern, because we live in an environment where violence, anxiety and fear have become ever more dominant in our thoughts and ever more relied upon as a means of dealing with problems. Our feeling of concern is growing and we are now at a stage where we have almost given up. We feel powerless in the face of these realities.

In the past few years, the violence around us has become impossible to ignore. Violence to our common sense. Violence to our minds and bodies. Many people use anger, capricious behaviour and weapons as a first resort when they come up against differences of opinion and things that annoy them.

Violence rules the streets. Mass brawls, robbery, murder and feelings of insecurity – they are present everywhere at all times. Social unrest as well as the decline in the threshold of tolerance is helping to strengthen institutionalised violence.

Violence has become a part of economic policy. Monopolies, free competition, bribery, the private control of public assets, forced evacuation and the corruption in the job market represent a direct extension of the culture of violence. Lotteries, criminally paraded under the name of charity and fate, taunt and deceive the poor with false hopes.

Violence pollutes our environment. It pollutes jungles and the soil, villages and cities, air and water. Violence is taking its revenge on the places we inhabit.

Violence has colonised the mind of the public. We are conditioned to receive information. Always the same monotonous sanitised news. We have come to believe that every form of art, sport and news is only worthwhile if it contains elements of violence and terror. Our language has been enriched in a strange way with words with violent overtones. 'Clean environment', 'national interests', 'subversion', 'secured', 'extreme right and left', 'fundamentalist' and 'participation'.[4]

Violence has overshadowed good intentions and public morality. Our leaders let their private anxieties become public fears. Religious leaders have lost their sense of responsibility. Intellectuals have taken a back seat. The violence done to the freedom of the press has numbed our sensibilities.

Violence has been spread and institutionalised by various means. Violence also claims its victims in various forms. We can remember clearly the bloody experience at Way Jepara in Lampung. We witnessed people who were killed on both sides. In Ujung Pandang, in Kedung Ombo, in Surabaya, in Aceh, in Tanjung Priok, everywhere.[5] Nobody in their right mind could be unaffected by this situation.

Call to action

If we genuinely want the men and women of this land to enjoy a proper and civilised standard of living, the time has come to concentrate our energies to act and take clear decisions.

The power holders, religious leaders, political leaders, non-government organisations, and important intellectuals are aware that it is not possible for violence to disappear without the existence of justice. Violence is rooted in injustice. Physical injustice and moral injustice. The economic conditions which lead to hunger, disease and poverty are in themselves an assault on human life. Likewise, the structure that deprives people of human rights and dignity obstructs the standing of justice. Those who hold the reins of power and the military must show initiative and give a strong example. Because if they are given authority and power to act unjustly, to torture and kill, it is only a matter of time before they provoke their victims to use the same methods.

We hope that public awareness can help to build a social and cultural system that respects civil rights as well as a willing acceptance of differences. We are trying to develop some instinctive and natural pattern to resolve conflicts and disagreements which does not have political overtones.

Individually, we must build a strong faith capable of breaking down that way of thinking which encourages us to receive facilities, to be indifferent and fearful as the only way of coming to terms with a situation.

Practically, we hope that we will all be able to restrain ourselves from using violence and weapons to overcome every conflict and disagreement. We have to return to a situation where we are genuinely committed to respecting public morality, conscience and life; more than we have done before. We hope that the press can play a larger and more creative role in defending awareness and guarding common sense.

But in all humbleness we are aware how difficult and dangerous it is to act without violence in a society which is easily aggravated and is marked by violence for the sake of violence. We are aware that all this is difficult to achieve. But what will be the consequences of us just going along with the situation? The simple answer is tears, fear and havoc.

Yogyakarta, 25 February 1989

7.4 SKEPHI: people-oriented forest management

This document was published by SKEPHI, the Network for Forest Conservation in Indonesia, in 1990. Linking structural inequality at the global level with injustice and bad management within Indonesia was typical of radical NGOs of the time. The extracts below are reproduced, lightly edited, from an English-language booklet entitled *Selling Our Common Heritage: Commercialisation of Indonesia's Forest* (1990).

Forestry and non-forestry policies in most Third World countries are never geared towards conservation and people's welfare. Rather, they are geared towards commercialisation that brings benefit to only a handful of capitalists from the ruling class or elite class. Naturally, this leads to forest destruction because the very people who know best how to manage the resources sustainably have been alienated....To a certain extent, international economic and political policies have made such destructive policies possible.

A set of integrated factors contributes to forest destruction. First, the industrial revolution has introduced the concept of 'man conquering nature through technology'....Indeed the tremendous development of sophisticated technology enables humans to exploit more natural resources more rapidly. Large-scale forest exploitation has been made possible by this technology.

The existence of the state is another factor. A state must exist, economically and politically. Unfortunately, conservation of natural resources conflicts with strategic economic and political moves in the competitive global context. The state becomes obsessed with its role in the international market. Fostering the interests of corporations to earn foreign exchange, the state's interests begin [to resemble those of a] corporation.... In order to succeed, the state becomes an instrument of foreign and domestic capital, collaborating with business elites and supporting their own depletion of natural resources....

When the colonial era ended, Third World countries desperately needed funds to develop their nations so as to prevent colonialism from transforming [itself] into imperialism. The G-7 countries came in with aid and loans of comparatively low value in exchange for natural resources of high value. They have the technology and processed goods, while the Third World has the raw materials and resources. So the arrangement helped the concept known as the 'international division of labour' [to] emerge....

The arrangement seemed good for a time. During the 1970s, when Third World countries began to review their development process, they still lagged behind in technology and found themselves facing subtle but definite ecological and economic imperialism...Third World countries found that their economic position was worse than before....

The means of production and technology have gone up in price, while the price of raw materials remained constant. This phenomenon...has caused international injustice as well as global ecological crisis. The G-7 and Second World countries are forcing the Third World countries to buy more but sell at a lower price. Third World countries have no choice, since the West practises protectionism, and international bodies such as GATT [the General Agreement on Tariffs and Trade] support its economic policies....

In 1967, [when] Indonesia started her economic development, forestry was seen as a potential contributor. In fact, Indonesia was advised to exploit the 'green gold'. This exploitation continues today. The current international trend of yen appreciation and rising debt-service ratio have led to new policies which may lead to further exploitation. For instance, there are deregulation policies on exports designed to get as much foreign exchange as possible. Once more, Indonesia is opening up its doors to foreign investors and loans.

The inequalities in international trade coupled with consumerism of the elites are actually the underlying factors behind forest destruction. The demand for tissues, for instance,...has led to [the] expansion of paper companies, especially multinational corporations that look at new possible exploitation sites. Intensive propaganda has brought in tissues, disposable chopsticks, Coca-Cola and a thousand other commodities, which directly or indirectly affects forest resources. Indonesia's plan to expand its pulp industry is prompted by the demand for paper in the First World. Pulp exports are being encouraged at the expense of domestic demand for pulp, and even ignoring the potential environmental and social hazards.

What can be done to correct the situation? First and foremost, return the forest resource to the people. Commercialisation has alienated the people from their resources. Consequently, the people cannot be blamed if they do not want to participate in forest conservation efforts.

People-oriented forest management can be undertaken through the community forestry concept, whereby the community owns forests. Through community forestry, the interaction between [the] social and ecological dimensions of forest management can be achieved and forest conservation secured.

Community forestry can be undertaken under the control of existing traditional institutions. *Hukum adat* (traditional law) and its related institutions should be revived and modified in Indonesia to enable the community to develop its own system. If a commercial venture has to be undertaken, then the companies involved will have to deal with the community directly, supervised by experts elected by the people.

The community should be assisted by its formal representatives who are elected to the People's Representative Council.... To date, logging concessions or non-timber forest product exploitation are decided solely by the Department of Forestry. This should be changed. The people's representatives should have a say in matters involving people's resources....

At the international level, several reforms should be implemented. First, a temporary moratorium on the timber trade should be formulated and undertaken until a point is reached where conservation efforts have been successful in 'returning' natural forest to existence. This will be useless without an effort at research and development of an alternative sustainable system. In addition, the timber trade moratorium should also be coupled with the development of sustainable, people-oriented non-timber forest products.

Such a venture will not be possible without a concurrent *moratorium on debts and a more humane international relationship*. There is no way this can be done on a bilateral or multilateral basis. It has to be done worldwide.

Second, a fair and just international trade system should be created. The prices of materials from tropical countries should be balanced with finished commodities and technology....

Third, consumerism should be decreased, as it contributes to nature destruction. Some 90 per cent of the resources and their products are consumed by hardly 1 per cent of the world's population. Therefore there should [also be a just distribution of resources].

The earth needs a balanced, egalitarian and harmonious international relationship, not a hierarchical one. A balanced division of functions is needed where Third World tropical countries develop their resources and First World countries develop their technology. But [fair trade] should be maintained.

The ecological, economic and cultural imperialism by the First World over the Third World should be halted if humans are to conserve forests and natural resources. For the people of tropical nations, sustainable forest management is a matter of justice, cultural identity, dignity and democracy. Only when these are kept intact can we talk about forest conservation.

To achieve this, a lot of concepts, actions, and attitudes have to be radically changed....

7.5 Nursyahbani Katjasungkana: gender equality, a universal struggle

This was written in response to an article by Bogor Agricultural Institute lecturer Ratna Megawangi in *Kompas* (6 September 1994). Ratna Megawangi drew on post-structuralist arguments about the collapse of the concept of individual autonomy and universalism, as well as the works of writers such as Colette Dowling and Wendy Kaminer, to attack mainstream feminism and make the case for the recognition of essential differences between the sexes and between cultures. Nursyahbani Katjasungkana, a well-known feminist and human rights lawyer, begs to differ. The article appeared in *Kompas* on 26 September 1994.

As one convinced of the view that freedom and equality (including gender equality and autonomy) are crucial to democracy and justice, Ratna Megawangi's article...certainly caught my attention. Ratna's argument rests upon two foundations: the specific context of society and women in America, and ambivalence towards the concept of gender equality.

Her article argues that modern feminism based on the struggle for freedom and equality is no longer relevant, or is at least brought into question. From this Ratna goes on to suggest that the women of Indonesia ought to construct their own concept of feminism, namely 'a concept which would give rise to a sense of self-confidence for women in their choice of vocation'. It is in this assertion, in my impression, that the contradiction and weakness of her argument lie.

One important precondition for the emergence of rights historically was a recognition of humans as free and autonomous beings. Accordingly, the right of individuals to their freedom and autonomy must first be recognised in order for them to actualise their other rights.

Ratna's recommendation that Indonesian women should construct their own concept of feminism raises the question of how women are able to determine their own choices in the absence of autonomy and freedom.

The rights to freedom and autonomy are natural rights which humans enjoy by virtue of being human. A diminution of these rights is therefore an infringement of a person's very nature as a human being. An understanding that the rights of freedom and equality are fundamental is a product of philosophers from the time of Aristotle to that of John Locke, and has been recognised in national and international legal instruments.

Consequently, Ratna denies reality in asserting (quoting from an article by Jamal D. Rahman in *Kompas*, 22 April 1994) that an understanding of freedom and equality, a central theme of modern feminism, is irrelevant.

The issue is that legal recognition of these as rights in many countries has yet to be fully implemented. For this reason, women in almost all parts of the world still struggle for these rights, demanding either their formal recognition or their implementation.

In fact, during the World Conference on Human Rights in Vienna last year, women sought to amend the Declaration of Human Rights. One proposal put forward by the Women's Action Forum from Pakistan stated that the declaration needed reinterpretation because it was formulated with conceptual parameters originating from a patriarchal worldview, namely a false dichotomy between what are termed the public and the private spheres. On the basis of this dichotomy, civil and political rights are categorised under the public sphere, while rights within the family are portrayed as belonging to the private sphere. As a consequence, women's rights fall outside this formulation of human rights.

This is just one example of how women nowadays are continuing the struggle not just to gain recognition, but to effectuate the recognition they have gained, and even to improve concepts of human rights in line with the times. In America itself, as outlined in Ratna's article, the struggle to gain recognition of rights and equality is not yet over, because the Equal Rights Amendment passed by congress in 1972 has yet to be ratified by all states.

This means the struggle of American women merely to gain juridical recognition of equality, not to mention actual equality in their everyday lives, has not yet been won, even though the struggle has been under way since 1923. The question here is whether one can legitimately claim that modern feminism has failed and is irrelevant simply because the struggle for *de jure*, let alone de facto, recognition of equality continues.

Ratna's argument, then, appears very simplistic since it considers the situation of women in America, as depicted in her article, as an endpoint rather than merely a symptom which will change in time, in line with other changes if and when the struggle eventually succeeds. The point I wish to make is that the women and the society Ratna uses as examples are also a part of what must be changed. For in the final analysis these women are products of a society that has yet to fully recognise the principle of equality, at least in the juridical sense. They live in a changing society; it is only natural that undesirable effects arise in periods of transition.

Such a process of transition is also occurring in our society and amongst our women. Even though some claim that our society is strong on family principles, the divorce rate is quite high. A friend who works for the Women's Legal Aid Institute (LKBH Wanita) says that in metropolitan Malang [population approximately 700,000] up to 200 divorce cases go before the courts every month.

Similarly, if we take a close look at magazines, many of our so-called career women feel guilty because they have their own careers. Nearly all of them say that, while they have a career, they still look after the house, their husband and their children. It is as if they had committed a dreadful sin, or that they fear harsh judgement if they fail to mention these matters – even though it may well be their maids who do all the real work.

Middle-class Indonesian women benefit greatly from a situation in which impoverished village women are forced to become housemaids for very little pay. In reality, middle-class women have never performed the dual role of which they are so proud.

For a majority of Indonesian women who are still in poverty, whether living in rural or urban areas, this dual role of earning a living and domestic duties at home is not a matter of choice. It is as if both roles are an inescapable fate prepared for them, a fate that must be accepted due to their poverty. They have no alternative but to work shoulder to shoulder with their husbands to keep the home fires burning.

Becoming a mother is a fate which culture also prepares for them because they are women. The tragedy of their fate is reinforced by state policy in all its instrumentalities, legal, institutional and ideological. A great many policies give rise to discrimination against women.

For example, because women are not considered to be primary breadwinners, they are paid less than their male colleagues (see decree of the Minister of Labour, no. SE.04/MEN/1988). Men's pay includes a supplementary family allowance, but because workers' incomes are still low women also shoulder the burden of their family's needs. The performance of women in their work very often actually surpasses that of the men who receive the allowance.

It is here that the importance of continuing to struggle for gender freedom and equality lies. Women's movements gain their legitimacy in this issue without needing to fear accusations that these ideas [about equal pay] originate from outside Indonesia. They are a logical consequence of our humanity.

These ideas have long been the central theme of the struggle of the leading figures of our women's movements. Read, for example, the letters of Kartini, where we will find that freedom and self-reliance are the fundamental ideas underpinning her whole struggle.

It must be acknowledged that there is a deep contradiction between wanting equal rights and still wanting special protection. I am very aware that such a desire automatically positions women as constituting a category of their own.

However, it is completely mistaken to take the examples of paid leave from work for menstruation and childbirth to demonstrate this contradiction, because they are the only areas in which there is a clear difference between men's and women's needs. It is natural for women to seek special protection concerning these two matters, which are tied up with their reproductive rights and functions.

These two forms of special treatment apply to the majority of Indonesian female workers, who labour for wages that remain far below minimum daily needs for physical survival. So leave for menstruation and childbirth provides a protection that is very empowering for them. With menstruation leave, for instance, a female labourer is able to make a choice: whether to rest her body [for a day] and still be paid, or whether to keep working on double pay, because she would be working on a day on which she is entitled to paid leave.

In the midst of the impoverished faces of our labourers, this right to paid leave really does add power and strength. While those from middle and upper classes do not actually need menstruation leave, it would be unjust to use this fact to do away with a right currently enjoyed by that majority of women who work as wage labourers.

For this reason, I am strongly opposed to those who say that the right to menstruation leave is in contradiction to the emancipation of women. The case of women labourers above clearly demonstrates that menstruation leave provides freedom and empowerment, which is what emancipation essentially means.

Leading figures in the Indonesian women's movement, who generally come from the middle and upper classes, have to be sensitive to the needs of the majority of their gender, those still left behind in poverty, because those women have never had a choice.

7.6 Wiji Thukul: a caution

Poet and activist Wiji Thukul wrote this poem in his home town of Solo in 1986. It is probably the best known of his poems because of its rousing final line, which was adopted as a slogan by protesting peasants and striking workers in the 1990s. After the PRD was formed in 1996 it was frequently read at meetings and included in party publications. This is a translation by the editors of the original, 'Peringatan', in Thukul (2000: 61).

> If the people leave
> during speeches of the powerful
> we must beware
> for they may have lost patience
>
> if the people hide
> and discuss in whispers
> their own problems
> the powerful must be wary and learn
> to listen
>
> if the people do not have the courage to complain
> the situation is critical
> and if the words of the powerful
> cannot be disputed
> then truth is threatened
>
> if suggestions are refused without heed
> voices silenced, criticism banned without reason
> accused of subversion and disturbing
> the peace
> then there is only one word: resist!

7.7 People's Democratic Party: manifesto

The People's Democratic Party (PRD) was founded at a congress in April 1996. It had previously existed as the People's Democratic Union, established in 1994. The following extract is from a manifesto the PRD issued in Jakarta on 22 July 1996.

There is no democracy in Indonesia. Democracy, meaning people's sovereignty, should be the basic principle and foundation for the formation of any state. As long as this sovereignty has not been given its rightful place in the political, economic and cultural life of a nation and people, history will continue to throw up resistance.

The state during the 30 years of Soeharto has become an institution that shackles and obstructs the opportunity for the development of popular participation in the process of determining social and political life. Executive power has become enlarged, is oppressive, uncontrollable and overrides the authority of the legislature and the judiciary.

Oppression under the New Order

The history of the Indonesian nation is actually the history of a people's struggle, a struggle famous for its tenacity in resisting all forms of exploitation and oppression with the aim of achieving humanism and peace. However, the coming to power of the New Order regime in 1965 has meant backward steps for Indonesian society when compared to Indonesian political life in the period of 1950–9. Basic rights of popular participation have been shackled, limited and cut off by the implementation of the five political laws and the dual function of the military (ABRI). The aim of independence, that is freedom to choose, to supervise and to determine the course of the political life of a country, has moved further and further away from everyday political life. Systematically, the authorities of the New Order regime dominate the political arena through brutal, cruel and unconstitutional methods. They do not value differences of opinion, criticism and do not want to hear the people's aspirations. The rise of the people's resistance – that is of civilians – is greeted with intimidation, terror, arrests, jailing, bullets and even with slaughter. Newspapers, magazines, books and other tools of education that are critical and dare to differ from the point of view of the authorities are banned and closed down. Journalists who do not favour one-sided reporting of the government's point of view are sent to jail. The working class, who are economically oppressed, are intimidated, terrorised and even killed. Peasants find it increasingly difficult to keep their land and defend their rights, as they are confronted by the military when they resist capitalist encroachment into their land. All these authoritarian strategies are employed, implemented, enacted and maintained with one aim in mind, to ensure the stability of capital accumulation.

Economic injustice

Until now, we have witnessed the widening of the gulf between the rich few and the poor majority. Workers are promoted by the Soeharto dictatorship and sold cheaply to invite investment and allow capital accumulation for the rich. Indonesia's economic growth of more than 6 per cent per annum is enjoyed only by a small minority group. Economic assets vital for the quality of life of the people are privatised, with concessions traded among Soeharto's cronies and their families. Monopolies and oligopolies that exploit the people are protected and facilitated by the powers that be. Economic hardship increases when the government is filled with corrupt people who are in collusion with bureaucrats working for private interests and their respective business groups. Imperialist organisations such as the World Bank and the International Monetary Fund continue to prop up its growth by pouring in millions in the form of foreign loans. As a result, Indonesia's foreign debt has now reached US$100 billion. This means that we occupy the third-highest rung on the foreign debt ladder, beneath Brazil and Mexico.

Indonesian economic development, which benefits the few owners of capital and exploitation by foreign investors, has resulted in a society which has become more brutal and further away from the people's aim of reaching prosperity and justice.

The people resist

After 30 years, eight months and 22 days of the New Order government, the Indonesian people can no longer accept and tolerate this government, economically, politically or socially. There are many examples that prove this: workers are striking in many industrial estates, peasants are actively resisting eviction, students are demonstrating against militarism, intellectuals resist attempts to stifle academic freedom, indigenous people in Kalimantan and West Papua are fighting back against Jakarta's exploitation. In East Timor, the Maubere people have never stopped fighting against the military invasion and occupation by the New Order.

The forms of resistance taken up by the people continue to increase – from mass actions, where many sectors of the population work together, occupying Parliament, invading police and military headquarters, confronting the military, to mass production of leaflets. The essence is this: popular dissatisfaction is everywhere. The people are no longer content to live under the New Order regime. The socio-economic and political system now, which is safeguarded by the regime, has proven itself unable to articulate, let alone resolve, the concrete problems faced by the people.

The current system is bankrupt. This is the time for the five political laws to be repealed and the time for the military, currently sheltering under the dual function of ABRI doctrine, to return to the barracks.

Political reforms

The package of five political laws is the government's justification for limiting the people's rights to political participation. The role of political parties as a channel for the people to become involved in politics, as the birthplace of popular sovereignty, needs to be established immediately. Fair and democratic elections, those that do not limit the participation and the political aspirations of people as given rights in a modern civil society, have never existed. The structure of the upper and lower houses of parliament reflects the tactics used by the regime to maintain power. Those belonging to cliques and the military have the special privileges of being appointed by Soeharto and have never had to subject themselves to elections. Laws governing mass organisations do not allow them to have political affiliations, and their formation is often obstructed. Finally, laws governing referenda are such that they have never been enacted to decide important questions, for example the appropriateness of the 1945 Constitution given the changing socio-economic and political world context. Instead the constitution has become something sacred. People who are sovereign are people who can learn about and have the opportunity and the ability to understand their sovereignty, and who can understand their ability to engage in politics. If we are to achieve these aims, there is no alternative but to repeal the five political laws of 1985....

Self-determination for East Timor

Foreign economic policies should have an anti-neocolonial character, as opposed to the policies of agreements such as those embodied in NAFTA [North American Free Trade Agreement], APEC [Asia-Pacific Economic Cooperation] and AFTA [Asian Free-Trade Area]. Internationalism must abide by the principles of peace and humanism. For that reason, the end of the Indonesian occupation of East Timor has to be part of our political program, not merely of us extending solidarity, but of fighting alongside the East Timorese for their right to determine their own destiny and to be independent. The Indonesian people's democratic struggle will not be complete and genuine unless it joins with the Maubere people's demand for independence. The PRD opposes national chauvinism and considers internationalist links as the mainstay of the people's struggle. The integrated nature of global capitalist power, with the support of governments who have no respect for democracy, necessitates an international resistance against it. For that reason, the PRD will actively support all international forums and actions that are of a grassroots character and are opposed to oppression.

The way forward

...To achieve clarity in direction towards a democratic society, we need to seek the forces from the people who have the strength to push towards this goal. Because of this, questions of strategy and tactics need to be formulated based on the potential existing among the people themselves. Of all the potential, we see the resistance put up by workers as the most significant potential force that will be harnessed and organised into the democratic struggle. Their increasing numbers, their continuing fightback and their strategic position in the capitalist system of the New Order will make the working class a stronghold of democracy now and in the future.

The second strength we see is that of students and intellectuals. This social layer has pioneered political resistance against the New Order. Their ideological, organisational and political ability are important contributions to the democratic struggle. The adventurism of the students' movement and the resulting loss of power of organised students can only be avoided if it is linked in with the people's democratic struggle as a whole.

The third proven force that is still developing is the urban poor. Their increasing numbers, marginalised state and the uneven development between city and countryside form the basis of the urban masses. In actions supporting Megawati, we can see how this sector militantly and tenaciously defended their rights. The last sector that is also important is the peasant sector. Brutal capitalism has impoverished them and robbed them of their land, which is their means of subsistence. It is not surprising that it is this sector, who are spread throughout Indonesia in large numbers, which will be an important supporting force in the democratic movement.

United front

To unify and mobilise the existing democratic forces, a common platform is necessary; one from which we can act in unity. It is not enough for unity in action to be represented by a common program and method; it needs also to have the ability to decipher the political situation in order to force wider popular participation....

PRD considers that a front that is supported by the masses needs to be built. As long as these mass 'pockets' are not mobilised into the democratic struggle, this front will be incapable of confronting the militaristic and domineering power of the New Order.

With all the problems of Indonesian society we have looked at above, we should also be able to envisage and articulate what a future democratic society might look like. PRD considers that it is more important to come up with political solutions to ease the way towards economic solutions for the problems of an Indonesia that has been exploited in a wholesale manner under capitalism. PRD sees that it is important in the future to build a modern civil society that respects popular sovereignty and institutionalises democratic practices with their own legislative, executive and judicial structures. The structures of true democracy must be subservient to the sovereignty of the people. For that reason, a popular democratic coalition government must be created for the future, in order to channel the aspirations of the people. This channelling of aspirations needs to be able to respect various ideologies and their respective methods without military intervention.

The development of a modern civil society in Indonesia that is based on popular sovereignty will depend on how we build a democratic movement now. Strategy and tactics need to be formulated now with the concrete state of the people in mind. Because of that, PRD believes and is confident that organising the masses is the only way to bring about popular sovereignty. The founding of the PRD is one manifestation of and an answer to the dysfunction of extra-parliamentary institutions. Its formation also aims to provide a clear goal for the people's struggle, towards a multiparty and peace-loving popular democratic society.

Notes

1   For a discussion of Wiji Thukul's role as a political poet, see Sen and Hill (2000: 42–5).
2   Serikat Pekerja Seluruh Indonesia (All-Indonesia Workers' Union), established in 1985 as a revamped, highly centralised version of the original FBSI. In 1995 the SPSI was yet again restructured, and renamed the FSPSI (SPSI Federation).
3   Both these figures met early deaths. They remain romantic symbols of youthful political idealism.
4   These were all familiar motifs in New Order political discourse. 'Clean environment' (*bersih lingkungan*) denoted political hygiene, or freedom from family ties with banned or suspect organisations; 'secured' (*diamankan*) meant to be arrested; while 'extreme right and left' were the twin bogies, communism and fundamentalist Islam.
5   In Way Jepara the military killed many villagers protesting over land in February 1989; in Ujung Pandang (Makassar) about a dozen students were killed in protests against the motorbike helmet law in 1987; Kedung Ombo is the name of a dam site in Central Java where protesting farmers were intimidated and evicted because of a dispute over compensation; Surabaya refers to the anti-Chinese violence there in the late 1980s; and Tanjung Priok is where the military shot scores of Muslim protestors in September 1984.

8 'Political openness' and democratisation

Democratisation was a key theme in public and intellectual debate in Indonesia for most of the 1980s and 1990s. Magazines, newspapers, seminars, public meetings and television talk shows dealt almost incessantly with topics such as democracy and the 1945 Constitution, democracy and Indonesian culture, and democracy and globalisation. This reflected, in part, a civil society whose aspirations were outgrowing the confines of the New Order's restrictive social and political framework. The rising urban middle class was growing more prosperous, and in some cases demanding, while the industrial working class displayed signs of restiveness. The rapid spread of communications technologies allowed some sections of society to plug into global information networks beyond the reach of government censors. Moreover, the international prestige of democracy was running high in the late 1980s with the revolutions in the Eastern bloc. Just as important to understanding the phenomenon in Indonesia, however, was the emergence of rivalries and divisions within the New Order political elite.

'Political openness' or '*keterbukaan*' was the term used to describe the period between 1989 and 1994 when intellectuals and activists experienced a relaxation of the official constraints they were used to. The period coincided with serious tensions between Soeharto and General 'Benny' Moerdani, Indonesia's powerful intelligence chief, who commanded the armed forces between 1983 and 1988. At issue were Soeharto's moves to establish bases of power independent of the military as an institution that threatened to diminish its autonomy. Soeharto frequently upset officers, for example, by personally promoting loyalists and former adjutants. Moreover, in the 1980s Soeharto had begun to transform Golkar from an appendage of the military into a cadre-based and more efficient political vehicle, under the leadership of minister of the State Secretariat, Sudharmono, a close aide. In this position, Sudharmono had also earned the military's ire by severely reducing its independence with regard to the lucrative business of procuring equipment (Pangaribuan 1995: 57). Soeharto removed Moerdani from his position as chief of the military after he attempted to block

Sudharmono's elevation to the vice-presidency in 1988, but many officers remained loyal to their former commander and he continued to exercise considerable influence as defence minister (1988–93).

Also troubling to the predominantly secularist military leadership at the time were Soeharto's moves to court political Islam. In 1990 he gave his blessing to the establishment of ICMI, the Indonesian Muslim Intellectuals' Association, under the leadership of trusted protégé B.J. Habibie. Soeharto was clearly trying to redress previously strained relations with organised Islam and establish a base of support among the rapidly growing constituency of educated urban Muslims. His overtures were largely successful, with many welcoming the initiative as indicating a genuine change of heart by Soeharto with regard to the place of Islam in society. Dawam Rahardjo's essay on ICMI's vision in Chapter 9 (Reading 9.8) exemplifies the new spirit of reconciliation between Muslim intellectuals and the government.

But while many middle-class Muslims welcomed ICMI's establishment as a new and important avenue to bureaucratic power, the military leadership saw it as a dangerously sectarian organisation that betrayed the New Order's commitment to keep politics and religion separate. Habibie was no favourite of the military either. Like Sudharmono he had undermined the military's material base, in this case by successfully extending his jurisdiction over strategic industries to include those in which the military had an economic interest. That Habibie was no friend of Moerdani only bolstered ICMI's popularity with the Islamic intelligentsia, for the Catholic general was vilified by large sections of organised Islam for his role in its suppression as a political force over the years.

The wrangling between Soeharto and sections of the military led each to attempt to coopt and direct the public debate on democratisation for their own purposes. Journalists found they were able to write more critically about the first family, and Jakarta audiences were treated to satirical plays, such as Nano Riantiarno's *Suksesi*, that would in the past have been banned immediately. Members of the armed forces faction in parliament also began to speak up, with Moerdani allies Major-General Samsudin and Police Colonel Roekmini Soedjono arguing for a relaxation of authoritarian controls. It was in this increasingly permissive atmosphere that General Soemitro, the former head of the internal security apparatus Kopkamtib, published a widely read article in the *Far Eastern Economic Review* calling for a return to 'normal' politics in Indonesia in accordance with 'international values and principles of democracy' (Reading 8.1). While Soemitro had long been retired, the central role he had played in establishing the New Order and presiding over the incarceration of tens of thousands of political prisoners gave his article particular gravity.

Soeharto's response to the groundswell was to declare his government's support for it. In his annual Independence Day address in August 1989 Soeharto reflected on the end of the Cold War and spoke positively about the 'winds of change', which would 'revitalise the ideas of democracy, freedom and openness' (Reading 8.2). A year later he reaffirmed his imprimatur, calling differences of opinion the 'very source of life's dynamism'.

Indonesia's press took him at his word, leading to a period in the early 1990s in which magazines such as *Tempo* and *Editor*, and most notably the tabloid *Detik*, strove to outdo each other in presenting 'daring' political news and interviews to an eager public. A recurrent call in the media was for a limit to be placed on the presidential tenure, preventing Soeharto being reappointed president when his fifth term came to an end in 1993. This became a priority not only among those who wished to see the restoration of democracy, but also among those who feared the chaos that would ensue were Soeharto, who was due to turn 72 in that year, to die in office without having groomed a successor.

Another common argument among proponents of political reform was that Indonesia's political stability no longer justified the use of emergency laws. An example is the 1990 submission a group of senior alumni of the prestigious Gadjah Mada University made to the People's Consultative Assembly (excerpted in Reading 8.3). Perhaps more fundamental, and less subtle, is the excerpt from Democratic Forum, a loose association of liberal political activists (Reading 8.4). It contends that the New Order had been detrimental to Indonesia in both the political and cultural senses, robbing the people of their 'critical capacities' through its propaganda and indoctrination, and therefore damaging democratic prospects.

By 1993 Soeharto was back for a sixth term, while Moerdani had been edged out of power and his followers in the military sidelined one by one, narrowing the space available for debate. The death knell for openness came in June 1994 with the sudden banning of *Detik*, *Tempo* and *Editor*, and the subsequent moves taken against critical academics and student, labour and NGO activists. The crackdown reaffirmed Soeharto's control over the political system, but at the same time left the New Order with a crisis of legitimacy.

It is a measure of this legitimacy crisis that in 1996 a group of researchers from the government's own Indonesian Institute of Sciences (LIPI) put together a report proposing a series of major reforms to the political system (Reading 8.5). The document can be read as a warning to the New Order leadership that urgent changes were necessary if it was to avoid collapsing under the weight of its inefficiency, corruption and authoritarianism.

But by this stage Soeharto was in no mood for reform, deciding instead to tighten the screws on dissent. In 1993 army officers aligned with Moerdani had covertly facilitated the popular Megawati Soekarnoputri's rise to lead the PDI. Threatened by Megawati's mass following, Soeharto engineered a clumsy party coup in 1996, which saw her replaced by her compliant predecessor, Suryadi. Rather than accept their fate, Megawati's supporters occupied the central Jakarta headquarters of the PDI, turning it into a bastion of resistance to the New Order supported by a range of groups including student radicals, independent unionists, East Timorese independence activists and some middle-class professionals. On 27 July 1996 military-sponsored thugs stormed the building, killing several people and cementing Megawati's status as Indonesia's de facto opposition leader. Reading 8.6, 'An agenda for reform', written the following year, provides a rare glimpse into the political thinking of the woman who would be president.

While the overwhelming majority of political activists – including Muslim political activists – were positive about democracy, there were some who were not. The final reading, written by the scholar Muhammad Shiddiq Al-Jawi, presents a rarely stated argument about the inherent incompatibility of Islam and secular, liberal democratic political arrangements. After Soeharto's fall, Islamist groups such as the Forum Komunikasi Ahlusunnah Wal Jamaah and Hizbut Tahrir Indonesia (which the author joined) became more vocal.

8.1 Soemitro: aspiring to normal politics

This article was written in English for the *Far Eastern Economic Review* (6 April 1989: 22) but was intended primarily for an Indonesian audience. It was regarded as an important intervention by a man who, as commander of the powerful internal security body Kopkamtib from 1973 to 1974, had played a crucial part in the consolidation of the Soeharto regime. By referring to international standards of democracy as 'normal', retired General Soemitro challenged the New Order directly and helped fuel demands that the regime adapt itself to the changed domestic and global environment. The article, which is reproduced here minus the magazine's editorial glosses, was also read as an appeal for Soeharto to step down in 1993.

With the end of the '45 Generation's service in Indonesia approaching in 1993, Indonesians increasingly feel that political life should return towards a normal condition, in which the values and systems stemming from the 1945 Constitution and in accordance with international values and principles of democracy will be re-established.

The instincts and aspirations of Indonesian political society, which have already undone an era of political development since the 1945 revolution, are regaining their strength, something reflected in the wish that from 1993 the life of the nation can get back to normal.

The expressions of this mainly focus on a longing for integrity and authority to be restored to the People's Representative Assembly and [the] People's Consultative Assembly; on the improvement of leadership, especially in the relationship between superior and subordinate, and on several basic social problems.

Conspicuous are statements desiring an end to the practice of 'drop-ping' [imposing the government's candidates] during the election of leaders for regions, provinces, non-government bodies and so on. The public has begun discussing openly matters concerning the succession of national political leadership, and questioning the calls to 'be sensitive', which ulti-mately could end in a feeling of fear towards higher-ups and the flourishing of a 'keep the boss happy' culture.

The need for a climate of openness is already pressing in the past five years of the '45 Generation's service. If the succeeding generation seems outspoken, that is fully within their rights. The year 1993 is on the threshold of the 21st century, which will be their charge. What we are experiencing now is the result of yesterday's policies. What is being drawn up today will shape tomorrow.

The leadership succession is closely related to the integrity of demo-cratic institutions. Three notable statements have been made recently about this. Soeharto said that when the time comes to change the leader-ship it should be carried out without disturbance. Coordinating Minister for Security Sudomo said the succession would proceed smoothly. DPR and MPR speaker Kharis Suhud said the president's period in office would be fully at the people's discretion.

These are very cautious statements, but bearing in mind that they are the products of a very different background to that of the young genera-tion, their attitude is fully understandable. Being quite aware that some of their fellows will soon have to leave the arena, a sense of solidarity, broth-erhood and the sharing of mutual trials motivates their instinct to shield one another's integrity.

Even so, the three statements give clear guidance for the generation coming after, and stress the need for genuine application of the 1945 Constitution to buttress the system. A crisis usually takes time and casual-ties to overcome and, most damaging, would require the application of extraordinary measures. A chaotic situation might bring forward into the national leadership a 'strong man', but one without the necessary physical and mental preparation for the task, as so far neither Golkar, the political parties nor any of the other political democratic institutions are yet prop-erly consolidated. The aftermath of a crisis would be that everything had to be started from zero again.

Speaker Suhud's statement implied that the succession question should be surrendered fully to the supreme institution of popular sovereignty, the MPR, and that it [should] be left to the succeeding generation to handle at its discretion, as long as attention is paid to the above-mentioned concerns. To suppress such an idea would be completely wrong.

For the sake of the growth of the culture of the nation, we should not be ashamed to admit that in the early days of Soeharto's New Order mistaken practices in the succession process were virtually institution-alised. People who felt they had a chance and prepared themselves for certain vacancies did not get them, while some who were uninterested and unprepared have been appointed.

Such a practice could be accepted at that time, but in the current climate of accelerating the modernisation process such a process becomes discordant, because the public feels it has lost its footing. In a modern society, leadership is institutional in nature, reflecting norms and systems to which a leader is expected to adhere. A succession process that does not follow a clear system is prone to create resentment among the people.

Concerning the succession question in 1993 and onwards, inevitably various essential aspects will turn up: the source of leadership, the number of potential leaders, whether the election procedure should be by voting or consensus, and other election criteria.

The source of candidates clearly cannot be separated from the current party system: the two political parties, Golkar and the armed forces. In all consciousness, these organisations should be made the seedbed of potential leaders of the nation. Since the individual chosen no longer is the leader of any one political force but of the nation, he ought to be able to place himself above all parties' interests, and should have reached political maturity through previous experience as a member of the DPR/MPR.

Clearly, as the leader of the nation is not a bureaucrat, it would be erroneous to create him through the path of an official career. The potential leader should meet the basic criteria of having demonstrated his potential and statesmanship. Therefore he must have years of experience in political life, among the political parties and Golkar as well as in the DPR/MPR, and should be mature in politics and accustomed to open dialogues with different parties having different interests.

Moreover, he should be conscious of the obligation of being elected and consequently representing the interest of the people, as their trustee. His fidelity to the constitution and the law must be proven under test. Experience as a member of the DPR/MPR would be very important, as he will be expected to be capable in executing all decisions and wishes of the people, and be able to account for himself either at the end of his term or at any time the mandatory body requires.

For the purpose of meeting the criteria, every political party, mass organisation and Golkar should be fully independent, relying on true democratic processes to thus build up a substantial leadership cadre. Cadres of substance can only be created when democratic practices are thoroughly maintained. Systems must be transparent, allowing growth of sound and open competition to avoid suspicion, and with a properly managed filtering system. Cliques as evident in the 1950s should be left behind.

Consensus should be reached on the election procedure as soon as possible. It must be acknowledged that with the system of the 1945 Constitution the MPR is the storehouse of democracy and as such the supreme authority. Its power is absolute and therefore should be free from direct or indirect pressure, specifically in deciding upon a president and vice-president.

Politics – the essence of Western political systems – has been a bad word in Indonesia. Through the Pancasila philosophy and system of democracy, the Indonesian people are convinced and determined to develop politics to keep national life dedicated to the national interest, not viewing political conflicts as intrinsic to the system. They want an orderly, civilised procedure, free from sordid intrigues. Therefore, all political 'games' may not be detached from the system mutually agreed upon. For instance, the forming of power bases or the developing of pressure through formations outside the system have to be terminated. For the sake of a healthy political life, all must become part of the system.

For that reason, resolutions handed to the MPR general session should be considered a thing of the past. The session must be relieved from any and all forms of pressure and influence, so that its self-reliance and authority will not be contaminated. The Indonesian people have to give their utmost efforts to have the absolute authority of the MPR respected within the context of leadership transfer over the coming five years.

In considering election, the terminology itself bears the connotation that the voter will have to confront more than just one choice. As such, it is reasonable to find more than just one candidate. The Indonesian people need not be very much concerned about ever being short of potential mandated leaders of substance, as long as the cadre formation and the practice of democracy are thoroughly implemented. To refer back to there being only one candidate, as in past presidential elections, is inconsequential.

The Indonesian people have never questioned the specific position of Bung Karno in his era of politics, nor Pak Harto's position as the Father of Development in the early days of economic development. Both have been accepted as leaders of the Indonesian people and nation, without match during their respective times.

Another thing that must be understood is the term 'leadership'. Confidence in the character of the individual to lead forms the kernel of leadership. Consequently, the election of the MPR mandatory must be free and confidential. This can only be ascertained via voting procedure and not through deliberation. MPR members must feel free in having dialogues with their own conscience, without any threats or influence.

It is hoped the succeeding generation will not be 'allergic' and view the terminology and procedure of voting as inadmissible in Pancasila democracy. The '45 Generation have their historical background in making them 'allergic' to voting. In the past (the 1950s) this procedure was part of the liberal democracy system, which through clash of interests, intrigues and power plays led ultimately to a critical situation.

Where state and governmental institutions have been well established, there should be no reason for the succeeding generation to hesitate from applying the vote wherever necessary. A clause in the constitution explicitly states that decisions be taken by the MPR by majority of votes. Hence, decision-making based [on a] vote has a strong constitutional basis. While voting could create problems in a decision-making system based on deliberation to reach consensus, the constitution obviously does [not] see them [as] in opposition to each other.

8.2 Soeharto: openness

In this state address, delivered on 16 August 1989, Soeharto signalled his readiness to tolerate a relaxation of the constraints on free speech. The speech was interpreted at the time as initiating a period of relative political openness. It is followed by a widely quoted extract from Soeharto's state address of the following year, in which he gave a clearer indication of his government's (apparent) willingness to tolerate diverse opinions (Soeharto 1989: 7–8, 10–17; 1990: 16–17).

On the occasion of delivering the state address in commemoration of Proclamation Day, the president asks the whole Indonesian nation to contemplate the past, the present and the future of our nation. During the days of the commemoration of the Independence Proclamation we, as a nation, engage in a dialogue with our own history.

Each time we contemplate and engage in a dialogue with history, we gain a fresh understanding of where we came from, where we are, and where we want to go on our historic journey. Thus, each year, we remind ourselves of the continuities in our national struggle....[Our] awareness of the need for such continuities must be balanced with the will to undertake reforms from year to year and from one era to the next....

The wheels of history never stop turning. New challenges emerge, new problems arise, new aspirations and new forces appear in our increasingly dynamic society. As our experiences multiply, our perspectives expand. We have to learn as much as possible from these experiences, including the mistakes. We have to channel creatively all the new aspirations and forces which continue to surface in our society by making the necessary adjustments.

But in continually adjusting and renewing we must preserve the historical continuity between the past, the present and the future. There is one very basic, persisting factor that we consider sacred and that unites us as a nation. This is Pancasila and the 1945 Constitution. Its essence must not change. It is up to us to exercise and implement it creatively in order to meet the challenges that continually arise in our society and in the world at large....

As part of an increasingly interconnected global society, Indonesia cannot isolate itself from the outside world. Indonesia is influenced by and helps to influence world developments. Both in Indonesia and in the world more generally, we are witnessing the end of an era that began in 1945 with the end of World War II. As the 21st century approaches, we are entering a new era in the history of humankind; new perspectives, new aspirations and new forces are emerging everywhere.

In a world shrunk by sophisticated science and technology, a new awareness has emerged that all nations, without exception, bear a common responsibility regarding the future of humankind. It is only by acting together that we can overcome the grave threats facing humankind and its civilisation – threats such as nuclear warfare, starvation, injustice and environmental degradation.

On the one hand, we have witnessed signs of the winding down of the Cold War, which was based on ideological conflict and competition between different socio-political and socio-economic systems. On the other hand, we feel the winds of change from the West, North, East and South; winds that reinvigorate moral, ethical, spiritual and religious values, that spread humanitarian values such as basic human rights and obligations, winds that strengthen national and international solidarity, that revitalise the ideals of democracy, freedom and openness, and rejuvenate the ideal of social justice....

The task ahead of us resembles, to some extent, the tasks we faced in winning and consolidating our national independence in 1945. When Indonesia became independent, our predecessors looked to the roots of our national character, unearthing its essence. The founders of this republic also took the essence of all the experiences of the independence movement, from the national awakening of 1908, and created Pancasila and the 1945 Constitution, the basic framework for subsequent struggle. In this way they made the transition from a colonised society to a national society within a free, united and sovereign state of the Republic of Indonesia.

Pancasila played a very important function in this transition. Without Pancasila, our national society would never have attained the resilience that we now enjoy. We will recognise this if we compare the national societies of many other countries that achieved their independence at almost the same time as we did....

In my 1984 state address I reiterated that we must develop our own concept and model of development, based on our own culture and values. We shall not imitate any other country's development model. Indeed there is no development model in the world that can simply be picked up and applied elsewhere.

In pursuing our own model of development we do not forget our past struggles. Neither do we allow ourselves to be divorced from our essential character as we make the transition from an agrarian society to an advanced and socially just industrial society. By implementing development in accordance with Pancasila, we continue, improve and renew all our accomplishments to date.

The transition process to take-off will continually give rise to new aspirations and forces. Failure may result if these new aspirations and forces are not channelled creatively, or if they collide.... National development guided by Pancasila provides us with a framework and instrument to reconcile all these different aspirations and forces. In this way they do not collide, but mutually reinforce each other so that they become a single harmonious entity.

By implementing national development guided by Pancasila, the industrial society that we build during the coming take-off era will not simply be a copy of the advanced industrial societies. We will build an advanced industrial society that continues to exhibit the character and ideals of our own national struggle, which we have made eternal in Pancasila and the 1945 Constitution.

Our main task, therefore, in the years to come, is to consolidate the basic framework of national development guided by Pancasila, leading towards the take-off stage.

To undertake this great task we require creative thinking in all fields. People from all walks of life in our society, all strata and groups, from every generation, must develop great creative ideas: those engaged in political groups and social organisations, intellectual life, education, culture and the arts, religion, business and the press.

This is why I put forward the idea of Pancasila as an open ideology a few years ago. By regarding Pancasila as an open ideology we can develop fresh and creative ways to implement Pancasila and respond to the changes and challenges of this restlessly dynamic age. The basic values of Pancasila never change. We can, however, adjust its implementation to the needs and challenges of our times. Our predecessors, the formulators of the 1945 Constitution, counselled us to pay close attention to the dynamics of society. In the 1945 Constitution they laid down only the ground rules for the republic. All of us who follow after them have been given the widest opportunity to develop ways of implementing them.

The consolidation of our political framework requires our greatest attention. The experience of all developing countries proves that if political development is neglected it can lead to stagnation and decline. It can even abort the entire development process. By the same token, political development that outstrips progress in other fields can also become the source of various difficulties and problems that may hinder development. What we need is the growth and development of a Pancasila democracy in step with progress in other fields; and which is always able to ensure national stability, dynamic growth, national unity and integrity, as well as the maintenance of national security and the enhancement of national resilience.

It is in this light that I view the national dialogue on political matters that has been preoccupying us for the past few months. Let us regard the recent voicing of political proposals and aspirations with calm hearts, clear heads and a great feeling of responsibility. Remember that all the changes we aspire to we will achieve in good time as long as we keep our wits about us, plan carefully and remain focused.

State address of 16 August 1990

It may seem that our diverse society is riven by competing demands and differences, but we will not let these become the source of contention and conflict. On the contrary, these forces can be harnessed and made to complement one another and contribute to progress.

Some time ago I stressed that we do not have to worry too much about the diversity of viewpoints and opinions in society. Democracy indeed requires a lot of consultation, discussion, exchanges of views and dialogue, both between the government and the society and between various groups in society. We should see differences of opinion as the very source of life's dynamism.

When our society was still divided by ideological differences we had reason to be concerned about differences of opinion. That time is now passing. Pancasila has taken firm root in our society. To fear diversity of opinion is to doubt Pancasila's power and to hinder the evolution of Pancasila itself.

8.3 Gadjah Mada alumni: the state of emergency is over

This submission to the People's Consultative Assembly, written in December 1990 by a group of senior graduates of the prestigious Gadjah Mada University in Yogyakarta, caused some controversy because it called on the government to set limits on the tenure of the president. Its major theme, however, was that the New Order's reliance on emergency powers – such as the 1988 law giving the president virtually unlimited authority – was no longer justified given the relative calm that prevailed in Indonesia. The unpublished document, issued in the name of 'Exponen Alumni Universitas Gadjah Mada' (1990), was a formal commentary on the draft Broad Guidelines of State Policy and also on the Second Long-Term Development Plan, both due to take effect in 1993.

In our efforts to draft the 1993 Broad Guidelines of State Policy we identified and made an inventory of problems in the fields of economics, politics and law, as well as in the socio-cultural realm. We were confronted by certain realities that need to be addressed:

1   In 1993 we are due to begin the Sixth Five-Year Plan and the Second Long-Term National Development Plan. The two years until that time constitute a crucial transition period because of the unresolved problems of the First Long-Term National Development Plan. We must also consider new problems that we will face in approaching the 21st century.

2   We need to be alert to the possibility of serious upsets or social unrest. These could be triggered by social disparities and distortions in all spheres, giving rise to jealousy, social ferment and an explosive degree of societal breakdown. Social developments such as these are very sensitive during this crucial transitional phase.

3   An absolute prerequisite for the 1993 Broad Guidelines of State Policy is to make the people more mature through their engagement in a more participatory style of Pancasila democracy, not simply through formal representation which only legitimises the wishes of the executive.

4   The current political system prioritises goals or targets, structures and procedures drafted during a state of emergency. Our national goals, or targets, were conceived to overcome the threats that gave rise to this emergency. Likewise our structures, our institutions. The procedures which have governed the formation of our institutions and the way they are run are determined by a set of laws commonly known as the [1985] 'political package', which regulate, among other things, the elections, Golkar and the political parties, social organisations, the composition and status of the MPR and the DPR, and referenda. Because this set of laws is the product of a nation in a state of emergency, their validity is questionable.

A state of emergency is by definition temporary. When order is restored, the legal products of the state of emergency must be regarded as void and inoperative.

There are many issues to be resolved during this two-year transition period, because it is impossible to enter the Second Long-Term National Development Phase, also our Era of Economic Take-Off, on the basis of temporary laws and institutions that are invalid and ought to be scrapped.

Most pressing, the laws pertaining to the general elections, to Golkar and the political parties, and to social organisations must immediately be examined in order that they can be changed, revised or replaced. This is critical because there is only a little over a year left before the general elections.

5   MPR Decision No. VI/1988[1] has had a negative impact on the legal system and on constitutional life generally. It obstructs, distorts and ultimately defeats efforts to build up participation in democratic life. Haunted by an atmosphere that distances them from the realisation of a Pancasila democracy, the people feel pressured. Constitutional life becomes sluggish or listless, and active citizen participation, so necessary to support development, atrophies. Development has deviated from its path, even coming into conflict with the 1945 Constitution and the spirit of the Pancasila. This has not met any overt reaction from the people, yet there is cause for concern that the pressures on people could trigger a rebellion.

8.4 Democratic Forum: rekindle society's critical capacity

According to the Democratic Forum (Forum Demokrasi), the pluralist organisation formed in 1990 under the patronage of Abdurrahman Wahid, democracy was not only a matter of presidential succession, but of transforming values. In this five-page statement (Forum Demokrasi 1992), issued on 19 April 1992, the Democratic Forum Working Group called on Indonesians to free themselves of apathy and acceptance and embrace a culture of criticism.

In the effort to introduce or to enhance democracy we face two kinds of obstacles, one external and one within ourselves....

The internal obstacle is the fading, the ebbing and the disappearance of a critical capacity, both in society and especially in ourselves. Without such a critical capacity democratic principles cannot be put into practice. Critical capacity implies the ability to evaluate an issue in a comprehensive, clear and incisive manner, distinguishing between right and wrong, form and content, appearance and reality.... [It entails] the capacity to check, investigate, test and reveal what is concealed – and never being resigned or submissive. Being critical does not mean carping or insulting people. This is a narrow-minded view of critical capacity.

Critical capacity means the ability to recognise and analyse a problem in order to distinguish its crucial elements. With its help we are able to differentiate between the make-believe democracy that has been served up to us all this time and democracy as it should be. This is why we say that democracy depends on society's critical capacity....

Uniformity tarted up as harmony is often preferred to truth. The repeated failure to defend the truth of an opinion eventually leads one to doubt the use of expressing it at all. This in turn creates a sense of futility about thinking and forming opinions of one's own. Society's critical capacity is then dulled and its horizons narrowed. If the situation is allowed to continue we will all be like 'buffalos led by the nose'. In this atmosphere of cultural decline, two things thrive: apathy and opportunism.

Neither is helpful in the effort to build democracy. People become preoccupied with adapting themselves to the situation or just playing it safe. What we have is a situation in which people simply defer to the strong. There is no sense of interdependency as there ought to be in a system inspired by a family spirit – a spirit that implies mutual respect and equal opportunity.

Apathy and opportunism benefit authoritarian systems, even totalitarian ones, in subtle and often imperceptible ways. They allow one group to set the agenda while the rest just go along with it.

In these circumstances, in which people have gone beyond caring, it is difficult to differentiate between fact and make-believe.

We have been dished up not only make-believe democracy but also make-believe policy reform, make-believe deregulation, make-believe abolition of monopolies, make-believe assistance for farmers, make-believe postponement of megaprojects, make-believe openness and so on.

In creating these illusions of normality, our critical capacity has been shackled and our nation's intelligence has been cynically insulted as well. It is as if they think us so bereft of common sense that we can be fooled time and again.

To rekindle our critical capacity we have to free ourselves from this world of make-believe, cast off our mental chains and see things once again as they really are....

Critical capacity should enable us to see beyond surface phenomena and get to the root of an issue. Take three recent cases: the clove monopoly, the orange monopoly in Kalimantan, and the TVRI [state television station] levy. Each case produced a quick and sharp popular reaction, indicating that there is no reason to believe that society's critical capacity is dead. What people failed to grasp, however, were the common roots of all three problems...the abuse of power, nepotism, and the paralysis of mechanisms of accountability....

Turning to the subject of the elections, we have to think deeply in order to identify what they are really about. The crucial thing about general elections is the opportunity they provide for the people to effect change. Change for the better, hopefully. Change is the key word. Elections that do not provide the opportunity for change are not worthy of the name. Change means something to the people only if it affects their wellbeing – changes to policy in other words. Elections have a bearing on policy only if they are able to influence policy-making – or the policy-makers themselves.

Fond as we are of the 1945 Constitution, we all realise that in policy-making the emphasis is on the position of the president. It follows that a general election...must provide for the possibility of a change of president. Or, in current terminology, it must enable a presidential succession.

Succession is therefore a natural and necessary process according to an honest reading of the 1945 Constitution. It is fully in tune with the 1945 Constitution to link the general elections with succession. Only pseudo-constitutional interpretations treat the general elections as something separate from the succession issue....

Finally, let us work together as one, first of all to empower society with critical capacity; second, to restore the people's sense of entitlement to a critical stance; and, third, to rely on society's critical capacity to ensure a more tranquil future. May this advance the process of democratisation without fear of impinging on the family spirit, or of disrupting harmony, or of disturbing national stability. Freedom!

Jakarta, 19 April 1992

8.5 LIPI: reforming the New Order

In 1996 a team of researchers from the Indonesian Institute of Sciences (LIPI) issued a report proposing a number of changes to the political system. While prescient in many respects, it is striking how cautious its recommendations for political reform were, given the sweeping changes that were to take place following the fall of Soeharto only two years later. It can be read as a failed attempt by conservative intellectuals to preserve the system from a crisis of legitimacy. The following extracts are from Tim PPW–LIPI (1996: 182–91).

One of the objectives of the New Order since its birth has been to correct totally the 'failure' of past political systems. The two main 'failures' were in the implementation of economic development and in creating a stable political system. These failures were reflected in the terrible decline of the economy in the mid-1960s, and in the emergence of various local rebellions which culminated in the G30S/PKI affair.

The objective of developing the economy and creating political stability has been the basis of the New Order political system that we have adhered to for the last 25 years. This system has the following characteristics:

1   The institutionalisation of ABRI's socio-political function (*dwifungsi*).
2   The formation of a 'semi-representative' system – that is, one in which part of the membership of the DPR is appointed besides the election system.
3   A 'closed' political party system and depoliticisation. Such depoliticisation is characterised by the floating mass policy.
4   The centralisation of government with an emphasis on responsible autonomy.
5   Economic development, which relies on foreign capital and foreign aid.

After more than 25 years, everyone acknowledges that this political format has resulted in high economic growth (averaging 6 per cent) and reliable and sustained political stability.

But these successes encompass only two of the three components of the New Order's development trilogy of economic development, political stability and equity. Furthermore, history has moved on and our society has undergone many political, economic, social and cultural changes. Although economic growth and political stability are still regarded as central, society has begun to ask for the fulfilment of other needs that it also regards as being important. These include broader political participation, greater opportunities and more equal distribution in the economic field, legal certainty, as well as protection of human rights and the upholding of social justice in general. At the same time economic development has resulted in the greater exposure of our society to the flow of information from the outside world. Thus we cannot avoid the influences of the wave of globalisation, especially those having to do with demands for democratisation, the upholding of human rights and sustainable development....

Main issues and recommendations

The institutionalisation of ABRI's dual function

Until now ABRI's dual function has been...quantitative in character. ABRI's presence as a political force in the New Order is characterised by ABRI personnel holding various government offices both in the centre and in the regions. This tendency, it is feared, will result in military domination of politics, suspicions on the part of civilians and a continued lack of readiness on the part of civilians to run the government.

Because the doctrine of dual function is not actually geared towards domination, it now seems time to emphasise quality over quantity. Accordingly, ABRI's socio-political function will continue to be recognised, but it no longer has to take a physical form....In this regard, it is also time to think about reducing the number of ABRI personnel appointed to the DPR, so that, in the end, ABRI faction members can be merged with the Golkar parliamentary faction....

The party and representation system

Our party system, determined by Law no. 3/1985, has indeed produced the 'political stability' that the New Order has aspired to since the beginning. However, in its later development the system has shown its limitations in accommodating society's growing aspirations. The three existing social and political organisations have not succeeded in carrying out their function as mediators between society and government. Their lack of autonomy is apparent in the way each of them depends on government-subsidised funds and 'blessings'. In addition, two of the organisations (the PPP and PDI) face a different problem, that is the government's preferential treatment of Golkar.

These limitations...result in various weaknesses in our representation system. This is reflected in the many demonstrations by peasants, workers and other lower-class people that would not be happening if our system of representation functioned properly.

This failure is also apparent in the fact that since 1971 the DPR has never successfully initiated a single piece of legislation. We have also seen that the parliament's other prerogatives have not been utilised optimally, such as the right to demand explanations and to launch inquiries.

To improve this situation, the government ought to take the following steps:

1   Gradually eliminate the policy of depoliticisation (i.e. the floating mass policy). This is pressing for four reasons: first, our society has matured, so it may be said that there is no possibility of a return to political groupism; second, the political participation of society will be broadened as a result; third, the elimination of this policy will allow for the growth of a political party which is more autonomous and well rooted in society; fourth, it will allow the DPR to truly voice the interests of the people it represents.

   During the next five-year development plan (Pelita VI), for example, this could begin at the level of the *kecamatan* (sub district), and in the next few Pelita it could be extended to lower levels, such as the village.

2   Equal recognition of the three social and political organisations. Given that Pancasila has been applied as the sole principle, it is now time to provide the three social and political organisations with truly equal standing, both legally and in practice. The steps that can be taken are as follows: first, we have to standardise the way the three organisations are referred to, whether they are called parties or groups; second, it is only right to allow the three organisations the same opportunity to seek support, including from civil servants – it is time that the Civil Service Corps (Korpri) was freed from the 'obligation' to vote for Golkar, enabling civil servants to return to their true position of serving the state, not a group or party; third, it would probably be helpful if the president were to act as patron either of all three social and political organisations, or of none of them at all; fourth, the government should limit the use of state facilities for social and political organisations, disallowing, for example, disproportionate access to the government's mass-media outlets.

3   The elimination of the government's authority to supervise, guide and freeze the executive bodies of the existing social and political organisations because all three have recognised Pancasila as their sole principle. This step will automatically enhance the autonomy of social and political organisations.

4   In the interests of improving the quality of the DPR, it would be better if its candidates were well known in and familiar with the areas they represent. The process of selecting nominees must therefore be inverted; it should start from the bottom up. This means that the candidates for the national parliament should be chosen by the executive body of social and political organisations at the provincial level, while nominees for the provincial and regional-level legislatures should be determined by the executive body at the regional level.

The centralisation and decentralisation of government

The success already achieved in the area of economic growth and political stability is inextricably linked to the government's centralistic approach. In the long run, however, this kind of approach is actually not very beneficial to the sustainability of development and to stability itself, because in the end it will result in power inequalities between the centre and the regions. This is all the more so because the aspirations and demands of society in the regions have also grown....If the centralisation approach is overused, it is feared that ever more intense 'uprisings' against the centre will emerge from the regions and their societies.

In this regard, it is probably time for the pendulum to swing back from centralisation towards decentralisation so that the ideal of regional autonomy referred to in Article 18 of the 1945 Constitution can be realised. For this to happen, the following steps have to be taken:

1 Limiting the policy of devolving central powers with the aim of, first, creating efficiency and effectiveness in the bureaucracy, second, reducing overlapping of duties and authority between central and regional offices and, third, increasing confidence in local capacities.
2 Applying a more just and proportional product-sharing system over regional economic assets without overlooking the special prerogative of the centre to manage state finances on the one hand and the needs of poor regions on the other....
3 Enhancing the functions of the national and provincial legislatures by gradually eliminating the appointment system. The regional parliaments' powers to act as a control on executive authority also need to be enhanced....

Policy choices that emphasise economic growth

We have enjoyed the fruits of economic development during our first 25-year long-term development...[but] there have been several failures of the chosen policy. First, it has not been successful in forming a strong and autonomous middle class. Second, the assumption of a trickle-down effect has not been realised. This is revealed by data which shows that only 1 per cent of the Indonesian population has enjoyed 80 per cent of the national income, while the other 99 per cent of the population at the lower and middle levels have only shared in 20 per cent. Third, although foreign investment has spurred growth, foreigners have in large part enjoyed the economic surplus. The data reveals that for every US$1 of foreign investment US$10.19 worth of financial resources flow out. Fourth, the phenomenon of corporatism, which has grown stronger, has allowed for the emergence of collusion, corruption and various other forms of abuse...on a massive scale....

We must therefore find a new approach to development, one that not only emphasises growth, but which also attends to the aspects of allocation, distribution, justice and equity. The following steps must be taken:

1   create policies that encourage the formation of a strong and autonomous middle class;
2   reduce reliance on foreign loans for development funding;
3   provide a more appropriate role for...cooperatives and the like;
4   organise a more just taxation system, one that applies progressive taxation for example.

Conclusion

It is clear from the above discussion that the political format that currently applies has resulted in quite high economic growth and long-term political stability. Nevertheless, the socio-political costs that society and the state have had to bear in the long term have been considerable. In order to reduce these costs a reconsideration of the New Order political format is an absolute necessity. Such reconsideration naturally does not require a total restructuring of the existing political format. Indeed change is necessary precisely to avoid a political crisis arising from a crisis of legitimacy of the existing system.

Thus, economic growth and political stability remain our mainstay. Our problem, however, during our second 25 years of long-term development, is how to ensure that democratisation, the upholding of human rights and social justice receive more attention than in previous times.

8.6 Megawati Soekarnoputri: an agenda for reform

Megawati issued this assessment of the state of Indonesian society and politics in April 1997. It appeared days after her followers had staged protests outside the national parliament condemning the conduct of the 1997 elections and demanding that Megawati be reinstated as the head of the PDI. The 20-page document, entitled 'Restoring democracy, justice, and order in Indonesia: an agenda for reform', was written in English.

During the last five years or so we have witnessed a continuing decline in our society with regard to how law is observed and how justice and order are maintained. We have also witnessed a steady decline among our public personalities in their observance of norms of decency in their public conduct. There is a strong impression that we are disintegrating as a pluralistic society, and that we are heading towards a society dominated by social jealousy and mutual distrust.

This situation cannot be left as it is. If we want to maintain our existence as a nation with genuine political and economic sovereignty in the face of globalisation forces that are certain to engulf our neighbours and us, then we have to do something to address all kinds of distortions that have plagued us. We have to do our best to reduce and finally wipe out corruption, collusion, and abuse of power. We have to strive towards clean and competent governments, both at the national and local levels. We have to stop monopolistic practices in our economy. We have to stop nepotism in our political life. We have to restore the independence of the judicial system, making it impossible in the future for any part of the executive system to interfere with the processes of justice. We have also to strengthen our legislative system to ensure that there is a healthy check and balance mechanism in our system of governance.

Failure to...restore and improve democracy in the future will make it impossible for our nation to have a political life that can channel all aspirations that live in the minds of our people. The popular desire to improve the conditions of everyday life, such as improvement of the daily minimum wage for our labourers, or improvement in the way government officials treat citizens, will never become a reality without a political system that is designed to accommodate and channel such popular aspirations....

I thus consider the restoration of democracy as the most important agenda in our effort to bring about improvements in our political, economic, social, and bureaucratic life. This does not mean, of course, that restoring democracy is the only struggle we have to carry out. It is the basis, the foundation, of our general struggle to improve the quality of life in our society, and on this basis we will have to build other structures – political, economic, and social structures – through which we will carry out other, more technocratic reforms. The entire process of reforming our present society, of bringing about a society free of corruption, collusion, abuse of power and nepotism, will have to be achieved through four agendas of reform, i.e. political reform, economic reform, socio-cultural reform, and legal reform.

Political reform: restoring people's sovereignty

Curtailments of people's sovereignty

According to Pancasila ideology and the 1945 Constitution, the Republic of Indonesia is a state based on law, and it is the people who hold the highest sovereignty of the state. In theory, it is the People's Consultative Assembly that has the highest power. The president of the republic is elected by this body and is responsible to this body. In practice, however, it is the president who wields the highest power in the state. A committee that works under the close scrutiny of the president selects members of the People's Consultative Assembly [and appointed] members of the House of

Representatives [DPR]. No one can become a member of the People's Consultative Assembly without the personal approval of the incumbent president. And it is these people who later re-elect the incumbent president for the nth time.

Control of political parties and mass organisations

'People's sovereignty' is just an empty phrase in Indonesia today. In reality the policy of the floating mass constitutes a big hindrance for the people to exercise their political rights. Through this policy political parties have been barred from operating in village communities. Only government bureaucracies – which include both civilians and military government personnel – have been allowed to enter them and conduct political operations. Other government policies that curb people's sovereignty include control of the press and the electronic media, and restrictions on freedom of speech....

Control of the press, radio and television broadcasting

The twisting of the concept of people's sovereignty is also reflected in the way the press is being controlled. If there were real people's sovereignty, then the press would have freedom in choosing their own news items and also freedom in choosing the format of each news item....In practice the government has exercised tight control over the press. The SIUPP policy – i.e. the policy that requires mass media publications to obtain a licence from the Department of Information before it can publish anything – is a very powerful instrument for controlling the press.[2] Each time a daily, weekly, or any other regular publication contains an item considered harmful to the government, the publishing licence can be withdrawn, and the daily or weekly in question has to be closed down....

Control towards radio and television broadcast is equally very tight. In the case of state radio and television broadcasts, the government simply decides in a very arbitrary way what can and cannot be broadcast....In this way the government tightly controls information that can be disseminated to the public. This has been the reason that many foreign radio broadcasts have become popular with the Indonesian public. It is only through these foreign broadcasts that Indonesians can have reliable information about significant events that happen in the country.

Restoring people's sovereignty

How can we put sovereignty back in the hands of the people? This is the most crucial part of our struggle.... Political organisations have to be really independent. The present practice that requires political organisations to consult the government for the appointment of members of the board of political organisations – whether at the national or at the regional or local levels – has to be dropped. Political organisations must have complete freedom in choosing their own members of their various boards. Political organisations must set up their own criteria concerning who can and cannot become members of their various boards.

Members of the House of Representatives – whether national, provincial or district (*kabupaten*) – must consist of those who are elected by the people. There must no longer be members who come into the House of Representatives by appointment. This practice must eventually be stopped, because it is a fundamental violation of the basic idea of people's representation. This same principle applies to membership in the People's Consultative Assembly. Every member of this most important political institution must be elected by the people....

Another step towards restoring people's sovereignty is to stop the present practice of conducting special investigations (*penelitian khusus* or *litsus*) [into the political backgrounds] of persons nominated to become members of parliament. The present practice of crossing out nominees the government does not like is tantamount to efforts to create a rubber-stamp parliament....

The present stipulation that the central board of any political organisation has the right to recall an incumbent member of parliament whenever he or she deviates from the 'party line' charted by the organisation is also an undemocratic practice that must be dropped. It should never be forgotten that any member of parliament ultimately represents the people, and not the organisation that nominated him or her. Any member of parliament must have full freedom in determining how he or she can best represent the interest of the people.

Still another step that must be undertaken to restore people's sovereignty is to stop the practice of the president summoning a member of parliament. If any summoning must be done, it must be by the chair of the People's Consultative Assembly and not by the president. We must keep in mind that the president is accountable to the People's Consultative Assembly....

Social reform and cultural transformation

Democratisation as a process of cultural transformation

The transformation of our society from a feudal society into a democratic one is in the first place a cultural transformation, a transformation of our value system both at the individual and at the collective level. In this process values and norms which were generated by our feudal way of life in the past have to be gradually dropped, and replaced by new values and norms that come from a democratic outlook....If we want to see a more rapid democratisation process taking place in our society, then we must be actively involved in the process of value transformation. We must actively reject values that put us in permanent bondage to feudalism and actively introduce values that change patterns of relationships within our society....

The growth of democracy in our society has been slow. This is because our people do not have sufficient understanding yet of what democracy essentially is. This is why providing education about democracy to the people is essential. We cannot move our society towards sustained democratisation unless the people understand that the struggle to defend democracy is a struggle to shield them from excessive practices of power abuse, a struggle to make others respect them. They will support efforts towards continuous democratisation only after they realise that democracy is relevant to their personal lives.

8.7 Muhammad Shiddiq Al-Jawi: must Islam accept democracy?

Although most Muslim parties and organisations support democracy, some campus-based groups emerged in the 1990s that rejected it as incompatible with Islam. In this early example, taken from a typescript circulated in Jakarta and beyond, the activist Muhammad Shiddiq Al-Jawi (c.1991) draws on the works of radical Middle Eastern thinkers to make a case against democracy.

There is no doubt that the idea of democracy has become part of world opinion. Since World War II, most countries in the world have been built on a democratic basis. UNESCO research in 1949 found that 'probably for the first time in history democracy is claimed as the proper ideal description of all systems of political and social organisation advocated by influential proponents' (Budiardjo 1972: 50).

The idea of (capitalist) democracy has come to rule the world and now underpins thinking in all sorts of subsidiary areas.

As the prevailing idea, democracy has become the only formula for building a government, as well as becoming a powerful means of changing and challenging governments regarded as undemocratic. All kinds of arbitrary behaviour and irregularities of a regime in various spheres of life have been criticised from a democratic standpoint. Democratic premises have become a standard for evaluating a diverse range of concepts. Only those concepts that are compatible with democracy are regarded as acceptable.

But public opinion in itself is not a sufficient test of the validity of an idea. Public opinion only indicates that an idea has been accepted by a majority of people and become the basis of their lives. It is therefore necessary that public opinion be evaluated according to a standard that there are no doubts about. It is only on this basis that we can either accept or reject an idea. Once an idea is accepted it is possible to plan how to implement it. This is how we must approach particular ideas.

On this basis, the Muslim community will evaluate democracy from the perspective of the Islamic faith. Muslims regard the Islamic faith as the basis for evaluating all other ideas (Shawwaf 1993). Having faith in Islam and making it the standard for evaluating other ideas entails demonstrating faith in and obedience to God's commands.

God ordained: 'Follow what was revealed to you by your God and do not follow other leaders'.

Democratic theory stems from an acceptance of the separation of religion and life (secularism), the ideological basis of Western capitalism.

Bearing in mind the separation of religion and the church from life and the state – which in turn distances religion from the formulation of legislation and the appointment of office-holders – it becomes necessary for people to *create their own set of rules to live by*. It is in this context that the idea of democracy arose.

Democracy is based on two fundamental ideas:

1   that sovereignty is in the hands of the people;
2   that the people are the ultimate source of power....

In order that these two ideas can exist without pressure or force, democracy gives the people *freedom*. Namely, freedom of religion, freedom of opinion, freedom of ownership and freedom of action....

Comparing Islam and democracy

Source of the idea

Democracy is a human creation. In the democratic system human rationality is the point of reference in judging the worth of deeds and of the things we use.

God bestowed the Islamic faith upon the Prophet Mohammed. In Islam, it is religious law – not human reason – that is the point of reference. In this regard the function of the mind is limited to understanding God's utterances.

God ordained: 'Determining law is the right of God alone' (Al An 'aam: 57).

God ordained: 'If there is still a conflict of opinion, refer it back to God (the Qu'ran) and the teachings of the Prophet (the Sunnah)' (An Nisaa': 59).

God ordained: 'Whatever you are in dispute about, leave the decision to God' (Asy Syura: 10).

Belief (the basis of thought)

Democracy is premised on the separation of religion from life and the separation of religion from the state. Democracy does not disavow religion, but it denies the role of religion in life and the state. Consequently it is left to people themselves to determine how life is to be lived and the state governed.

In Islam, built on the foundations of Islamic faith, all matters of life and state are subject to the rules and prohibitions of God as contained in *syariah*. Humans must obey the rules decided for them by God; they have no right to decide for themselves the rules to live by. God ordained: 'And you will decide disputes among them according to God's teachings, not according to their base desires' (Al Maaidah: 49).

Sovereignty and power

Democracy holds that sovereignty is in the hands of the people. It is the people who have the right to make – and to annul – constitutions, rules and any legislation according to their priorities. The people are the lawmakers (*Musysyari'*).

Democracy holds that power originates from the people, meaning that it is the people who chose the leaders they want to implement the laws that the people have made. The people have the right to dismiss their leaders because they have the power.

In Islam, sovereignty is determined by Islamic law, not the people. So it is God alone who acts as lawmaker (*Musysyari'*). The people have no right to make even a single law. God ordained: 'Making laws is the right of God alone' (Al An 'aam: 57)....

With regard to power, Islam takes the view that power is in the hands of the believers. It is the believers who have the right to choose their rulers so that the rulers implement God's rules and prohibitions. This is based on the Hadith that determines that Muslims have the right to appoint a caliph, to carry out the teachings of the Qu'ran and His Prophet. As the Prophet said: '*Whoever has sworn allegiance to the caliph and has given with his whole heart, he will obey him as much as possible.*'

But *syariah* determines that the believers do not have the right to dismiss a ruler, as is the case in democracy. This is based on the Shahih Hadith, which obliges people to be obedient to the caliph, even if he sins and acts tyrannically. The Prophet said,

> Listening (to the pronouncements of the caliph) and obeying them is obligatory for all Muslims whether they like it or not, as long as they are not ordered to sin.... If they are ordered to sin, there is no need to heed his commands.

Thus it is justified to revolt against the ruler only if he is brazenly heathen. The only body that can legitimately dismiss the caliph is the Mahkamah Mazhalim (supreme court in a caliphate).

The majority principle

Democracy considers that the opinion of the majority represents the true voice of the people. The opinions of minorities must submit to majority opinion.

In Islam the issue is very different. To be specific:

1   Issues surrounding the making of laws (*tasyri'*) do not depend on the extent of public support for them but rather on the articles of *syariah*, because the only lawmaker is God, not the believers. The precedent is the Prophet's rejection of the opinion of the Muslims in the Hudaibiyah agreement, even though they were in a majority.
2   In matters concerning knowledge (such as science and technology) and where expertise is required (such as military matters) the emphasis is on correct opinions (*shawab*), regardless of whether a majority agrees. The precedent is the Prophet's choice to endorse the opinion of Habbab bin Mundzir – a strategist of his time – in the Badar War. The Prophet abandoned his original opinion and he did not ask for the opinions of other advisers.
3   In technical matters that do not require special expertise, decisions can be made on the basis of majority opinion. The precedent is the Prophet's actions during the Uhud War. At that time the majority wanted to fight the war outside the city of Madinah, while the Prophet and his senior advisers did not want to leave the city.

Attitudes towards freedom

Democracy holds that individual freedom encompasses the freedom of belief, the freedom of opinion, the freedom of ownership and the freedom of action. The freedom of ownership gave birth to the capitalist system based on advantage and profit alone. Each of these freedoms conflicts with Islamic law. To clarify these points:

1   Freedom of belief. Muslims are not free to choose their faith; they are obliged to be Muslims. The Prophet said, 'Whoever changes their religion, kill them.'
2   Freedom of opinion. Muslims' beliefs must be grounded in an Islamic outlook and be based on Islam.
3   Freedom of ownership. Muslims have a right to ownership only within the constraints specified by *syariah*. Ownership must be guided by what is held to be religiously sanctioned or proscribed.

4 Freedom of action. There is no formula guaranteeing freedom of action in Islam. The behaviour of Muslims must be governed by *syariah*, with those who violate *syariah* liable to be punished.

Therefore democratic freedoms are in sharp conflict with the freedoms found in Islam.

Notes

1 Article 2 of MPR Decision No. VI/1988, dated 9 March 1988, 'Bestows on the President/Mandatory of the MPR the authority to take whatever measures [are] required to ensure the security and maintenance of national unity in order to confront and cope with social unrest, the danger of a repeat of the G30S/PKI and other threats of subversion in order to safeguard national development and the implementation of Pancasila and Pancasila Democracy as well as preserving Pancasila and the 1945 Constitution' (Majelis Permusyawaratan Rakyat 1988: 114).
2 SIUPP stands for *Surat Izin Usaha Penerbitan Pers* (Press Publishing Licence). The Habibie administration abolished the press licensing system in June 1998.

9   State and society relations

This chapter explores how individuals and groups sought to stake out claims against an overbearing yet fractured state. Most of the readings are from the last decade of Soeharto's rule, when it was becoming increasingly clear that the New Order's rigid political architecture was ill suited to accommodate the demands of the new social groups that economic growth had generated. It would be a mistake, however, to view this period as one in which the New Order was in terminal decline. Until the mid-1990s the Soeharto government had in place a formidable system of legal, ideological and repressive controls capable of quashing open dissent and preventing the establishment of effective vehicles through which a political challenge could be organised. The New Order's capacity to guarantee continued economic growth also helped to a considerable extent in legitimising the repressive aspects of its rule.

The foundations of this system were laid down in the early New Order with the military takeover, the mass killings of suspected communists and the attempt to eliminate or coopt all organisations independent of the state. Existing parties, labour unions, youth groups and other mass organisations were dissolved into corporatist bodies aligned with the government's election vehicle Golkar. As we mentioned in Chapter 4, a compliant legislature passed a set of laws in 1985 institutionalising this corporatist system. Restrictions on expression were also an important part of the Soeharto regime's concept of order. The government used a range of instruments to intimidate critics, including informal threats, *lèse majesté* and 'hatred-sowing' criminal charges, as well as a system of press licensing that enabled the authorities to close down offending publications at will. Both sets of restrictions were publicly justified on the grounds that political stability was an absolute prerequisite for development, and that to this end the government and the armed forces had to protect society from the forces of disorder, whether in the guise of sectarianism, liberalism or communism.

We open this chapter with a political questionnaire produced by the powerful internal security organisation Kopkamtib in about 1985 (Reading 9.1). Administered in written form and via interviews to tens, possibly hundreds, of thousands of workers in vital industries, the questionnaire reveals the extraordinary importance the regime attached to ideology as a means of social control.[1] Data collected through this kind of intelligence gathering exercise gave the security authorities considerable leverage over the lives of ordinary Indonesians. 'Incorrect' responses saw thousands fall under suspicion and lose their jobs in the late 1980s (Motek 1988: 5–8). At the same time, the questionnaire unwittingly provided a valuable insight into the anxieties of the regime.

Control was, of course, never complete or uncontested. The period saw numerous protests by displaced farmers and poorly treated industrial workers in Java and Sumatra. It was also a period in which some middle-class groups showed a willingness to risk defying the authorities. Readings 9.2 and 9.3 are by two of Indonesia's best-known artists, W.S. Rendra and Iwan Fals. Rendra was a major figure in the protest movement in the 1970s, not only for his poems but also for his essays and plays, including the biting satire *The Struggle of the Naga Tribe*. 'Poem of an angry person' captures well the sense of distance between the ordinary people and the privileged elite, but also the promise that resistance will overcome in the end. Iwan Fals' song 'Bento' also targets the idle rich, sarcastically celebrating the success of a ruthless, well-connected young entrepreneur resembling Soeharto's playboy son Hutomo 'Tommy' Mandala Putera. Fals gained a huge following in the 1980s and 1990s among youths and the urban poor for his songs about corruption, injustice and suffering. The popularity of Rendra and Fals protected them to some extent, but this did not stop the authorities banning several of their performances and detaining Rendra.

The language of rights came to the fore much more strongly than ever before in the 1980s, especially in relation to the right to organise and the right to free expression. This trend was encouraged by the worldwide rise in the stocks of liberal democracy at the end of the Cold War and by the relaxation of domestic constraints during the so-called era of 'openness' between 1989 and 1994. As discussed in Chapter 8, it was also facilitated by a power struggle between Soeharto and some sections of the military establishment.

Senior political activist and former student leader Marsillam Simanjuntak captured the mood of the times in a 1990 *Tempo* article in which he appealed to Indonesians to put aside their fears and exercise their constitutional right to 'Speak out' (Reading 9.4). More broadly representative of the concerns of community organisations is the 1991 aide mémoire of the International NGO Forum on Indonesia (INGI), excerpted in Reading 9.5. This document's emphasis on the right to organise reflected the sharp growth in pressures during the period among groups in society – particularly workers, farmers, students and women – to organise independently of the officially licensed corporatist bodies established in the 1970s.

Some professionals, too, were attempting to shake free of the state corporatist system. Reformist lawyers, for example, were largely successful in gaining control of successive official bar associations in the 1980s (Peradin and Ikadin). Following the precipitous banning of the news weeklies *Tempo, Editor* and *Detik* in June 1994 – which brought an end to 'openness' – dozens of journalists, backed by several prominent cultural figures, turned their back on the official Indonesian Journalists' Association (PWI) to form their own body, the Alliance of Independent Journalists (AJI). The Sirnagalih Declaration (Reading 9.6), which brought AJI into existence in August 1994, marked a crucial moment both in the history of Indonesian journalism and in the unravelling of the New Order's system of corporatist control (see Sen and Hill 2000: ch. 2).

As was detailed in Chapters 3 and 6, corporatist mechanisms were also a key means of controlling Islamic groups in the 1970s and 1980s. But once Soeharto was convinced that the threat of Islamic radicalism was past he embarked on a much more conciliatory policy. The most obvious manifestation of his new approach to Islam was his sponsorship of ICMI in 1990. Sections of the new Muslim urban middle class embraced ICMI, but its establishment also gave rise to – or, perhaps more accurately, exacerbated – an important schism among Muslim intellectuals. Abdurrahman Wahid was a leading critic of the group, arguing that it represented a cynical attempt to coopt Muslims to the purposes of the New Order by encouraging a dangerous re-politicisation of religion (Reading 9.7). Supporters of ICMI, on the other hand, such as former NGO activist Dawam Rahardjo, refuted such charges, holding that Indonesia's Muslim majority had benefited under the New Order and that ICMI provided an overdue opportunity for Muslims to exercise real political influence (Reading 9.8).

Yet while some saw the last few years of the New Order as a time of opportunity, the government's legitimacy in the public's view was clearly in sharp decline. From 1996 it increasingly resorted to violence and intimidation to persecute political rivals such as Megawati Soekarnoputri, labour leaders, including Muchtar Pakpahan, and student-based groups like the left-leaning PRD (People's Democratic Party). The last excerpt in this chapter was written in the aftermath of the riots that shook Jakarta on 27 July 1996 following the military-orchestrated storming of the PDI headquarters – riots that the authorities said were instigated by people using 'communist methods'. In an essay thick with irony, the distinguished novelist, priest and social commentator Y.B. Mangunwijaya questioned the government's charges, suggesting that the New Order itself more closely resembled the 'totalitarian bureaucratic collectivism' that characterised many communist states (Reading 9.9).

Soeharto's fall in May 1998 in the midst of a deep economic crisis precipitated the partial unravelling of the framework of state and society relations built during his long presidency. The speed with which new parties and labour unions were formed afterwards was a measure of the bankruptcy of the old structures, essentially proven to be unviable without Soeharto himself at the helm. Elements of his old New Order were to realise that their own political survival would now require them to reinvent themselves in new alliances and vehicles within a much more open and democratic social and political framework. The struggle still continues, however, to ensure that Indonesia's new democracy provides genuine opportunities for those most systematically marginalised by the New Order – such as peasants and workers – to influence the direction of politics and society.

9.1 Kopkamtib: intelligence test

This set of questions was drawn up by the internal security agency Kopkamtib and administered in the mid-1980s to oil industry workers in Sumatra. It was then extended to workers in other 'vital industries', including state-run and private enterprises connected with sea, rail and air transport, mining, electricity, postal services and banking. The document was first published in *Inside Indonesia* (no. 8, October 1986: 8) and is rendered here with minor changes based on the original document.

1 Describe your family background and that of your spouse, starting with your grandparents and those of your spouse. Mention which religion(s) and the organisations/parties they have followed. Tell the story of your family since you were small, from the time you started primary school. Was it on the whole comfortable or difficult? If you were adopted, say who your foster parents were. Also give the full names of your brothers and sisters, brothers-in-law and sisters-in-law. Then give the names of your closest acquaintances during the last three years.
2 If you have ever received a scholarship, where was it from and on what conditions was it issued?
3 The basis of your convictions/religion. Do you practise these (convictions/religion) diligently? Which parish/church/mosque are you part of?
4 Your attitude towards mystical sects.
5 Say which national/world heroes you admire, and give your reasons.
6 Recite the Pancasila. Describe your attitude towards the Pancasila.
7 What would you think if the Pancasila were altered?
8 Explain P4.[2]
9 Your view of G30S/PKI.[3] Your reaction.
10 Were any members of your family involved?

11 Marxism/Leninism. When did you hear of it, come to understand it, in what circumstances? Communism is a latent danger, do you agree?
12 Your attitude towards protest demonstrations with banners.
13 Your attitude towards the dual function of the armed forces.
14 Your understanding of the New Order. What is it? What is its basis?
15 Your attitude to citizens who reject or do not take part in the general elections.
16 The monoloyalty of public servants/the armed forces towards the government. What is your opinion?
17 Is the existence of the Indonesian Civil Servants Corps [Korpri] in accord with Article 28 of the 1945 Constitution?[4]

These questions are for you alone.

If as a consequence of this you are dismissed from your company, what would your attitude be?

Be prepared to accept the risks if you make an erroneous statement.

9.2 W.S. Rendra: poem of an angry person

Written in 1978, this poem remained popular through the 1980s and 1990s. Rendra read it at the Trisakti University campus in May 1998 following the student shootings, and again at the parliament on 15 May at the height of the anti-Soeharto demonstrations. This translation by Max Lane was published in *Inside Indonesia* (no. 2, 1984: 25).

> Because we eat roots
> And flour piles up in your warehouses...
> Because we live all cramped up
> And your space is so abundant...
> So we are not your allies.
>
> Because we are soiled
> And you are shiny bright...
> Because we feel suffocated
> And you lock the door...
> So we distrust you.
>
> Because we are abandoned on the streets
> And you own all the shade...
> Because we endure floods
> And you party on pleasure boats...
> So we don't like you.
>
> Because we are silenced
> And you never stop nagging...
> Because we are threatened

And you use violence against us...
So we say to you NO.

Because we may not choose
And you are free to make plans...
Because we have only sandals
And you are free to use rifles...
Because we must be polite
And you have jails...
So NO and NO to you.

Because we are the current of the river
And you are the stones without heart...
So the water will erode away the stones.

9.3 Iwan Fals: Bento

A folk hero to the urban poor in the 1980s, Iwan Fals' songs were widely circulated on cassette and his live concerts attracted huge and sometimes unruly crowds. 'Bento', one of his best-loved songs, was co-written with Naniel and first recorded with the group Swami on the album *Swami I* in 1989.

My name is Bento and I've got it all
plenty of cars, a big solid house
people call me the executive boss
everyone knows I'm the one
unreal...!

I'm handsome as hell, the women adore me
one glance and they're mine
trading's my business, I'll cut any throat
as long as I'm happy, as long as I win
to hell with the losers who get in my way
as long as I'm happy, once more
unreal...!

Sermons about morality and justice
I have them for breakfast
deceit, lobbying and graft
I'll show you how it's done!
small-time crooks, street-corner bandits
they know nothing
if you want to get serious,
I'm the one to teach you how
just say my name three times: Bento, Bento, Bento
unreal...!

9.4 Marsillam Simanjuntak: speak out!

This extract, by Democratic Forum member Marsillam Simanjuntak, is translated from an article he wrote for the popular magazine *Tempo* (15 September 1990). Marsillam would later serve as cabinet secretary and attorney-general to President Abdurrahman Wahid.

Someone asked my response to President Soeharto saying in his recent state address, 'Differences of opinion are permitted', particularly in connection with the current state of the Indonesian press. Before answering this question, some preliminary clarification of basic concepts is necessary.

To begin with, it should be understood as a fact of life that, for as long as people think and have interests, they will always have opinions. And at the same time it follows that there will always be a variety of different and even opposed opinions about any issue. These obvious statements need to be made in order to lay to rest the notion that differences of opinion exist only because they are sanctioned by the authorities. Opinions and differences of opinion existed before government decreed them and before they were regulated by any constitution.

Openly asserting or expressing opinions is another matter, which leads us to the next point. While 'the right to hold opinions' is incontestable, 'the right to express opinions' came into being, or, more precisely, was codified, through constitutional regulation – in our case in Article 28 of the 1945 Constitution.

It follows that the freedom to express opinions is the constitutional right of every citizen. However, in our society we are not yet accustomed to understanding and exercising our constitutional rights. The significance of a constitutional right is that it is a basic right that must become the standard for all subsequent laws and regulations. Violating this basic right, by whatever means, violates the 1945 Constitution. In other words, it is *unconstitutional*.

So the issue of constitutionality does not relate only to the issue of the presidential succession or the procedures of lofty state institutions. To obstruct, repress, block, hamper or impede the channels for free expression is also unconstitutional. And it is not only those outside the government who are capable of unconstitutional behaviour. Anyone can be guilty of it, and they all ought to be 'clobbered'[5] – in accordance with constitutional procedures of course.

The third point is that the president's recent statement that people no longer need to be concerned about differences of opinion implies acknowledgement that differences of opinion were not given the opportunity to develop freely in the past. Significantly, in his state address of 16 August 1990 President Soeharto used the phrase 'when our society was still ideologically divergent'. If that is the case, what mechanisms existed (or still exist) for controlling the expression of opinions? Does the president's state address signal that all controls and constraints are to be lifted?

The press facilitates the expression of public opinion (and, by extension, differences in opinion). Therefore a free press guarantees the exercise of the constitutional right to free expression of opinion. By the same token, blocking or obstructing such a channel for public opinion is tantamount to breaching the obligation to uphold this constitutional right. As I said, this is unconstitutional.

On this basis, it can be inferred that the government is acting unconstitutionally when it exercises the right to withdraw publication permits in response to certain news being printed. The issuing of publication permits, which are actually only business licences, is in practice frequently used as a threat to the survival of publishing enterprises. This gives rise to a good deal of worry and insecurity on the part of the media about how free they are to communicate news. Experience has shown that the threat of having publishing permits revoked has been highly effective. With the threat of closure hanging over the heads of publishers, the channels of public opinion have been blocked.

We have learned not to be too optimistic about what President Soeharto says in his speeches. Almost a year after proposing in a speech to the DPR that [corporate leaders] transfer as much as 25 per cent of their shares to cooperatives, we find that they have only transferred 1 per cent, and grudgingly at that. If we relate this to President Soeharto's recent state address about 'differences of opinion' we may have a long wait before we see an end to violations of the constitutional right to speak and write freely.

As with many older people, President Soeharto does not like to be 'preempted'. But if there is one concrete consequence of the president's statement it is surely that ministers must end their intimidating practice of threatening to withdraw publishing permits.

Rather than discussing whether or not they are allowed to express themselves, the people at large, including journalists, would do better to go ahead and start exercising their constitutional rights: so have opinions, and express them!

9.5 International NGO Forum on Indonesia: democracy and the right to organise

This aide mémoire was prepared for the seventh conference of the International NGO Forum on Indonesia (INGI), held in Washington, DC, in April–May 1991. INGI was an association of Indonesian and foreign NGOs set up to lobby major donors such as the Inter-Governmental Group on Indonesia (IGGI), a multilateral aid consortium that channelled billions of US dollars into Indonesia annually. The Dutch Development Cooperation Minister and IGGI chair, Jan Pronk, angered the Indonesian regime by meeting with a range of NGO, worker and human rights groups in Jakarta in May 1991 and conveying their concerns in blunt terms to the government. In a flamboyant gesture, Soeharto rejected future development aid from the Netherlands in 1992. IGGI was also dissolved as a consequence but soon re-emerged as the Consultative Group on Indonesia.

INGI began its communication with the IGGI Chair in June 1985. Six years later, INGI appreciates the IGGI Chairperson's and the World Bank's acceptance of the invitation to speak on [the] occasion of the opening of the Seventh INGI Conference in Washington, DC, USA.

The presence of the IGGI Chairperson at the INGI Conference reflects the objectives of INGI to have the IGGI consider and take positive action on important issues affecting the poor and disadvantaged, and to strengthen people's participation in development, especially in Indonesia. INGI welcomes Mr Pronk's statement that INGI's concerns are also concerns of the IGGI.

In his opening address, the IGGI Chairperson dwelled on the progress of development in Indonesia. He noted that compared to other developing countries, absolute poverty in Indonesia declined at a remarkable rate. However, as he suggested, development is more than finding the right mixture of economic growth, appropriate adjustment policies and an anti-poverty campaign. Development is also a question of good governance. The IGGI Chairperson defined good governance as consisting of five factors: appropriate choice of targets and tools; good management and implementation; attention to societal norms and values; an equitable decision-making process; and the existence of democratic institutions. There is a danger that even if we recognise the importance of non-economic factors in development we would still focus on quantitative rather than qualitative results.

Although we appreciate the IGGI Chair's commitment to good governance, we believe that the real question is empowerment. INGI believes that if the quality of life of the Indonesian people is to be enhanced, development must be consciously linked to democratisation or a greater participation of all sectors of society in allocating resources and sharing power. Democratisation in Indonesia should involve respect for the basic freedoms of expression, assembly and association; that is, an 'openness' not just tolerated but gradually institutionalised in the form of independent organisations, unrestricted publications and speech, and academic freedom. It should lead to the mutual independence of the executive, legislative and judicial branches of government, a strengthening of the judiciary and legal system, and equal access of all, including minorities, disadvantaged groups and women, to justice. Democratisation would lead to a reduction in the role of the military in government and less reliance on the use of force and coercion.

INGI acknowledges the importance of political stability and achieving economic growth. But the understanding of political stability as a situation where conflicts have to be avoided or eliminated instead of being resolved by open debate and democratic procedures has had the undesired effect of enforcing conformity and preventing constructive dissent. Too much emphasis on economic growth has obscured the question of equity and distributive justice, which has been the concern of INGI since its first Aide Mémoire in 1985.

INGI believes that sound and sustainable development depends on unhampered access to information from governments, multilateral agencies and others; on absence of fear, intimidation, harassment or physical abuse of those who challenge authority or decline to take part in programs which they believe are unsound; and on accountability of officials for abuses or mistakes.

INGI believes that democratisation in Indonesia is essential if development is to be equitable across social strata and between genders – humane and sustainable.

Recommendations

The right to organise

Article 8 of the 1945 Constitution guarantees the right to organise. However, the interpretation of this article in laws, regulations, decrees and instructions (e.g. Law no. 5/1985 on political parties and Law no. 8/1985 on mass organisations) has limited the full exercise of this right.

This limitation is primarily the result of the paradigm of political stability as a precondition for development and economic growth. A more participatory and sustainable concept of development would allow for a more open, non-repressive and democratic concept of political stability.

Changing the very concept of development could ensure a pluralistic system of representation of sectoral interests for Indonesians at all levels of society and in all professions, including minorities, women, child workers, labourers, farmers and migrant workers.

1   INGI urges the Government of Indonesia to protect the right of workers, men and women, to organise both in the formal and informal sectors, as guaranteed by the 1945 Constitution, Law no. 18/1956 (ratification of the ILO [International Labour Organisation] Convention no. 98) and Law no. 14/1969. Ministerial decrees and other regulations which contradict the above-mentioned laws must be abolished, such as Ministerial Decree no. 1109/1986 and no. 5/1987.

2   Workers should be free to form organisations of their own choice to represent their interests and settle their disputes with employers by and among themselves. Trade unions – such as Setia Kawan free trade

union – should be accorded autonomy consistent with relevant inter-national labour standards (ILO conventions 87, 98 and 151 in particular).... Farmers must be given the freedom to form and manage organisations such as farmers' unions and cooperatives. International aid agencies and donors should refrain from funding projects in which workers and farmers are not allowed to organise independently.

3   Recognising that disadvantaged populations consist of both men and women but that women experience additional problems not faced by men, INGI recommends that disadvantaged women have the right to organise and the right to opportunities to improve their lives. These groups include domestic servants, migrant workers, prostitutes, house-wives, women in the informal sector, industrial workers and home-based workers.

4   The corporatist drive towards single organisations is contrary to the reality of Indonesian diversity as well as the spirit of democratisation. Therefore, the right of Indonesian citizens should be respected not to join official or officially approved organisations such as Korpri (Indonesian Civil Servants' Corps), HKTI (All-Indonesia Farmers' Association), SPSI (All-Indonesia Workers' Association), PWI (Indonesian Journalists' Association), PGRI (Indonesian Teachers' Association), KOPMA (Student Cooperatives), Dharma Wanita[6] and PKK (Program for Family Welfare).

Political democratisation

LIFTING CONTROLS

The emphasis on security in Indonesia has restricted popular participation in development, as illustrated by the Kedung Ombo case.[7] In order to contribute effectively in the development process, individuals, communities and organisations need to be able to do the following:

a   to meet without requiring a permit;
b   to speak, publish and distribute materials critical of government and development policies without fear of intimidation, imprisonment and ill treatment;
c   to demonstrate peacefully without fear of reprisal;
d   to make decisions, in the case of farmers, on planting and marketing without undue government intervention;
e   to ensure that civil and military authorities are fully accountable to the people for their actions;
f   to have the freedom to question or challenge executive decisions and practices without harassment or intimidation both directly or before an independent judiciary and/or through parliament. In order to achieve this, INGI recommends:

- to elect directly local representatives, which implies a revision of the Law on the Regional Governments no. 5/1974 and the Law no. 3/1985 on General Elections;
- that the proportion of appointed members in parliaments at all levels be reduced;
- that the proportion of military officials in civilian positions directly affecting the civilian population be reduced....

9.6 The Sirnagalih Declaration

In this landmark document, signed in the West Javanese village of Sirnagalih on 7 August 1994, 58 journalists and cultural figures declare their opposition to censorship, intimidation and media bans. Some of those sacked for signing the statement helped pioneer the boom in Internet media, including *Tempo Interaktif*, which evaded official restrictions. The document was posted in Indonesian and English versions on the Indonesia Publications e-mail list (apakabar@igc.apc.org) on 8 August 1994.

We acknowledge freedom of speech, access to information and freedom of association as a basic right of all citizens.

We recognise that the history of the Indonesian press is marked by struggles to uphold truth and justice as well as to oppose all types of oppression.

In carrying out its mission, the Indonesian press places national unity and national priorities above individual and group interests.

Indonesia is a constitutional state. Because of this the Indonesian press bases its struggles on legal principles rather than power.

Based on these principles:

- we reject all kinds of interference, intimidation, censorship and media bans which deny the freedom of speech and open access to information;
- we reject all efforts to dissipate the spirit of the Indonesian press venturing to fight for their concerns;
- we reject one-sided information advanced for the benefit of individuals or groups in the name of the national interest;
- we reject any deviations from the law that conflict with Pancasila and the 1945 Constitution;
- we reject the concept of a single compulsory organisation for journalists;
- we proclaim the establishment of the Alliance of Independent Journalists as an organisation which upholds the struggles and concerns of the Indonesian press.

Sirnagalih, 7 August 1994
Signed[8]

9.7 Abdurrahman Wahid: Islam and the state in the New Order

In this 1991 discussion paper, the influential Nahdlatul Ulama leader surveys the range of attitudes to state power on the part of Islamic organisations during the New Order, making clear his disapproval of the recently established Indonesian Muslim Intellectuals' Association (ICMI). The paper was presented at the Society for Political and Economic Studies (SPES) in Jakarta on 27 November 1991.

When we look at how various key issues have been resolved during the first 25 years of the New Order, a very interesting pattern emerges in the relationship between Islam and the state. An assortment of images comes to mind regarding the dynamics of the relationship between Islamic movements and the government, between Islamic movements themselves, external relations with Islamic movements overseas, and relationships between non-government movements both domestically and internationally. Images also arise concerning the main modes of operation adopted by various Islamic movements during the New Order.

Before looking at these different aspects, we need first to consider underlying factors in the relationship between Islam and the state during the New Order. Especially interesting here is that there appear to be two contradictory developments. On the one hand it is apparent that Islam has been removed from the stage as a formal political force through a government-imposed policy of dismantling the vertical alignments or confessional affiliations in Indonesian politics. With the requirement that all civil servants support Golkar as the 'government party' in the 1971 general elections, the simplification of the number of political parties in 1973 (resulting in the fusion of Islamic parties in the PPP), as well as the policy since 1984 to make nearly all Islamic organisations adopt Pancasila as their sole basis, the separation of Islam from formal political life was completed relatively quickly, in around 15 years.

Yet it is also true that over the past 25 years the potential of Islamic movements as informal political forces has grown. Because it needs legitimacy to implement its development programs, the New Order government has had to seek backing from various quarters, including Islamic movements. A constructive response from these movements has seen the government become partly dependent on them in areas such as family planning, the environment, campaigns to improve family nutrition, all aspects of education, the maintenance of socio-political stability and the development of national law. This dependence has also manifested itself at the intra-governmental level in the intensive interaction between a diversity of power centres vying for national influence.

Nurcholish Madjid's slogan of the late 1960s and early 1970s of 'Islam yes, Islamic parties no', must now be read as 'Islamic political parties no,

Islamic political forces yes'. It is interesting to observe the dynamics that have unfolded in arriving at this position, because within them are hidden patterns that provide insights into the future political development of various Islamic movements. The divergent, if not conflicting, strategies adopted by various Islamic movements will also be exposed. Or, more precisely, it will be shown which movements are consciously developing a particular strategy, and which are just being swept along without any strategy whatsoever....

Being mindful that various factors influence the 'Islamic agenda' and stance of each movement, it is possible for us to categorise the relations between Islamic movements and the government and observe the orientations within each category. Of course in so doing we must always keep in mind the possibility of various Islamic figures performing concurrent roles in institutions with dissimilar orientations.

On the one hand are those who consider that joining the power structure is crucial, either as direct participants or as formulators of policy and/or as king-makers for those in government circles. Because this approach gives priority to harmonious relations with government, everything else takes second place, including the process of political democratisation focused on the struggle to build a more just social structure. Their inclination is to surrender these issues to the political will of the government, if necessary by allowing the possibility of friction with groups struggling for human rights, the environment and so on. ICMI is the prime example of this attitude and perspective.

On the other hand are those who give more importance to developing a capacity to effect change, without having to be incorporated in the system. Such groups consider that as long as relations with the government are maintained at a reasonable level they can concentrate on the internal transformation of the lives of their members. This is the approach taken by NU, with the result that it is easier for its activists to join in the struggle for political democratisation via 'alternative institutions' such as the Democratic Forum.

Of course, between these two opposing views other perspectives will emerge which attempt to accommodate both perspectives, but we are yet to see what form their activities will take. If such an approach does develop, relations between Islam and the state in the New Order will certainly become even brighter, opening up further possibilities in our national life.

There could be said to be three approaches to accommodating the two views outlined above. First, the socio-political approach emphasises the need to participate in the current power structure. Adherents of this approach tend to see Islam in ideological terms, drawing a sharp distinction between Islam and other religions, ideologies and theories. Its creed is 'Islamic interests', and Islamic solidarity is its common bond. Sectarianism breeds easily in such an environment, as is clear from the raging anti-Christian and anti-Chinese sentiment within certain Islamic circles these days. Their absolute demand that the 'Islamicisation process' be carried through to the end rests on an assumption that the entire national interest was being threatened, even though this is not the case.

Second is the cultural approach that aims to realise an awareness of Islam in everyday life, without being excessively tied up with institutional forms. Where some institutionalisation is necessary, it is done only in the context of supporting the spread of Islam in a cultural way, as we have seen with the setting up of the Paramadina Foundation, the growth of 'middle-class Qu'ran readings' and so forth. Actually this approach emphasises a universalist perspective of Islam as the manifestation of a world civilisation rather than being concerned with any particular system of power.

But proponents of this approach are not always consistent. Some of them have suddenly turned on others, who they accuse of disturbing the power structure they wish to be a part of. This inclusive cultural approach can thus quickly take on a 'historical' flavour that involves blaming other ethnic and religious groups for the disadvantaged status of the Muslims. It then becomes indistinguishable from the socio-political approach described above. The 'Islamic agenda' is promoted at the expense of the 'national agenda'.

Third is the socio-cultural approach, which can be placed between the other two. This approach emphasises the need to develop cultural perspectives and mechanisms while at the same time building institutions in civil society that accord with its cultural vision. It stresses a cultural orientation in the context of working to develop institutions capable of changing the structure of the society incrementally over the long term. The question of whether to get involved in power structures therefore becomes irrelevant. It is this approach that now characterises Muslim activists in all kinds of NGOs, as well as large Islamic social organisations such as Muhammadiyah and NU, in *pesantren* circles, and so forth. Their relationship with the existing power structures makes it easy for them to introduce an 'Islamic agenda' into the 'national agenda' of this nation.

In examining these approaches taken by Islamic movements in Indonesia over the past two decades, it is evident that the relationship between Islam (represented by Islamic movements) and the state (represented by the New Order government) has followed a very complex pattern. Awareness of this complexity is a vital starting point for new research programs or historical studies.

9.8 Dawam Rahardjo: ICMI's vision

Writing in his capacity as a member of the board of experts of the Indonesian Muslim Intellectuals' Association, the economist Dawam Rahardjo (1995: 25–43) explains the organisation in sociological terms and defends it from charges of sectarianism and opportunism.

Early one wet December in the cool climate of Malang, hundreds of people gathered at a symposium at the recently renovated student centre at Brawijaya University and established ICMI, the Indonesian Muslim Intellectuals' Association. It was very reminiscent of the birth of Boedi Oetomo on 20 May 1908 at the Stovia Medical College in Jakarta.[9] Boedi Oetomo's pioneers were students at the college led by Soetomo. Many of them are forgotten to our generation, even though their role in our national awakening was very significant. But Soetomo and his friends were inspired by the ideas of Dr Wahidin Soedirohoesodo, a senior Javanese doctor who took early retirement to concentrate on encouraging *priyayi* (members of the indigenous civil servant class) to think about the education of the younger generation of *priyayi* and later also the fate of Javanese culture. Like Boedi Oetomo, it was students who gave birth to ICMI, especially students from the engineering faculty as well as activists from the campus mosque, Masjid Raden Patah. The students were backed in their initiative by a number of intellectuals who supported the students' project....

The establishment of Boedi Oetomo was one step in the development of a civil society in Indonesia, because in fact it was a kind of NGO. But Boedi Oetomo did not set itself up in opposition to the colonial government. This was to be expected from a group made up of the indigenous *pangreh praja* (administrative officers) who the organisation was set up to represent. In the 1930s this group were called 'cooperators', as opposed to the non-cooperators.

Soetomo had been forced to be a cooperator, because if he opposed the government the movement he had developed would have been closed down or persecuted by the colonial government, as was to happen to the radical nationalist movements led by Tjipto Mangoenkoesoemo and later by Sukarno and Hatta. By remaining on the side of the cooperators, Soetomo and his friends could help build a civil society and thereby contribute to the process of social formation in Indonesia.

The pattern of events leading to the formation of Boedi Oetomo is similar to that encountered by ICMI, with Dr Imaduddin Abdurrahim (who we know as Bang Imad) playing the role of Dr Wahidin Soedirohoesodo....An intellectual preacher, Imad...had long been concerned to bridge the differences between Muslim intellectuals, especially in the wake of the disagreements surrounding the renewal of Islamic thought sparked unintentionally by Nurcholish Madjid in 1970 (see Reading 3.3). [He was especially troubled by] the potential for leading participants in the debates...to retreat into exclusive groups defined by sectarian and primordial allegiances....

Another of Imad's motivations was his passionate advocacy – remembering that he was an electronics graduate whose Ohio University PhD was in personnel management – of science and technology among Indonesian Muslims. It was because of this that he looked to Habibie....As it happens, the students at the Brawijaya University engineering faculty also idolised Habibie, especially after reading about his vision for Islam and technology in an interview with the Muslim magazine *Kiblat*....

In 1987 a book was published entitled *Islamic Perspectives on National Development*.[10] It comprised 18 papers that had been presented at the first 'Congress of Muslim Intellectuals'....If we look at the structure of the book, it is obvious that Muslim intellectuals had a wide range of concerns. But what is clear is that they were much less interested in politics than they were about culture, society, theology, economics and development. A great deal of attention was focused on technology, even among the theologians. If there was a central theme in all the papers, it was the need for a renewal of Islamic thinking arising from a dialogue between Islamic traditions and modern Western science.

There are a number of empirical phenomena that help explain the preoccupations of these writers. First is the growth of institutions concerned with education and thought. Two of the most prominent are the Wakaf Paramadina Foundation and the Institute for the Study of Religion and Philosophy (LSAF).[11] Similar institutes have been set up in Yogya, Bandung and Semarang. Second are the NGOs. While many of them do not identify themselves as Islamic, professional Muslim intellectuals play a large role in them, whether they are secular or even Christian-oriented. Third is the fact that the government bureaucracy now employs many Muslim graduates. Education has fundamentally changed their priorities: from the world of small family businesses they now aspire to join the ranks of the government bureaucracy. This is what is popularly referred to as the *priyayi*-isation of Muslim families....

Many observers view the birth of ICMI as a symptom of the 'bureaucratisation' of Islam; in other words, the 'domestication' of the Islamic community....But the upward mobility of Muslim intellectuals into the government bureaucracy began well before ICMI was founded, especially among former members of HMI, the Muslim Students' Association, including Mar'ie Muhammad, Akbar Tanjung, Ibrahim Hasan, Azwar Anas, Saadilah Mursyid, Syarifuddin Baharsyah, Tarmizi Taher, Saleh Afif and Djamaluddin. Of course these people wanted the Islamic community to be close to the New Order government and the armed forces; they also wanted Muslims to support and participate in development efforts. Educated young people from pious Muslim families have indeed been upwardly mobile since the beginning of the New Order. We have to remember that many young Muslims were on the front line in establishing the New Order. They were part of youth organisations such as HMI, PMII, IMM, PII and graduate organisations including KAHMI and PERSAMI....[12] So it is not altogether true to characterise political Islam as an opposition force during the New Order....

Little by little, the struggle from within – both within the government bureaucracy and within Golkar – produced results, namely the

Islamisation of the civil service and of Golkar. This phenomenon may have confused outside observers, because many analyses, both in articles and books, depicted the New Order government and the armed forces as 'anti-Islamic'. That depiction was linked to incidents like the suppression of various actions or movements, such as the case of the Bank Central Asia bombing, the hijacking by Imron and his associates, the Tanjung Priok riot, Lampung and the Aceh insurrectionists.[13] The Muslim community itself views the role of figures such as the late Ali Moertopo and Benny Moerdani as having contributed to that image. As foreign observers have pointed out, Muslims have also tended to blame the government's 'anti-Islamic' attitude on Catholic and Protestant elements in the armed forces (especially in intelligence) and Golkar, even though this perception may not be justified, or at least not entirely so.

Although there is good evidence for the argument that there were elements within the New Order pushing an anti-Islamic or secularist agenda, it cannot be denied that there was also a process of Islamisation occurring. The evidence for this includes the granting of increased leeway (as well as facilities) for religious activities, the absence of discrimination against pious civil servants and – most importantly – the incorporation of religious values in the development process....

What the Muslim community has achieved is an integration of Islam and the state.... Interpretations that place intellectuals outside power and in an antagonistic relationship with it become irrelevant. The process of integration [of Islam and the state] would be occurring with or without ICMI. The problem was that the Muslim community needed 'accelerated evolution' and this could not happen without some form of organisation. Whether it was ICMI or another group that took on the task, the appearance of some such organisation was determined by historical necessity....

If ICMI was simply a government creation, or an organisation designed to serve the political interests of a number of individuals – or even of one person in particular – it is inconceivable that ICMI would have grown so quickly all over the country and among Indonesian communities abroad during the past five years. And if ICMI was only a vehicle for the sectarian and primordial spirit of one group, it could not possibly have attracted the support of nearly all sections of society.

In his popular book *A Nation in Waiting: Indonesia in the 1990s* (first edition 1994) Adam Schwarz argued that there were three groups supporting ICMI, government bureaucrats, modernists who aspired to build an Islamic state and a group of neo-modernists. He depicted the three groups as having distinctive, and contradictory, aspirations, ideas and interests.

If Schwarz is correct, it is clear that ICMI is neither primordial nor sectarian. It would be more accurate to describe ICMI as a pluralist, democratic and egalitarian community. Pluralist in the sense that it values diversity, as long as each group understands and respects the other. Democratic, because each group agrees to negotiate when taking decisions that affect their joint concerns and interests. And egalitarian in that all identify themselves as servants of God with equal rights and obligations.

While valuing pluralism, ICMI's mission is political, social and cultural integration. Contrary to Schwarz's schema, ICMI has NGO people as well as bureaucrats. From a theological perspective, ICMI accommodates modernists, neo-modernists, and even traditionalists and neo-traditionalists. It has Western-educated intellectuals as well as religious teachers with traditional Islamic education. But in ICMI no distinction is made between *abangan* and *santri*. In ICMI, bureaucrats work alongside NGO activists....

ICMI also has a mission to encourage the participation of Muslims and to improve the quality of that participation. The current lack of Muslim participation has more to do with the quality of the labour force than with any theological or doctrinal obstacles, such as a belief in fatalism. Therefore ICMI focuses on the issue of quality, symbolised by the five Qs: quality of faith, quality of thought, quality of work, quality of service and quality of life. This is ICMI's vision of development and its interpretation of the phrase in the Broad Guidelines of State Policy, 'to build a complete human being and society'.

A further mission of ICMI is social change and development. This mission arose out of an awareness that most Muslims live in a state of backwardness and poverty.... In concrete terms, ICMI believes that development should not simply aim for growth, but also for more just, advanced and egalitarian social conditions.

9.9 Y.B. Mangunwijaya: communists

This article was written in response to official charges that the riots sparked by the violent destruction of Megawati's PDI Jakarta headquarters were communist inspired. It first appeared in *Forum Keadilan* on 26 August 1996, but this version is translated from a compilation of Mangunwijaya's essays (1997: 23–5).

Recently we have been reawakened by the communist issue. Therefore it is important for us to have an understanding of the practice of communism itself. Its practice. Not just its philosophy, the genesis of its development, its economic theory or its sociological theses. This is for no other reason than that we may correctly understand how we must be anti-communist or, more precisely, how we must be opposed to communist praxis. How gullible we would be if we were anti something without knowing what we were opposing. Worse still would be to be anti something abstract and theoretical, while warmly embracing the implementation of the very thing we were opposing. So it is praxis that is important. In concrete terms, what are the characteristics of communist praxis?

A concrete example is the former Soviet Union, where one party held power and determined everything. But, please remember, the Soviet Union and even the People's Republic of China had multi-party systems, with several small parties existing alongside the Communist Party. These, however, were merely appendixes. At best they served to liven things up. The Soviet Union, the People's Republic of China, Vietnam, Cuba and other communist countries all called themselves democracies – more precisely, people's democracies. But were their people sovereign, in the sense that Mohammad Hatta, Syahrir and the other founders of the Indonesian Republic spoke of? Clearly not. The formation or election of the leadership and cadres of the party is not transparent, but very mysterious, full of manipulation by the ruling elite and collusion within a murky crony system. But it is effective.

Essentially, in a country where communist praxis prevails, unless you join the dominant party it is impossible for you to become a civil servant, a bank manager or join the army. Yes, an army employing communist practices always sides with that one party, the government party. The other parties, well, they are only appendixes.

The term communist is related to the word *commune*, a group based on mutual cooperation. The collective or government interest always takes absolute precedence over the interests of the private individual, even though individual interests are legitimate, a fundamental right, humane, just and very civilised. To ensure subordination of individual interests any means are justified, whether honest or deceitful, fair or foul, whether by free choice or intimidation, or through physical terror, corruption or bribery. Essentially the end justifies the means.

From the erroneous perspective of communist praxis, the government is identical to the state and the society, while the dominant party is identical to the people and the state. So in communist terms even the most corrupt and lazy government officials are identical to the state and the constitution (and ultimately equivalent to God). So it is clear why we oppose the practice of communism in all its forms.

Other features of communist praxis are also clear. Because communist praxis is a form of totalitarian, bureaucratic collectivism, it finds expression in a slavish devotion to all things uniform. Clothes, trousers, shoes, hats, opinions, information, statements, figures of speech, argumentation, tastes, professional organisations, youth affairs, sports, in short every single thing without exception must be uniform. And this is why they are so enraptured by the movement of steps taken in unison, otherwise known as marching formations with military-style salutes.

The problem with all this is that a nation is not a colony of ants. A nation always has a great diversity of opinions. So in a system employing communist methods the rulers have to force, either crudely or subtly, a uniformity of opinion. This is achieved by employing an intelligence and spy network, censorship, terror, confinement or exile, with systematic use of torture. The entire people is struck dumb by all sorts of intimidation and media restrictions and then made to parrot the official line. This system always seeks the acclamation of so-called people's representatives chosen with the guarantee that they will agree to whatever their superiors have directed. Those singing a different tune are labelled opponents of the state or its ideology and are immediately purged as instigators of subversion or as liberal democrats condemned as opponents of the national culture.

While communist praxis is officially anti-capitalist, it is actually a system of state capitalism completely controlled by a collusion of the bureaucratic elite, technocrats, the controllers of capital and information, industrial managers, the military and the leadership of the dominant party. Accordingly, in the model of communist praxis the entire judiciary is under the control of the executive or the ruling party. Justice is defined as that which accords with the wishes of the executive.

What we need to pay special attention to is the fact that, from the perspective of the common people, the results of communist and capitalist praxis are not markedly different. Both, for example, shackle ordinary people and suck them dry. They both like to get their way through brainwashing, the only difference being that, while communist methods are brutal and unimaginative, capitalist practice is subtle and sophisticated. Capitalist practice gives the appearance of defending freedom, while in actuality virtually all desires and tastes, private and public, are driven to uniformity through the world of advertising and subliminal ideology. Moreover, under capitalism diverse forms of collaboration, coalition and collusion are invariably allowed to flourish beyond the reach of laws that would effectively protect ordinary people.

So the one is just a variant of the other, applying apparently contradictory methods that are, nevertheless, in essence equally anti-democratic and against the interests of the majority of ordinary people. It is only the ruling elite which is permitted the power to direct affairs (to make the cake), while the majority is left to accept directives (and the crumbs the elite is pleased to leave them). It is the elite that can soar skyward, while the others, the majority, are the runway that enables the elite to take off. So we understand and agree that we must be alert and oppose the communist praxis that has quietly been making a comeback.

Notes

1 See the careful analysis of the questionnaire in Tanter (1991: 398–400).
2 P4 refers to the government-run courses in Pancasila state ideology compulsory for civil servants and private enterprise employees. See Chapter 4 in this volume.
3 G30S/PKI was the official designation for the 'attempted communist coup' of 30 September 1965.

4 Article 28 reads: 'Freedom of association and assembly, of verbal and written expression and the like, shall be prescribed by law.'

5 Marsillam's use of the term '*digebuk*' plays on Soeharto's September 1989 threat to 'clobber' anyone who behaved 'unconstitutionally' in the upcoming MPR session to select a new president and vice-president.

6 Dharma Wanita was the official organisation of the wives of civil servants.

7 In 1988 government attempts to expropriate land for a dam at Kedung Ombo near Salatiga in Central Java saw local villagers team up with university students to protest against the minimal rates of compensation they were offered. The campaign was well publicised and Kedung Ombo soon came to symbolise an attitude of callous developmentalism.

8 Achmad Taufik; Andreas Harsono; Ardian T. Gesuri; Arief Budiman; Aristides Katoppo; Asikin; Ati Nurbaiti; Ayu Utami; Bambang Harymurti; Bina Baktiati; Candra Negara; Christianto Wibisono; Dadang Rachmat H.S.; Dhia Prekasha Yoedha; Didik Budiarta; Diah Purnomowati; Didik Supriyanto; Goenawan Mohamad; Happy Sulistiyadi; Hasudungan Sirait; Heddy Lugito; Hendrajit; Ida Farida; Idon Haryana; Imran Hasibuan; Indrawan; Jalil Hakim; Janoe Arijanto; Keliek M. Nugroho; Lenah Susianty; Liston P. Siregar; M. Faried Cahyono; M. Thoriq; Fikri Jufri; M. Anis; Moebance Moera; Nuruddin Amin; Putu Wirata; Ragawa Indra Marti; Rinny S. Doddy; Rustam Fachri Mandayun; Rudy P. Singgih; Santoso; Satrio Arismunandar; T.J. Wibowo; Yopie Hidayat; Yopie Lasut; Yosep Adi Prasetyo; Zed Abidin; Jus Suma di Pradja; Budiman S. Hartoyo; Yoanida Rosita; Wahyu Muryadi; Toriq Hadad; Saifullah Yusuf; E. Djarot; Amira Jufri; Dwi Setyo Irawanto.

9 The comparison with Boedi Oetomo is telling because in official narratives of the nation Boedi Oetomo is the prototypal nationalist organisation, despite its conservative and almost exclusively Javanese membership. The implication is that ICMI is not only nationalist but also heralds a new era.

10 The Indonesian title of this book is *Perspektif Islam dalam Pembangunan Bangsa* (Hasan and Achmad 1987).

11 Among Paramadina's key figures was Nurcholish Madjid (see Reading 3.3), while LSAF was founded and headed by Dawam Rahardjo himself.

12 PMII: Pergerakan Mahasiswa Muslim Indonesia (Indonesian Muslim Students' Movement); IMM: Ikatan Mahasiswa Muhammadiyah (Muhammadiyah Students' Association); PII: Pelajar Islam Indonesia (Indonesian Muslim Secondary School Students); KAHMI: Korps Alumni HMI (Muslim Students' Association Alumni Corps); PERSAMI: Persatuan Sarjana Muslim Indonesia (Indonesian Muslim Graduates' Association).

13 Originally 'GPK Aceh'. GPK stands for Gerakan Pengacau Keamanan, the Security Disruptors' Movement, the New Order military's standard appellation for armed nationalist movements in Aceh, West Papua and East Timor.

10 Human rights and the rule of law

From its earliest days, Soeharto's New Order claimed for itself extraordinary powers that allowed it to act with virtual impunity. The military used these powers to sanction the killing of hundreds of thousands of its enemies and to incarcerate many more without trial. Over the next three decades Soeharto presided over a system of government that gave short shrift to human rights and the rule of law, whether dealing with Acehnese, Papuans and East Timorese resisting Jakarta's rule, peasants and slum dwellers standing in the way of the development of private projects, striking workers, Muslim demonstrators or student activists.

The New Order government came to power proclaiming its support for the rule of law and promising a total correction of the abuses that had taken place under Sukarno. It did this because its supporters, especially educated civilian groups, wanted to hear this. Given the marginalisation of these groups described in earlier chapters – and of course the dangers involved in propagating alternative ideologies – it is perhaps not surprising that the rule of law emerged in the 1970s as an important rallying point for opponents of the government (Lev 1978). Typically the call was for the establishment of a *negara hukum*. This is the Indonesian term for *Rechtsstaat*, best translated into English as a 'state governed by law'. Many looked to the 1945 Constitution, which declares Indonesia to be a *Rechtsstaat*, not a *Machtsstaat*, a state based on coercion.

Some of the first leaders of the pluralist opposition were lawyers associated with the Indonesian Legal Aid Foundation (YLBHI), such as Adnan Buyung Nasution, T. Mulya Lubis and the late Yap Thiam Hien. These lawyers and their colleagues made a point of taking on politically sensitive cases and used law courts as an arena to denounce not only the injustices perpetrated by the government but also its hypocrisy. With the demise of the political parties, Legal Aid Foundation figures became leading spokespeople for human rights, social justice, workers' rights, press freedoms, constitutionalism and the rule of law (Lev 1987).

The worldwide growth of interest in human rights in the late 1970s and 1980s gave the movement a significant boost in Indonesia, leading to increased political pressure on the Soeharto government both domestically and from abroad. One response on the part of the government was to formulate constitutional arguments that would wrong-foot its critics. In the mid-1980s, government ideologues began giving increasing prominence in their writings, and in the curricula of compulsory Pancasila indoctrination courses, to Supomo, the customary law expert who had put forward in the constitutional debates of 1945 the idea that Indonesia ought to follow an 'integralist' philosophy. Supomo had stressed that Indonesia's government should reflect a pattern of traditional village governance in which the rulers lived in harmony with the ruled, obviating the need for checks, balances and rights to be written into the constitution. In the first reading (10.1) Hamid S. Attamimi, a constitutional lawyer and long-serving bureaucrat in the powerful State Secretariat, summons Supomo's authority to argue that the 1945 Constitution was inspired by an indigenous Indonesian theory of statecraft and therefore did not provide for the separation of powers.

The legal scholar Padmo Wahyono was another figure who provided much theoretical ammunition for the government's position. In Reading 10.2 he attempts to articulate an Indonesian theory of human rights, arguing that in the integralist conception the relationships between people were defined in terms of obligations to the community rather than in terms of individual rights. This was to be a recurring theme in official discourse, and was used on many occasions to label advocates of human rights 'Western minded', 'liberal' or 'un-Indonesian'. In 1993 Armed Forces Commander Try Soetrisno went as far as accusing human rights and democracy activists of being 'fourth generation communists' (*Straits Times*, 14 March 1993).

Liberal scholars, however, fought back. Marsillam Simanjuntak, a founding member of Democracy Forum, launched a scathing attack on Padmo Wahyono and other ideologues, pointing out the fascist nature of Supomo's ideas and arguing that integralism had been soundly defeated in the constitutional debates of 1945 by the democratically minded Mohammad Hatta and Mohammad Yamin (Simanjuntak 1994). Reading 10.3 presents a debate between Harry Tjan Silalahi and Adnan Buyung Nasution on the question of human rights and the 1945 Constitution. Buyung was one of the few people openly to propose that the constitution was due for an overhaul. Considered radical at the time, Buyung's proposal was adopted soon after the fall of Soeharto.

In Reading 10.4 the senior legal practitioner and activist Harjono Tjitrosoebono tackles integralism head on, arguing that it has been used as a means of concentrating and perpetuating power. Its logic, he says, has pervaded the entire system of government, making democracy more remote than ever and making it impossible for the legal system to function impartially. This argument was relevant not only to democrats and human rights activists, but to business as well. The government's decision to deregulate sections of the economy in the late 1980s saw a rapid increase in the number of firms doing business in the major cities. In order to feel secure, investors, both international and domestic, required some measure of legal certainty. Intellectuals and professionals associated with the interests of the mushrooming business and middle classes therefore started to voice their opposition to arbitrary decision-making and extraordinary powers. This is essentially the argument put by Budiono Kusumohamidjojo (Reading 10.5), who sees the pursuit of more liberal economic policies as demanding a fair and reliable legal system.

International pressure on Indonesia to improve its human rights record increased sharply with the end of the Cold War and particularly after the massacre of East Timorese demonstrators was broadcast to the world in November 1991. The reaction was a mix of two parts nationalist pique and one part diplomatic accommodation. Critical comments made by Jan Pronk, the Dutch minister responsible for international development assistance, saw Soeharto unilaterally and publicly refuse to accept any more Dutch official aid. Sections of the government were also incensed with the Americans for tying aid to improvements in human rights, a sentiment expressed in forthright terms by Juwono Sudarsono in Reading 10.6. On the other hand, the Indonesian government set up a National Human Rights Commission that, despite legitimate doubts about its independence, helped keep human rights abuses in the public eye and paved the way for later investigations into abuses by the military.

The final two readings illustrate the way in which the battle lines in human rights in Indonesia were influenced by global debates. Especially important were the preparations for the World Conference on Human Rights held by the United Nations in Vienna in June 1993. At preliminary meetings in Bangkok in March–April 1993, the Indonesian government – together with Malaysia, China and Singapore – was a leading proponent of the argument that human rights standards should take into account individual countries' unique social and cultural circumstances, and that more emphasis ought to be given to the individual's duties and responsibilities to society and the state. Indonesian NGOs, on the other hand, liaised with other Asian NGOs to formulate a position that stressed the universality and indivisibility of human rights. This position is stated clearly in a document issued in May 1993 by a broad coalition of Indonesian NGOs (Reading 10.7). Reading 10.8 presents the government's position, formulated in the late New Order, after compromises were made in Vienna. Given that this document remained posted on the Indonesian Department of Foreign Affairs website from 1997 until at least December 2001, we can assume that it represents a relatively enduring position.

10.1 Hamid S. Attamimi: the separation of powers is alien to our constitution

Hamid Attamimi was one of the most influential constitutional lawyers advising the government throughout the 1970s and 1980s. A keen advocate of Supomo's integralist theory and the idea of Indonesia as a 'village republic', his arguments helped the New Order justify a reading of the 1945 Constitution that annulled its potentially democratic and rights-supporting elements. This extract is translated from his doctoral dissertation (Attamimi 1990: 144–6).

As its drafters explained, the 1945 Constitution follows its own system, not Montesquieu's separation of powers theory in which state power is divided and exercised separately by the legislature, executive and judicial branches of government. Supomo, the chair of the constitutional drafting committee, said, 'In my opinion, Mr Chair, in this draft of the constitution we are not following a system that draws any distinction in principle between these three bodies.' Responding to one of the members of the Committee for the Investigation of Indonesian Independence, Supomo stated, 'We are using our own system, as Sukiman has said.'[1]

So why, in the elucidation of the 1945 Constitution, do we find the terms legislative power, executive power and *pouvoir réglementaire* [regulatory power] and so forth?

As stated above, the drafters of the 1945 Constitution, through the drafting committee chairman Supomo, were quite firm that the 1945 Constitution does not follow the separation of powers theory. Therefore if we find in the elucidation some terms that derive from the separation of powers system, or some other system, they have to be understood merely as an attempt to describe what is meant in the main body of the constitution – to explain, that is, the difference between the system used in the constitution and other systems. In other words, even though the elucidation of the 1945 Constitution contains words and phrases such as legislative power, executive power and *pouvoir réglementaire*, they have to be interpreted in accordance with the system used in the main body of the 1945 Constitution, which was based on a conception of the state and a theory of statecraft rooted in the Indonesian nation itself.

10.2 Padmo Wahyono: Indonesian human rights

This is included to illustrate the sometimes convoluted efforts of New Order ideologues to articulate an alternative, Indonesian view of human rights. Padmo Wahyono was professor of law at the University of Indonesia and, from 1978 to 1999, deputy director of BP7, the body that determined the curriculum for the nationwide Pancasila indoctrination program, P4. It is taken from one of Padmo Wahyono's many books on constitutional law (1989: 109–111).

Human rights are often represented in the general literature as universal. Sometimes they are also said to stem from a liberal or individualistic way of thinking. In essence, they are regarded as relating to the life, liberty and property of individuals, and sometimes also to the pursuit of happiness. When applied, these three fundamental elements translate into political, economic and social-cultural rights....

Are there other ways of approaching human rights?

If we accept that implementing Pancasila and the 1945 Constitution gives rise to certain basic rights and obligations, then it is clear that these rights and obligations will have their own special character. The same is true when Pancasila is brought to bear on citizens' rights and obligations. A people's worldview can make a real difference.

We can therefore assume that different worldviews will give rise to different philosophical constructions, and that this will affect the way in which human rights are conceived.

Individualistic ways of thinking, including liberalism...assume that people are born in a 'state of nature', without any bonds to their group. They are said to enter into a social contract later on with the state that guarantees their freedom in a legal form (civil rights).

In this approach, people's inborn human rights set them apart from the state. The logical consequence of this dualistic way of thinking is that people's human rights have to be protected by laws.

According to the Indonesian integralist approach, referred to in the 1945 Constitution, and its elucidation as the 'family spirit', people were not born free but rather into an existing matrix of human relationships, integrally connected to their society.

In this system, people's rights and responsibilities depend on their existence in a group. Their rights as an individual will be recognised only in the context of their obligations to the life of the group (which values harmony, reciprocity and balance).

This is why, in the non-dualistic integralist way of thinking, the management of the state...must be based on *musyawarah* [deliberation].

What *musyawarah* means in constitutional terms is implied in the elucidation of Article 3 of the Constitution, which specifies that the People's Consultative Assembly will take account of all circumstances and all streams of opinion – so it differs from the notion of the general will – in order to decide issues either on the basis of unanimity, a simple majority vote or a two-thirds majority.

So it is clear that in the integralist way of thinking citizens' rights and responsibilities depend on their being a member of a collectivity, or what is more commonly called living as part of a society, nation and state.

10.3 Harry Tjan Silalahi v. Adnan Buyung Nasution: human rights and the constitution

This is a summary of a 1993 debate between Harry Tjan Silalahi, the deputy director of the Centre for Strategic and International Studies, and Adnan Buyung Nasution, a well-known human rights lawyer and legal historian. While Harry Tjan did not speak for the government, his references to the customary law expert Supomo, the family principle [*kekeluargaan*] and to the importance of the cultural context reflect common themes in the official discourse of the time. Both contributions highlight the continuing relevance of the key figures in the constitutional debates of 1945, including Supomo, Mohammad Yamin and Mohammad Hatta. The article appeared in *Forum Keadilan* (21 January 1993).

Harry Tjan Silalahi

The Magna Carta of 1215 was a product of the struggle of the nobility to have the rulers of the time grant them basic rights. It was not a popular struggle but rather one between the nobility and the English Crown.

Our 'human rights' charter, the 1945 Constitution and its preamble, were born of a different kind of conflict – the struggle of an Eastern people against colonisation by another nation.

In this atmosphere, more prominent was the family principle – or what is often called integralism and totalism. This theory of Dr Supomo's is often regarded as related to Hegel's integralist theory, which underpinned Nazism, fascism and totalitarianism. In actual fact, Supomo's definition of totalism was 'a state that does not align itself with the largest or strongest group but that transcends all groups and individuals, uniting itself with the people as a whole'.

The 1945 Constitution was born in this familial atmosphere. For this reason, the kind of individual human rights we know from the West and the Magna Carta are not to be found spelled out in detail in the 1945 Constitution. If we accept that any document must be interpreted in the context of its creation, however, we sense that the 1945 Constitution does embody human rights.

Article 1 of the 1945 Constitution stresses that Indonesia is based on popular sovereignty. This is the essence of the entire constitution. Based on this Article, human rights – mentioned explicitly in Articles 27–34 – should be viewed through the prism of popular sovereignty.

This means that in any given situation human rights must be implemented in accord with the interests of the people. What constitutes a human right will depend on the situation. For instance, restricting the freedom to inflame ethnic, religious, racial and group sentiments, known as SARA, actually curtails human rights. But of course we all agree that this is necessary for the sake of stability and the survival of our nation. Here we can see that, although the concept of human rights is universal, local circumstances do matter.

It is a political fact that human rights cannot be treated in isolation from the problems of the world. I am reminded of Yap Thiam Hien. He was a master at detaching himself from politics. But could someone like him be a successful leader?

On the other hand, integralism is grounded in an understanding of family that is essentially paternalistic. Here, the relationship between the government and the governed is like a father and his child. A good father will protect the human rights of his child.

This brings us back to a society's culture and the ability of the actors to advance human rights and democracy in the system as it exists. If we cannot dance, let us not blame the floor for being slippery.

Adnan Buyung Nasution

The 1945 Constitution was drafted in a time of great political and intellectual ferment. Hatta and Yamin, both of them educated in the West, did their utmost to have human rights provisions included in it.

They argued, and I agree, that there are three rights fundamental to public life. First is the right to express opinions. Second is the right to organise, because there is no use people having opinions if they are not allowed to express and act on them. Third is the right to associate, so that opinions can attain a certain authority.

These three rights are fundamental to public life and must be stoutly defended. They are the wellspring of other human rights. This is what Hatta and Yamin demanded.

But Sukarno and Supomo thought otherwise. Sukarno was impressed by the arguments of Supomo, a former civil servant in the Japanese administration who had apparently clung to authoritarian concepts adopted from the Japanese. Drawing on his well-known theories of state organisation – integralism and totalism – Supomo, as well as Sukarno, opposed all efforts to have human rights incorporated into the 1945 Constitution. They did this on the grounds that all [political] systems that emphasised human rights were inherently in conflict with the concept of integralism. At that time Supomo attached the greatest importance to concepts. Systems were subordinate, and could not contradict the concepts that defined them.

Ultimately the founding fathers compromised, which resulted in provisions such as Article 28 of the 1945 Constitution, which states: 'The freedom to organise and associate, to speak and write and so forth, will be determined by law.' The inclusion of these articles is testimony to the resoluteness of Yamin and Hatta's belief in human rights in the face of Sukarno and Supomo's objections. But it did little to guarantee the rights themselves.

If we read the text more critically, Article 28 does not provide any guarantees at all for the rights to organisation, association and expression. Rather, it gives the government, or the legislators, the opportunity to neuter those fundamental rights.

I am always reminded of an interesting exchange during the Constituent Assembly debates in 1958. Responding to a proposal that the 1945 Constitution be adopted permanently in its entirety, Asmara Hadi, a member of parliament regarded as a follower of Sukarno, said, 'We have no monopoly on truth and wisdom. If anybody has the right to decide to enshrine the 1945 Constitution for ever it is the future generations.'

The time has arrived for us to make a change.

10.4 Harjono Tjitrosoebono: the concept of the integralist state hinders democracy

Harjono Tjitrosoebono was a prominent advocate for victims of human rights abuses and for the legal profession itself. This short piece was his contribution to a collection of position papers presented at a human rights forum timed to coincide with the Non-Aligned Movement summit in Jakarta in September 1992.

Our problems are not new, in fact they have become a longstanding chronic illness. Perhaps we can attempt to diagnose the sickness that has frustrated the realisation of the *negara hukum* of our hopes. Why does the law not play a role, why is there no supremacy of law, why doesn't legislation reflect community aspirations, why do basic human rights remain neglected, and so on? If we wish to find the underlying answer to these questions we have to go back to the origins of our conception of the *negara hukum*.

The most important issues in discussing the *negara hukum* lie in the connection between law and power, and in the concept of the *negara hukum* itself. The way we think about the *negara hukum* is fundamental and has far-reaching consequences for the implementation of law, yet it is still imprecise and a subject of discussion and debate.

In these discussions the problem is that our *negara hukum* is based upon an integralist concept of the state. According to this concept, the state is regarded as an integral entity, dominating and encompassing everything else, with citizens relegated to a subsidiary position. In such an integralist structure the interests of the state are paramount. Everyone must submit to the interests of the state. Citizens' and human rights take second place. In a situation such as this, regulations or legislation are issued to support the interests of the state, setting aside, if necessary, the interests of citizens. In such a context human rights are automatically subordinated to the rights of the state. This is why many questions arise, like why is the law unjust? This begs another question, unjust from which perspective? From the perspective of the state the law could be said to be just since it upholds order, security and defence. But at the same time this can mean sacrificing citizens' rights or human rights.

This policy has produced excesses. An example is the right to freedom of thought and expression in the press law. How can freedom of the press exist when the law provides for the Minister or Director-General of Information to head the Press Council? How can freedom of the press exist when a government official controls the council? Such a predicament is only made possible by the integralist concept, or the concept of the state interest, or what is often referred to as the public good or security and order.

Others have discussed how the labour law prohibits workers from striking. Affording workers basic rights is said to be against the public or community interest. Why is workers' pay so low, and even below the minimum rates? This is because the community or public interest supersedes that of individual workers. As a result, everything has to be sacrificed to the interests of development, including human rights. So the integralist state exerts an enormous influence, and accounts also for the paralysis of the Supreme Court. Everything within the purview of the state, including the legal apparatus and the judiciary, must be subordinated to the integralist system.... This in reality is what has occurred. For instance, judges are unable to take an independent position because they are members of the Indonesian Civil Service Corps and must submit to its discipline. Why, for example, is the Supreme Court not allowed the right of review, namely the right to test whether a piece of legislation is in conflict with the 1945 Constitution? It is because of fear that the Supreme Court might pass down interpretations which go against the government or the authorities, who defend the integralist system and who consider that the 1945 Constitution must be implemented purely and consistently without even the slightest revision.

This is despite the fact that the elucidation of the 1945 Constitution itself states that the Constitution must be adapted to changing circumstances. But in the interests of retaining power, the elucidation of the 1945 Constitution has been sacrificed. As long as the integralist system is retained, the Supreme Court will have no right of review, because the right to interpret the 1945 Constitution is regarded as the sole preserve of the authorities, not the Supreme Court. Integralism is intrinsically incompatible with the *negara hukum* because the integralist system is principally concerned with the perpetuation of power.

Our state is ruled by force and based on the integralist system. Without first getting rid of the integralist system it will be impossible for legal and judicial institutions to function freely. These legal institutions are still shackled and caged because they exist as part of an integralist state. If judicial institutions are to perform the roles they ought to, the integralist state must go. But who can effect this, and who would want to, since it would indeed involve a very great change to the system. The current DPR could not possibly do this, because it does not actually represent the people. Its members are only able to be members because they have undergone ideological screening (*'litsus'*).

Actually at the moment we are striving for something that we cannot possibly achieve without rethinking our basic assumptions. But we must continue to fight on regardless in reaching towards the change we desire.

To return to the question of human rights, it makes sense to regard these as second-order concerns, as in the case of press freedoms. Real freedom of the press cannot exist for as long as the Press Council, with the Information Minister as its chair and the Director-General of Information is its secretary, continues to oversee and direct media institutions. Freedom, in terms of fundamental rights, is actually not freedom when it is subject to surveillance or even direction.

There are other examples of what we often face in daily life, such as the code of criminal procedure. In this code it is the role and power of the police, the prosecutor and the judge which have precedence, not the rights of the defendant or the convicted. We can say whatever we like, but if we are then accused of subversion we are finished. This is because, regardless of the defence, the outcome is still determined by the authorities, while the Supreme Court merely goes along with whatever the authorities decree. The Supreme Court previously had some room for manoeuvre on this matter because it could declare that the subversion law did not apply to actions that were not linked to an attempt to overthrow the government. But the Supreme Court's courage to defend this point of law did not last long. As the integralist political system became entrenched, the Court's courage was soon eroded. As a result, what the authorities held to be subversive was upheld by the Supreme Court, and the Supreme Court has never since had the courage to reject a charge of subversion made by the authorities. This has been able to happen because they have all been dragged into this integralist system. Whenever the government, for the sake of holding on to power, needs to declare someone subversive, then that person becomes a subversive. In such an atmosphere, fundamental rights have no chance to develop.

We often hear the authorities stating that the fundamental rights proclaimed by the United Nations or international conferences are liberal concepts that conflict with Indonesian culture. Labelling as liberal the broad array of human rights found in the United Nations Charter (even though we are a member state of the UN) or raised in European conferences means there is little chance of seeing them ratified here. A committee of the Interim MPR once [in 1996] attempted to formulate a set of human rights, many of which were taken from the United Nations Charter. But this formulation of human rights came to nothing because it was considered to be liberal and out of tune with our culture. The integralist concept that gives the authorities pride of place is strongly supported by our nation's paternalistic culture, which always confirms what the father or the authorities say.

10.5 Budiono Kusumohamidjojo: the need for a reliable legal system

This article was published in April 1988 against a backdrop of rapid deregulation of the banking and finance sector. Budiono, a legal practitioner and law lecturer at Parahyangan University, called for urgent legal reforms to keep pace with economic reforms. The reading is translated from an article in *Kompas* (Kusumohamidjojo 1988).

Economic deregulation inevitably brings with it changing political values. The issue here is that economic deregulation must be supported by some mechanism capable of maintaining a degree of order in political and market processes. Without this regulatory mechanism the political process, market processes and other social processes will descend into absurdity.

The legal bureaucracy can perform this function, but it first has to be made more reliable – all the more so because of the massive shifts taking place in the global environment.

As economic and trade deregulation starts to bear fruit we are now hearing demands from other sections of society to extend the reforms to such areas as law, education and health.

People do not have to be economists to arrive at this conclusion. We all have a basic interest in increasing our prosperity and security. The problem is that many people in sectors other than production and trade will be unable to take advantage of the changes, leading to frustration and possible social conflict. Furthermore, if the increasingly efficient management of economic deregulation is not matched in other areas of the administration, systematic distortions will appear within the state. Whether we like it or not, state administration is an integrated system and we cannot just deregulate one sector and not others.

While economic deregulation will undoubtedly change political values, we risk a major crisis if people at large are led to expect this spirit of deregulation to translate automatically into the political sphere. This risk can be avoided if deregulation is applied across the board, not only to producers and traders, but also to professionals and others. In this broader approach, deregulation of the legal sector is important, because law is the principal mechanism guaranteeing that transactions between people – which are multiplying as a result of deregulation – do not lead to anarchy.

As transactions and economic activities multiply, they also become more complex and involved, increasing the risk of unilateral default. The entities involved will always need a normative structure to ensure that the benefits, and the risks, are not all borne by one side.

The results of this can be anticipated: there will be a rapid increase in the number of people seeking a fast and effective means of resolving disputes. Whenever legal systems are slow and inefficient in responding to this tendency they will produce judgements that are ineffective and unreliable to litigants. Where the litigants are active in trade and production, this will be regarded as a cost that needs to be taken into consideration in any investment decision. They take note of the high costs they will incur if they need to resort to the courts in the course of their business. No investor, trader or producer is happy with these risks.

Outside the armed forces, traders, producers and investors are the most pragmatic groups in society. All losses are compensated for quickly and without fuss. If creditors find that their loans will not be repaid and that the courts are unlikely to support them, they simply raise interest rates, restrict credit or take other measures to protect themselves.

This situation also affects development on a national scale since we depend on foreign credit being invested mostly in private enterprise projects. Negative perceptions of the ability of our legal system to defend their legitimate rights will frighten off future investors, impeding the national development process.

When traders and producers find themselves in the same situation as investors, the outcome for consumers and society as a whole is obvious, and indeed is acknowledged by the government and by non-official groups: a high-cost economy.

So it is clear that the high risks that result from our slow and inefficient legal system are a factor, if not the main factor, behind our high-cost economy. Our slow and inefficient legal system certainly does not help national development. Meanwhile its corollary, 'high-cost law', is a reflection of our regulatory system, our bureaucracy, as well as our process of political decision-making. So where should we begin?

Dr Thee Kian Wie [in *Kompas*, 17 and 18 March 1988] has written that our tortuous and often inconsistent system of licences and restrictions can be traced back to the vested interests of particular groups. If this is correct, every genuine deregulation initiative must be able to give a clear-cut answer to the question of whether vested interests or the public interest are going to be given priority. Only if this question can be answered logically, consistently and firmly will it be possible to implement broad-based deregulation and to avoid systemic distortions.

First of all, though, we need deregulation of the legal sector. Because of its normative character, law can play a very decisive role in minimising anarchy in transactions between people in other sectors of life. But law can only serve as an effective standard in regulating behaviour and transactions between people if it is capable of abiding by the standards it sets itself. In order for this to happen, law – meaning in this case the legal system as well as the legal bureaucracy – needs to meet a number of criteria.

Most crucial is that normative legal decisions, which in trade and production are manifested as regulations governing the granting of permission and the imposition of prohibitions, be made clear and simple in order that the people they affect will not be confused by them. Unclear legal norms erode people's legal consciousness, making the job of implementing these legal norms increasingly difficult and leading people to lose faith in the law.

Second, legal norms must be unequivocal so that they will be clearly recognised by all. If they are not explicit, each side can interpret them in their own way to their own advantage.

Third, the various norms that come into being as a result of statutes, regulations or as products of the legislature (and, in practice, the executive also) must be consistent, so that what is done with the right hand is not undone with the left. Inconsistent legislation will in the long term turn the country into a 'leaking ship', and the benefits of development will drain away.

The construction of a simple, clear, unequivocal and consistent system of law will depend upon a legal bureaucracy that is also simple, clear, unequivocal and consistent. This kind of legal bureaucracy can only come about if the power to fine, impose sanctions and make binding decisions resides with the courts rather than being distributed over several institutions. The current situation only confuses the legal authorities.

We ought to be able to rely on the courts to issue clear and strictly enforceable decisions. Let us not get into a situation where creditors who are invited to invest their money in development projects suddenly find themselves having to go cap in hand to the debtors if they make a legitimate decision to withdraw their funds! Also, the courts, especially the Supreme Court, need to be consistent in their decisions. Do not decide one year that a creditor has a right to demand their loan be repaid and the next year favour the debtor as the weak party in need of protection.

Clarity and consistency in legal thinking will make it much easier for both ordinary citizens and litigants to follow and understand the politics of law. After two decades of political and governmental stability, the time has arrived for the government to provide and guarantee a just, consistent and reliable legal system and legal bureaucracy.

This hope is quite natural: in order to facilitate national development we need to present ourselves as a country with a stable government and political system, as well as a just and orderly legal system. We need to present ourselves as a country that can be relied upon in planning a better future in more difficult times.

10.6 Juwono Sudarsono: the diplomatic scam called human rights

The Soeharto government's public rejection of official aid from the Netherlands in 1992 helped license a degree of pugnacity in foreign affairs discourse not witnessed since the Sukarno years. In this article, excerpted from the *Jakarta Post* (11 April 1997), Juwono Sudarsono, a US- and British-educated international relations specialist, castigates the West for hypocrisy on human rights. Juwono was serving at the time as deputy governor of the National Resilience Institute, a military think tank and elite officer school. The article was reproduced on the Indonesian Department of Foreign Affairs website, where it remained in late 2001.

Because human rights is a nebulous concept, its use as a political weapon in diplomacy and international business has led to it being applied more often by developed nations facing growing economic competition from emerging markets.

In Western industrialised countries, intricate and well-financed human rights networks have been developed, giving rise to a thriving conscience industry binding the interests of thousands of politicians, lobbyists, academics, civic groups and media celebrities. Though they deny it, there are clear links between human rights activists and businesses affected by growing international competition.

In this light, the principles and practices of human rights need to be affirmed in a more balanced and proportionate manner. First and foremost, in conceptual terms the 1948 Universal Declaration on Human Rights calls for the advancement of all rights – civil, political, economic, social and cultural.

After the adoption of the International Covenant on Civil and Political Rights and the Covenant on Economic, Social and Cultural Rights in 1966, over 80 per cent of advanced industrialised countries focused their concern on civil and political issues in communist and developing countries.

In 1986 the United Nations General Assembly broadened the conceptual definition of human rights to encompass 'the right to development', in which all states are ensured 'access to basic resources, education, health services, food, housing, employment and the fair distribution of income'.

It was no coincidence that advanced industrialised countries' focus on civil and political rights issues in East Asia grew with the increasing competitiveness of those new industrialising economies. Even after the 1993 World Conference on Human Rights in Vienna affirmed that 'all human rights are universal, indivisible, interdependent and interrelated', advanced industrialised countries incessantly focused attention on civil and political issues in developing countries.

No nation, not even the most industrially advanced, can achieve a perfect score in broadly defined human rights.

But the hypocrisy of governments and rights advocates in industrialised countries is particularly stark in their arrogant assumption that civil and political rights in their countries are irreproachable and must become the benchmarks by which developing countries are judged.

Politicians and rights advocates in advanced industrialised countries disingenuously claim that economic, social and cultural rights are 'unjustifiable', not subject to verifications through a country's legal system.

It is worth remembering that the International Commission of Jurists' Bangalore Declaration of 25 October 1995 reminds human rights commissions and advocacy groups all over the world that the economic, social and cultural dimensions of human rights are 'just as urgent and vital as civil and political rights'.

There must be less vehement insistence on immediate rectification of civil and political rights flaws, and more humility based on the reality that there can often be only gradual and deliberate ways to progress with a balanced view encompassing all categories of human rights, especially in developing nations.

The tendency of media in advanced industrialised countries to adhere to the credo that 'if it bleeds, it leads' makes it hard to have a comprehensive and balanced viewpoint. It is always tempting to present in a news feature 10 paragraphs on issues of civil and political liberties in a country of 1.2 billion people such as China, particularly if they obscure the one or two lines of grudging acknowledgement of China's economic success and its need to maintain social and cultural cohesion.

Can it be purely coincidental that the attention of governments, parliaments, the press and non-governmental organisations and other self-styled concerned citizens of the industrialised world are focused on human rights issues in economies that are increasingly becoming more competitive in international trade and business?

Would the United States place that much attention on civil and political rights issues in China if trade surplus figures were more favourable to them than the Chinese? Would there have been much concern about civil and political rights in Indonesia if the manufacturing industries in Indonesia had not eroded the competitiveness of comparable goods made in the advanced industrialised countries?

Have not the United States and Europe been more selective and coy about their human rights concerns in the strategically oil-rich states in the Middle East, particularly if these countries purchase surplus NATO arms, fighter planes and tanks, and order European Airbuses and American Boeings?

Human rights in international diplomacy should be affirmed for what it really is: a big scam that seems destined to last as long as nations compete for economic advantage through political subterfuge on behalf of noble ideals.

10.7 Indonesian NGOs for Democracy: joint declaration on human rights

This statement was issued in Jakarta on 3 May 1993 by a coalition of NGOs called IN-DEMO, which included INGI, the International NGO Forum on Indonesia (1993). It appeared in advance of the World Conference on Human Rights held by the United Nations in Vienna in June 1993.

Motivated by a feeling of responsibility as citizens of the world and specifically as citizens of Indonesia who revere the values of humanism, and for the sake of strengthening the belief in human rights, in the dignity and value of humankind, in equal rights for both men and women, and in the equality of big and small nations, and for the sake of advancing the progress of society and a better life for the individual in a free environment, we, Indonesian human rights activists, both individuals and from a range of organisations, feel that it is necessary to clarify our position on human rights. We hope that such clarification, in the form of this statement, will have an influence on the formulation of human rights concepts and declarations at the national, regional and international levels.

Given the above, our declaration of our views on human rights is as follows:

1   We affirm that human rights adhere to every human being from birth until death. Because of this, human rights are essentially universal in nature.

2   As a consequence of the acknowledgement of the universality of human rights, we assert that such rights apply to all people all over the world, and are not dependent on their acknowledgement by states. Because of this, the Universal Declaration of Human Rights, issued by the UN in 1948, is morally binding and must be adhered to by all member countries of the UN. This declaration should also be the foundation of international human rights law, and it should be the obligation of all countries to respect it. Emphasising the importance of particularities in cultural values, historical backgrounds and religious differences will in essence only undermine the importance of the very universality of human rights.

3   Human rights are often formulated in terms of civil and political, social, cultural and economic rights. In reality, there is no dichotomy between these rights. All of these rights should be viewed as a whole and as being indivisible. Any trade-off of such rights, no matter what it is in the name of, is unacceptable.

4   We affirm the belief that development directed at advancing the welfare of the people is the right of every human being, of all groups and of all nations. The actual process of development must advance human dignity. At the same time, development must include the free and full participation of the people and, in the process of development, the just and equal distribution of the benefits of development, and the principles of the sustainability of the natural environment.

5   We re-emphasise that respect for human rights applies to the actual process of development as well as to its objectives. And so the right to development must stress respect for human rights in economic, social, cultural and environmental, as well as civil and political rights. These

represent the principal elements upon which the process of development should be based. These rights are interdependent and indivisible.

6 We reaffirm that it is the individual who is the subject of the right to development. And so the realisation of human potential, in harmony with society, must be viewed as the principal objective of development. Every individual must be viewed as the subject, rather than as the object, of development. Every individual must be able to participate fully and actively in development as part of the process of self-actualisation.

7 Participation in development means that the right to associate must be guaranteed, both for individuals and collectively. People must be able to organise themselves, whether as producers, workers, consumers, groups who have been harmed, or as citizens on a local, national and international level. And, in order to make the right to free association effective, the rights to freely express opinions and to access information must also be respected.

8 We stress that the implementation of all the aforementioned rights should be viewed as being in the national interest, in its most whole sense. Therefore, in this context sovereignty must be viewed as the sovereignty of the people.

9 We stress that implementing all the aforementioned rights should be viewed as being the responsibility of all parties – the states and citizens of UN member countries, with no difference being drawn between the superpowers and other countries. Thus it is necessary to question the continued relevance of the UN Security Council veto power. This has been used to provide de facto legitimation of human rights violations committed by a number of the superpowers in other countries....

Signed[2]

10.8 Government of Indonesia: rights and obligations

This undated English-language statement represented the government of Indonesia's position on human rights in early 1998. The statement borrows phrases from speeches by Indonesian Foreign Minister Ali Alatas, Indonesia's ambassador to the Vatican Irawan Abidin, and Wiryono Sastrohandoyo, former director-general of the Indonesian Foreign Ministry's Political Department. It is excerpted from a posting on the Indonesian Department of Foreign Affairs website.

As a people, Indonesians feel that, having once been colonised for more than 350 years, they know only too well the true meaning of human rights. In any discussion on this subject they readily point out that

Indonesia was born out of a struggle for the most fundamental of human rights – the right to be free. And that includes not only the right to political freedom, but also the right to be free from want, ignorance, social injustice and economic backwardness.

The Indonesian concept of human rights emanates from the state philosophy, Pancasila, particularly its second principle that calls for 'a just and civilised humanity'. It is also reflected in the four companion principles that together advance the idea of the essential nobility and dignity of the human being both as a member of society and as an individual.

In this, Indonesia is no different from other Asian and African nations endowed with age-old and highly developed cultures and which have not gone through the same history and experience as the Western nations in developing ideas on human rights and democracy. They often developed different perceptions based on different experiences regarding the relations between man and society, man and his fellow man, and the rights of the community as against the rights of the individual.

A complex issue

But Indonesia does not propose an alternative concept of human rights. As a committed member of the United Nations and, since 1991, a member of the UN Human Rights Commission, it accepts and recognises the universal validity of basic human rights and fundamental freedoms. It stresses, however, that there should be greater recognition of the immense complexity of the issue of human rights due to the wide diversity in the history, culture, value systems, geography and phases of development among the nations of the world. All nations should therefore be more sensitive towards this complexity.

Consistent with this view, Indonesia fully adheres to the policy in the United Nations Charter placing the promotion and protection of human rights within the context of international cooperation. There is now a body of conventions, declarations and common understandings on their implementing measures developed by the United Nations since 1945. Indonesia regards these as representing the beginning of a universal culture on human rights which makes feasible international cooperation on this issue.

International cooperation, however, presupposes respect for the sovereign equality of states and the national identity of peoples. Indonesia therefore holds the view that in such international cooperation there should be no room for unfounded accusations or preaching self-righteous sermons, or interference. No country or group of countries should reserve unto itself the role of judge and jury over other countries on this critical and sensitive issue.

The Indonesian view

...It is now generally accepted that all categories of human rights – civil, political, economic, social and cultural, the rights of the individual and the rights of the community, the society and the nation – are interrelated and indivisible. The promotion and protection of all these rights should therefore be undertaken in an integrated and balanced manner. Inordinate emphasis on one category of human rights over another should be eschewed. Likewise, in assessing the human rights conditions of countries, particularly developing countries, the international community should take into account the situation in relation to all categories of human rights – following the principles contained in the Universal Declaration of Human Rights. Article 29 of that declaration addresses two aspects that balance each other: on the one hand, there are principles that respect the fundamental rights and freedoms of the individual; on the other, there are stipulations regarding the obligations of the individual towards the society and the state.

A balanced relationship

The implementation of human rights implies a balanced relationship between individual rights and the obligations of individuals towards their community. Without such a balance, the rights of the community as a whole can be denied, which can lead to instability and even anarchy, especially in developing countries. In Indonesia, as in many other developing countries, the rights of the individual are balanced by the rights of the community. The culture of Indonesia as well as its ancient customary laws have always stressed the rights and interests of the society or nation, without, however, in any way minimising the rights and interests of individuals and minorities. The interests of the latter are always fully taken into account on the basis of the principle of '*musyawarah-mufakat*' (deliberation in order to obtain consensus), which is firmly embedded in the nation's socio-political system and form of democracy.

Right to development

Indonesia is now at a stage of development that requires increasing focus on its people as both the principal agent and ultimate beneficiary of development. This is why Indonesia, like most developing countries, attaches great importance to the right to development and to the right to pursue development in an environment of peace and national stability. The Vienna Conference on Human Rights, which was held last year, supports this view and reaffirms that the right to development is a universal and inalienable right. Therefore, poverty, hunger and other denials of economic, social and cultural rights render impossible the full enjoyment of all human rights.

Indonesia holds that, although human rights are universal in character, their expression and implementation in the national context remain the competence and responsibility of each government. This means that the complex variety of problems, of different economic, social and cultural realities, and the unique value systems prevailing in each country should be taken into consideration. This national competence not only derives from the principle of [the] sovereignty of states, but also is a logical consequence of the principle of self-determination. Recognising the important role that could be played by national institutions in the promotion and protection of human rights, Indonesia in 1993 established a National Commission on Human Rights.

The complete picture

Indonesia is also of the firm view that, in evaluating the implementation of human rights in individual countries, the characteristic problems of developing countries in general, as well as the specific problems of individual societies, should be taken fully into account. The complete picture rather than the partial view should be presented.

Indonesia finds it regrettable that the way in which concerns on human rights are expressed at the international level has so far failed to reflect the immense political, economic, social and cultural diversity of the world. When this diversity is disregarded, as it often is, imbalances occur in such forms as politicisation, selectivity, double standards and discrimination. As a result, some countries have become the targets of unfair censure and trial by prejudicial publicity. On the other hand, there are countries that deserve but are spared from criticism for reasons that have nothing to do with human rights.

It would help the cause of human rights if these imbalances were addressed through an integrated and balanced approach that takes into account the diversity of the societies in which human rights are to be observed and implemented; the indivisibility and non-selectivity of all human rights; and the inherent relationship between development, democracy, social justice and the universal enjoyment of human rights.

A universal culture

Indonesia therefore stands committed to the declaration and program of action adopted at the Vienna Conference on Human Rights and supports the work being undertaken by the United Nations High Commissioner on Human Rights (UNHCHR).

Indonesia and like-minded developing countries worked hard to realise the mandate of the UNHCHR so that he may be able to bring greater coordination to UN human rights activities, to give balance to these activities so that all categories of human rights are duly emphasised, including the right to development, and to place them in [the] rightful context of international cooperation.

Indonesia regards the concepts, the instruments and the international understandings on human rights as constituting the beginnings of a universal culture that should be nurtured and built upon so that in time it may be able to bridge the vast diversity of cultures, traditions, and social, economic and political systems in the world today without disregarding any of them or allowing any one of them to dominate the others.

Notes

1   Dr Sukiman Wirjosandojo was a medical practitioner who was part of the subcommittee that drafted the constitution in 1945. He became a Masjumi politician after independence and served as prime minister from 1951 to 1952.
2   Centre for Human Rights Studies (YAPUSHAM); Indonesian Legal Aid Foundation (YLBHI); Indonesian Forum for the Environment (WALHI); Bandung NGOs Forum; Association for the Management of Population Issues (PPMK-SA); Institute for National Development (LBB); Forum for Social Study; People's Movement for Democracy; Development of Indonesian Citizens' Rights Foundation; West Java Farmers' Association (SPJB); Bandung Legal Aid Institute (LBH Bandung); Indonesian Forum for the Environment, West Java (Forda WALHI Jawa Barat); Bandung Group for Children; Student Movement Committee of the Indonesian Peoples (KPMURI); Pribumi Cultural Institute of Bandung; YSPM Solo; Yogyakarta Legal Aid Institute; Society for Human Rights Studies (LEKHAT); Society for Environmental Study and Action (SENSA); Tjut Nyak Dien Women's Forum; Yogyakarta NGO Forum; Institute for Study and Social Development (LSPS); Society for Social Study, Lombok (HMPES); Institute for Study and Legal Aid Consultation, Surabaya (LSKBH); Humanika Foundation, Surabaya; Daya Parakarsa Foundation; Centre for Information Study and Data (P2ID); Indonesian Scavenger Association (IPI); Institute for the Defence of Human Rights (LPHAM); Solidarity Forum for Labour (FORSOL); Indonesian Front for the Defence of Human Rights (INFIGHT); International NGO Forum on Indonesian Development (INGI); Adhikara Indonesiana Foundation, Surabaya; Centre for Human Rights Education and Information (PIPHAM); Indonesian Interreligion Forum for Human Rights (FAHAMI); Women's Solidarity (SP); Network for Social Information (JARIM); Women's Liberation Foundation (YPM); Indonesian Centre for Environmental Law; Regional Council of Human Rights in Asia; Secretariat for Cooperation of Volunteers for the Protection of the Environment (SKREPP); Sejati Foundation; Foundation for Indonesian Legal Service, Solo (YAPHI); Frans Winarta & Partners; Indonesian Consumers' Organisation (YLKI); Jakarta Legal Aid Institute (LBH Jakarta); Institute for Social Science Study (LSIS); Pijar Foundation; Democracy Forum, Yogyakarta Student and Youth Group; and 109 individual activists not named in the document.

11 Federalism, regionalism and the unitary state

Indonesia inherited its far-flung borders from the Netherlands East Indies. That they remain intact is remarkable, given the country's ethnic and religious, not to mention geographical, diversity. Probably the most important reason for this has been the success of the nationalist project. National unity has been a central theme of Indonesian nationalist discourse since at least the 1920s. It was inscribed in the preamble to the 1945 Constitution and was constantly reiterated by both the Sukarno and Soeharto regimes.

Jakarta's vision of national unity, however, has always been contested. In the mid-1950s autonomist movements sprang up in several of the resource-rich islands outside Java. With the backing of local military commands, and in some cases the CIA, these movements posed a significant challenge to the central government and to the coherence of the newly independent state. In Aceh, South Sulawesi and some other strongly Islamic regions, the Darul Islam movement also rejected the authority of the republic until the early 1960s. General Nasution's forces crushed both the regional rebellions and Darul Islam, bringing the military prestige as the 'guardian of national unity' and instilling within it a deep suspicion not only of political Islam but also of regionalist sentiment.

Upon its inception, the New Order tightened the grip of central control – over the military apparatus, bureaucracy and over the country as a whole. Thousands of active military officers were appointed to strategic 'civilian' positions, and a parallel military and intelligence structure reporting to the central command shadowed every layer of civilian government in the regions. Law no. 5/1974 laid the foundations for a quarter of a century of central domination of the administrative apparatus. Although it was presented as extending a degree of autonomy to the regions, its effect was to make provincial and regional government heads responsible to Jakarta. Central control was further institutionalised with Law no. 5/1979, which standardised village administrative structures throughout Indonesia on the Javanese model. Village heads would no longer be elected, but civil servants appointed by provincial governors, who were in turn appointed by the president (A.R. Kahin 1994: 209–10; MacAndrews 1986: 39).

While it is true, as Amal (1994: 219) has argued, that the New Order was able to inspire greater loyalty from the regions than previous governments, resentment over the concentration of administrative and economic power in Jakarta was never far from the surface. This often manifested itself in disputes over the appointment of outsiders (more often than not Javanese) as provincial governors. Grievances over the government's handling of its relations with the regions were typically expressed with circumspection. In the first extract (Reading 11.1) Frans Seda, a former finance minister from the eastern Indonesian island of Flores, suggests that the New Order's policies on regional autonomy and government failed to live up to the 1945 Constitution, whose authors, he argues, had envisaged a more diverse and decentralised system of administration.

In three areas, West Papua, Aceh and East Timor, there was overt resistance to the central government. In West Papua wholesale exploitation of the island's fabulous mineral resources, as well as an insensitivity to local culture and land ownership practices, helped spark an armed independence movement, known as the Organisasi Papua Merdeka (OPM, Free Papua Movement). In Reading 11.2 Manuel Kaisiepo, a veteran journalist from West Papua, appeals to an Indonesian audience in 1993 to understand that the roots of the OPM's appeal lie in the unfair and often brutal treatment of the local population by the civil and military authorities. He was later to serve as minister for East Indonesian affairs.

Discrimination is also a major issue in Aceh, where discontent over the perceived lack of local benefit from the lucrative oil and gas projects in the territory has helped fuel a significant armed separatist movement. Gerakan Aceh Merdeka (GAM, Free Aceh Movement), headed by the businessman in exile Dr Teungku Hasan di Tiro, has waged a low-level war against the Indonesian government since the mid-1970s. In response the military launched a major counter-insurgency operation, peaking in the late 1980s and early 1990s, in which large numbers of Acehnese villagers were killed, tortured and raped. GAM's military activities were severely curtailed, but grievances against the central government spread to broad sectors of the population. Recognising this, President Habibie and his defence minister General Wiranto apologised to the Acehnese people in August 1998, but the momentum for independence only grew after Habibie promised East Timor a plebiscite on its future. In Reading 11.3 Mohammad Daud Yoesoef, an academic based in Aceh, puts his case for Aceh's secession from Indonesia, focusing in this case mainly on historical and constitutional arguments. He did this in a major regional newspaper, *Serambi*, indicating how mainstream separatist arguments had become by March 1999.

Resistance in East Timor started as soon as the Indonesian military invaded the former Portuguese colony on 7 December 1975. Indonesia established full control over the territory by the early 1980s, but at an enormous cost. It is estimated that approximately one-third of East

Timor's 600,000 residents died as a result of the anti-insurgency campaign, which involved military operations as well as strict controls on the movement of the population, leading to famine and disease. Indonesia lost about 10,000 soldiers and attracted regular criticism in international forums, including the United Nations, which refused to recognise the incorporation. In an effort to ease international condemnation and win over the East Timorese, the government poured money into infrastructure projects, including roads and schools. To Indonesia's dismay, many of the youths it educated affiliated themselves with clandestine groups working for independence. Reading 11.4 was written by an Indonesian-educated East Timorese activist in 1992, not long after the massacre of pro-independence youths at Dili's Santa Cruz cemetery in November 1991 had brought the conflict to the world's attention in dramatic fashion. Writing for an Indonesian audience, the anonymous author adapts a well-known anti-Dutch tract by the Indonesian nationalist Soewardi Soerjaningrat (also known as Ki Hadjar Dewantoro) to draw parallels between Dutch and Indonesian colonialism. Equally galling for many Indonesians at the time were the casual analogies the writer made between East Timorese and Indonesian nationalisms. Mainstream Indonesia's denial of the reality of East Timorese nationalism helps explain the genuine shock that greeted the announcement that 78.5 per cent of the East Timorese population had voted for independence in the United Nations-sponsored ballot on 30 August 1999.

For the duration of the New Order, any public advocacy of federalism was taboo. It had been so since 1950, when the newly independent republic emphatically rejected the Dutch-inspired 1949 Constitution creating a federated United States of Indonesia. Despite a quiet interest in the idea among some non-Javanese intellectuals, federalism was officially associated with divide-and-rule tactics and foreign manipulation. The break-up of the Soviet Union and Yugoslavia only reinforced unitarist sentiment in Indonesia. After the fall of Soeharto, though, the concept began to be floated once again, perhaps most notably by Amien Rais's National Mandate Party. In Reading 11.5 the late, renowned intellectual, social activist and priest Y.B. Mangunwijaya puts the case for a federal Indonesia. Far from precipitating the break-up of Indonesia, Mangunwijaya argues that federalism provides the best means to hold the country together. Two controversial pieces of legislation introduced in the early post-Soeharto period, Laws nos. 22 and 25/1999, transferred significant administrative powers to the sub-provincial level and introduced new revenue-sharing arrangements between Jakarta and the regions.

Introduced during the Habibie presidency, the laws received only lukewarm support from the governments of presidents Abdurrahman Wahid and Megawati Soekarnoputri. The staunchly nationalist Megawati, in particular, has been keen to slow or even reverse the trend for decentralisation and regional autonomy, supported by allies within her party and sections of the military. In Reading 11.6, armed forces spokesperson Major-General Sudrajat puts the military's case against federalism, arguing that Indonesia is still too fragile and riven by ethnic tensions to embark on 'experiments' of this type. Outbreaks of ethnic and religious violence in many parts of Indonesia from 1999 have strengthened the hand of those arguing for strong central government, but others argue that the decentralisation process simply needs to be better regulated. Whatever the outcome, debates over the distribution of power have become much more important in recent years and seem likely to remain a crucial issue in the future.

11.1 Frans Seda: regional autonomy, a constitutional right

This extract is taken from a book of essays by the seasoned economist and Catholic politician Frans Seda (1996: 157–62).

Many political, social and economic crises, such as in East Timor and Irian Jaya, have been closely connected with the issue of autonomy. Autonomy has also played a decisive part in sub-regional cooperation schemes with neighbouring countries....

In setting out some basic ideas about regional autonomy and its implementation, my point of reference is not the discipline of Indology, which the Dutch used to teach their bureaucrats before being posted to Indonesia, and which has sometimes influenced the perspective and thinking of our own experts. Nor is it Law no. 5/1974 on Regional Administration, which I consider to have been an attempt to bulldoze regional autonomy and impose Javanese administrative conventions across the country – to the extent of adopting Javanese nomenclature for village heads (*lurah*), subdistrict heads (*camat*) and so on.

My point of reference here is instead the 1945 Constitution and the aspirations of the society that produced it. Regional administration was regarded as so important then that it was given precedence in the constitution over regulations governing the parliament....The elucidation of Article 18 reads: 'Because Indonesia is a unitary state (*eenheidstaat*), there shall be no separate states within its boundaries...but rather a system of autonomous or administratively autonomous districts.'

But the issue of autonomy is not simply about government, even though this is an important aspect. Autonomy is about communities, about the way people live and behave, and local aspirations. What defines an autonomous district is the nature of its local community – that is, whether it is an ethnic group/folk society or a local or regional traditional law community/legal society.[1] So the sentence of the elucidation that reads 'Indonesia shall be divided into provinces and the provinces shall be divided into smaller districts' should rightly continue thus: 'inhabited by ethnic groups and autonomous traditional law communities'....

Nowadays the issue of regional autonomy is focused upon decentralisation of power or conferment of governmental authority to certain levels of administration (for instance the district level). But administrative autonomy is only one aspect or element of authentic autonomy as a right belonging to local communities. Authentic autonomy, as intended in the 1945 Constitution and by the founders of the republic, is the right of local communities to sustain and develop themselves in matters relating to their own prosperity and welfare.

The 1945 Constitution also recognises special regions, namely regions inhabited by local communities which have their own unique structures of authority, 'such as the *desa* in Java and Bali, the *negeri* in the Minangkabau region, and the *dusun* and *marga* in Palembang' (Article 18). But while such entities are afforded special status in the 1945 Constitution, this is not recognised in our current administrative structures. We do indeed have special regions today, but these are based on considerations that have little to do with the 1945 Constitution.

So, when we consider how autonomy is dealt with nowadays, it is clear how far we have strayed from the purity of purpose that shaped the thinking and the hopes of the founders of the republic.

We must quickly reclaim that purity, for there can be no other basis for implementing the 1945 Constitution and Pancasila purely and consistently, bearing in mind the need to ensure that this republic and this nation remain completely united as we enter the era of globalisation, free competition, economic openness and the 21st century.

The founders of the republic who proclaimed the independent state on 17 August 1945 conceived of it as having three dimensions. It would be at once a nation-state based on Pancasila, a republic based on popular sovereignty and a unitary state based on regional autonomy....

The unitary state has been realised, but it has been bound together so tightly, with such a centralised bureaucracy and concentration of power, that all sorts of problems have arisen. Regional autonomy as an aspect of the unitary state has been shunted aside and considered a potential threat to unity, as something to be experimented with at best. Consequently our unitary state has yet to function as it should.

Autonomy is a right of regional communities, not something to be granted as a gift or delegated by and from the centre, as many central government officials seem to think. This attitude, this perception, needs to be corrected, because it disturbs the functioning of the unitary republic and, accordingly, the integrity of the nation and its society....

I am reminded of how we reacted when the Dutch colonialists used to consider us not yet able and competent to be independent, telling us that a period of probation and transition was required. At that time we took it as an insult. But how is this colonial attitude essentially any different from the approach of current power-holders to the question of regional autonomy?

Related to the question of regional autonomy is the matter of finance. Financial self-sufficiency has been made one of the key conditions for granting autonomy. Here the issue of the division of finances between the centre and regions has been a matter of contention. Indeed centre–region financial relations have often been linked to the question of decentralisation of governmental authority. But autonomy is more than simply an issue of decentralising governmental authority. When we are talking about the division of finances, we have to ask exactly what and how much is to be divided. Since the centre currently funds all routine and project expenditure, any reassessment of centre–regional financial relations that led to a reduction in central government subsidies would do nothing to improve the state of regional finances.

Making financial self-sufficiency a condition for conferring regional autonomy is unfair, since the regions have been given neither the means nor the freedom to develop their own financial potential. Imposing this condition is intended to obstruct the conferment of regional autonomy, which is misconceived as a delegation of authority from the centre, rather than as a right of local communities.

Regional autonomy is essentially about the freedom of regions to run their own affairs and to develop their own natural and human resources. So as well as setting up finance-sharing arrangements, the regions also need to be funded directly....

My determination to defend the right of regions to enjoy autonomy does not diminish my realism concerning their shortfalls in human resources as well as finances, together with regional bigotry and the attitude of quite a few regional officials who still behave like small-time royalty in their local domains. These shortcomings need to be overcome and sorted out. But they do not diminish the urgency for a breakthrough in the issue of regional autonomy, because this is a matter of survival for the unity and integrity of the Indonesian Republic.

11.2 Manuel Kaisiepo: the trouble in Irian Jaya

This extract from a seminar paper by moderate Papuan journalist Manuel Kaisiepo highlights some of the key grievances of the Papuan people under New Order rule. It also illustrates the difficulties of raising the issue of regional nationalism in a political atmosphere that denied the very idea. The paper, entitled 'Irian-ness and Indonesian-ness: examining nationalism in the local context', was presented at a seminar on 'Indonesian Nationalism in the 21st Century' in Salatiga in June 1993 (Kaisiepo 1993).

It is important to understand that the sporadic acts of resistance in the last few years are no longer driven by separatist aims or the desire to create a 'Papuan state', but more by other factors such as social dissatisfaction.

These sporadic resistance movements, although still bearing the name OPM [Free Papua Movement], are in reality OPM in name only and are not based on firm beliefs, ideals or clear political aims.

The pressing issue now is why these resistance movements, although no longer significant either politically or militarily, are still in evidence today. Without a clear understanding of the roots of the issues related to these movements we will always be sidetracked into reaching false conclusions as to the cause of these acts of resistance.

There are clearly two factors which, either directly or indirectly, relate to the appearance of these resistance movements: first, the side-effects of the security approach implemented in Irian Jaya over an extended period; and, second, the effects of various development programs that local communities felt actually hurt rather than helped them.

The 'OPM' trauma

The security approach, implemented over an extended period in Irian Jaya in the form of intensive military operations, was aimed at eradicating OPM resistance between 1965 and 1970. These intensive military operations succeeded in crushing the OPM resistance groups but they also left behind deep-seated feelings of fear and trauma among the Irianese.

They are always haunted by the fear of being labelled 'OPM', a trauma resembling that experienced by sections of the population in Javanese rural communities at the time of the crushing of the G30S/PKI in 1965/6, who were terrified of being labelled 'PKI'.

Certain unscrupulous officials, from both the government and the private sector, have unfortunately taken advantage of this fear of being labelled 'OPM' in order to intimidate local communities. If, for example, local people refuse to relinquish their land for the requirements of private or government development projects, they can easily be accused of belonging to the OPM.

Fear of persecution has often been a factor motivating sections of the Irianese population to flee to the jungle or even cross the border into Papua New Guinea [PNG]. Their flight into the jungle or into PNG is, in reality, only an attempt to find a safe haven – an act of self-defence in other words.

Yet fleeing to the jungle can backfire, because in doing so people are all the more likely to be considered genuine members of the OPM and find themselves targeted by military operations. This happened at the time of the so-called exodus of a large number of Irianese to Papua New Guinea at the beginning of 1984.

Development and poverty

Development programs carried out by the government in Irian Jaya since its integration into Indonesia have succeeded in several sectors and its people have experienced real benefits.

On the other hand, the development model that was applied and several programs disadvantaged the people of Irian Jaya. This gave rise to dissatisfaction and disappointment, and in some extreme instances even motivated local people to carry out acts of resistance. Some examples are outlined below.

The requisitioning of lands traditionally owned by local communities for forestry-industry concessions, for transmigration programs and for other projects without taking into consideration local customs and laws has often led to dissatisfaction and eventually to acts of resistance against the government.

The flood of transmigrants from Java and the steady flow of migrants from South Sulawesi, and their domination of almost all sectors of the economy, have created a situation that the Irianese people see as very unjust.

According to the Transmigration Department's Irian Jaya office, the number of transmigrants from Java grew steadily between the First Five-Year Plan (Pelita 1) to the Fifth Five-Year Plan. As of April 1993 the number totalled 23,947 families, or 102,941 people.

According to research carried out by George Aditjondro (1986), as many as 3,000–4,000 people migrate from South Sulawesi to Irian Jaya every year. Between 1970 and 1985 he estimated that 60,000 people from South Sulawesi had migrated to Irian Jaya, a total that is bound to have increased since.

The presence of these migrant groups has clearly brought with it various negative effects, including:

1   unfair trading methods;
2   an imbalance in business competition between migrants and local people;
3   depletion of marine and terrestrial resources;
4   land conflicts;
5   business-oriented marriages;
6   crime.

(*Ibid.*)

Dissatisfaction is also widespread among young high-school and university graduates who are unemployed, because a large proportion of job vacancies have been filled by 'newcomers' (a term that has negative connotations in Irian Jaya).

Data from the Department of Labour and Industry's Irian Jaya office in 1992 revealed that the largest number of job-seekers were high-school graduates, numbering 67,418, followed by 23,018 primary graduates, 15,369 junior high-school graduates and 5,902 tertiary graduates. The existence of such large numbers of unemployed young people obviously creates difficult social problems.

Other negative effects are apparent if we examine the issue of poverty in Irianese communities, especially those living in remote villages. Of the 11 provinces with percentages of poor people above the national average in 1987, Irian Jaya was the worst affected (Booth 1992: 348).[2]

Figures on development investment and per-capita income in Irian Jaya highlight another important issue. Investment is quite large in the mining and forestry sectors. According to the 1990 Business Activity Report, the mining sector made up 31.55 per cent of the province's gross domestic product.

The problem is that profits from these mining projects go to the central government and only a small fraction of the benefits are enjoyed by the people of Irian Jaya. Ironically, these mining operations give Irian Jaya the highest per-capita income in Indonesia, yet the population is much worse off than in other provinces....

Accumulated feelings of dissatisfaction and disappointment towards the negative effects of development and the reality of poverty which envelops the daily life of the people of Irian Jaya are clearly factors which often motivate sections of the population to flee to the jungle, to form armed groups to oppose the government, or to cross the border into PNG.

The acts of resistance we have witnessed since 1970 clearly stem from these feelings of dissatisfaction and poverty, not from a determination to create a 'Papuan state', as was the case during the period from 1965 to 1970. It is too easy simply to brand them 'OPM'.

11.3 Mohammad Daud Yoesoef: Aceh might still secede

At the time this article (Yoesoef 1999) appeared in the Banda Aceh newspaper *Serambi*, on 7 March 1999, the campaign for a referendum on independence in Aceh was well under way. Mohammad Daud Yoesoef was a lecturer in law at Syiah Kuala University in Banda Aceh.

In re-examining historical narratives of the birth of the Indonesian Republic, we ought to reconsider events preceding the proclamation of the independence in 1945. This examination can be approached historically and from a constitutional perspective. First of all, historical research needs to investigate which ethnic groups in the archipelago were represented at the assembly that subsequently gave birth to the Youth Pledge of 28 October 1928.[3] According to historical data, there was not a single Acehnese delegate present.

Even during the process that led to the formation of the 1945 Constitution, only one Acehnese was included in the Preparatory Committee for Indonesian Independence, namely the late Teuku Mohammad Hasan. However, it should be noted that he could not be said to have represented the Acehnese nation. He owed his appointment to the committee to the fact that he happened to live in Batavia as a student in the Dutch colonial era. He was chosen because he was descended from one of the regional rulers in Aceh who had been appointed by the Dutch.

If we look at the issue from a constitutional angle, colonialism clearly influenced the philosophy behind the 1945 Constitution. This influence is reflected in the granting of enormous powers to the president, who as bearer of executive power also holds legislative power, and who is further able to intervene in matters pertaining to justice. The very broad presidential powers conferred by the 1945 Constitution are a carry-over from the powers of the Governor-General in the colonial era. It is common knowledge that in those times the distance between the Netherlands and the Dutch East Indies made communication very difficult. Consequently, the government in the Netherlands delegated enormous powers to the Governor-General of the Dutch East Indies.

It should also be noted that a majority of the committee put in charge of drafting the constitution were Dutch educated.

Aside from these issues, it is necessary for a constitution to contain basic stipulations, not only on government bodies and their essential functions, the basis of the state and the rights of citizens/human rights, but also to specify the territorial extent of the state. In other words, a constitution needs to list all the regions included under its territorial sovereignty. We can see such specifications in the constitutions of the Netherlands, Malaysia, the Philippines and of other states.

It was never clearly stated in the 1945 Constitution, or in its elucidation, which regions were to be included in the territory of the Republic of Indonesia. The only mention of territories is in the elucidation of Article 18, where examples are given of customary modes of organisation in Java, Bali, Palembang and the Minangkabau lands. Consequently, it is actually unclear just which regions are covered by the territory of the state of the Republic of Indonesia in constituting its territorial sovereignty. On the basis of these facts, regions outside Java are entitled to demand their secession from the Republic of Indonesia. Since 1945, regions outside Java have been incorporated in the republic without regard to the aspirations of the majority of their populations. In reality, the 1945 Constitution was written to represent Javanese interests, ignoring the interests of the other regions. Therefore people in areas outside Java have the right to reject or demand changes to the 1945 Constitution. This is especially true for Aceh, which has been exploited for decades, while its people were cruelly repressed during the period when the territory was designated a 'military operations zone'. It is entirely legitimate for Aceh to demand secession from the Indonesian Republic. It is also perfectly legitimate to demand self-determination via a referendum, or at the very least a federal state.

In a federal state there are laws demarcating the powers of the central, federal government and the regional, provincial government. Federal systems of government are ideally suited to states whose territory stretches across a wide area (such as archipelagos), and to states whose regional diversity is a consequence of socio-economic inequality and cultural difference. The Indonesian state, which has long been controlled by a centralised government, is one such example. So say the political scientists.

For Aceh, the demands mentioned above are matters of absolute importance. This is because the central government, in particular the leadership of the armed forces, have not to date shown that they have the political will to resolve the cases [of human rights abuse] that occurred both during and after Aceh was a 'military operations zone'. The government has closed its eyes and ears to the heartfelt cry of the people of Aceh. Despite this, those in government are perhaps aware that the people of Aceh still have a survival instinct to continue to live in a humanitarian way. The people of Aceh have a dignity that the armed forces have trampled all over. For the sake of national prestige, the people of Aceh are ready to sacrifice everything if the government fails to open the way for a face-saving exit as a response to the grief and oppression Aceh has suffered.

Whether we look at the issue historically or from a constitutional viewpoint, and especially when we take into consideration the present crystallisation of Aceh's spirit and determination, there are no particularly significant obstacles to Aceh seceding from the Republic of Indonesia. If East Timor is to be given the opportunity, why not Aceh? The only issue is whether the republic is prepared to let go of the territory that has done so much to fatten up the capital.

11.4 Anonymous: if only I were free

In 1913 the Indonesian nationalist Soewardi Soeryaningrat created a scandal when his article entitled 'If only I were a Dutchman' appeared in the Dutch-language newspaper *De Express*. The well-known tract exploited Dutch nationalist feeling in the lead-up to the centenary of Holland's independence from Napoleonic rule to argue that Indonesians too had legitimate aspirations for independence. In this document, circulated on e-mail networks in 1992, an anonymous East Timorese nationalist deliberately adopts the same tactics, and much of the same language, to appeal to Indonesians to recognise the aspirations of the people of East Timor. This abridged version of the Indonesian-language typescript first appeared in *Inside Indonesia* (December 1992: 7–8).

The church bells ring throughout the land of Maubere.[4] Flags and ribbons of all colours are hanging in the city streets. The governor's office and the military post's walls have been freshly scrubbed and painted. The people, as required, have hung out red and white flags in their yards. The wives of government officials can be seen busily preparing for the celebration. A stage has also been built for the music, dance and drama performances on the night. During the afternoon there will be sports competitions with prizes. The festivity is everywhere.

According to a newspaper report, all this activity is to celebrate the anniversary of Indonesia's independence. In August, on the 17th to be exact, the independent Indonesian nation became a united republic.

According to the historians, Indonesia was colonised by the Dutch for three and a half centuries and then by the Japanese for a further three and a half years. Colonial practices, which the Indonesians cannot easily forget, included cruelty as well as expropriating the people's property....

So the celebration is of course significant now that the Indonesian nation is independent. Like many Indonesians, I have great respect for this important day, because there is no happiness for a people suffering oppression under colonial domination.

Like many Indonesian nationalists who love their homeland, I also love my homeland, in fact more than I can express in mere words.

I would cheer aloud to be able to celebrate a day as important as this. How happy I would be, yelling in anticipation of the long-awaited day of independence celebrations. How relieved my heart would be at seeing the red and white flag fluttering. My voice would become hoarse from singing 'Indonesia Raya'.[5] I would be proud and would thank God in the mosques for His generosity, and I would pray for the welfare of the people of Indonesia, including those in occupied areas, so that this great and glorious power would remain for generations to come.

I would gladly pay taxes in order to implement General Try Soetrisno and General Benny Moerdani's plan to increase the size of our nation's army to safeguard Indonesia's independence. I would...actually I do not know what else I would do if I were an Indonesian because I feel capable of anything.

But obviously it is not like that. Even if I were a free person I would not be able to do whatever I fancied. I have the greatest respect for the forthcoming Independence Day celebrations, but I would curb the desire of the people in occupied territory to join in the festivities. In fact I would prefer that they were banned from the celebrations altogether so that none of the Maubere people could see our elation at commemorating our day of independence.

In my view there is something not quite right with this celebration. It is immoral to make the Maubere people join in our Independence Day celebration parties. While we are celebrating 47 years' liberation from foreign rule we are trampling on another people's independence and occupying their territory. Do we not consider that these unfortunate creatures are also yearning for a moment like this when they, like us, could celebrate their independence?

Considering this, it is not only unfair but also wrong to demand they pay taxes to support our country's independence. As if the idea of preparing for the Independence Day celebration is not humiliating enough for them, we now steal from their pockets. It is morally and materially degrading.

If I were a free person, I would curb Independence Day celebrations in the land where the people have been robbed of their independence.

What do we actually gain from organising remembrance ceremonies on Maubere territory? If this commemoration expresses the Indonesian nation's happiness, it is not very tactful to celebrate it in colonised territory. It will cause opposition within the community, pitting one against another. Or is that what we really desire, to boast about our political authority? Such tactics only provide them with an example of how they should celebrate their own independence.

We are unintentionally arousing their noble aspirations for independence. When the month of August ends this year, Indonesian colonialism will have implemented an irresponsible policy. I would not want to be responsible for that.

If I were a free person now I would protest against organising a celebration like this. I would write in all the newspapers that ideas like these are wrong. I would warn my fellow colonists about the danger of organising an Independence Day celebration in these times. I would advise all Indonesians not to offend the Maubere people, who have already begun to turn against us. I would protest with as much power as I could summon.

But I am not a free person, I am only a colonial native from the soil of East Timor, a person who every day is lashed by Indonesian colonial law because I do not have the power to protest any more.

Because if I did actually protest the government would be angry with me and think that I was insulting the Indonesia that now rules my land. That is why I cannot do any more.

They would also consider that I had an improper attitude towards His Excellency the President, and that is unforgivable because I am a native of his colony and I must always be loyal to him.

Because of this I cannot protest. It is better if I join these celebrations. As natives of this colony it is our responsibility to participate in the independence celebrations of the coloniser of our homeland because it is a good opportunity for us to demonstrate loyalty to the Indonesian Republic.

Thank God I am not a free person and an Indonesian.

Well, I am starting to get sick of these sarcastic words of mine so I will put them aside. What it is that really hurts my fellow countrymen and me is the idea that native people must finance celebrations from which they cannot benefit. At most it only reminds us that we are not free citizens and that 'Indonesia will never grant us our independence'. At least not as long as His Lordship Theo Syafei rules this country.[6]

We, the people of Maubere, gained our freedom from foreign colonists when the Democratic Republic of East Timor was formed on 7 October 1975. But then, on 15 July 1976, a claim was filed for East Timor to become part of the territory of Indonesia regardless of the East Timorese people's independence or sovereignty.

So it is very hard for me to trust a government administration that is based only on slogans which, however beautiful, even sacred, they may be, are expressed without regard to true humanitarianism, justice or the rights of other nations.

The Maubere people realise that the Indonesian government is no different than other world colonists. The hands of the Indonesian military have shed blood on Maubere soil. If the Dutch colonists, from J.P. Coen and Daendels to Westerling,[7] butchered the Indonesian people, the Indonesian military is doing nothing less to the people of Maubere. In 1985 the London-based Amnesty International reported that the Indonesian occupation force had killed around 200,000 East Timorese people during its 16 years of colonisation. And acts of terror continue every moment and every hour, as if we were animals.

The brutal incident at the Santa Cruz cemetery last November [1991] showed the true face of colonial Indonesia. It seems like human souls have no meaning for them.

Because they did not want to be blamed for the incident the Indonesian military said that our people were responsible. Those of us who protested about that brutal action were instead accused of creating a disturbance in this land that holds freedom in such high esteem. No members of the Indonesian military responsible for brutally killing our people were sentenced to more than 10 months, whereas we, who have had our independence and our human dignity trampled on, were sentenced to life imprisonment.

It is now clear to me that the nation whose constitution and Pancasila philosophy exalts freedom is no more than a bunch of pirates in the Timor Sea. Since early in the independence struggle, during the negotiations about the future of our nation, the Indonesian government was never sympathetic to the true liberation of the East Timorese people.

At that time it said total independence was not possible because the East Timorese people did not yet have the educational standard to form a capable government administration or sufficient national resources to sustain a sovereign state.

How arrogant and haughty their words were. I was reminded of the excuses the Dutch masters gave to the enslaved Indonesian nation. Now the Indonesian government are the masters, they give the same excuses to us, the people of Maubere.

The once-enslaved nation has forgotten that even the development of Indonesian nationalism came about as a result of changes introduced under the Ethical Policy.[8] How can a person who has once suffered oppression now practise oppression on other people?

Was the spirit of the Indonesian nation's nationalism not based on justice and humanity? Our people are constantly amazed by the way the Indonesian government continues to extract our wealth. Our massive oil and gas reserves, with an estimated value of US$261.72 billion, are being plundered by Indonesian robbers and other Western capitalists, whereas every day the people of Maubere receive in return only rebukes, harsh words and killing, as well as accusations of subversion.

Can I believe in a justice that is forced on us by the Indonesian government? We have been pauperised and robbed of our right to life, but we are still required to praise the Indonesian Republic for upholding justice and humanity.

For me the idea of Independence Day celebrations in East Timor has little meaning. If I really were a free person I would never celebrate independence in a country that was still colonised. I would first give independence to the people who we colonise, because only then would we be able to truly celebrate our independence.

11.5 Y.B. Mangunwijaya: federalism as an antidote to separatism

Mangunwijaya was one of the first New Order era intellectuals to challenge the shibboleth of 'national unity and oneness'. The following extract is from an article published in the *Jakarta Post* on 4 August 1998 in the wake of demonstrations in West Papua and Jakarta calling for independence for the territory. This piece and other articles in Mangunwijaya (1998) helped spark an important debate on the once-taboo subject of federalism.

Papuan...patriots have openly demanded freedom. The demand was made without fear in the centre of Jakarta. Had they done so in Jayapura or Biak they would have been shot dead.

Gubernare est previdere et providere, goes an ancient Roman saying. Have a forward vision and make appropriate arrangements. Understand the signs of the time, please, and weigh the natural consequences of 30 years of Soeharto's iron-fisted security and self-censoring fear.

In the 1950s a unified state with a firm centralised rule was necessary to confront our former colonial masters. Even during the years of economic growth from 1965 onwards, a centralised state was a prudent and appropriate superstructure for the country. But the iron rule of Soeharto since that time was too cruel to bear. Fascistic methods became all too common, and the further you travelled from Jakarta the more common Nazi SS-style practices became.

Wisdom and courage are required to learn from the ancient principle of Roman statesmanship *lex agendi lex essendi*, the law of action is the law of doing.

A peaceful and democratic centralised government can rule a nation of 5 million people. But for a similar governing institution to rule a huge and heterogeneous mass is impossible unless it resorts to the language of violence. Is that really what we want?

Even the late President Sukarno himself, as chair of the Committee for the Independence of Indonesia, declared to the Central National Committee of Indonesia (an embryonic Indonesian parliament) on 18 August 1945 that the proposed constitution was a 'somewhat tentative constitution, a lightning constitution or, you could say, a revolutionary constitution. Later we should make a constitution which is more complete.'

Thus the 1945 Constitution was not meant to last for ever.

A nation with such a diversity of people, spread as they are across an area larger than Europe, can only develop in a democratic fashion if a decentralised state becomes a reality. The young generation, which will guide our republic in the 21st century, need explicit guarantees to protect their basic human rights, and this would best be served by a federal framework for the state.

But do the young generation demand federalism?

Yes, the concerned and the committed do.

They never knew Sukarno and Mohammad Hatta. They cannot appreciate the enormous difficulties that they both had to face. They did not experience first hand the heady rush of excitement as Indonesia took its first tentative steps as a free and democratic nation. The young generation only know what they have been taught about Sukarno in the New Order's brainwashing Pancasila courses.

Although our young generation did not taste the early joys of independence for themselves they have experienced the New Order regime at first hand.

They are now fed up with great leaders, corrupt authoritarian bureaucrats and threatening generals with their one-way command over a centralised state and society. Indonesia Incorporated.

They do not want another big leader. Gadjah Mada University rector Dr Ichlasul Amal pointed to the very heart of the matter when he said in a seminar some time ago that 'the new generation is basically federalist'.

The 1950s required unity and so a strongly centralised state was created. However, in seeking a model for the state as we approach the 21st century I would like to draw your attention to the famous message of our great democrat and independence fighter Mohammad Hatta, who knew his own people's character very well. He warned against the wrong kind of unity when he said, 'We too struggle for *persatuan* [unity] and that's why we reject *persatean* [being stuck together like meat on satay skewers].'

So, if we earnestly wish to avoid a wave of separatism triggered by the demands of our Papuan brothers; if we do not want to imitate a crumbling Yugoslavia, with ethnic divisions widened by the ambition to create a Greater Serbia, or Greater Java for that matter, then we should stop and think. We should ask if a government which greedily sucks the wealth from the outer regions of our country is really the best way to organise Indonesian society in the 21st century.

If the answer to this question is no, then we must prepare – through studies, seminars, discussions, discourses and the drafting of a wise and strong constitution – to build a country that will genuinely suit the needs of Indonesians in the 21st century. We must prepare to build a United States of Indonesia.

11.6 Major-General Sudrajat: federalism is not right for Indonesia

In this contribution to a panel discussion on autonomy and federalism in Jakarta on 16 December 1999, the armed forces information service chief Major-General Sudrajat put the military's perspective on federalism (2000: 183–6).

There is really no need to debate the question of whether the unitary state in Indonesia is final. Nothing that humans create is final. But sometimes natural factors determine what we do. As far as federalism is concerned, the van Mook issue tends to be a psychological barrier for us, because van Mook was Dutch.[9] Federalism was in fact conceived a long time ago by the English, who…passed on their system to Malaysia, Australia and the United States.

Indonesia's unitary state stems from a different history. We became a new country because of colonialism. Without colonialism our country would comprise several kingdoms like Aceh, Mataram and Kutai. Our 350-year struggle against colonialism produced a united Indonesia. With the possible exception of the kingdoms of Aceh, Banten and Mataram, there were not many political entities of any real significance; most were just tribal and ethnic groupings. In order to become independent, they had no choice but to unite, and it was this spirit of unity that has been proclaimed since 1928.[10] After a long struggle that was at once political and academic, we eventually achieved independence and claimed all the areas under Dutch colonial rule from Sabang to Merauke as part of the Indonesian Republic.

When people like Anhar Gonggong[11] speak of resistance to the idea of federalism, they may be referring to resistance by the military. The military does indeed resist federalism because it is not something that should be considered lightly. The military resists the idea not because of van Mook or because we are opposed to federalism *per se*. We only ask that the matter be considered more soberly and maturely. A state's configuration is fundamental to the life of a people and is not something that should be altered on an experimental basis. Australia, for instance, held a referendum before adopting a federal system.

The world consists of about 180 countries, 18 of which are true federations and 17 of which have federal arrangements, such as Monaco and France, and to some extent America and Puerto Rico. So only 35 per cent of the world's states are federations. We have to look at the pros and cons very carefully before establishing any kind of federal system in Indonesia. The danger is that federalism will lead our nation to disintegrate along ethnic lines, so we are talking about something far more serious than the secession of a couple of provinces. Experience tells us that our real problem is ethnic conflict.

Whatever the failings of the New Order, it never allowed communal hatreds to blow up. Ethnic, religious, racial and inter-group conflict remain very sensitive issues. We should remember that the recent troubles in Situbondo, Ketapang, Ambon, Aceh and other places have had to do with ethnic conflict. What would happen if a federal state were established?...Our country consists of 260 ethnic groups. With Banten and mainland Riau now asking to be new provinces, it is not hard to imagine Indonesia having 50 provinces even without a federal system. Also, if we were to move to a federation, where would we start? Would it be based on provinces or ethnic groups? We certainly do not want to follow the European example of ethnically based states. This would be extremely dangerous. The military resists the idea because the military thinks about security.

What system is best depends on the circumstances. The leaders of the People's Republic of China, a country of 1 billion people, did not opt for a federal system because they knew very well the condition of their country. They have managed to keep a tight rein on all aspects of administration. But for Indonesia, with its relatively low levels of education and high levels of emotionalism, it does not make sense to move to a federal system within the next five to 10 years.

Notes

1 The author here is paraphrasing the official elucidation of the 1945 Constitution, which uses the Dutch terms '*volksgemeenschappen*' and '*rechtsgemeenschappen*'.

2 The author, Manuel Kaisiepo, includes a table at this point, derived from Table 10.18 in Booth (1992), showing that, of the 11 provinces with the highest levels of poverty, Irian Jaya ranked top in both urban and rural areas (33 per cent and 67 per cent, respectively).

3 This refers to the landmark *Sumpah Pemuda*, declared at a Youth Congress held in Batavia. The delegates pledged: 'One motherland, Indonesia; One nation, Indonesia; One language, Indonesian.'

4 Maubere is a Tetun word for the 'rural poor' popularised by Jose Ramos Horta in the 1970s as part of Fretilin's appeal to East Timor's rural population.

5 The Indonesian national anthem.

6 Brigadier-General Theo Syafei was field commander in East Timor from January 1992 until March 1993.

7 January Pieterszoon Coen was the first Governor-General in Indonesia, from 1619 to 1623; Herman Willem Daendels was Governor-General from 1808 to 1811; and Raymond 'Turk' Westerling was the notorious Dutch commando responsible for massacres of nationalists in Sulawesi in 1947.

8 Under the Ethical Policy, implemented from 1900, the colonial regime invested in education and industrialisation, among other things, in the name of the people's welfare.

9 Hubertus J. van Mook was the Dutch Lieutenant-Governor whose efforts to create a federation in the late 1940s came to be seen as an attempt to preserve Dutch influence in Indonesia.

10 See note 3 in this chapter.

11 Dr Anhar Gonggong, a historian at the Indonesian Institute of Sciences, presented a paper at the same seminar entitled 'Resistance to federalism; the van Mook trauma and centralist political culture'.

Part IV
Crisis and reform

12 Looking beyond the New Order

Soeharto dominated Indonesian politics for longer than the life of the Berlin Wall, and for most Indonesians he had come to seem just as immobile a fixture. Even in mid-1997 there was no opposition group that posed a threat to his power. As recounted in the Introduction, the deepening Asian economic crisis brought profound changes. Rocketing prices and unemployment told ordinary people that something had gone very wrong with their government. The international financial community also turned their backs on the president they had once lauded. Soeharto was thrown onto the defensive and his opponents began to smell defeat – and opportunity. In November 1997 Amien Rais, head of the modernist Muslim organisation Muhammadiyah and a former leading ICMI figure, declared that he was ready and willing to take over the reins of the presidency. In this chapter Rais outlines the reasons why he thought Indonesia needed a new national leadership (Reading 12.1). In January 1998 Megawati Soekarnoputri, who in 1996 had been unceremoniously toppled by the government as head of the PDI, declared that she too was prepared. In the first months of 1998 there were calls for a 'change of national leadership' from an exponentially increasing number of organisations. In Reading 12.2 we present one of the most controversial, a bold statement by civil servants at the government-sponsored Indonesian Institute of Sciences (LIPI) lambasting the government for its nonchalance towards the suffering of the people and bluntly demanding a new leadership.

Food shortages and anger at the government had led to several riots across Java in early 1998. Momentum was also building among students and democracy activists, who held demonstrations demanding an end to 'corruption, collusion and nepotism', as well as the removal of Soeharto. Following the fatal shooting of four students at Trisakti University on 12 May, cross-campus coalitions formed rapidly, as students prepared for a showdown. Reading 12.3, a call to action issued by the PRD, represents the position of some of the more militant groups involved. On 18 May thousands of students, joined by groups of workers and urban poor, began a five-day occupation of the parliamentary complex, turning it into a forum where Soeharto was openly denounced by student leaders and figures like Amien Rais. The final straw for Soeharto came on 20 May, when his key economic ministers refused to serve in a reshuffled cabinet. The next day the unimaginable happened and Soeharto tendered his resignation, inspiring uninhibited jubilation and thanksgiving from the thousands of protestors who had only days earlier risked being shot.

Some students went home convinced that the New Order was finally over and were pleased that Indonesia had a genuinely Muslim president in B.J. Habibie. Others, however, saw Habibie as a Soeharto stooge and immediately put forward bold demands for his resignation and a complete overhaul of the New Order political system. There was also real consternation at the prospect of the 1997 parliament, stacked as it was with New Order cronies, presiding over any process of reform. In Reading 12.4, students from a range of campuses in Jakarta and surrounding areas propose the establishment of a broad-based People's Committee to run the country until elections could be held.

Habibie's initial failure to remedy Indonesia's desperate economic situation only increased the pressure on him to take decisive action to restore confidence in the government. As the rupiah hit new lows in June 1998, even moderate figures like the former Minister of the Environment Emil Salim were suggesting that political change needed to take place more quickly and fundamentally in order to produce a credible, legitimate administration that could oversee economic recovery and avert collapse (Reading 12.5). While the rupiah did regain some of its value over the next few months, interest rates remained exorbitant, hitting the middle classes hard. In Reading 12.6 a group of young urban professionals lament the ongoing corruption and lack of security, declaring their refusal to pay taxes until transparency and justice are realised. This kind of declaration was still unusual at the time, but it does suggest that sections of the professional middle class were beginning to overcome their ingrained reticence to involve themselves in overt political campaigns.

Compounding Habibie's problems was the reluctance of Chinese Indonesians to repatriate their money from overseas. This had to do with the deep sense of insecurity caused by the riots of 13–15 May 1998. Over a hundred young Chinese women were gang raped during the riots, sometimes in public (Heryanto 1999). These events led to many suicides and traumatised the community in ways that are yet to be fully understood. In the face of official scepticism about the rape reports and a sometimes hostile public reaction, a number of women activists, including Ita Nadia, undertook detailed investigations. They uncovered not only the extent of the rapes but also disturbing similarities between them, leading them to conclude that they were systematic and targeted. Reading 12.7 is from a statement by the Jesuit priest Sandyawan Sumardi, whose Team of Volunteers for Humanitarian Causes compiled these and other reports to produce the first comprehensive analysis of the riots. His evidence played an important role in initiating a government inquiry that cautiously confirmed his claims that the riots were linked to elite conflicts and that the military was culpable, if not for its actions, at least for its failure to act.[1]

Habibie's successes were mainly on the domestic political front. Indeed, under his brief rule Indonesia adopted all the trappings of a multi-party democracy: a free press, multiple parties, free elections and an empowered parliament. Habibie in fact had little choice but to embrace democratisation, since the authoritarian structures that Soeharto had carefully crafted had become untenable in his absence. But he was happy to take the credit. In his Independence Day address in 1998, sections of which are presented in Reading 12.8, Habibie took care to distance himself from the New Order and presented a confident vision of a democratic future. He was ultimately a victim of his own reforms though, as he had little of the authority Soeharto enjoyed over the institutions of state power, including parliament, the military and, most decisively, the former state party, Golkar. In October 1999 Habibie's re-election bid failed when a large number of Golkar delegates to the MPR deserted him.

The end of the New Order saw many of its shibboleths attacked publicly. Tabloids re-examined the 1965 coup, airing every possible theory in large type. The military's dual function was openly condemned. There were calls for Indonesian history to be completely rewritten. Others argued that Pancasila should be scrapped as the state ideology. The former political prisoner Ibu Sulami led groups to unearth victims of the anti-communist pogroms of the mid-1960s.[2] Reading 12.9 is an editorial from the mainstream nationalist newspaper *Media Indonesia* that captures the changed mood. It urges its readers to sympathise with families of communists who were persecuted during the New Order and support legislation giving them the right to vote and be elected.

Least willing of all groups to embrace meaningful change were the military. Their language throughout 1998 and 1999 reflected their ongoing preoccupation with stability, unity, order and the dangers of communism. Yet they were in such disgrace for their record of abuses under the New Order, compounded by their involvement in the kidnapping, torture and murder of activists in 1997 and the Trisakti University shootings of 1998, that they had no alternative but to accept a winding back of their political role. In September 1998 a seminar was held at the Armed Forces Staff and Command College at Bandung, where a 'New Paradigm' was discussed (Reading 12.10). In this meeting a number of broad principles were accepted that would see, among other things, an end to the secondment of active military personnel to civilian positions. Soon afterwards, the military would also accept a reduction in their reserved seats in parliament. But as the 'New Paradigm' made clear, they continued to see themselves as responsible for the welfare of the nation and reserved the right to revert to a 'security approach' if the situation warranted it. It was only later, in 2000, that the military were to declare that their socio-political role had ended (ICG 2000: 14).

The last reading is by the late Lieutenant-General Agus Wirahadikusumah, the leader of a reformist faction of the military in favour of much more sweeping reforms than his commanding officers were prepared to countenance. His main target was the territorial apparatus, the nationwide hierarchy of military commands designed to shadow the civilian administration at all levels. It remains crucial in allowing military officers to enter into political and business alliances at the local level. In a remarkable series of interviews given in December 1999, Agus Wirahadikusumah suggested that, in many areas, soldiers in the territorial apparatus, especially at the lower levels, served no other purpose than to prey on the civilian population. Promoted to head the Army Strategic Reserve by the newly elected President Abdurrahman Wahid, he set about uncovering large-scale graft by his predecessor. Resistance, however, by the military leadership forced Abdurrahman Wahid to remove Agus and other members of his faction in late 2000 in what was widely seen as a defeat for military reformers. Agus Wirahadikusumah died the following year.

12.1 Amien Rais: succession in 1998 – an imperative

Muhammadiyah leader Amien Rais was the first high-profile national figure to call for Soeharto's resignation. The following excerpts are from an essay in one of many books to be published in 1998 about the man who would be president (Najib *et al.* 1998: 25–31). A version of the essay was written in 1993, but it was apparently revised and published only in January 1998.

To determine whether 1998 is the time to change the nation's leadership or whether it should be preserved until 2003 it is necessary to look over the past 25–30 years and draw up a very elementary balance sheet of the achievements of development and the shortcomings that need to be remedied.

There are at least five achievements of the New Order to be thankful for. First, the realisation of financial stability and steady economic growth....Second, and closely related, is Indonesia's self-sufficiency in food....Third, the relatively stable political system we have enjoyed for the past 30 years....Fourth, the unity and integrity of the nation of Indonesia that is now a proud, living reality....And, fifth, the improvement of Indonesia's international image over the past 25 years.

However, we need to acknowledge several problems that have been building up chronically over the past 10–15 years in the life of the Indonesian nation. First, although economic growth has been satisfactory, the twin problems of poverty and unemployment persist. The number of people still below the poverty line in both rural and urban areas is perhaps two or three times the official statistic of 27 million, depending on where the line is drawn. The unemployment figures are also hard to ascertain given the difficulty of defining the phenomenon itself. Recent findings on the alarming number of poor or backward villages suggest that poverty and unemployment are already so chronic that a structural approach is needed to address them.

Second, corruption remains rampant and appears to be worsening by the year. Professor Soemitro Djojohadikusumo's statement at the Indonesian Economists' Association Congress in 1993 that the squandering or leakage of development funds has risen to 30 per cent, shows that corruption is a major and ongoing problem. Efforts to overcome corruption have not succeeded – indeed, sometimes such efforts are simply cosmetic. Displaying pictures of several 'corrupters' on television, for instance, shows how naïve efforts to eliminate corruption have been. Besides, the popular perception is that small-time corruption gets all the attention while institutionalised corruption, which poses a real threat to our national life, is left alone.

Third, the process of democratisation is still far from adequate. It would not be going too far to say that the Indonesian system is democratic more in form than in substance. Concepts such as the 'floating mass', the 'single majority' and 'election targets', which we accept without question, are actually unknown in true democracies. So we have to ask in all seriousness how far we have democratised. At the same time it must be said that democratisation is always a slow process.

In addition to these three major problems, there are of course many other issues to be resolved. For example, foreign debt, which has reached US$83 billion, with a debt-service ratio of around 35 per cent, a legal system that is losing more and more of its authority as a result of constant outside interference, the problem of upholding basic human rights, a welter of land disputes laden with potential for explosive social conflict and so on. But it is the chronic problems discussed above (poverty, unemployment, corruption and democratisation) that demand the wholehearted efforts of the entire nation.

If the current national leader is reinstated for the 1998–2003 period, I do not believe that these three problems will go away. They may instead grow larger and more complex. It is therefore imperative, in my opinion, that there is a succession, a change of national leadership, in 1998.

There are five further arguments why succession must take place in 1998.

First, the current national leadership has been in place since 1967. In 1998 it will have been in power for 31 years. Given the time they have been in power, all the national leaders are surely wise enough to understand Lord Acton's political axiom, 'power tends to corrupt and absolute power tends to corrupt absolutely'. This political axiom is universal; it applies both in the West and in the East.

Second, staying in office for too long can breed a 'cult of the individual' among the national elite. We have witnessed how we, as a nation, got caught up in a cult of the individual in the past, the Interim People's Consultative Assembly going so far as to bestow a life presidency on Bung Karno. Of course we do not want to let our fear of nominating an alternative figure as national leader lead us to make the same mistake. Our respect and love for a leader should not overwhelm healthy thought.

Third is the matter of rotation or regeneration in a democratic system. Unlike monarchies, where successions occur only when the monarch dies, democracies manage the rotation of the elite through constitutional means. In a democratic system, a leader's tenure is usually limited to one or two terms. The absence of limits on the tenure of the head of state can cause the political process to become more and more undemocratic and can entrench the vested interests of the elite in an irrational way.

Fourth, the vision and creativity of an elite group that has ruled for too long tend to dull. This matter is easily understood, remembering that a national leader who has long been trapped in routine can become less sensitive to the dynamics of change around him. Decisions made by elements of the national leadership become out of touch with reality, making them anachronistic and inappropriate to the needs of the society.

Fifth, an elite group that has held power for too long can slowly come to regard itself as the personification of stability and, indeed, the state itself. This is not a healthy thing for democracy. If a leader is affected by the Louis XIV syndrome, '*L'état c'est moi*', he will consider every criticism directed at him a criticism of the state as an institution or, even worse, as a criticism of the state ideology.

General arguments such as this can clarify why we must have a succession of national leadership in 1998. Succession is part of God's plan, a process in accordance with the laws of nature, rationality and reality.

12.2 LIPI researchers: restore our dignity as a nation

The following denunciation of the government and call for Soeharto's resignation is significant for both its audacity and its timing. Issued in January 1998 by 19 researchers from the Indonesian Institute of Sciences, it was the first public call by a non-political body for Soeharto to resign. The signatories to the document, *Pernyataan Keprihatinan 19 Peneliti LIPI*, were all public servants.

The accumulated effects of the crisis that has swept our people has reached a point where we, 19 researchers at the Indonesian Institute of Sciences (LIPI), feel compelled to issue a statement of concern. Our statement should be read as reflecting the feelings and conscience of the people to those who have closed their hearts and minds to the reality around them.

In surveying the current crisis, it is our view that the lower classes are suffering the most. While prices continue to rise, the wages of day labourers are falling drastically, making it impossible for them to preserve their dignity in a country supposedly self-sufficient in food. Every day the rate of unemployment rises, with no prospect of any expansion in job opportunities in sight.

Every household is now suffering a fall in the quality of life because of declining or stagnant incomes at a time when the prices of basic commodities are climbing. Beyond these economic issues, the volatility of prices has stretched people's patience to breaking point, driving them to turn against one other. Social solidarity has plunged to an all time low, making the notion that we are living together as a nation quite meaningless.

Meanwhile the managers of state power have closed their hearts, carrying on as if nothing had changed. The government has grown lethargic, stubborn and unyielding. There has been no attempt to overcome the crisis with wise statesmanship; rather, the government has sought scapegoats. Instead of addressing the problems, it has responded with threats. Not a single member of the government has been willing to take responsibility, to acknowledge that the current crisis is a result of the accumulated mistakes of its own development policies.

The managers of state power never welcome ideas that come from outside their circle as positive contributions. They are always viewed with suspicion and prejudice. The closing down of the public realm means that there are no longer any controls on the power they wield.

The managers of state power have more faith in the ideas of foreigners than they do in their own country's thinkers. Some of the most important components of the IMF's reform program, for instance, have long been proposed by various domestic groups. The managers of state power have closed their eyes to their own feelings and consciences. They have disregarded the sovereignty of the people.

We conclude that the root causes and implications of the crisis sweeping our people go well beyond economics. We are facing a crisis of dignity as a nation.

We believe that the managers of state power have failed to carry out the people's mandate. There is therefore a need for a new national leadership, one that can peacefully bring about a comprehensive renewal in both politics and economics. As well as restoring the economy, a rejuvenated national leadership will restore our dignity as a nation.

LIPI Jakarta, 29 January 1998
Signed[3]

12.3 People's Democratic Party: end the dictatorship!

The national leadership committee of the People's Democratic Party (PRD) issued this statement on 14 May, a day that saw large and destructive riots in Jakarta and other cities. The sentiments expressed here were similar to those of the more militant student groups demonstrating in Jakarta. The statement was published in the Australian newspaper *Green Left Weekly* on 20 May 1998.

Today, students and other people rose up in a mass battle in Jabotabek [Greater Jakarta], while students in cities throughout the country held demonstrations. The people's battle in Jakarta is widespread and has paralysed the city. Hungry people are taking goods from the supermarkets and setting fire to buildings and vehicles.

The authorities have not been able to confront the people's resistance. Everywhere, the masses cannot be prevented from carrying out the attacks. Many in the armed forces are demoralised.

President Soeharto has said that he is prepared to step down if the people do not support him. This indicates that the regime is cornered by the continued attacks on the dictatorship.

To the people

1   Do not let the rioting become an ethnic, religious, racial or inter-group conflict. We must not destroy, take from or kill our Chinese brothers and sisters. The source of the people's suffering is not the Chinese, but Soeharto and the dictatorship. Many Chinese have also suffered and been oppressed by Soeharto. The attacks and looting of our Chinese brothers and sisters will only weaken our struggle and benefit Soeharto by becoming a battle between the people.
2   Focus the attacks and looting on what is owned by capitalists, the government, government officials and the armed forces. Don't damage or take that which is owned by your own people.
3   Rally to the centre of the city, to places like government offices, and the police and military headquarters.

To all pro-democratic figures

1   To Megawati, Amien Rais, Budiman Sujatmiko [jailed chair of the PRD], Sri Bintang Pamungkas [jailed chair of the Indonesian United Development Party] and others: it is time for you to state your readiness to replace Soeharto. This must be done soon, because Soeharto is no longer wanted by the people and is ready to step down.

2 We must reject collaboration with the armed forces. In a modern democracy, the military must not be allowed to meddle in political affairs. The political violence and the destruction of democracy in Indonesia are a result of allowing the military to enter the world of politics, legitimised by the dual function of the armed forces.

3 We must quickly prepare an independent people's council to replace the parliament and the People's Consultative Assembly.

To the soldiers and civil servants

1 Remove your uniforms and join with the people. It is time for you to abandon Soeharto.

To the New Order dictatorship

1 End the brutal actions against the people. The destruction that has occurred so far has been a result of repressive actions by the military. If the students and people are given permission to hold a rally, they will do it in a peaceful manner.

2 President Soeharto must step down. Don't let his latest statement that he is prepared to step down be just political rhetoric.

3 The commander of the armed forces, the military and police commanders of Jakarta must step down, because they have taken brutal action against students and the people and can no longer carry out their functions.

4 The armed forces must end their activities in the political arena, because the involvement of the armed forces in political matters has resulted in political violence and the death of democracy.

12.4 Jakarta students: proposal for an Indonesian People's Committee

Produced in the name of 'the Greater Jakarta Student Community' (1998), this piece represented the views of the cross-campus activist coalition known as the Forum Kota (City Forum). The members of this group tended to hold more militant views than most other student groupings. They saw the student movement as a pure 'moral' force and were especially indignant about the New Order's rapaciousness.

Thirty-two years of Soeharto's leadership has left a legacy of large-scale corruption, collusion, nepotism, killings and human rights abuses. People have been robbed of their rights and the constitution has been perverted.

These longstanding abuses bred a rotten mentality and culture that afflicted almost all government agencies and even the people at large. Right and wrong were confused, the boundaries between good and bad were blurred, and morality and ethics were increasingly ill defined. All in all, this has been an undeniable tragedy for the country.

Soeharto's advancing age apparently did nothing to make him realise the error of his ways. In his last years and days he planted a time-bomb, bringing destruction, division and a series of calamities to the people, the nation and the state. Examples were the 27 July 1996 incident, the Ujung Pandang tragedy and the killing of the Trisakti University students. Other examples that underscore his greed were the National Car project, the Clove Marketing Body (BPPC), the citrus monopoly in Pontianak...and the like, which led eventually to the national economic crisis.[4]

In the political field, Soeharto often acted in unconstitutional ways to preserve his power and satisfy his greed. One example was his removal of Megawati from her position of General Chair of the PDI, which set in train a series of events leading to the illegal and unconstitutional [1997] general elections. Even in his last moments in power Soeharto continued to act unconstitutionally by resigning and avoiding accountability. By simply transferring the presidency to Habibie without following constitutional procedure, he left behind a time-bomb.

Legal, moral, political and constitutional defects in the conduct of the [1997] general elections render their products, the DPR/MPR, the president and vice-president, as well as the cabinet and a range of other products, similarly flawed and unconstitutional. To force the people to accept the elections and their products is to foist upon them a national, collective fraud.

Rampant nepotism in the DPR/MPR further reinforces the impression that the parliament, the president, the vice-president and the cabinet do not represent the aspirations of the people but the interests of a clique.

The Indonesian people are being given no choice but to go along with the national hypocrisy, the national collective fraud and be caught up in an endless cycle of deceit which can only give legal validity to the unconstitutional deeds of the Soeharto regime. Is this a wise way to ensure the integrity of the nation and the state, or will it only plunge the people into an abyss?

No resolution to this chaotic situation will come of forcing 210 million people to endorse the mistakes, to consecrate the sins, to make constitutional the unconstitutional acts of the past. The only solution is to act in a bold, honest, objective and pure way, motivated by a desire for oneness and unity as well as a deep love for the people and the motherland.

To this end, and based on our noble desire for reform, the Greater Jakarta Student Community hereby calls on the entire people of Indonesia as the legitimate bearers of sovereignty to reject the special session of the DPR/MPR as:

1   illegitimate from a legal, moral, political and constitutional standpoint;
2   full of corruption, collusion and nepotism.

For this reason, and motivated by the noble desire for reform, the Greater Jakarta Student Community calls on the entire population of Indonesia as the legitimate bearers of sovereignty to back the speedy formation of an Indonesian People's Committee.

Indonesian People's Committee

This temporary committee will have supreme executive and legislative powers vested in it and will also serve as an interim cabinet. Its members will be drawn from among the people of various groups. We are optimistic that, based on calculations that have been made, this committee will be capable of producing a leadership representative of the entire Indonesian population of 210 million people.

This committee will be charged with annulling the five political laws and the anti-subversion law. It will also compile a list of amendments to articles of the 1945 Constitution that are frequently misinterpreted, as well as compile new political laws and carry out fresh general elections to elect a new DPR/MPR. This new DPR/MPR will be free from collusion, corruption and nepotism. It will be capable of fighting for the aspirations of the people, empowering the people and constructing a democratic framework for the state and for the government that is clean, committed to human rights and able to guarantee the pure and consistent implementation of the Pancasila and the 1945 Constitution....

The Indonesian People's Committee will dissolve itself when:

1   the new DPR/MPR has elected, appointed and ratified a new president and vice-president;
2   the elected president and vice-president [have resolved to] try Soeharto;
3   the president and elected parliament have taken responsibility for political, economic, legal and educational reforms.

These are the ideas put forward by the Greater Jakarta Student Community in an attempt to extricate the people, nation and state from the political, economic, legal, educational, moral and ethical crisis, and return the sovereignty of our beloved Republic of Indonesia to its rightful owners, the people. We also hope very much that the entire people, from Sabang to Merauke, can unite and fight for the formation of an Indonesian People's Committee with pureness of heart and solidarity.

Jakarta, 28 May 1998
Greater Jakarta Student Community[5]

12.5 Emil Salim: total reform

A long-serving cabinet member under Soeharto, the author had by 1998 emerged as one of the informal leaders of the opposition to the New Order, forming a group called Gema Madani. In this piece, written in mid-June 1998, Salim called on the Habibie government to yield power immediately, arguing that it could not deal with the crisis because it lacked legitimacy (Salim 1998).

Because the role of the state is too great, constraints are necessary. This entails measures including:

a   Wiping out monopolies, cartels, special treatment, excessive protection, corruption, collusion and nepotism, which centralise economic power in the hands of state officials.
b   Eliminating the means by which state officials centralised power in their hands, such as the appointment of the president without time constraints, the arbitrary appointment of the majority of People's Consultative Assembly members, etc.

Because the role of society is too weak, it is necessary to strive to empower social groups, such as:

- political parties;
- businesspeople;
- civil society groups.

To achieve these aims, total reform is required in various sectors: economic, political, social, legal, cultural, etc. Because this process will take a long time, a primary program is required most urgently within the timeframe of the next year.

A primary program must entail:

- Political reform: change the current political system to a multi-party system that accommodates to the greatest possible degree the aspirations of the people, and is selected via a general election held by the people themselves. As a result it is necessary to strive for new regulations regarding general elections, social and political organisations, and the composition of the central and regional legislatures. Based upon these new regulations it is necessary as soon as possible to hold:

a   a general election;
b   session of the People's Consultative Assembly to choose a president and vice-president.

- A schedule for a general election and a People's Consultative Assembly session, paying special attention to:
a eliminating economic uncertainty as quickly as possible, preferably within six months;
b the socialisation of a new general election system and the formation of social and political organisations within a year.
- The addressing of corruption, collusion and nepotism via:
a the mobilisation of public opinion;
b the implementation of corrective measures initiated by the president/vice-president, cabinet members, military leaders and other high officials in the capital and the regions.
- Striving to fulfil the people's basic necessities, including food, medicines and education, through, among other things, the 'social security net program' in collaboration with non-government organisations.
- Actively pursuing social reconciliation between ethnic groups, religions and races in order to develop the plurality and unity of the nation with the involvement of volunteers.
- Fostering a feeling of security in the hearts of the people by thoroughly investigating numerous incidents of political violence, such as the murder of students from Trisakti University and the disastrous looting of Black Thursday, 14 May 1998.

Timeframe

This program of reform ought to be implemented by a government that has legitimacy in the eyes of the people. For this, agreement between reform groups and the government will be sought regarding:

- the content of the concept of a general election and the emergence of new social and political organisations.

The direction of the total reform program

A reasonable timeframe for holding a general election and the emergence of social and political organisations.

The economic situation

In considering total reform it is necessary to pay attention to the following economic conditions in Indonesia:

- The poor exchange rate of the rupiah (hovering now at Rp15,000 [to the US dollar], one-sixth of its value in July 1997) compared to the Thai baht (which has lost only half its value in the same period).

- With this poor exchange rate the price of imported goods, including food, has increased. This has contributed to the high rate of inflation.
- Distribution networks have suffered damage, especially those managed by non-indigenous people, impeding the smooth flow of goods.
- There is a large difference between interest on savings and interest on credit, which has been shouldered by the banks and has eaten up their financial capital.
- Government subsidies of various consumer goods, including petroleum, presuppose an exchange rate of Rp6,000 to the dollar. If the value of the rupiah continues to weaken, then the subsidy rate will increase, burdening the budget and increasing the rate of inflation.
- The buying power of consumers has decreased because wages have gone down as a result of job severances and growing unemployment.

The matters mentioned above stem from a lack of confidence in, and the poor economic performance of, the government. This is connected to the attitude of the transitional cabinet towards President Habibie.

In order to overcome this economic crisis it is extremely important that the term of the transitional cabinet and its president be shortened by hastening a general election and a session of the People's Consultative Assembly based on its results.

Jakarta, 17 June 1998
Emil Salim

12.6 Indonesian professionals: no justice and transparency, no tax

This reading is translated from a press release issued in the name of 'Indonesian professionals' after a rally in Jalan Thamrin in central Jakarta on 3 September 1998.

Declaration of Indonesian professionals

The crisis battering Indonesia has shown no sign of abating. Making things worse, several problems that have tainted the Indonesian nation have shown no signs of resolution. Cases of abduction and rape, uncontrolled hyperinflation, lay-offs everywhere, and the widespread loss of a sense of security among citizens prove that the government has failed to carry out the people's mandate.

As citizens who have faithfully paid our income tax, we feel compelled to question the actual use of the income tax we pay every month via the companies and institutions that employ us. Over the last five years the total amount of income tax the government has collected has more than doubled, from Rp12,516 trillion in 1992/3 to Rp28,458 trillion in 1997/8.

Such large sums demand transparent financial management and accountability to ensure a sense of justice and confidence among the entire Indonesian people. To date the quality of government service has been very poor. Moreover, corruption, collusion and nepotism have spread throughout the entire body of the government.

We want the income tax we pay to be used in the people's interests. Accordingly, we, as professionals of Indonesia, declare:

1   We will refuse to pay taxes to this government as long as the government is not managed in the interests of the entire people. Part of our income tax should be directly allocated to the ordinary victims of this economic crisis.
2   We demand the resignation of Mr Habibie and the entire Reform Cabinet, which is a continuation of the Soeharto regime, because they have failed to implement the people's mandate.
3   We call on other professionals and the entire society not to pay income tax to this regime until justice and transparency are realised.

Jakarta, 3 September 1998
Jalan Thamrin, Central Jakarta
In the name of Indonesian professionals:

1   The Society of Professionals for Democracy (MPD)
2   The Graduates of Jakarta (GSJ)
3   The Midday Saturday Movement (Gersang)
4   Professionals in Solidarity with Reform (SPUR)

12.7 I. Sandyawan Sumardi: crimes against humanity

This is an abridged and lightly edited version of the address given to a congressional committee in the United States on 28 July 1998, entitled 'Condition of our shared life: the May 1998 tragedy in Indonesia' (Sandyawan Sumardi 1998). The author, who was speaking in his capacity as secretary of the Team of Volunteers for Humanitarian Causes, is a well-respected Jesuit priest active for many years in Indonesia as an advocate of the poor.

I have come here on behalf of 'Tim Relawan untuk Kemanusiaan', the Indonesian name for the 'Team of Volunteers for Humanitarian Causes'.

The Team was formed in the aftermath of the urban riots in Jakarta, Indonesia, following the attack on the headquarters of Indonesian Democratic Party on 27 July 1996. As [has] repeatedly happened in the history of Indonesia in the past 30 years, it was the ordinary people who bore the burden: 5 dead, 149 injured, 136 arrested and 23 missing. The concern of the Team was to help the victims from among these ordinary people. Since the incident in mid-July 1996, political events in Indonesia have been unfolding in a chaotic way, almost all marred by unnecessary violence and bloodshed. The political system has gone bankrupt, and the severe monetary and economic crisis that started in July 1997 has intensi- fied the magnitude of the crisis. Again, it is the ordinary people who have to bear the suffering. Gone is politics as a noble vocation, for it has simply become a barbaric venture. The word 'barbaric' is to be understood liter- ally, that is, hundreds or thousands disappear or die from organised violence. One of the horrors in a long series of such barbaric politics is what happened in May 1998.... I am speaking about this particular event because, in terms of magnitude and methods of violence, it has become the most dramatic manifestation of politics as practised by the elites in Indonesia. We are not concerned here about politics as such, but about the consequences of these barbaric politics on the future of Indonesia. At your invitation, we have come here to make an appeal to your solidarity with and for the victims of the tragedy.

The horror

The May 1998 tragedy was preceded by the shooting-to-death of four university students on the occasion of student demonstrations at Trisakti University in Jakarta on 12 May 1998. On that day the political tempera- ture rose suddenly, and sporadic violence began to show its face. On the morning of 14 May 1998, a series of violent incidents started to break out, and by midday the city of Jakarta and its surroundings were on fire. Thousands of commercial buildings, business offices, supermarkets, resi- dential houses, public utilities, buses and private cars were burned down or simply ransacked on the streets. Amidst the riots, widespread looting and torture took place in an incomprehensible manner. By 9 June 1998, the Team of Volunteers for Humanitarian Causes had catalogued 2,244 dead bodies (mostly burned), 91 injured and 31 people missing. Again, most of the victims were ordinary people. The casualties, however, are only part of the story. It was soon discovered that the horror also involved a series of gang rapes of Chinese women. As of 3 July 1998, we found that 152 women had been gang raped, of whom 20 are dead. The following is a random example of how these gang rapes were perpetrated:

> A group of unknown persons were looting the victims' house. By
> threatening to burn down the house, some of them forced the victim's

son to rape his younger sister. They also coerced the male house-help to rape the mother of the family. The gang rapes were then continued by the group and other unknown persons. The victims' house was burnt down, the siblings were thrown into the burning fire and the mother threw herself into the fire.

(As told confidentially by an eyewitness; the gang rape occurred in Jakarta on 13 May 1998)

The pattern

Being shocked, we may ponder: who planned such barbaric acts on such a massive scale? We may suspect that they were spontaneous acts by the mobs, the crowd of ordinary people. The answer is 'NO'. From our ongoing investigations, we began to see clearly that the May tragedy involved a highly systematic and organised plan and its execution. It was not a 'coincidence', for the coincidence-factor simply cannot explain (a) the scale and (b) simultaneity...of the tragedy in an area as vast as Jakarta and its surroundings, (c) the similarity of their *modus operandi*, and (d) the systematic selection of targets in the case of gang rapes of Chinese women. With regard to the similarity of *modus operandi*, we have uncovered the following pattern:

- First, the looting and burning were not initiated by people from the neighbourhood, but by groups of strangers not known by the local people. These strangers were transported in a bus or truck coming from unknown places. They incited, provoked and encouraged the local people to do the looting.
- Second, the leaders of the looting/burning and the perpetrators of gang rapes were described by eyewitnesses and local people as muscular persons, wearing military boots, having the appearance of goons and hitmen.
- Third, this group of unknown persons disappeared while the buildings were on fire, and while adults and children from the neighbourhood were helplessly trapped inside.

Indeed, our investigations show that the May tragedy is inseparable from the power struggle that intensified in the days prior to the outbreak of the riots. And this is a recurring pattern in the elite politics in Indonesia in the last 30 years. A similar pattern, leading to similar consequences, was evident in the riots in Surabaya, Solo, Palembang and Medan. They also happened in Aceh, Irian Jaya, East Timor, Banjarmasin, Tasikmalaya, and Situbondo, as well as in the 27 July 1996 incident. The past was soaked in violence and blood. The present is simply another space and time for similar blood-spilling politics. If we do not break this recurring pattern, the future will never become the realm of civilisation....

The cover-up

...First, the Indonesian government and the old guard in the military show a lukewarm attitude even in admitting that systematic and organised acts of looting, burning and gang rape have been committed. Among their official ranks, there is a tendency to cover up the fact of the May tragedy. They repeatedly say that what happened were spontaneous acts by the crowd, or they simply keep quiet as if nothing has really happened. Another political move by official ranks is to make the tragedy appear as a natural disaster, comparable with an earthquake or a hurricane. Behind such a move is an agenda, or rather a non-agenda, that 'nothing can be done'. As [was] repeatedly done in the past, a deliberate amnesia is again being injected into public life. It is a betrayal of history, a denial of collective memory.

Second, there is a blatant move by official ranks to construe the events to look like a racial conflict. Based on our ongoing investigations, we assure you that it was not a racial conflict. The 'racial-conflict claim' can never explain why the organised gangs burned down buildings in which thousands of non-Chinese adults and children were helplessly trapped. Racial differences are not the main problem. They are a solution repeatedly employed by the government every time its power is under threat, or a method repeatedly used by some power contenders in their attempt to capture political power.

Third, the old method of scapegoating is currently being employed again. The official ranks have a tendency for making it appear that the perpetrators of the May tragedy are the urban poor. Since most of the victims are also the urban poor, the case is made so that it appears that it was the urban poor who killed the urban poor. In the language of Indonesian politics, it is the same as saying that 'nothing can be done'. No wonder that there is an increasing moral outrage among the urban poor towards political authority.

Fourth, with regard to the gang rapes, there is a move from some quarters within official ranks to separate the acts of rape from the organised riots, looting and burning. The purpose of such a move is clear, that is, to strip gang rapes of their political connection. By so doing the gang rapes will look like ordinary 'criminal' acts rather than part of an organised 'political' move.

Fifth, gang rapes, using similar *modus operandi*, continued until at least mid-July 1998. It is clear that the continuing gang rapes have become part of terrorism currently being waged against the wider population and humanitarian activists. Members of the Team of Volunteers for Humanitarian Causes have been subjected to various forms of terror and threat from unknown sources, from death threats to abduction. This alone gives an undeniable proof that democracy has never been seriously given a chance to surface in Indonesia. The irony is that, instead of receiving moral support, our humanitarian Team has become the accused. We are constantly blackmailed and accused of defending the interests of the ethnic Chinese, without the accusers admitting that we also are helping the non-Chinese victims.

The urgency

...There is an urgent need to unearth the facts of the May 1998 tragedy. No crime against humanity happens without criminals.... To unearth the facts of the May 1998 tragedy is to uncover an organised plan and its execution, as well as the planners and perpetrators of the tragedy. This seems to be the key to reviving the ethics of social life, of politics, of the economy, or even one of the keys to economic recovery. The reluctance on the part of the Indonesian authorities to carry out such agenda is usually expressed in the rhetoric of 'due process', while the legal system in Indonesia has long been known as the 'dark road to justice'. Only concerted efforts among various groups within the Indonesian 'civil society' and international support for such efforts can gradually unravel the puzzle....

We have to say clearly that the authoritarian arrangements of the past and the present state in Indonesia have been part...of the problem. Within such authoritarian arrangements is the deep-seated power of the Indonesian military, from the palace politics and economy to the structure of village life. It is no secret that dominant groups within the military have always been involved in all political proceedings in Indonesia. There is a big irony behind the May 1998 tragedy. For many decades Indonesian military intelligence has been very stern in conducting surveillance on all aspects of social life: from workers' gatherings to the contents of newspapers, from [the] geographical movement of street children to the schedule of student discussions. It is indeed impossible that the military intelligence, with such a vast experience, [was] unaware of the network of organised riots and gang rapes as colossal as the May 1998 tragedy. Or should it be said that the dominant groups within the Indonesian military may have given their tacit blessing or were even involved in the tragedy?

12.8 President B.J. Habibie: a new beginning

In this state of the nation address, delivered in parliament on 15 August 1998, Habibie sums up the problems facing Indonesia and outlines his vision. The translation below is abridged from the *Jakarta Post* (16 August 1998), with amendments based on the official Indonesian transcript (Habibie 1998).

The twenty-first of May 1998 was an historic milestone marking the change in the national leadership and the beginning of the Era of Democratic Resurgence. This historic turning point cannot be understood in isolation from the demands for all-encompassing reform pioneered by the young generation and students. The history of the nation records 12 May 1998 as the day four Heroes of Reform died, sparking the events that saw the emergence of the democratic era.

The struggle to develop a nation and a state forms an unbroken chain. History records that successful nations must always be prepared to revise the path to realising their ideals.

On historic days like this one we assess what should be enhanced, expanded and corrected, and what should be renewed. Therefore, allow me to convey to you a summary of those matters as inputs to the whole nation through this honourable House of People's Representatives. The preamble of the 1945 Constitution expresses the wishes and desires of Indonesian people to live in an independent, unified, sovereign, just and prosperous state. We are now free, unified and sovereign. However, we still have a duty to perform, namely to realise a just and prosperous society through a long process of national development.

Since the outset of the First Five-Year Development Plan in 1969, we have endeavoured to achieve national development goals. We were able to achieve progress in various fields, which the majority of our people enjoyed until we were jolted by the monetary crisis in July 1997. This was part of the Asian monetary crisis, which has not yet been fully overcome.

Since the middle of 1997, the standard of living of Indonesian people has dropped sharply. Prior to that, we had managed to reduce the proportion of people living in poverty to 11 per cent; it is now estimated to have soared to about 40 per cent. Indeed, it is no exaggeration to say that the achievements of three decades of national development have been wiped out in the space of several months.

We never suspected that such a crisis would happen. More startling still, we never imagined that our economic order and our national financial institutions would be unable to withstand the violent tremors that shook the nation's economic foundations. We also felt, and admitted, that moral impropriety may have weakened our resilience in various areas of national life.

Efforts to prevent the people's standard of living from deteriorating, let alone lifting it to the level reached before the crisis, were not easy. Most national production and distribution has been crippled and the exchange rate of the rupiah has declined sharply. This has seen rises in the price of daily necessities, basic materials and imported spare parts. Government and private-sector external debt repayments also increased.

One after another, large, medium-sized and small enterprises were compelled to wind down production or stop it altogether, leading to a great many employees being laid off. The number of unemployed people continues to increase, leading to social, economic and security problems, especially in big cities.

Various policy alternatives have been tried, but to little avail. Gradually, the monetary crisis developed into an economic crisis. The only sectors which withstood it were those which did not rely on imports such as the mining, agribusiness and agro-industrial sectors, as well as a number of export-oriented businesses.

The decline in the people's standard of living was aggravated by various political tensions arising from the 1997 general elections. The political system that had been developed since 1966 turned out to be unable to accommodate the dynamism of the aspirations and interests of the community, which had far outgrown it. Riots and disturbances took place in various places. To a certain extent, these events reflected a breakdown of the political system and of the government's capacity, finally causing this situation to develop into a political crisis.

The economic and political crises together gave rise to something graver: a crisis in confidence. This affected not just officials and state institutions, but also began to touch on the system of values and the legal foundations that underpin the state institutions. Critical moments prevailed in the capital, Jakarta, and other cities between 12 and 21 May 1998....

The political situation developed in such a manner that the only alternative for the president in order to save the nation and the state was to declare that he would step down from his position. Man proposes, but God disposes, and history keeps a record. Pursuant to Article 8 of the 1945 Constitution and the People's Consultative Assembly Decree no. VII/1973, concurrent with the resignation, the vice-president got the mandate to lead and the honour of leading the nation and continuing the development process. He became the third president of the Republic of Indonesia.

The change in the presidency was a logical consequence of the demand to make changes in the life of the society, nation and state. All constituted a part of the national reform movement that continues to unfold.

The essence of the national reform movement is a planned, institutionalised and continuous correction of all deviations which have taken place in the economic, political and legal spheres. The target is our ability to recover and forge ahead in a more open, well-ordered and democratic climate. Included in the important agenda of the national reform movement is the abolition of corruption, collusion and nepotism, which have proved to be the main cause of the weakness and vulnerability of our economy....

The program to get the wheels of the national economy turning again requires the restoration of a feeling of security among members of the society. I would like to call the attention of the House to the fact that our business community is still suffering from the trauma inflicted by the riots that took place in mid-May. Not many of the business people whose companies were destroyed have begun to rebuild their businesses. They are still awaiting further developments.

They are also still haunted by memories of the mass riots triggered by the demise of the four Heroes of Reform on 12 May. The riots, which involved looting and the burning of shopping centres and people's houses, were aggravated by violence and sexual harassment against women, especially ethnic Chinese. All of these irresponsible acts are very disgraceful; they have shamed our nation, a nation renowned for its good character and high morals. As a civilised and religious nation, we curse these barbaric acts....

Honestly, we must admit that one of the causes of the current crisis is that the rule of law was often disregarded, not only in the political and economic domains but also in the socio-cultural realm. The law has often been used as an instrument of power, deviating from the goal of enforcing justice and creating welfare for the people.

Therefore legal reforms should be carried out with a view to making the law truly authoritative, both as a means of creating order and of realising a just and prosperous Indonesian society based on Pancasila. In the context of implementing reforms in the legal domain, we want all of us to be consistent by properly regarding Indonesia as a law-based state. By the same token we should try our best to realise and enforce the supremacy of the law in our activities as members of society, the nation and the state. In that regard, we should be aware that a democratic government can only be effected if we always place the supremacy of the law as one of its main pillars....

In the political domain, reforms aim at reinforcing democracy based upon popular participation. This is brought about by providing rights to ensure space for opinions to be expressed orally or in writing; by expanding opportunities for people to participate in the political domain through various political and social organisations; by organising people's consultative and representative institutions to uphold sovereignty vested in the people; and by maintaining the independence of such institutions in carrying out legislative and monitoring functions with a high degree of credibility.

Some political reform activities have been consolidated through the formation of political parties. Some other activities are still taking the form of mass demonstrations. I would like to call upon community leaders to seriously consider this mass mobilisation. Experience has proved that mass movements cannot always be kept under control. Uncontrolled mass movements can also give rise to fear, which does not contribute to the restoration of our economy. Thus it is necessary to balance the demand for democracy (which guarantees freedom of assembly and freedom of expression) with the need to maintain public order, as stated in the UN Universal Declaration on Human Rights.

The press has been able to communicate news and opinions freely. The government has also abolished the threat of revoking printing permits, which up to now the press has regarded as a barrier in exercising its rights as a free and responsible press.

Reforms of the government and state administration are a crucial part of political reform. In this regard, I have communicated to all parties responsible for state administration that the priority of reforms in this domain consists of creating clean and authoritative government free from corrupt, collusive and nepotistic practices – government that is accountable to the people and able to render services to the community in a just and equitable manner. Reform measures towards that end have been taken in the context of creating a responsive and responsible administration.

The armed forces form a part of the state apparatus that must also undergo thorough reform. Reforms in the rank and file of the armed forces have been and are being exercised in a serious, conceptual and systematic fashion. Please do not forget that the initial impetus for openness and reforms came partly from the armed forces faction in the House of Representatives prior to the reforms of last May.

In relation to the latest cases, I have specifically instructed the commander of the armed forces to thoroughly investigate the matter of the abduction of a number of political activists and the shooting of the Trisakti University students, so that these cases can be resolved in accordance with the law. Transparency in dealing with these matters is imperative to restore the dignity and honour of our armed forces.

In line with the spirit of reform in enforcing human rights, we announced the National Action Program for Human Rights towards the end of last June. In the National Action Program we confirm our national commitment to ratify and access the UN human rights instruments, but also to popularise and implement them in all areas of society, state and national life.

Thus we have left behind us once and for all the notion that human rights are a product of Western culture. We state clearly that human rights imply a commitment by all of us to respect the honour and dignity of humankind irrespective of race, ethnicity, skin colour, sex or social status. Needless to say, efforts to promote and protect human rights must be accompanied by a sense of responsibility. Indeed, there are no rights without responsibilities....

In our seriousness to respect and enforce human rights I, on behalf of the government, would like to express through this grand forum my deepest regrets for past human rights violations in several regions committed by individuals from the state apparatus in operations against separatists. It is my conviction that all of us are concerned and troubled by violations against the dignity and honour of citizens and of humanity. In full awareness of my mandate to respect and implement human rights, I hereby offer my apology to the Indonesian people, in particular to the families of the victims....

I will now turn to the third major element of our economic stabilisation and reform program, which involves the productive or the non-financial sector. Here we have to eliminate various procedures that gave rise to economic rents and excessive or unnatural profits in some economic activities. We have to abolish exclusive permits and business rights that cause economic inefficiencies. Likewise, procedures for awarding business permits, tendering processes, and provision of goods and services by the government and state-owned enterprises must be carried out openly and competitively. In this way the economy will be capable of prospering in an increasingly global environment....

Another reason why a healthy competitive climate is necessary is that companies that prosper because of special facilities or through corruption, collusion and nepotism are often vulnerable to economic turbulence. A competitive economy is highly resilient to the fluctuations of the world economy. In the years to come, we can be sure that only companies which come into being and develop on the basis of healthy commercial and financial principles will be able to survive, while businesses which rely on monopoly rights and special facilities will not....

We must eradicate corruption because if it is not cured this disease will spread, damaging institutions and undermining the foundation of the social order and the political system. The legal and political reforms we are implementing underpin our efforts to eradicate corruption. We must develop the government bureaucracy into an efficient organisation oriented to providing services that really satisfy the needs of society, free from intervention and political influence. I am sure that in this new social atmosphere we will be able to create clean and transparent government and business practices....

Permit me now to convey an evaluation of the current stage of the development of our life as a society, nation and state.

It is only natural that in this time of reform we should ask ourselves whether it is worth preserving any of the policies and structures of the pre-reform period. Does reform mean that we have to rebuild everything from scratch? I would like to invite all of us seriously to ponder these matters. Whatever the case, we do not intend to establish a new state.

One legacy we must maintain and even further refine is the spirit of nationalism of our highly diverse society. It was the spirit of nationalism professed by people from all walks of life and from various and diverse groups that enabled independence to be proclaimed and has allowed the unitary Republic of Indonesia to be maintained since 1945. Without this national spirit, there could have been tens, perhaps hundreds, of small, mutually hostile states in this archipelago....

We should not consider the spirit of nationalism as something static. In the current climate of reform, we need to take steps so that on 28 October, the 70th anniversary of the Youth Pledge, we reaffirm our nationalistic spirit. The objective is that every person and every group, whether native or naturalised, indigenous or non-indigenous, minority or majority, should feel that he or she is a legitimate citizen on a par with anyone else within the body of this large nation of ours....

Openness goes to the essence of human values and is the air the reform movement breathes. Based on the fundamental perspective of openness, we must create a transparent socio-political system with structures and processes that truly and effectively reflect the sovereignty of the people. Effective control from below is one of the ways in which the practices of corruption, collusion, cronyism and nepotism can be eradicated. Effective control by the people will pave the way for an honest and clean government to be realised and morality upheld in our society, nation and state.[6]...

The political crisis which emerged at the end of 1997 and climaxed on 21 May 1998, when the Development Reform Cabinet was formed, has made us more and more aware of the need for a basic review and a change in the paradigm which then constituted the basis on which national development programs and policies were formulated. The stability paradigm adopted until recently, which was translated into a security approach and a mechanism of top-down of strong government, turned out to be antiquated and no longer suited to the demands of the situation and the progress of society.

If we pay attention to the most outstanding events in various corners of the world towards the end of the 20th century, we can perceive three events that will usher nations into the 21st century: first is the resurgence of nations in the world; second, awareness of human rights; and, third, rapid progress in science and technology. The progress made by telecommunications and information technology in the last two decades has made the world more open and encouraged a high level of interdependency between and among nations. Openness in almost all spheres of life, coupled with high levels of interdependency between and among nations, will be the main features of globalisation in the 21st century.

These three events have given rise to fundamental changes in the social, economic and political life of many nations, including ours. The social and political volatility that peaked on 21 May was evidence that the old paradigm emphasising stability through a security approach was no longer adequate to respond to the fast-changing demands and aspirations of the people.

A new paradigm needs to be developed that gives more emphasis to a democratic and welfare approach. This new approach, the essence of which is transparency and bottom-up mechanisms – in matters relating to the working of the nation and state as well as to national development activities – is the right response to the demands of a society with increasingly high levels of education and social awareness. Furthermore, the new paradigm is also in line with the characteristics of the civil society we are developing.

12.9 *Media Indonesia*: an ideology of tolerance

This editorial in the secular nationalist newspaper *Media Indonesia* appeared on 16 January 1999, the same day as a report by key members of a parliamentary review committee announced that grandchildren of PKI members would be granted the right to vote and be elected. This move was seen as marking the end of the elaborate regime of screening and surveillance of former members of communist organisations and their families.

PKI. The very term is like a hurricane. In the past, to be branded PKI was as good as a death sentence. It meant not only physical death but also civil death. It was also a potent weapon in the hands of the authorities to silence those who did not go along with them.

Is it any surprise that being branded PKI was more feared than any court sentence? People involved with the PKI, including those with only tenuous family links to the party, have been held hostage to a historical trauma. New Order figures who escaped the cruelty of the PKI in 1965 declared the PKI to be their ideological enemy, the enemy of the age, the enemy of Indonesian-ness.

Now, 34 years on, the stigma has begun to fade. Members of parliament debating the draft law on politics have decided to restore to families of PKI members the right to vote that has been denied them all this time. So after three decades their political rights have been resurrected. Imagine what this meant for children whose grandparents might have belonged to a PKI family. It was most unfair for them to have to bear the burden of the 'political sins' of their family. Especially as the PKI has long been dissolved and banned.

Indonesian society is entering a more enlightened era. There is a very strong awareness now that history needs to be totally corrected. 'Stability', which was used as a pretext for the preservation of the status quo, is now seen as the very source of political and ideological repression.

Part of the correction process is the abandonment of institutionalised Pancasila indoctrination courses, as these did little to change anyone's behaviour. Indeed corruption, collusion and nepotism, the very antithesis of the noble values taught in these courses, flourished under the New Order.

The fall of communism in the Soviet Union put an end to antagonism between peoples based on ideological difference. Capitalism, liberalism and socialism these days are all adaptable and tolerant.

It would therefore be very unfortunate if our Pancasila ideology was to be used to encourage hostility to other ideologies, including communism. It would be worse still if Pancasila was used to concoct verbal or ideological instruments to ensnare its own citizens.

Is Pancasila ideology really that bad? Of course not.

The weaknesses we have seen have to do with how Pancasila has been implemented. It is as though Pancasila has been off in a fantasy world, ignoring reality and practice on the ground.

And herein lies the danger. We have all been making light of Pancasila without any real awareness of [the importance of] ideology. In these circumstances we should not be surprised to find that religion is moving in to fill the void.

The granting of political rights to the families of former PKI members must be seen as a fulfilment of human rights and not as a denial of ideology. Using ideology to make enemies of citizens only creates totalitarian regimes, but ignoring ideology altogether will only lead to anarchy.

12.10 The armed forces: a new paradigm

This important but often opaque document summarises the outcome of a seminar held at the Armed Forces Staff and Command School (Sesko TNI) in Bandung on 22–3 September 1998. The selections that follow are from a short book prefaced by General Wiranto the translated title of which is *The Armed Forces in the 21st Century: Redefining, Repositioning and Remaking the Role of the Armed Forces in National Life* (*TNI Abad XXI* 1999: 14–18, 22–9).

In the New Order era under President Soeharto we saw the armed forces playing the most prominent role in the socio-political arena. Indeed, according to some senior officers who had helped formulate the concept of the dual function, this role had gone beyond what they originally intended. The dual-function concept was not able to anticipate that the presidency would be held by someone with a direct position in the command structure who would use his influence over the command structure for his own socio-political interests....

This situation was made possible because society was still, at that stage, conditioned by its experience under the Old Order; that is, it was oriented towards ideology. The difference between society in the Old Order and the New had to do with its orientation. While under the Old Order society was oriented to political ideology, under the New Order it was oriented to development ideology. The logical consequence of this was that not much attention was given to ensuring participation and the popular will in the process of decision-making....

We now turn to the present situation regarding the socio-political role of the armed forces. Actually we are now facing the biggest challenge ever to the continuance of this role. There are six reasons for this.

1   The emergency conditions of the past are over and no longer justify a large expansion of the armed forces' role beyond its defence and security function.
2   The emergence of anti-military sentiment in society. Many now regard the military as an obstacle to the process of democratisation and the observation of human rights. This is occurring in the context of a shrinking and increasingly integrated world in which national boundaries are dissolving due to the revolution in information technology. In these circumstances it is increasingly difficult to declare any issue purely domestic in character.
3   Economic development has led to increasing levels of education in society, making people more aware of their right to political participation and more attentive to the process of political decision-making....
4   Globalisation has blurred international boundaries, leading to a global convergence of value systems but also a demand for effective national management to ensure our competitiveness with other nations.
5   Indonesian society is modernising rapidly....
6   Indonesia's productive population is increasingly made up of people who neither experienced nor comprehend the historical events that underpin the legitimacy of the dual function....

Having undertaken a review of the conditions we have faced both in the past and in the present, and in view of the future challenges to the socio-political role of the armed forces, we have concluded that a paradigm shift is now necessary. We have been led to rethink our old paradigm, which was often based on a 'security approach', in favour of a new paradigm. The security approach encouraged the armed forces to see themselves as having a determining role in any decisions that affected the running of the state and lives of the people. Because security is the main concern of the armed forces, or at least because the armed forces cannot be divorced from security interests, this approach was usually referred to as the security approach.

The security approach made the armed forces feel that they had to take full responsibility for everything that affected the nation's life, whether it had to do with the political format of the New Order or other factors. The new paradigm, on the other hand, is analytical and forward looking. It is based on a comprehensive approach in which the armed forces are seen as part of the national system. In this environment, national objectives have to be formulated in an integrated way by all components of the nation, guided by a single national vision. Where they see shortcomings in other departments, the armed forces will not, therefore, take over their functions directly. This would suggest we were still in a state of emergency. Rather, they will be obliged and duty bound to help strengthen all components of the nation and help revitalise all functions of government.

In socio-political terms, the new paradigm entails:

1   A change of position and method to one where [the armed forces] are not necessarily in the forefront. This means that the prominent role the armed forces once played – necessarily in the circumstances – as pioneers and paragons of social, national and state life will now give way to one in which they are used [to support] functional institutions. Exactly how they are used will be determined by national agreement according to the prevailing circumstances. While we will abide by the role we are allotted in the system of national management, we remain, as committed soldiers, always ready to respond to a range of situations. In quiet times we are prepared to implement a functional approach and in emergency situations we are prepared to defend the state by applying the security approach.

2   A change from the concept of occupying to influencing. This means that the socio-political role of the armed forces will no longer involve military personnel occupying civilian positions. But on the other hand they will always contribute constructive ideas because they always feel responsible for and attentive to the nation's fate.

3   A change from direct to indirect methods of exerting influence. If in the past people understood the armed forces' socio-political role to mean that they took an active role in practical politics, the new approach is to exert influence through indirect means. From now on they will contribute ideas and concepts to institutions to be carried out in an integrated way by the relevant institutions and components of the nation in the framework of the national system.

4   A readiness to engage in political role-sharing (joint decision-making in the case of important national and government issues) with other components of the nation. This means that every time the armed forces take an initiative in social, national and state life, this will always be done in partnership with other components of the nation in a national integrated system. All components of the nation must be aware that they constitute inseparable, interlinked subsystems, each contributing to the success of national management....

The placing of armed forces personnel in non-military positions will from now on depend on the capacity and acceptability of the individual. The best man will be selected through a general and transparent electoral process. When armed forces personnel are chosen via this process, a process that reflects the national will, they will have to resign from active service in the military. Military personnel serving in non-military jobs will therefore no longer represent the armed forces as they did in the past, but will be selected on the basis of their individual merit and serve in a civilian capacity.

In line with the new paradigm, the armed forces faction in the People's Consultative Assembly will be pared down. This also reflects the fact that Indonesian society is becoming more mature in its practice of democracy as it moves towards the realisation of a civil society.

Likewise, the abolition of the position of the armed forces chief of staff of socio-political affairs (Kassospol TNI) and the creation, in its place, of the armed forces chief of staff for territorial affairs (Kaster TNI) is only a first step towards giving the armed forces an integrated role. This refers to the armed forces' devotion to the state and the nation, not only in the area of defence and security, but also in the more general area of nation-building....

The armed forces remain conscious of their rights and responsibilities towards the nation, and are aware that this state was built on a fundamental commitment to the family principle.

12.11   Agus Wirahadikusumah: overhaul the military

The following extracts are from a series of hard-hitting interviews given to news magazines by the military reformer Major-General Agus Wirahadikusumah, head of the Sulawesi military command. They date from the last weeks of 1999, soon after he had been removed from his job as head of planning to the armed forces commander in a reshuffle widely seen as a setback for the reform movement in the armed forces. They are taken, in sequence, from *Gatra* (23 December 1999), *Tempo* (26 December 1999) and *Tajuk* (31 December 1999).[7]

Q: *You have been quoted as recommending that the military should eliminate village-level non-commissioned officers (*Babinsa*) and military posts at the sub-district level (*Koramil*).*

A: That is needed to show that the military is responding to the real changes taking place among the Indonesian people. The territorial command structure was set up to serve as the eyes and ears of the military, but then it became an instrument of control and an instrument of political manipulation. Now that Indonesian society has become more advanced, the territorial structure is no longer necessary, particularly if the military is going to be truly committed to promoting democratisation and the empowerment of the people. The territorial structure is precisely what is obstructing democratisation, and it also conflicts with the armed forces' own efforts to carry out internal reform.

Q: *So when should the dismantling of the territorial system begin?*

A: The sooner the better. I have commissioned an academic survey on the effectiveness of the territorial system in my military region, Sulawesi, and I will submit the results to the army chief of staff. It's what the people want. There have been all sorts of demands for us to get rid of the system, from the regional commands (Kodam) down to the Koramil level. We'll be looking at the whole thing to see whether there is any use in keeping it or not.

Q: *Are you sure that the territorial system is really no longer necessary?*

A: It's possible that the territorial system is still needed in some areas – for example, in a few areas where the civilian administration is not yet in full control. In other areas, however, we all know that the military is acting as a parasite. Who backs and supports the discothèques, brothels and narcotics rings if not the military or police? Let's be honest about it....

Is our territorial supervision so great? It's rotten! Let's not talk about theories – this is a fact that has to be addressed. For two years now the Indonesian people have been restless. Everyone has been gripped by fear, everyone has been afraid. Let's not lie to the people any more! Let's not lead the people into flights of fancy. It is an embarrassing fact that the people no longer trust the military.

Q: *Is that why you issued a formal apology?*

A: Precisely. On behalf of the Indonesian military, I ask forgiveness. Where are there soldiers who ask for forgiveness? What's so difficult about apologising? All this time there were mistakes being made. Show me an officer who says that the military is not to blame. This has to be repaired now, so that the military can once again engender the trust of the people. For the top commanders: I hereby ask them to look at the facts on the ground.

Q: *And the military's dual function is no longer appropriate, either?*

A: Clinging to dual function is an anachronism. The armed forces have delved too deeply into practical politics. How can security personnel possibly garner respect if they are said to be Golkar cadres, and told to wear yellow jackets?[8] That's a very fundamental mistake. How else can you put it? That was a mistake, politically.

Q: *What about the military's business interests? Is that tolerable, because of the limited budgetary resources available for the military?*

A: No. The system's wrong and it has got out of hand. This is a major reason why the authorities find it so hard to foster professionalism. The military's businesses interfere with the economy, because they receive so many different types of facilities. Look into it – you'll find all sorts of weaknesses in military businesses. Their management is a mess. Businesses continually make losses, without ever reporting a profit. Just look at PT Asabri [the military's pension fund]. More than Rp200 billion has gone missing! Those funds are entitlements for soldiers! What more do you want to say about the management of military businesses? Don't use excuses about limited budgetary resources any more! What actual benefit has there been for the armed forces as an institution? In the end, it's all for the individuals running the businesses....

Q: *There are still trouble spots in several areas. What do you think the armed forces should do?*

A: What are you calling trouble spots? Irian? Why are we fighting our own people? Injustice is what it is all about there! It's about an imbalance in the management of natural resources, as well as issues to do with politics, nationhood and statehood. So why respond with military means? Separatism cannot be solved with violence. In Ambon, for instance, they set up a new regional command. Has it solved the problem? They wanted to do the same in Aceh, but this was eventually rejected.[9]

When I was called to testify at the People's Consultative Assembly recently I tried to get them thinking about these things, and not to lose themselves in theories from the past. Look at the conditions on the ground today: times have changed. If we go on the way we have, there is no way we will rebuild our image.

Q: *If the military isn't sent in against the separatists, what should the military be doing?*

A: Look at what General Jasin did. He said, 'I brought [Aceh rebel commander] Teungku Daud Beureueh down from the mountains without using a bullet.[10] All it took was a letter, addressed "Beloved Father…".' After that, Daud came down and embraced Jasin. This approach was sharper than any bullet. But look what goes on now. It seems the young generals just want to use force, use weapons. I'm ashamed. Really, as a young general, I'm ashamed.

Notes

1 The findings of a joint fact-finding team on the 13–15 May riots in Jakarta, Solo, Surabaya, Medan and Palembang are summarised in the *Jakarta Post*, 4 November 1998.

2 Several books have been written documenting and analysing the reform movement. (See, especially, Budiman *et al.* 1999; Manning and van Dierman 2000; Lloyd and Smith 2001. On Ibu Sulami, see, for example, Mares 1999.)

3 Dra Adriana Elisabeth, MsocSc, Dr Asvi Warman Adam, Dra Awani Irewati, MA, Drs Dhuroruddin Mashad, Edison Muchlis S.H., Dra Ganewati Wuryandari, MA, Dra Hargyaning Tyas., Dr Hermawan Sulistyo, MA, Drs Heru Cahyono, Dr Ikrar Nusa Bhakti, Drs M. Hamdan Basyar, Drs Moch. Nurchasim, Drs M. Riefqi Muna, MdefStud, Dr M. Riza Sihbudi, Drs Muhammad Rum, Drs Muridan S. Widjojo, Dra R. Siti Zuhro, MA, Dra Sri Yanuarti, Drs Syamsudin Haris.

4 BPPC was a monopoly under the control of Soeharto's youngest son, Hutomo Mandala Putera, while the citrus monopoly was under the control of his second son, Bambang Trihatmodjo.

5 The list of institutions appended to this statement included STIE Swadaya, Univ./Akad Kertanegara, Univ. Borobudur, Univ. Krisnadwipayana, Unika Atmajaya, APP, Pancasila, IAIN Jakarta, Gunadarma, ITI, IKIP Jakarta, UIC, Univ. Sahid, STEI Nusantara, UID, STT Jakarta, STF Drikarya, ABA–ABI, Mpu Tantular, Univ. Djuanda Bogor, Atahirriyah, YAI, UMJ, ATGI, PTI–Q, Univ. Pakuan, Tarumanegara, USIP, ATST, Jayabaya, Ukrida, STIE LABORA, Inter Studi, STIE Jagakarsa, STIE Rawamangun, STEKPI, Univ. Islam Assyafiyah, Univ. Trisakti, STMI Jakarta, LPK Tarakanita, IIBI, STMT, UKI, LPI, AMI, IISIP, YARSI, ISTN, Univ. Nasional, UPN, Univ. Dr Moestopo, UIC, Univ. Ibnu Saut, UNIJA, UNKRIS, UNTAG, Univ. Syahid, UNTAR, ATGT, AKASTRI, SPPJ and AKPM.

6 The last two sentences here appear only in the English version.

7 The editors wish to acknowledge that parts of the translation in this reading are taken from a profile of Agus Wirahadikusumah in the *Van Zorge Report* of 7 January 2000, accessed at www.vanzorgereport.com/reports/agusall.html.

8 The author refers here to the 1995 proclamation by the then army commander, General Hartono, that all military officers were Golkar cadres, contradicting the doctrine of military neutrality in politics.

9 This was premature. In February 2002 the Iskandar Muda Military Command was revived in Aceh.

10 General Jasin, deputy army commander between 1970 and 1973, served as commander of the Aceh military region between 1960 and 1963. On this episode, see *Tajuk*, 4–17 March 1999.

Bibliography

Aditjondro, G. (1986) 'Datang dengan kapal, tidur di pasar, buang air di kali, pulang naik pesawat: Telaah dampak migrasi suku-suku bangsa Sulawesi Selatan dan Tenggara ke Irian Jaya sejak tahun 1962', unpublished typescript, Jayapura: YPMD Irian Jaya.

Al-Jawi, Muhammad Shiddiq (c.1991) *Haruskah Islam menerima demokrasi?*, typescript, Bogor: Lingkar Studi Islam An Nur.

Amal, Ichlasul (1994) 'The dilemmas of decentralisation and democratisation', in D.M. Bourchier and J.D. Legge (eds) *Democracy in Indonesia, 1950s and 1990s*, Melbourne: Monash University Centre of Southeast Asian Studies: 214–22.

Amin, S.M. (1970) *Polemik dengan 'Berita Yudha' mengenai Dwi-Fungsi ABRI dan Civic Mission*, Jakarta: Hudaya.

Anderson, B.R.O'G. (1972) *Java in a Time of Revolution*, Ithaca, New York: Cornell University Press.

—— (1983) 'Old state, new society: Indonesia's New Order in comparative historical perspective', *Journal of Asian Studies* XLII(3): 477–96.

Anderson, B.R.O'G. and McVey, R.T. (1971) *A Preliminary Analysis of the October 1 1965 Coup in Indonesia*, Ithaca, New York: Cornell University, Modern Indonesia Project,.

Anonymous (1992) 'If Only I Were a Free Person (Or: Soewardi Soeryaningrat lives again)', *Inside Indonesia* 33, December 1992: 7–8.

Anwar, Dewi Fortuna (1999) 'The Habibie presidency', in G. Forrester (ed.) *Post-Soeharto Indonesia: Renewal or Chaos*, Bathurst: Crawford House Publishing: 33–47.

Anwar, M. Syafi'i (1995) *Pemikiran dan Aksi Islam Indonesia*, Jakarta: Paramadina.

Aspinall, E. (1996) 'The broadening base of political opposition in Indonesia', in G. Rodan (ed.) *Political Oppositions in Industrialising Asia*, London: Routledge: 215–40.

Attamimi, A. Hamid S. (1990) 'Peranan Keputusan Presiden Republik Indonesia dalam Penyelenggaraan Pemerintahan Negara: Suatu studi analisis mengenai keputusan Presiden yang berfungsi pengaturan dalam kurun waktu Pelita 1 – Pelita IV', unpublished dissertation for the degree of Doctor of Laws, Postgraduate Faculty, University of Indonesia, Jakarta.

Awanohara, S. (1983) 'Firming up a philosophy', *Far Eastern Economic Review*, 11 August: 37–8.

Barton, G. (1994) 'The impact of neo-modernism on Indonesian Islamic thought: the emergence of a new pluralism', in D.M. Bourchier and J.D. Legge (eds) *Democracy in Indonesia, 1950s and 1990s*, Melbourne: Monash University, Centre of Southeast Asian Studies : 143–50.

—— (1999) *Gagasan Islam Liberal di Indonesia: Pemikiran Neo-Modernisme Nurcholish Madjid, Djohan Effendi, Ahmad Wahab dan Abdurrahman Wahid, 1968–1980*, Jakarta: Paramadina with Pustaka Antara, Yayasan Adikarya and the Ford Foundation.

Besar, Abdulkadir (1972) 'Academic appraisal tentang tata tertib MPR', *Laporan Pimpinan MPRS tahun 1966–1972*, Jakarta: Penerbitan MPRS: 493–548.

—— (1978) 'Dwifungsi ABRI, Diungkapkan oleh Brigjen TNI Abdulkadir Besar', typescript (marked 'Restricted'), Bandung: Seskoad.

Boileau, J.M. (1983) *Golkar: Functional Group Politics in Indonesia*, Jakarta: Centre for Strategic and International Studies.

Booth, A. (1992) 'Income distribution and poverty', in A. Booth (ed.) *The Oil Boom and After: Indonesian Economic Policy and Performance in the Soeharto Era*, Singapore and New York: Oxford University Press: 323–62.

Bourchier, D.M. (1987) 'The Petition of Fifty', *Inside Indonesia* 10, April 1987: 7–10.

—— (1990) 'Law, crime and state authority in Indonesia', in Arief Budiman (ed.) *State and Civil Society in Indonesia*, Melbourne: Monash University Centre of Southeast Asian Studies: 177–212.

—— (1996) 'Lineages of organicist political thought in Indonesia', unpublished PhD, Monash University, Melbourne.

—— (1999) 'Skeletons, vigilantes and the armed forces' fall from grace', in Arief Budiman, B. Hatley and D. Kingsbury (eds) *Reformasi: Crisis and Change in Indonesia*, Melbourne: Monash Asia Institute: 149–71.

—— (2000) 'Habibie's interregnum: reformasi, elections, regionalism and the struggle for power', in C. Manning and P. van Dierman (eds) *Indonesia in Transition: Social Aspects of Reformasi and Crisis*, Singapore: Institute of Southeast Asian Studies: 15–38.

Bourchier, D.M. and Legge, J.D. (eds) (1994) *Democracy in Indonesia, 1950s and 1990s*, Melbourne: Monash University, Centre of Southeast Asian Studies .

Bresnan, J. (1993) *Managing Indonesia: The Modern Political Economy*, New York: Columbia University Press.

Budiardjo, M. (1972) *Dasar-dasar Ilmu Politik*, Jakarta: Gramedia.

Budiman, A., Hatley, B. and Kingsbury, D. (eds) (1999) *Reformasi: Crisis and Change in Indonesia*, Melbourne: Monash Asia Institute.

Chalmers, I. and Hadiz, V.R. (eds) (1997) *The Politics of Economic Development in Indonesia: Contending Perspectives*, New York and London: Routledge.

Cribb, R. (ed.) (1990) *The Indonesian Killings of 1965–66: Studies from Java and Bali*, Monash Papers on Southeast Asia No.21, Melbourne: Monash University Centre of Southeast Asian Studies.

Cribb, R. and Brown, C. (1995) *Modern Indonesia: A History since 1945*, London and New York: Longman.

Crouch, H. (1979) 'Patrimonialism and military rule in Indonesia', *World Politics* 31(4): 571–87.

Departemen Penerangan (1983) *Himpunan Pidato Menteri Penerangan RI 1978–1982, Peningkatan Penerangan yang Berwibawa*, Jakarta: Departemen Penerangan.

Dewan Redaksi Api (1965) *Harian 'Api' Mengganjang Nekolim-PKI-Gestapu*, Jakarta: Merdeka Press.

Dharsono H.R. (1986) 'Demanding the promise of the New Order (Menuntut Janji Orde Baru)', *Indonesia Reports*, no. 17, August 1986: 2–17.

Dinuth, A. (ed.) (1997) *Dokumen Terpilih Sekitar G.30S/PKI*, Jakarta: Intermasa.

Eklöf, S. (1999) *Indonesian Politics in Crisis: The Long Fall of Suharto, 1996–98*, Copenhagen: Nordic Institute of Asian Studies.

Eldridge, P.J. (1995) *Non-Government Organizations and Democratic Participation in Indonesia*, Singapore: Oxford University Press.

Elson, R.E. (2001) *Suharto: A Political Biography*, Cambridge: Cambridge University Press.

Emmerson, D.K. (1976) *Indonesia's Elite: Political Culture and Cultural Politics*, Ithaca, New York, and London: Cornell University Press.

Exponen Almuni Universitas Gadjah Mada (1990) 'Garis Besar Haluan Negara dan Pembangunan Nasional Jangka Panjang Kedua 1993–2018', unpublished typescript, Jakarta, 27 December 1990.

Fadhali, Amak (ed.) (1969) *NU dan Aqidahnya*, Semarang: CV Toha Putra.

Fealy, G. (1994) ' "Rowing in a typhoon": Nahdlatul Ulama and the decline of parliamentary democracy', in D.M. Bourchier and J.D. Legge (eds) *Democracy in Indonesia, 1950s and 1990s*, Melbourne: Monash University, Centre of Southeast Asian Studies: 88–98.

—— (1998) 'Ulama and Politics in Indonesia: A History of the Nahdlatul Ulama Party, 1952–1967', unpublished PhD thesis, History Department, Monash University.

Feillard, A. (1999) *NU vis-à-vis Negara: Pencarian Isi, Bentuk dan Makna*, Yogyakarta: LKiS Yogyakarta with the Asia Foundation.

Feith, H. (1962) *The Decline of Constitutional Democracy in Indonesia*, Ithaca, New York: Cornell University Press.

—— (1989) 'Indonesian political thinking in the late 1980s: democratisation and the new interplay of three perspectives', paper presented to the Australian National University Conference on Indonesia's New Order, Canberra, 8 December 1989.

Feith, H. and Castles, L. (eds) (1970) *Indonesian Political Thinking, 1945–1965*, Ithaca, New York, and London: Cornell University Press.

Forum Demokrasi (1992) 'Tumbuhkan Kembali Daya Kritis Masyarakat', unpublished typescript issued by Kelompok Kerja Forum Demokrasi, Jakarta, 19 April 1992.

Greater Jakarta Student Community (1998) 'Pernyataan Profesional Indonesia', press release, 3 September 1998, available at http://basisdata.esosoft.net/1998/09/04/0014.html (13 March 2002).

Greater Jakarta Students' Committee (1998) 'Pernyataan Bersama Komunitas Mahasiswa Se-Jabotabek', unpublished typescript, Jakarta, 28 May 1998.

Habibie, B.J. (1998) *Pidato Presiden RI pada Sidang Paripurna DPR-RI tanggal 15 Agustus 1998*, Indonesian Department of Foreign Affairs website, available at http://www.dfa-deplu.go.id/policy/statements/president/paripurna150898.htm (15 March 2002).

Hadiz, V.R. (1997) *Workers and the State in New Order Indonesia*, London: Routledge.

Hasan, A. Rifa'I and Achmad, Amrullah (eds) (1987) *Perspektif Islam dalam Pembangunan Bangsa: Pertemuan Cendekiawan Muslim Pertama*, Yogyakarta: PLP2M.

Hefner, R.W. (1993) 'Islam, state, and civil society: ICMI and the struggle for the Indonesian middle class', *Indonesia 56*, October 1993: 1–35.

Heryanto, A. (1993) 'Discourse and state terrorism: a case study of political trials in New Order Indonesia', unpublished PhD Thesis, Department of Anthropology and Sociology, Monash University, Melbourne.

—— (1999) 'Race, race and reporting', in Arief Budiman, B. Hatley and D. Kingsbury (eds) *Reformasi: Crisis and Change in Indonesia*, Melbourne: Monash Asia Institute: 299–334.

Hill, D.T. (1995) *The Press in New Order Indonesia*, Perth and Jakarta: University of Western Australia Press in association with the Murdoch University Asia Research Centre and *Sinar Harapan*.

ICG (International Crisis Group) (2000) 'Indonesia: keeping the military under control', *International Crisis Group Asia Report No. 9*, Jakarta/Brussels: ICG, 5 December 2000.

'Ideologi yang toleran' (1999) *Media Indonesia* (editorial), 16 January 1999.

Indonesian NGOs for Democracy (IN-DEMO) (1993) 'Joint Declaration on Human Rights', unpublished typescript, Jakarta, June 1993.

International NGO Forum on Indonesia (INGI) (1991) 'Aide Mémoire', unpublished typescript produced for the Seventh INGI Conference, 29 April–1 May 1991, Washington, DC.

Jayasuriya, K. (1998) '"Asian values" as reactionary modernisation', *Contemporary Politics* 4(1): 77–91.

Jenkins, D. (1984) *Suharto and His Generals: Indonesian Military Politics 1975–1983*, Ithaca, New York: Modern Indonesia Project, Cornell University.

Kahin, A.R. (1994) 'Regionalism and decentralisation', in D.M. Bourchier and J.D. Legge (eds) *Democracy in Indonesia, 1950s and 1990s*, Melbourne: Monash University Centre of Southeast Asian Studies: 204–13.

Kahin, G.McT. (1952) *Nationalism and Revolution in Indonesia*, Ithaca, New York: Cornell University Press.

Kaisiepo, Manuel (1993) 'Ke-Irian-an dan ke-Indonesia-an: Mengkaji Nasionalisme dalam Konteks Lokal', Paper presented at the Seminar 'Nasionalisme Indonesia Menjelang dan Pada Abad XXI' convened by Yayasan Bina Darma, Salatiga, 2–4 June 1993.

Karim, M. Rusli (1999) *Negara dan Peminggiran Islam Politik*, Yogyakarta: PT Tiara Wacana Yogya.

Kusumohamidjojo, Budiono (1988) 'Harga birokrasi hukum dalam deregulasi', *Kompas*, 29 April 1988.

Lev, D. (1978) 'Judicial authority and the struggle for an Indonesian rechtsstaat', *Law and Society Review* 13(1): 37–71.

—— (1987) *Legal Aid in Indonesia*, Working Paper No. 44, Melbourne: Monash University Centre for Southeast Asian Studies.

Lloyd, G. and Smith, S. (eds) (2001) *Indonesia Today: Challenges of History*, Singapore: Institute of Southeast Asian Studies.

Lowry, R. (1993) *Indonesian Defence Policy and the Indonesian Armed Forces*, Canberra Papers on Strategy and Defence No.99, Canberra: Research School of Pacific Studies, Australian National University.

Luwarso, Lukas (ed.) (1997) *Jakarta Crackdown*, Jakarta: Alliance of Independent Journalists, Asia-Forum for Human Rights and Development, Institute for Studies on Free Flow of Information.

Lyon, M. (1970) *Bases of Conflict in Rural Java*, Berkeley, California: University of California Center for South and Southeast Asian Studies.

MacAndrews, C. (1986) 'The structure of government in Indonesia', in C. MacAndrews (ed.) *Central Government and Local Development in Indonesia*, Singapore: Oxford University Press: 20–41.

Mackie, J. and MacIntyre, A. (1994) 'Politics', in H. Hill (ed.) *Indonesia's New Order: The Dynamics of Socio-economic Transformation*, St Leonards, Sydney: Allen & Unwin: 1–53.

Madjid, Nurcholish (1987) 'Keharusan pembaruan pemikiran Islam dan masalah integrasi umat', *Islam: Kemodernan dan Keindonesiaan*, Bandung: Mizan: 204–14 (first published 1970).

Mahasin, Aswab (1996) 'Empowering civil society: the NGO agenda', in Rustam Ibrahim (ed.) *The Indonesian NGO Agenda*, Jakarta: CESDA-LP3ES: 1–9.

Majelis Permusyawaratan Rakyat (1988) *Ketetapan-Ketetapan Majelis Permusyawaratan Rakyat Republik Indonesia*, Jakarta: Kreasi Jaya Utama.

—— (1989) *Inventarisasi dan Himpunan Ketetapan-Ketetapan MPR RI 1960–1988*, Jakarta: Badan Penerbit Alda.

Mangunwijaya, Y.B. (1996) 'Komunis', in Y.B. Mangunwijaya (1997) *Politik Hati Nurani* (compiled by Ignatius Haryanto), Jakarta: Grafiasri Mukti: 23–5.

—— (1998) *Menuju Republik Indonesia Serikat*, Jakarta: PT Gramedia Pustaka.

Manning, C. and van Dierman, P. (eds) (2000) *Indonesia in Transition: Social Aspects of Reformasi and Crisis*, Singapore: Institute of Southeast Asian Studies.

Mares, Peter (1999) 'Indonesian activist calls for inquiry into 1965 massacre', transcript of radio programme *Asia Pacific*, Australian Broadcasting Corporation; first broadcast 9 July 1999, available at http://www.abc.net.au/ra/asiapac/archive/1999/jul/raap-15jul1999–3.htm (1 March 2002).

Megawangi, Ratna (1994) 'Feminisme pascaambruknya otonomi dan persamaan gender', *Kompas*, 6 September.

Mietzner, M. (2001) 'Abdurrahman's Indonesia: political conflict and institutional crisis', in G. Lloyd and S. Smith (eds) *Indonesia Today: Challenges of History*, Singapore: Institute of Southeast Asian Studies: 29–44.

Mintaredja, H.M.S. (1972) *Islam dan Politik, Islam dan Negara di Indonesia: Sebuah Renungan dan Pembaharuan Pemikiran*, Jakarta: Permata.

—— (1973) *Islam and Politics, Islam and State in Indonesia: A Reflection and Revision of Ideas*, Jakarta: Permata.

Moertopo, Ali (1970) *Politik Nasional: Strategi, Taktik dan Teknik Implementasinja (Tjeramah Brigadir Djenderal TNI Ali Moertopo pada kursus up-grading karyawan teras ABRI tingkat pusat di Djakarta, tanggal 20 Agustus s/d 17 Oktober 1970)*, Jakarta: Departemen Pertahanan Keamanan.

—— (1972) *Dasar-Dasar tentang Akselerasi Pembangunan 25 Tahun*, Jakarta: Centre for Strategic and International Studies.

—— (1973) *The Acceleration and Modernization of 25 Years' Development*, Jakarta: Yayasan Proklamasi/Centre for Strategic and International Studies.

Morfit, M. (1981) 'Pancasila: the Indonesian state ideology according to the New Order government', *Asian Survey* XXI(8): 838–51.

Mortimer, R. (1974) *Indonesian Communism Under Sukarno: Ideology and Politics, 1959–1965*, Ithaca, New York: Cornell University Press.

Motek (1988) 'Reviving the communist threat', *Inside Indonesia* 16, October 1988: 5–8.

Najib, M., Supan and K. Sukardiyono (eds) (1998) *Suara Amien Rais, Suara Rakyat*, Jakarta: Gema Insani Press.

Nasution, A. Buyung (1992) *The Aspiration for Constitutional Government in Indonesia: A Socio-legal Study of the Indonesian Konstituante 1956–1959*, Jakarta: Pustaka Sinar Harapan.

Nursyahbani Katjasungkana (1994) 'Relevensi otonomi dan persamaan gender', *Kompas*, 26 September.

Paget, R. (1967) 'Djakarta newspapers, 1966–1967: preliminary comments', *Indonesia* 4, October.

Pangaribuan, R. (1995) *The Indonesian State Secretariat 1945–1993*, trans. and ed. V.R. Hadiz, Murdoch, Western Australia: Asia Research Centre, Murdoch University.

Pengurus Besar Himpunan Mahasiswa Islam (1984) *Pandangan Kritis terhadap RUU Keormasan*, Jakarta: Himpunan Mahasiswa Indonesia.

People's Democratic Party (1996) *Manifesto of the PRD*, available at http://www.peg.apc.org/stan/asiet/prddoc/manifes2.htm (29 January 1998).

—— (1998) 'People's Democratic Party calls for an end to New Order regime', trans. James Balowski, *Green Left Weekly*, no. 318, 20 May 1998; available at http://www.greenleft.org.au/(16 March 2002).

Prawiranegara, Sjafruddin (1983) 'Pancasila Sebagai Azas Tunggal' (facsimile of a letter to President Soeharto dated 7 July 1983), in *Perihal: Panca Sila Sebagai Azas Tunggal*, Jakarta: DDII, Jl Kramat Raya no. 45 (n.d.): 7–18.

Rahardjo, Dawam (1995) 'Visi dan misi kehadiran ICMI: Sebuah pengantar', in Nasrullah Ali-Fauzi (ed.) *ICMI Antara Status Quo dan Demokratisasi*, Bandung: Penerbit Mizan: 25–43.

Rahzen, Taufik (1989) 'Students' Statement of Belief: Violence and Conscience', *Inside Indonesia* 19, July 1989: 15.

Ramage, D. (1997) *Politics in Indonesia: Democracy, Islam and the Ideology of Tolerance*, London: Routledge.

Reeve, D. (1985) *Golkar of Indonesia: An Alternative to the Party System*, Singapore: Oxford University Press.

Richburg, K. (1998) 'Seven days in May that toppled a titan: back-room intrigue led to Suharto's fall', *Washington Post*, 24 May.

Robison, R. (1986) *Indonesia: The Rise of Capital*, St Leonards, Sydney: Allen & Unwin.

—— (1993) 'Indonesia: tensions in state and regime', in K. Hewison, R. Robison and G. Rodan, *Southeast Asia in the 1990s: Authoritarianism, Democracy and Capitalism*, St. Leonards, Sydney: Allen & Unwin: 39–74.

Robison, R. and Hadiz, V.R. (1993) 'Privatisation or the reorganisation of dirigism?: Indonesian economic policy in the 1990s', *Canadian Journal of Development Studies*, special edition: 13–32.

—— (forthcoming) *Oligarchy and Capitalism: Reorganising Power in Indonesia*.

Salim, Emil (1998) 'Reformasi Total', unpublished typescript, Jakarta, June 1998.

Sandyawan Sumardi, I. (1998) 'Condition of our shared life: the May 1998 tragedy in Indonesia', testimony before a US Congressional committee, 28 July 1998, available at http://basisdata.esosoft.net/1998/08/04/0008.html (1 March 2002).

Sanit, Arbi (ed.) (1992) *Analisa Pandangan Fenomena Politik Golput*, Jakarta: Sinar Harapan.

Schwarz, A. (1999) *A Nation in Waiting: Indonesia in the 1990s* (2nd edn), St Leonards, Sydney: Allen & Unwin.

Seda, Frans (1996) *Kekuasaan dan Moral Politik Ekonomi, Masyarakat Indonesia Baru*, Jakarta: Grasindo.

Sekretariat Dewan Perwakilan Rakyat Gotong Royong (1970) *Undang-undang Pemilihan Umum dan Undang-undang Susunan dan Kedudukan MPR, DPR dan DPRD*, Jakarta: Sekretariat Dewan Perwakilan Rakyat Gotong Royong.

Sen, K. and Hill, D.T. (2000) *Media, Culture and Politics in Indonesia*, Melbourne: Oxford University Press.

Shawwaf, Munir Muhammad Tahir (1993) *Tahafut Al Qira'at Al Mua'shirah*, Limassol: al-Shawwaf lil-Nashr wa-al-Dirasat.

Sim, S. (1998) 'May 14 meeting "pivotal" to Suharto's downfall', *Singapore Straits Times*, 5 November.

Simanjuntak, Marsillam (1994) *Pandangan Negara Integralistik: Sumber, Unsur dan Riwayatnya dalam Persiapan UUD 1945*, Jakarta: Grafiti.

Smith, R.M. (ed.) (1974) *Southeast Asia: Documents of Political Development and Change*, Ithaca, New York: Cornell University Press.

Soeharto (1967) *Pidato Kenegaraan PD. Presiden Republik Indonesia Djendral Soeharto Didepan Sidang DPR-GR 16 Agustus 1967*, Jakarta: Departemen Penerangan RI.

—— (1982a) 'Laporan stenografi amanat Presiden Soeharto pada malam ramah tamah dengan pengurus KNPI tanggal 19 Juli 1982 di Jalan Cendana No 8 Jakarta', unpublished typescript, Jakarta.

—— (1982b) 'Presiden Soeharto tentang Ha-Na-Ca-Ra-Ka dan sangkan paraning dumadi', *Mawas Diri*, October 1982: 4–8 (continued in the November 1982 issue: 8–12).

—— (1988) *Soeharto: Pikiran, Ucapan dan Tindakan Saya: otobiografi seperti dipaparkan kepada G. Dwipayana and Ramandan K.H.*, Jakarta: PT Citra Lantoro Gung Persada, available in English translation as Soeharto *My Thoughts, Words and Deeds: An Autobiography as Told to G. Dwipayana and Ramandan K.H.*, trans. Sumadi, ed. Muti'ah Lestiono, Jakarta: Citra Lamtoro Gung Persada.

—— (1989) *Pidato Kenegaraan Presiden Republik Indonesia Soeharto di depan Sidang Dewan Perwakilan Rakyat 16 Agustus 1989*, Jakarta: Republik Indonesia.

—— (1990) *Pidato Kenegaraan Presiden Republik Indonesia Soeharto di depan Sidang Dewan Perwakilan Rakyat 16 Agustus 1990*, Jakarta: Republik Indonesia.

Soekarnoputri Megawati (1997) 'Restoring democracy, justice, and order in Indonesia: an agenda for reform', unpublished typescript, Jakarta, April.

Soemardi, Sulaiman (1968) 'Penstrukturan Politik', unpublished typescript prepared for an Intermediate Leadership Training Course, Ikatan Mahasiswa Djakarta (IMADA), Ciloto, West Java, 25–8 January 1968.

Soemarno (1967) 'Zaman Sesudah Sukarno', typescript, Jakarta, 18 February 1967 (published in the West Java edition of *Mahasiswa Indonesia* shortly afterwards).

Soemitro, General (1989) 'Aspiring to Normal Politics', *Far Eastern Economic Review*, 6 April: 22.

Sudarsono, Juwono (1997) 'A diplomatic scam called human rights', *Jakarta Post*, 11 April.

Sudrajat, Major-General (2000) 'Federalisme masih diperdebatkan', in B. Simorangkir (ed.) *Otonomi atau Federalisme: Dampaknya Terhadap Pembangunan*, Jakarta: Pustaka Sinar Harapan: 183–6.

Sukarno (1966) *Under the Banner of Revolution*, vol. 1, Jakarta: Publication Committee.

Supreme Executive Council, Setiakawan Free Trade Union (1991) 'Thoughts and ideas presented to the Sixth Parliamentary Committee', unpublished typescript, Jakarta.

Tanter, R. (1991) 'Intelligence agencies and third world militarization: a case study of Indonesia, 1966–1989', unpublished PhD dissertation, Monash University, Melbourne.

Tanter, R. and Young, K. (eds) (1990) *The Politics of Middle Class Indonesia*, Melbourne: Monash University Centre of Southeast Asian Studies.

Thukul, Wiji (2000) *Aku Ingin Jadi Peluru: Kumpulan Sajak Wiji Thukul*, Magelang: IndonesiaTera.

Tim PPW-LIPI (1996) 'Menuju reformasi politik Order Baru: Beberapa usulan perbaikan', in S. Haris and R. Sibudi (eds) *Menelaah Format Politik Orde Baru*, Jakarta: Gramedia: 182–91.

Tjitrosoebono, Harjono (1992) 'Konsep negara integralistik menghambat demokrasi', *Menyingkap Arah dan Dampak Globalisasi: Prosiding Diskusi Informal Mengenai Hak Azasi Manusia Sekitar KTT Non Blok*, Jakarta: 52–5.

TNI Abad XXI: Redefinisi, Reposisi dan Reaktualisasi Peran TNI dalam Kehidupan Bangsa, Jakarta: Jasa Buma (fourth printing), June 1999.

van Marle, A. (1974) 'Indonesian electoral geography under ORLA and ORBA', in Oey Hong Lee (ed.) *Indonesia after the 1971 Elections*, Hull Monographs on Southeast Asia No. 5, London, Kuala Lumpur: Oxford University Press: 37–59.

Vatikiotis, M.R.J. (1993) *Indonesian Politics under Suharto: Order, Development and Pressure for Change*, London: Routledge.

Wahid, Abdurrahman (1990) 'Indonesia's Muslim middle class: an imperative or a choice?', in R. Tanter and K. Young (eds) *The Politics of Middle Class Indonesia*, Melbourne: Monash University Centre of Southeast Asian Studies: 22–4.

—— (1991) 'Islam dan Negara Dalam Masa Orde Baru', Discussion paper prepared for SPES (Society for Political and Economic Studies), Jakarta, 27 November 1991.

Wahyono, Padmo (1989) *Pembangunan Hukum di Indonesia*, Jakarta: IHC: 109–11.

Ward, K.E. (1970) *The Foundation of the Partai Muslimin Indonesia*, Ithaca, New York: Interim Report Series, Modern Indonesia Project, Southeast Asia Program, Cornell University.

—— (1974) *The 1971 Election in Indonesia: An East Java Case Study*, Melbourne: Centre of Southeast Asian Studies, Monash University.

Wertheim, W.F. (1979) 'Whose plot? New light on the 1965 events', *Journal of Contemporary Asia* IX(2): 197–215.

White Book of the Students' Struggle (1978) *Indonesia*, April 1978.

Winters, J.A. (1996) *Power in Motion: Capital Mobility and the Indonesian State*, Ithaca, New York, and London: Cornell University Press.

Wirahadikusumah, Agus (2000) ' "I'm just anticipating change earlier than the others": Profile: Maj. Gen. Agus Wirahadikusumah', *Van Zorge Report*, II.i, 7 January 2000, available at http://www.vanzorgereport.com/reports/agusall.html (11 January 2000).

Wirahadikusumah, Agus, Sumarkidjo, Atmadji, Warouw, Stella, and Iswanti (1999) *Indonesia Baru dan Tantangan TNI: Pemikiran Masa Depan*, Jakarta: Pustaka Sinar Harapan.

Yamin, Mohammad (1959) *Naskah Persiapan Undang-Undang Dasar 1945*, vol. 1, Jakarta: Jajasan Prapantja.

Yayasan Lembaga Bantuan Hukum Indonesia (1984) *Hukum, Politik dan Pembangunan: Pokok-Pokok Pemikiran Yayasan LBH Indonesia tentang Perundang-Undangan Pembangunan Kehidupan Politik*, Jakarta: Yayasan Lembaga Bantuan Hukum Indonesia.

—— (1987) 'Problems of the legislation concerning social organisations', *Indonesia Reports Human Rights Supplement* no. 20, February 1987.

Yoesoef, Mohammad Daud (1999) 'Aceh masih mungkin pisah dari RI', *Serambi*, 7 March.

Index

Abadi 13, 57, 58, 76–80
Abdul Gafur 146, 148
Abdulkadir Besar, Brigadier-General xi, 28–9, 41–3, 99, 115–17
Abdurrahman Wahid xi, 21, 22, 28, 120, 136–8, 141, 155–6, 197, 214, 224–6, 257
Abikusno Tjokrosujoso 156
ABRI *see* military
Accounting Office (BPK) 125
Aceh 18, 20, 107, 229, 255, 256, 263–5
Aditjondro, George 262
Agus Wirahadikusumah, Lieutenant-General xii, 280, 306–8
Ahmad Wahib 167
Al-Irsyad 91
Al-Wasliah 91
Ali Alatas 250
Ali Moertopo, Lieutenant-General xii, 12, 13, 21, 28, 29–30, 58, 76, 97, 139, 229; on dual function of the armed forces 34–6; on 'floating mass' concept 29–30, 45–9; on national political history 43–5; on Pancasila 46, 98, 110–12
Ali Sadikin, Lieutenant-General 14, 58, 75, 76, 118, 119
All-Indonesia Labour Federation (FBSI) 165
All-Indonesia Workers' Union (SPSI) 166, 222
Alliance of Independent Journalists (AJI) 214, 223
Amak Fadhali 84
Ambon 20
Amien Rais xii-xiii, 257, 277, 280–2
Amin, S.M. xiii, 76–9, 80
Amir Biki xiii, 140, 151–5
Anderson, Benedict R.O'G. 3, 4, 6, 21

Anhar Gonggong 271
Ansor 82
anti-communism 2, 4, 5–6, 27, 28, 30–1, 33–4
anti-violence manifesto 162, 170–2
Anwar, Dewi Fortuna 20
Anwar, M. Syafi'i 83
APEC (Asia-Pacific Economic Cooperation) 182
Api 28, 30–1
Arbi Sanit 75
armed forces *see* military
ASEAN Free-Trade Area 182
Asian currency crisis (1997–8) 18–19, 277, 296–7
Asmara Hadi 241
Aspinall, Edward 17
Attamimi, Hamid S. xiii, 235, 237
Awanohara, Susumu 140
azas tunggal legislation *see under* Pancasila
Aziz, Harry Azhar 148

Bandung Institute of Technology (ITB) Student Council 119, 120–6
Beautiful Indonesia in Miniature project xiii, 30, 50–2
Berita Yudha 58, 76–80
Boedi Oetomo 227
Booth, Anne 263
Bourchier, David 8, 20
Brown, Colin 15
Buddhism 6, 106, 107, 145, 147
Budiardjo, Miriam 207
Budiman, Arief 12, 58, 73, 74–6
Budiono Kusumohamidjojo xiii, 236, 244–6
bureaucracy 97, 129, 204, 214, 228–9, 232, 244, 245, 246

capitalism 2, 22, 29, 168, 232, 302
Castles, Lance 2, 5, 7
Catholics 139, 229
centralisation 202, 255
Chalmers, Ian 2
China 5, 231, 236, 272
Chinese Indonesians 139, 155, 278, 284, 292, 293, 298
Christian parties 6, 12
Christians 12, 139, 142, 147
City Forum 285
civil rights 238, 247, 248, 249
civil servants 134, 165, 201; *see also* Korpri
civil service 229; *see also* bureaucracy
colonialism 2, 264
communism 2, 5, 7, 8, 23, 29, 37, 105, 107, 110, 114, 230–2; *see also* anti-communism
Communists 3, 4, 5, 6, 7, 28, 279, 302–3; *see also* PKI (Indonesian Communist Party)
Constitution (1945) 22, 29, 41–3, 103, 263, 270; and colonialism 264; and human rights 218, 235, 239–41, 242; and regionalism 258, 259; revision of 100–1; and separation of powers 78, 79, 237
consumerism 174, 175
corporatism 8, 29, 202, 212, 213–14, 222; *see also* social organisations
corruption 12, 281, 289, 300
coup attempt (1965) 6–7, 28, 30–1, 59, 68, 80 n.2, 100, 101, 104, 108, 134, 199
Cribb, Robert 7, 15
critical pluralism 118–38
Crouch, Harold 97
CSIS (Centre for Strategic and International Studies) xii, xvi, 28, 34, 139
Cuba 231
cultural nationalism 2–3
cultural rights 247, 248, 249
cultural transformation 206–7
currency crisis *see* Asian currency crisis

Darul Islam movement 100, 143, 255
Daud Yoesoef, Mohammad xiv, 256, 263–5
Dawam Rahardjo, Mohammad xiv, 186, 214, 226–30
debt, foreign 281

decentralisation 20, 202, 259
Declaration of Indonesian professionals (1998) 278, 290–1
Deliar Noer 82
democracy 2, 4–5, 9, 41, 58–9, 60–1, 62, 279, 298; and Islam 207–11; and right to organise 219–23; *see also* Pancasila democracy
Democratic Forum (Forum Demokrasi) xi, xviii, xx, 58, 187, 197–8, 225
democratic socialism 7, 59
democratisation 185–211, 222–3, 281, 304
deregulation: economic 244; of legal sector 244, 245
Detik 187, 214
developmentalism 9, 27, 29, 45–9, 92, 194
Dewantoro, Ki Hadjar (Soewardi Soerjaningrat) 257, 265
Dharma Wanita 222
Dharsono, Lieutenant-General H.R. xiv, 14, 118, 119, 132–5, 141
Dinuth, Lieutenant-Colonel Alex 31
Djarek 59, 81 n.3
Dowling, Collete 175
DPR (People's Representative Council) 67, 100, 101–2, 188, 199, 200, 201, 204–5, 206, 242–3, 286, 287
Dutch 3–4, 236

East Timor xv, 18, 20, 23, 182, 236, 256–7, 265–9
economic rights 247, 248, 249
economy 6, 13; crisis in 18–19, 277, 289–90, 296–7; deregulation of 244; growth and development 9, 10, 13, 27, 29, 50–1, 92, 180–1, 199–200, 202–3; reform of 289–90, 299–300
Editor 187, 214
electoral procedures and systems 57, 69, 182, 190–1, 198, 288, 289
Elson, Robert E. 98
emergency powers 187, 195–6
Emil Salim xv, 122, 278, 288–90
Emmerson, Donald K. 14, 83
environmentalism 10, 161, 163, 172–5

family planning 153
family state 28, 29, 41–3, 238, 239, 240
Far Eastern Economic Review 186, 188

farmer organisations 165, 222
farmers, protests by 213
Fazlur Akhmad (pseud.) 162, 167–70
FBSI (All-Indonesia Labour Federation) 165
Fealy, Greg 83
federalism 257–8, 264–5, 269–72
Feillard, Andree 83
Feith, Herbert 2, 4, 5, 7, 71
feminism 10, 161, 163, 175–9
financial relations, centre–regional 260
'floating mass' concept 29–30, 45–9, 57, 70–1, 97, 199, 201, 205
forest management 172–5
Forum Keadilan 230, 239
Forum Komunikasi Ahlusunnah Wal Jannah 188
Forum Kota (City Forum) 285
freedom, and Islamic faith 210–11
freedom of association 129, 147, 164, 165, 220, 223, 240, 250
freedom of expression 147, 164, 205, 213, 218–19, 220, 223, 240, 242, 250, 298

G30S/PKI *see* coup attempt
Gadjah Mada University alumni 187, 195–6
GAM (Free Aceh Movement) 256
gang rapes 278, 292–3, 294
Gatra 306
Gema Madani xv, 288
GEMSOS (Socialist Student Movement) 167
gender equality 175–9
Gestapu *see* coup attempt
globalisation 17, 185, 192–3, 301, 304
Golkar xix, 5, 14, 15, 18, 20, 57, 97, 165, 185, 190, 200, 212; Dharsono on 133–4; and Islam 139, 142–3, 228–9; and the military 99; and Moertopo 12, 29, 48–9; student critique of 126
Golput (White Group) 58, 73–4, 75, 76
Graduates of Jakarta (GSJ) 291
Greater Jakarta Student Community 285–7
Guided Democracy period 5, 8, 11, 59, 78
GUPPI (Union of Endeavours to Renew Islamic Education) 141, 142, 143

Habibie, B.J. xv, 19–20, 227–8, 256, 278, 279; and East Timor 23, 256; and ICMI 16, 186; state of the nation address (1998) 279, 295–301
Hadiz, Vedi R. 2
Hamka xvi, 83, 85–8
Hankamnas Rata doctrine 77, 78, 81 n.5
Harian Kami 75, 77, 85, 141
Harjono Tjitrosoebono xv–xvi, 235, 241–3
Harry Tjan, Silalahi xvi, 235, 239–40
Hasan di Tiro, Teungku 256
Hasbullah Bakry, K.H. xvi, 139, 141–4
Hatta, Mohammad 2, 3, 82, 235, 239, 270
Hefner, Robert W. 16, 141
Heryanto, Ariel 278
Hill, David 13, 17
Hindus 6, 8
Hizbut Tahrir Indonesia 188
HKTI (Cooperative Farmers' Association) 165
HMI (Muslim Students' Association) xviii, xix, 140, 146, 148–51, 167, 228
HMI-MPO 140
human rights 9, 17, 176, 199, 203, 234–54, 281, 298, 299, 301, 304

ICFTU (International Confederation of Free Trade Unions) 165
Ichlasul Amal 256, 270
ICMI (Indonesian Muslim Intellectuals' Association) xiii, xiv, xv, xix, 16, 141, 155, 186, 214, 224, 225, 226–30
ideology 2–10; *see also* Pancasila
Idham Chalid xvi–xvii, 82–3, 84–5
IGGI (Inter-Governmental Group on Indonesia) 219–20
Ikadin 214
ILO (International Labour Organisation) 165, 221, 222
Imaduddin 227–8
IMF (International Monetary Fund) 19, 23
Imron 229
IN-DEMO 248–50
individualism 22, 29
Indonesia (journal) 144
Indonesia Raya 13
Indonesia Reports 132, 151

Indonesian Democratic Party *see* PDI
Indonesian Democratic Party of
    Struggle *see* PDI-P
Indonesian Journalists' Association
    (PWI) 214, 222
Indonesian Legal Aid Foundation
    (YLBHI) xiv, 234
Indonesian Legal Aid Institute (LBH)
    15, 74, 120, 128–32
Indonesian NGOs for Democracy
    248–50
Indonesian People's Committee 278,
    287
industrial action 17, 162
industrialisation 10
informal sector 166
INGI (International NGO Forum on
    Indonesia) 169, 213, 219–23, 248
Inside Indonesia 170, 215, 216, 265
Institute for the Study of Religion and
    Philosophy (LSAF) 228
'integralism' xi, 8, 17, 41–2, 136,
    235–6, 237, 238, 239, 240, 241–3
International Commission of Jurists
    248
international trade 173–4
Irawan Abidin 250
Irian Jaya *see* West Papua
Islam 2, 3, 5, 7, 8, 10, 14, 23, 97, 120,
    139–56, 186, 188, 224–6; and
    democracy 207–11; and freedom
    210–11; Islamic law (syariah) 86,
    87, 210, 211; marginalisation of 56,
    82–93, 139–56; and the marriage
    law 14, 83, 85–8; and Pancasila
    144–7, 224; and power 209–10;
    reform movement 83, 91–2;
    sovereignty in 209
Ita Nadia 278
Iwan Fals xvii, 213, 217

Jakarta Charter 86
Jakarta Post 246, 269, 295
JAKKER (People's Art Movement) xxii,
    163
Jamal D. Rahman 176
Japan 3
Jasin, General 308, 309 n. 10
Java 6
Javanese traditionalism 2–3, 7–8
Javanese transmigrants 262
Jayasuriya, Kanishka 29
Jenkins, David 13
Juwono Sudarsono xvii, 236, 246–8

Kahin, Audrey 255
Kahin, George McT. 3
Kaisiepo, Manuel xvii-xviii, 256, 260–3
Kaminer, Wendy 175
Karim, M. Rusli 82
Kedung Ombo dam 222
Kharis Suhud 189
KNPI (National Committee of
    Indonesian Youth) 103
Kompas 57, 70–1, 88, 136, 175, 244,
    245
Kopkamtib xxi, 134–5, 212–13,
    215–16
Korpri (Indonesian Civil Servants
    Corps) 134, 165, 166, 201, 222

labour movement 17, 161, 162, 163–7,
    183, 187, 213, 221–2
Lampung 229
Lane, Max 216
leadership succession 189–91, 198,
    280–2
legal profession 214, 234
legal system 236, 242–3, 244–6, 281
legislative bodies *see* parliament
legitimacy, crisis of 187
Lenin, V.I. 1
Lev, Daniel 234
liberal democracy 29, 46, 136–8, 188,
    213
liberalism 8, 22, 29, 105, 107, 120,
    136–8, 212, 235, 236, 238, 302
Liem Sioe Liong 141
LIPI (Indonesian Institute of Sciences)
    187, 199–203, 277, 282–3
Lubis, T. Mulya 234
Lyon, Margo 6

MacAndrews, Colin 255
MacIntyre, Andrew 14
Mackie, Jamie 14
McVey, Ruth T. 6
Madiun uprising 4, 100
Mahasiswa Indonesia xx, 59, 71–3
Malari riots (Malapetaka Limabelas
    Januari) xviii, 13, 58, 139, 167,
    168
Malaysia 5, 236
Mangunwijaya, Yusuf B. xvii, 214,
    230–2, 257, 269–71
Manipol 45, 54 n.5, 59
Mao Zedong 5
marriage law 14, 83, 85–8
Marxism 3, 10, 28, 33, 105, 107, 114

Masjumi 4, 6, 7, 9, 13, 56, 82, 84, 139, 169

mass organisations *see* social organisations

Mawas Diri 103

media 16–17, 187, 205, 219, 223; *see also* press

Media Indonesia 279, 302–3

Megawati Soekarnoputri xi, xviii, 18, 21, 22, 187–8, 203–7, 214, 257, 277, 286

Midday Saturday Movement (Gersang) 291

middle class 16, 169, 177, 185, 186, 202, 203, 236, 278; Muslim 16, 141, 155–6, 214

Mietzner, M. 22

military (ABRI/TNI) 4–6, 11, 13, 15, 16, 20, 40–1, 115–17, 119, 127, 143, 162, 185–6, 190, 255, 299; business interests 307; and the constitution 100–1; dual function (dwifungsi) xi, 28, 34–6, 52, 58, 76–80, 103, 116–17, 143, 199, 200, 279, 285, 303–4, 307; and federalism 258, 271–2; and Golkar 99; and ICMI (Indonesian Muslim Intellectuals' Association) 186; reform of 279–80, 303–8; territorial command structure 306–7

military culture 27

Mintaredja, H.M.S. xviii–xix, 84, 92–3

modernising pluralism 56–81, 118

Moerdani, General L.B. (Benny) 15, 16, 97, 140, 185, 186, 187, 229

Mohammad Hasan, Teuku 263

moral force, student movement as 58, 74–6

Mortimer, Rex 5

MPR (People's Consultative Assembly) 28, 42, 43, 67, 100, 101–2, 124–5, 134, 188, 190–2, 204, 206, 286, 287

Muhammadiyah xii, 2, 63, 91, 226, 277

Muslims 3, 4, 6, 7, 12, 13, 14, 16, 21, 56, 58, 97, 214

NAFTA (North American Free Trade Agreement) 182

Nahdlatul Ulama *see* NU

Najib, M. 280

Nano Riantiarno 186

Nasakom 5, 37, 45, 59, 81 n.3

Nasution, Adnan Buyung xiv, 15, 58, 74, 234, 235, 240–1

National Commission on Human Rights 17, 236, 253

nationalism 5, 23, 300–1; cultural 2–3; radical 7, 8; regional 255, 256–69; secular 2, 3, 4

Natsir, Mohammad 156

Network for Forest Conservation in Indonesia (SKEPHI) 163, 172–5

new social movements 161–84

non-governmental organisations (NGOs) 10, 15, 120, 128–32, 163, 168, 169, 187, 213, 228, 236, 248–50; *see also* individual organisations

NU (Nahdlatul Ulama) xi, xvii, 4, 6, 7, 8, 11, 56, 82, 83, 91, 120, 169, 225

Nurcholish Madjid 13, 29, 70, 83–4, 88–92, 224, 227

Nursyahbani Katjasungkana xix, 163, 175–9

OPEC 13

OPM (Free Papua Movement) 256, 261

organicism 8–9, 12, 23

organisation *see* right to organise

P4 *see under* Pancasila

Padmo Wahyono xix, 235, 237–8

Pakistan, Women's Action Forum 176

Pakpahan, Muchtar 214

Palapa satellite 122

PAN (National Mandate Party) xiii, 21, 257

Pancasila 16, 24 n.3, 27, 28–9, 127, 141–4, 259, 279, 302–3; and human rights 251; indoctrination program (P4) 14, 97–8, 110–12, 235; and Islam 14, 144–7; and liberal democracy 136–8; Moertopo on 46, 98, 110–11; Soeharto on 28, 37–41, 99–109, 192, 193–4; as 'sole principle' (*azas tunggal*) legislation 14, 28, 98, 112, 113, 118–19, 120, 128, 140, 144–51, 152, 224

Pancasila democracy 14, 28, 37–41, 97–8, 99–109, 131, 141–4, 191, 192, 193–4

Pancasila socialism 59, 61, 62

Pangaribuan, Robinson 15, 185

Paramadina Foundation 226, 228

Parindra (Greater Indonesia Party) 3, 4

parliament: composition of 67–9, 100, 101–2, 124, 134, 182, 204–5, 206;

student critique of 122–5; *see also* DPR; MPR
parliamentary democracy 4–5, 9, 279
Parmusi (Muslim Party of Indonesia) 82, 84, 92, 93
party system 5, 56–7, 60–3, 97, 108, 126, 133–4, 182, 199, 200–1, 205; multi-party 11, 23, 56, 288; two-party 56–7, 61–2, 97
patrimonialism 97
PDI (Indonesian Democratic Party) xviii, 12, 18, 58, 126, 136, 187–8, 200
PDI-P (Indonesian Democratic Party of Struggle) xv, xviii, 20, 23, 163
peace movement 162, 170–2
peasant sector 183
People's Consultative Assembly *see* MPR
People's Democratic Union 179
People's Representative Council *see* DPR
Peradin xvi, 214
Permesta/PRRI xx, 5, 6, 82, 143
Persis 91
Petition of Fifty (1980) xx, 14, 98, 119, 126–7
PIR (Greater Indonesia Unity Party) 4, 8
PKB (National Awakening Party) xi, 21
PKI (Indonesian Communist Party) xxi, 4, 5, 6, 7, 8, 27–8, 30–1, 33–4, 68, 82, 104, 139, 302, 303
pluralism 2, 8, 9, 14, 23, 56–81
pluralist critiques 118–38
PNI (Indonesian Nationalist Party) 4, 6, 7, 8, 11, 56
political openness 9, 185, 192–5, 213
political parties *see* individual parties; party system
political rights 247, 248, 249
poverty 139, 183, 263, 280–1, 296
PPP (United Development Party) xi, xix, 12, 14, 21, 58, 92, 93, 98, 139, 142, 146, 200, 226
Prabawo Subianto 19
PRD (People's Democratic Party) 18, 162–3, 179–84, 214, 277, 284–5
press 16, 20, 212, 214, 219, 223, 242, 243, 298; licencing policy 205
Prisma xiv, 167
Professionals in Solidarity with Reform (SPUR) 291
Pronk, Jan 219–20, 236
proportional representation 57, 69

PRRI/Permesta *see* Permesta/PRRI
PSI (Indonesian Socialist Party) xx, 4, 6, 7, 9, 11, 13, 56, 57, 168

radical nationalism 7, 8
radicalism 8, 10, 17–18, 161–84
Ramage, Douglas 16
Ratna Megawangi 175–7
Reeve, David 5, 8
Regional Legislatures (DPRD) 67
regionalism 255, 256–69
religion 97, 106–7, 109; *see also* Islam
Rendra, W.S xx, 213, 216–17
resistance/separatist movements 256–7, 261, 308
Richburg, Keith 19
right to organise 131, 148–50, 166, 213, 219–23, 240
rights 213, 218; *see also* freedom of association;; freedom of expression; human rights; right to organise
riots (May 1998) 278–9, 297–8
Robison, Richard 11
Roekmini Soedjono, Brigadier-General 186
rule of law xv, 9, 78, 120, 234–54, 298

Samsudin, Major-General 186
Sandyawan Sumardi, I. xx, 278–9, 291–5
santri community 6
Sarbini Sumawinata 57
Sarbumusi (Indonesian Muslim Workers Union) 165
Sarekat Islam 2
Schwarz, Adam 229
secular nationalism 2, 3, 4
secularisation 89–90
Seda, Frans xv, 256, 258–60
self-reliance 22–3
Sen, Krishna 17
separation of powers 17, 43, 78, 79, 237
separatist/resistance movements 256–7, 261, 308
Serambi 256, 263
Setiakawan 162, 163–7
Shawwaf, Munir Muhammad Tahir 208
Shiddiq Al-Jawi, Muhammad xii, 188, 207–11
Sim, Susan 19
Simanjuntak, Marsillam xviii, 213, 218–19, 235

Sinar Harapan 57, 142
Singapore 236
Sirnagalih Declaration 214, 223
SIUPP policy *see* press
Sjafruddin Prawiranegara xx, 140,
 144–7
Sjahrir, Sutan 3
SKEPHI 163, 172–5
Smith, Alan 71
Smith, R.M. 70, 71
SOBSI (All-Indonesia Central Workers
 Organisation) 5
social democrats/democracy 2, 4, 9, 59
social justice 22, 199, 203
social organisations 62–3, 112–14,
 118–20, 128–32, 205, 212, 221,
 222; and Pancasila ideology 14, 28,
 98, 112, 113, 118–19, 120, 128,
 140, 144–51, 152, 224
social rights 247, 248, 249
social security net 289
socialism 59, 60, 62, 302
socialists 3, 12
Society for Political and Economic
 Studies 224
Society of Professionals for Democracy
 (MPD) 291
Soe Hok Gie 167
Soeharto, General xxi, 1, 6, 7, 8, 12,
 15, 21, 22, 23, 27–8, 99–109, 185,
 186–7, 189, 218, 277; on
 democratic rights 30, 49–54; and
 economic crisis 19; and Islam 16,
 82, 186, 214; on Javanese
 mysticism 105–7; and Pancasila
 democracy 14, 28, 37–41, 97–8,
 99–109, 192, 193–4; and the party
 system 11, 108; and Petition of
 Fifty 119; and political openness
 192–5; and religion 16, 82, 106–7,
 109, 186, 214; resignation of 278
Soelaiman Soemardi xxi, 57, 64–6
Soemarno xxii, 57, 58, 59–63
Soemitro Djojohadikusumo 281
Soemitro, General xxi, 13, 58, 186,
 188–92
Soerjadi 18, 187
Soetomo 227
Soewardi Soerjaningrat *see* Dewantoro
South Sulawesi 255, 262
sovereignty: in Islam 209; popular 41,
 183, 184, 204–6, 209, 259, 298
Soviet Union 231
Special Operations (OPSUS) group 58

SPSI (All-Indonesia Workers' Union)
 166, 222
student movement 13, 17, 57–8, 71–6,
 119, 120–6, 161, 162–3, 167–72,
 183, 187, 277–8, 284–7; in
 Yogyakarta 170; *see also* HMI
 (Muslim Students' Association)
study groups 168–9
Suardi Tasrif xv
succession, leadership 189–91, 198,
 280–2
Sudharmono, Lieutenant-General 15,
 185–6
Sudomo, Admiral 189
Sudrajat, Major-General xxi, 258,
 271–2
Sugianto, Colonel Aloysius 76
Sukarno 3, 5, 7, 11, 14, 22, 23, 104,
 145, 147, 191, 240; on the
 Constitution 270; economic policy
 6; and Pancasila ideology 105; and
 party system 5, 9; on separation of
 powers 79; signing of Supersemar
 document 28, 31
Sulami, Ibu 279
Sulawesi 4–5
Sumatra 4–5
Supersemar 28, 31–2
Supomo, Dr Raden 8, 17, 29, 42, 235,
 237, 239, 240
Supreme Court 125–6, 242, 243
Sutjipto, Brigadier-General 27
Suwarto, Lieutenant-General 27
syariah *see under* Islam

Tajuk 306
Taman Mini *see* Beautiful Indonesia in
 Miniature
Tanjung Priok killings 14, 97, 140, 141,
 151, 169, 229
Taufik Rahzen xxii, 170–2
Tavip 59, 81 n.3
taxation 203, 291
Team of Volunteers for Humanitarian
 Causes 278–9, 291–5
television *see* media
Tempo 187, 213, 214, 218, 306
Tempo Interaktif 223
Thee Kian Wie 245
TNI *see* military
tolerance, ideology of 302–3
Tolleng, A. Rahman xix–xx, 57, 58,
 67–9
Tony Ardhie 139

tourism 50–1
trade, international 173–4
trade unions 162, 163–7, 221–2; *see also* labour movement
traditionalism 2–3, 7–8
Trisakti University 19, 277, 286, 292, 299
Try Soetrisno, General 235

Ujung Pandang 169, 286
unemployment 262, 280–1
UNESCO 207
unitarist state 255, 257, 258, 259, 271
United Development Party *see* PPP
United Nations 23, 243, 247, 249, 250, 251, 253
United States 6, 23, 236
Universal Declaration of Human Rights 176, 247, 249, 252, 298
Untung 'coup' *see* coup attempt
Usdek 59, 81 n.3

van Marle, A. 12, 84
van Mook, Hubertus J. 271
Vatikiotis, Michael R.J. 15
Vienna Conference on Human Rights (1993) 176, 236, 247, 248, 252, 253

Vietnam 231
Volksraad (People's Assembly) 3
voting rights 68

wages 164, 177–8
Wahid Hasjim, A. 156
Wahidin Soehirohoesodo 227
Ward, Kenneth E. 57, 70, 82
Wertheim, W.F. 6
West Irian *see* West Papua
West Kalimantan 20
West Papua (Irian Jaya) 5, 18, 20, 256, 260–3
White Book of the Student's Struggle 119, 120–6, 167
Widodo, Major-General 70
Wiji Thukul Wijaya xxii, 163, 179
Wiranto, General 256, 303
Wiryono Sastrohandoyo 250
Women's Action Forum (Pakistan) 176
women's issues 163, 175–9, 222
worker protests *see* labour movement

Yamin, Mohammad 42, 235, 239
Yap Thiam Hien xv, 234, 240
YTKI (Indonesian Manpower Foundation) 166